DISTILLED SPIRITS

New Horizons: Energy, Environmental and Enlightenment

Distilled Spirits

New Horizons: Energy, Environmental and Enlightenment

Edited by

G.M. Walker[1]
P.S. Hughes[2]

[1]*Professor of Zymology, Yeast Research Group, Food Division, School of Contemporary Sciences, University of Abertay Dundee, Dundee DD1 1HG Scotland, UK;* [2]*Director, International Centre for Brewing and Distilling, Heriot-Watt University*

Nottingham University Press
Manor Farm, Main Street, Thrumpton
Nottingham, NG11 0AX, United Kingdom

NOTTINGHAM

First published 2010

British Library Cataloguing in Publication Data
Distilled Spirits - New Horizons: Energy, Environmental and Enlightenment
I. Walker, G.M., II. Hughes, P.S.

ISBN 978-1-907284-45-8

Disclaimer

Typeset by Nottingham University Press, Nottingham
Printed and bound by CPI Antony Rowe, Wiltshire

Foreword

Despite the undoubted traditions of the global distilling industry, it is fully cognisant of the environments in which it operates. With this in mind, the contents of this volume reflect the presentations and discussions at the third Worldwide Distilled Spirits Conference, held in Edinburgh in September 2008. Organised under the auspices of the Scottish Section of the Institute of Brewing and Distilling, more than 300 delegates from around the world met to consider the three key themes of Energy, Environment and Enlightenment. As the distilling industry moves forward, it is acutely aware of these issues, so the timing of these deliberations is timely indeed.

It was a pleasure to serve as Chairman of the Organising Committee for the 2008 Conference. I would like to thank my colleagues who worked with me on the Committee, and the generous sponsors who unstintingly supported the Conference. I would like to say a special thank you to the Chairman of the Scottish Section at that time, Richard Beattie, and my co-editor and Chair of the Programme Committee, Professor Graeme Walker. I hope that you find the contents here enlightening!

Paul S. Hughes

Director, International Centre for Brewing and Distilling, Heriot-Watt University

Chair of the third Worldwide Distilled Spirits Conference Organising Committee

Contents

PART 4: CONSUMER-PRODUCT INTERACTION

PART 5: GLOBAL OPPORTUNITIES AND THREATS

Preface

The distilled spirits industry is rapidly embracing new technologies to save energy, protect the environment and apply new scientific approaches to improve efficiencies. These issues are covered in this book which originated from the Worldwide Distilled Spirits Conference held in Edinburgh in the Autumn of 2008 and organised by the Scottish Section of the Institute of Brewing & Distilling. More than 300 international delegates at that conference discussed key scientific and technological challenges facing the modern distilling industry under the main themes of Energy, Environment and Enlightenment. These topics are comprehensively discussed in these proceedings with chapters dealing with raw materials, yeast and fermentation, energy conservation, co-product treatment, process efficiencies, impact of new technologies on flavour and consumer-product interaction.

Part 1 of this book (Raw materials & Fermentation) includes Chapters dealing with diverse starting materials for various distilled spirits, ranging from cereals for whiskies to molasses for rum and Agave for Tequila. The inter-relationship between the potable and fuel alcohol industries – especially food-to-fuel issues – is discussed in an early chapter by Charles Abbas. Undoubtedly, the bioethanol sector is growing rapidly and is impacting significantly on global distilled spirits producers. Microbiological aspects of various spirits, including cachaca, malt whisky, brandy, rum and tequila also feature in part 1 which concludes with a summary of the distiller's yeast Discussion Forum.

Part 2 deals with Energy & Environment which was a key theme of the conference and includes contributions on new technologies not simply to treat residues from distilleries, but to recover some useful renewable energy (biogas, bioethanol) in the process. Novel process developments for co-products are also discussed as well as the important topic of water conservation and recycling. Environmental challenges faced in building a new malt whisky distillery are described in chapter 15.

Part 3 of the Conference considered enhancements in the efficiency of the distilling process. Key aspects included sophisticated data handing/process management tools – such as fuzzy logic controllers and multivariate analysis of dynamic process data – these having been shown to have real relevance to the contemporary management of distilling operations.

Part 4 is concerned with consumer-facing issues, such as flavour, health-related aspects and a consideration of the positioning of distilled spirits and their provenance to consumers. Thus the contribution of Japanese oak to the flavour of Japanese whisky, the structure of ethanol-water mixtures at the molecular level and the opportunities to expand the alcoholic beverage product map by introducing new ingredients were all explicitly discussed. The impact of alcohol on cardiovascular health was eruditely and objectively explored by cardiovascular expert Dr Arthur Klatsky.

Part 5 of the Conference looked to the future, with Alan Rutherford challenging for instance the need for an age statement on a whisky package and Ian Buxton discussing the perceived notions of whisky tradition and authenticity. The Conference was concluded by brief presentations from three distilling

CEOs: Paul Walsh of Diageo, Ian Curle of the Edrington Group and Mike Keiller of Morrison Bowmore, each giving their insight on the way ahead for the distilling industry.

We wish to thank session chairs at the Worldwide Distilled Spirits Conference for their assistance in editing some of the manuscripts, all authors and presenters and finally Sarah Keeling at Nottingham University Press for her expert help in publishing this book.

Graeme Walker,
University of Abertay, Dundee

Paul Hughes,
ICBD, Heriot-Watt University, Edinburgh

Chapter 1

Sugar cane for potable and fuel ethanol

Luiz Carlos Basso[1] and Carlos Augusto Rosa[2]
[1]Biological Science Department, ESALQ/USP, 13418-900, P.O. Box 9, Piracicaba (SP), Brazil; [2]Department of Microbiology, ICB/UFMG, 31270-901, P.O. Box 486, Belo Horizonte (MG), Brazil

Summary

Sugar cane is a crop that has been used in Brazil since the colonial period for sugar production, and subsequently for a distilled spirit called "cachaça". Today, sugar mills (*ca.* 400 plants that produce both cane sugar and fuel ethanol) are big industries while most of the cachaça is produced in small plants in a traditional fashion, although a few plants produce cachaça in a large scale. In the 2008 crop season, cane sugar and fuel ethanol production consumed nearly 500 million tons of sugar cane, and 52% of this raw material was used for fuel ethanol production (estimated at more than 24 billion litres). Most of the fuel ethanol produced is used internally for transportation, representing more than 40% of the total volume of gasoline consumed. Total cachaça production volume amounted to 1.3 billion litres in 2008 (only 1.2% is exported), produced by 30,000-35,000 small plants (alambiques) and some larger capacity distilleries located mainly in Sao Paulo Estate. It is proposed that an additional sugar cane production of 7 million ton may be used for cachaça production.

Both fuel ethanol and cachaça are produced by *Saccharomyces cerevisiae* yeasts fermenting substrates based on cane juice, but these processes are quite different from each other. For fuel ethanol production, both sugar cane juice and molasses (the by-product of the sugar industry), in varying proportions, are used as substrate, while for cachaça production only the fresh juice is used. In both fermentation processes, the yeasts are submitted to several stressful conditions and a succession of indigenous yeast strains carry out the fermentations. These strains do not necessarily have desirable fermentation traits, but among them suitable strains have been selected. Due to the differences in both fermentation processes (fuel ethanol and cachaça), strains with different features are required. For fuel ethanol, the priority is the productivity, while for cachaça production, strains with a suitable balance between secondary products (associated with cachaça flavour) are required.

Sugar cane – a suitable crop for fermentation processes

Sugar cane was early introduced to Brazil by the Portuguese colonizers at the beginning of the XIV century and the first mills for cane sugar production (to be consumed in Europe) were established around 1530 in the Southeast region (today the State of Sao Paulo). Later on sugar cane was also introduced in the Northeast region (Amorim and Leão, 2005) and nowadays is grown in several other regions, with a noticeable increase in the Centre-western region due to available land and suitable climate.

Today sugar cane is an important crop in Brazil occupying *ca.* 7 million hectares with a production of 500 million tons per year, making the country the world largest sugar cane producer. Nevertheless, the sugar cane cultivation area corresponds to only one tenth of that used for corn, soy and other crops. As a C-4 photosynthetic species, sugar cane presents very high biomass productivity and up to 60% of its nitrogen demand can be supplied by nitrogen-fixing endophytic bacteria, at least in low fertility soil . These attributes, namely: its drought tolerance, high fermentable sugar content and other desirable agricultural features, make sugar cane an economically and environmentally suitable feedstock for fermentation processes. Sugar cane productivity amounts to 80-120 ton/ha year with an industrial ethanol production of 8,000 litres/ha, higher when compared to maize (3,000 litres/ha) (Wheals *et al.*, 1999).

Sugar cane contains 11-18% (wet basis) of total sugar (90% of sucrose and 10% of glucose plus fructose) and 8-14% of fibre. For industrial processes, the average extraction efficiency to produce cane juice by crushing is *ca.* 95% of the total sugar and the remaining solid residue is the cane fibre or bagasse. Bagasse is used for steam generation and supplying the energy for crushing, heating, juice concentration and ethanol distillation. There is a 20% surplus that is used in the co-generation of electricity, which can be sold to electricity companies during the dry season in Brazil, when the electricity demand is high and hydroelectric supplies are at their lowest. Bagasse is also an attractive lignocellulosic substrate for second generation ethanol production and when pre-treated (steam explosion) is used as an animal feed (Wheals *et al.*, 1999).

Cachaça – the Brazilian distilled spirit

Cachaça has been produced in Brazil since the introduction of sugar cane crop, and was ruled by Federal Legislation and assigned as a Brazilian typical distilled spirit with 38-48% ethanol (v/v at 20°C) obtained from fermented fresh cane juice with a Standard Quality according Table 1. It is very distinct from rum produced in Caribbean countries, that relies on fermentation of sugar cane molasses and/or cooked cane juice. Production of cachaça amounts to approximately 1.3- 1.6 billions litres per year, most of it being consumed within Brazil. The Brazilian consumption is about 11 litres/year per capita and only 1% is exported, mainly to Europe (Germany is the main importer). Cachaça is the second most consumed alcoholic beverage in Brazil, exceeded only by beer, and is the third most consumed distilled beverage in the world (exceeded only by vodka and *shoju*, a Korean beverage) (Faria *et al.* 2003a; Verdi, 2006).

Table 1. Standard quality of cachaça according Brazilian Federal Legislation Act number 2314 of September 4th, 1997, fixing limits of some components.

Components	*Maximum values (mg/100 ml of anhydrous ethanol)*
Volatile acidity (as acetic acid)	150
Esters (as ethyl acetate)	200
Aldehydes (as acetic aldehyde)	30
Furfural	5
Higher Alcohols	300
Methanol	200
Copper	5

Basically there are two kinds of cachaça: artisanal (300,000 litres/year produced by *ca.* 30,000 small plants) and industrial (1,300,000 litres/year produced by less than 10 big distilleries). They differ not only in terms of the plant capacity, but also on the technology used, yeast fermentation and distillation equipment. Industrial cachaça is produced by bigger distilleries, very similar to fuel ethanol process, using centrifuge for yeast recycling, baker's or selected yeast strains as starters, and distilling in stainless-steel columns. On the other hand, artisanal (traditional or "alembic cachaça") cachaça is produced in small plants (*alambiques*), using open vessels (sometimes wooden vats) where fermentation normally occurs spontaneously by indigenous yeast strains and the distillation is performed in copper pot stills. These traditional distilleries do not use centrifugation for cell recycling. Batch distillation, conducted in one, two, or three alembics (pot stills), usually made of copper, continues to be the process used in most traditional distillery plants (Rosa *et al.* 2008).

Traditional cachaça

In traditional cachaça ("alembic cachaça"), the fermentation process is spontaneous, and involves exclusively the indigenous microbiota present in the must and equipment (Morais *et al.*, 1997). It has already been demonstrated that in such systems there occurs a succession of yeasts, with the prevalence of *Saccharomyces cerevisiae* strains. (Morais *et al.* 1997; Schwan *et al.* 2001; Araujo *et al.* 2007). The freshly-cut sugar cane juice is fermented in a simple, open vat sometimes after adjusting the sugar concentration and with the addition of small amounts of crushed corn as used in most of the traditional distilleries.

Natural microbial starter cultures can be prepared with sugar-cane juice, rice, maize flour and lemon (to reduce pH) to favour growth of indigenous *S. cerevisiae* strains. Fresh addition of sugar cane juice occurs each day for five to seven days. This starter culture is used to inoculate the main vat that is typically less than 1,000 litres, and the single batch fermentation is often complete in 24 hours. The starter culture, in general, corresponds to 25% of the vat's total volume. At the end of the fermentation, the yeasts sediment and the fermented liquor is transferred to a copper alembic for distillation. The vat is left with around of 25% of the liquor and contains most of the yeasts. The process is repeated by slowly refilling the vat with fresh juice (Rosa *et al.* 2008; Schwan *et al.* 2001).

Although *S. cerevisiae* has been shown to dominate during cachaça fermentation, other yeasts species are normally found in the microbiota: for example, *Candida apicola, Candida maltosa, Candida guilliermondii, Debaryomyces hansenii, Hanseniaspora uvarum, Kloeckera japonica, Kluyveromyces marxianus, Pichia subpelliculosa, Pichia heimii, Rhodotorula glutinis, Schizosacccharomyces pombe* and others (Morais *et al.* 1997; Pataro *et al.* 2000; Schwan *et al.* 2001; Gomes *et al.* 2007).

The microbial populations not only affect ethanol yield and other physiological parameters of fermentation but also the flavour of cachaça (Gomes *et al.* 2007; Oliveira *et al.* 2008). It is suspected that the frequent contamination with *Lactobacillus* (Schwan et *al.* 2001) could contribute to the aroma of cachaça, as has been suggested for rum. *Lactobacillus* also improves the sedimentation rate after fermentation, causing yeast cell flocculation. Similar to other spirits, cachaça is organoleptically characterised by the content of secondary metabolites, such as higher alcohols, esters, carboxylic acids, and carbonyl compounds, which contribute to the peculiar flavour of the spirit. Cachaças produced in copper alembics possess higher contents of ethyl acetate and ethyl lactate than those produced in stainless steel columns, whereas cachaças produced using stainless steel columns possess a higher content of ethyl octanoate, ethyl decanoate and ethyl laurate. (Nascimento *et al.* 2008). Indeed these two types of cachaça present different aroma and flavour.

There is an effort to improve the sensory quality of cachaça, not only selecting proper yeast strains but also evaluating several Brazilian wood casks as substitutes for oak barrels for ageing. After a single distillation, Brazilian cachaça already has a sensory quality that is acceptable for drinking, which may explain why the ageing of cachaça is not a common practice in Brazil. However, this process certainly leads to a significant improvement of cachaça flavour (Faria *et al.*, 2003b).

Regarding yeasts, it is desirable to use strains with no production of hydrogen sulphide, as well as high flocculation rate to favour the sedimentation step in cachaça production (Silva *et al*. 2006). It is expected that with good microbiological control, traditional cachaça will be significantly improved in quality.

Fuel ethanol – a renewable energy source for transportation in Brazil

Energy crises and environmental concerns are making bioethanol an attractive renewable fuel source. Fuel bioethanol for transportation has received much attention in Brazil, mainly after the first oil crisis of 1973, leading the country to launch a national program to replace part of gasoline by ethanol (Amorim & Leão, 2005). Since then, ethanol production has greatly increased making Brazil the largest producer and exporter for many decades (Richard, 2006). Recently, however, Brazil has been surpassed in terms of volumetric bioethanol production by the USA (Valdes, 2007), reaching 21 billion litres per year during the 2007/2008 crop season (Oliveira, *et al*., 2007). In the USA, most of ethanol is produced from corn (maize), amounting to 24 billion liters in 2007 (RFA, 2008), with an estimated energy balance of 1.3 (units of energy from the produced ethanol per 1 unit of energy used for its production). On the other hand, Brazil produces ethanol from sugar cane with an estimated energy balance of 8.0 for this particular crop (Leite, 2005). In Brazil, nearly all produced ethanol is used as biofuel, today representing more than 40% of total gasoline consumed in the country. Scientific and technological advances, for example, regarding sugar cane varieties, agricultural and fermentation process management and engineering have led to increased efficiency in Brazilian distilleries.

The Brazilian fermentation process is quite unusual in that yeast cells are intensively recycled (more than 90% of the yeast is reused from one fermentation to the next), resulting in very high cell densities inside the fermenter (10 to 17% w/v, wet basis) which contributes to very short fermentation times. Sugar cane juice and molasses (in varying proportions) are used as substrates, and ethanol concentrations of 8-11% (v/v) are achieved within a period of 6-11 hours at 32-35°C. After fermentation, yeast cells are collected by centrifugation, acid washed (the yeast slurry is treated with diluted sulphuric acid at pH 2.0-2.5 for 1-2 hours in order to reduce bacterial contamination) and re-pitched, comprising at least two fermentation cycles per day during a production season of 200-250 days (Basso *et al*., 2008; Wheals *et al*., 1999). High cell densities, cell recycling and high ethanol concentration, all contribute to reduced yeast growth, which in turn leads to high ethanol yields (90-92% of the theoretical sugar conversion into ethanol).

Ethanol plants in Brazil traditionally use baker's yeast as starter cultures, because of its low cost and availability at the required amount. For example, some distilleries start with 1 to 12 ton of pressed baker's yeast. Karyotyping analyses of yeast samples from distilleries using baker's or other available *Saccharomyces cerevisiae* strains showed that these strains were unable to compete with indigenous (wild) yeasts that contaminated the industrial processes (Basso *et al*., 2008).

The reason why such starter yeast strains were unable to survive could be due to the stressful conditions imposed by industrial fermentation. High ethanol concentration, high temperature, osmotic stress due to sugar and salts, acidity, sulphite and bacterial contamination are recognized stress conditions faced by yeast during the industrial processes (Alves, 1994), some of them acting synergistically (Dorta *et al*., 2006), and particularly with cell recycling.

Additional factors can act upon yeast affecting fermentation performance, such as the presence of toxic levels of aluminum and potassium in the medium. The acidic condition of fermentation renders aluminum (absorbed by sugarcane in acid soils) in its toxic form (Al^{+3}), reducing yeast viability, cellular trehalose levels and fermentation rate with negative impacts on ethanol yields (Basso *et al*., 2004). Toxic effects of aluminum can be partially alleviated by magnesium ions, and completely abolished in a molasses rich medium, suggesting the presence of chelating compounds in this substrate (Basso *et al.*, 2004). High potassium levels, especially in molasses, also exert a detrimental effect upon yeast performance (Alves, 1994).

Great yeast biodiversity is observed in Brazilian industrial fermentations, each distillery with its own population, showing a succession of different strains. Prevalent strains were found infrequently, and even more rarely, strains with persistency. Prevalent and persistent strains were isolated from distilleries suggesting competitiveness and stress tolerance during industrial fermentation, respectively. Such strains were screened for desirable fermentation features for fuel ethanol production (high ethanol yield, reduced glycerol and foam formation, maintenance of high viability during cycling and high implantation capability into industrial fermenters). These selected strains presented remarkable physiological and technological parameters (Basso *et al.*, 2008). Table 2 shows the fermentation characteristics of one selected strain (PE-2) as compared to baker's yeast. Ethanol yield, as the fraction of metabolized sugar converted to ethanol, was higher for the selected strain. Table 2 also indicates that glycerol formation is inversely related to ethanol yield and that low glycerol-producing strains would have a great impact on industrial yields. Reduced cell viability, as well as low intracellular glycogen and trehalose levels, observed in baker's yeast, indicates that this strain does not survive during these fermentation conditions, and this might explain the short-lived nature of this yeast in industrial fermentations

The selected strains also present reduced foam formation and no flocculation, although this last feature is desirable in cachaça fermentation. High foam producing strains do not allow the use of fermenters' total capacity and also consume more antifoam products, thus increasing ethanol production costs. Additionally, flocculent or high sedimentation strains impair the centrifugation step of the fuel ethanol industrial process. Most of the foam producing strains also lead to yeast flotation, and both flotation and flocculation reduces the yeast contact with the substrate, increasing fermentation time and resulting in high residual sugar concentration after fermentation. The industrial processes as employed in most Brazilian plants operate better with a homogeneous yeast suspension during fermentation (Basso et. al., 2008).

In only a few distilleries non-*Saccharomyces* (mainly *Schizosaccharomyces pombe, Dekkera bruxellensis* and *Candida krusei*) could be identified, and even so with low prevalence (these non-*Saccharomyces* yeasts represent less than 5% of the total strains observed), but their presence are frequently associated with low ethanol yield (Basso *et al.*, 2008). Nevertheless in cachaça fermentation, non-*Saccharomyces* are

Table 2. Physiological and technological parameters of selected PE-2 strain and baker's yeast strain during fermentation cycles using sugar cane juice and molasses as substrate at 33°C and attaining up to 9.1% (v/v) ethanol. Data are the average (±S.D.) of 5 fermentation cycles run in triplicate. (Basso *et al.*, 2008).

	Strains	
Fermentation parameters	*Baker's yeast*	*PE-2*
Ethanol yield (%)[a]	88.1 (±1.01)	92.0 (±1.12)
Glycerol (%)[a]	5.40 (±0.25)	3.38 (±0.33)
Biomass gain (%)[b]	5.8 (±0.61)	8.2 (±0.84)
Viability (%)[c]	48 (±1.1)	94 (±1.9)
Trehalose (% dry basis)[d]	4.0 (±0.22)	9.5 (±0.29)
Glycogen (% dry basis)[d]	9.0 (±0.43)	16.0 (±0.51)

[a]sugar fraction converted into either ethanol or glycerol (g/100g sugar)
[b]average biomass increase per fermentation cycle
[c]cell viability at the end of the last fermentation cycle (% viable cells)
[d]cell storage carbohydrate at the end of the last fermentation cycle

more frequent contaminants, probably due to the lower ethanol content (5 – 7% v/v) compared to fuel ethanol fermentation.

Few selected yeast strains appear to be useful for industrial fermentations and consistently able to contribute good fermentation performance for many distilleries and for many seasons. Table 3 presents the best performing strains with their implantation capabilities, showing their dominance and prevalence in industrial fermentations. It can be seen in Table 3 that, during 12 crop seasons, PE-2 strain, for instance, was implanted in 58% of the distilleries where it was introduced, representing 54% of the yeast population at the end of the crop season (160-200 days of recycling). PE-2, CAT-1 and BG-1 showed a remarkable capacity of competing with indigenous yeast, surviving and dominating during industrial fermentations, and they are currently the most widely used strains in ethanol plants in Brazil. During 2007/2008 crop season, PE-2 and CAT-1 strains were used in about 150 distilleries, representing ca. 60% of the fuel ethanol produced in Brazil (Basso *et al.*, 2008).

Table 3. Implantation performance of different strains, evaluated by their persistence and prevalence in industrial fermentations of 20 to 78 distilleries during 12 crop seasons (1993-2005). Data are presented as the average (± S.D.) of the values at the end of each crop season (collected between 160-250 days of recycling). (Basso *et al.*, 2008).

Introduced strains	*Permanence (%)*[a]	*Prevalence (%)*[b]
PE-2	58 (±4.1)	54 (±5.2)
CAT-1	51 (±4.3)	45 (±5.8)
BG-1	42 (±5.1)	65 (±4.8)
SA-1	32 (±5.0)	44 (±6.6)
VR-1	25 (±4.3)	15 (±3.0)
CR-1	7 (±6.2)	6 (±6.3)
Others[c]	0	0

[a]proportion of distilleries (%) where the introduced strain was able to be implanted
[b]strain proportion (%) in distilleries where it was implanted
[c]all others introduced strains

Once implanted into a distillery, selected strains may reduce ethanol production costs not only by increasing ethanol yield or simplifying fermentation handling/operations, but also through reducing antifoam consumption, helping Brazilian fuel ethanol to be very competitive in relation to fossil fuel.

References

Alves DMG (1994) *Fatores que afetam a formação de ácidos orgânicos bem como outros parâmetros da fermentação alcoólica.* MS Thesis, ESALQ Universidade de São Paulo, Piracicaba, SP.

Amorim, HV & Leão, R.M. (2005) A experiência do Proálcool. *Fermentação alcoólica: Ciência e Tecnologia* (Amorim HV, ed), Fermentec, Piracicaba (Brazil), pp 190-191.

Amorim HV & Lopes ML (2005) Ethanol production in a petroleum dependent world: the Brazilian experience. *Sugar Journal* **67:** 11-14

Araujo RAC, Gomes FCO, Moreira ESA, Cisalpino PS and Rosa CA (2007). Monitoring Saccharomyces cerevisiae populations by mtDNA restriction analysis and other molecular typing methods during spontaneous fermentation for production of the artisanal cachaça. *Brazilian Journal of Microbiology,* **38**: 217-223.

Basso, L.C., Amorim, H.V., Oliveira, A.J. and Lopes, M.L.(2008) Yeast selection for fuel ethanol in Brazil. *FEMS Yeast Research* **8**: 1155-1163.

Basso LC, Oliveira AJ, Orelli VFDM, Campos AA, Gallo CR & Amorim HV (1993) Dominância das leveduras contaminantes sobre as linhagens industriais avaliada pela técnica da cariotipagem. *Anais 5º Congresso Nacional da STAB* **1**:246-250.

Basso LC, Paulilo SCL, Rodrigues DA; Basso TO, Amorin AV & Walker GM (2004) Aluminium toxicity towards yeast fermentation and the protective effect of magnesium. p. PB-14. *International Congress on Yeasts – Yeasts in Science and Biotechnology The Quest for Sustainable Development, Book of abstract* Rio de Janeiro (Brasil), p PB14.

Dorta C, Oliva-Neto P, Abreu-Neto MS, Nicolu-Junior N & Nagashima A I (2006) Synergism among lactic acid, sulfite, pH and ethanol in alcoholic fermentation of *Saccharomyces cerevisiae* (PE-2 and M-26). *World Journal of Microbiology & Biotechnology* **22**:177-182.

Faria, JB, Cordello, H.M.A.., Boscoso, M., Isique, WD., Odello, L. and Franco, D.W. (2003a) Evaluation of Brazilian woods as an alternative to oak for cachaças aging. *Eur. Food. Res. Technol.* **218**:83-87

Faria JB, Loyola E, López MG and Dufour PD (2003b) Cachaça, Pisco and Tequila. In: *Fermented Beverage Production* 2nd ed pp 335–363. Eds AGH Lea and JR Piggott Kluwer Academic/Plenum, New York.

Gomes F C O, Silva C L C, Marini M M *et al* (2007) Use of selected indigenous *Saccharomyces cerevisiae* strains for the production of the traditional cachaça in Brazil. *J Appl Microbiol* 103:2438-2447.

Leite, RCC (2005) Biomassa, a esperança verde para poucos http://www.agrisustentavel.com/san/biomassa.htm (accessed on 28 January 2008)

Morais, P. B.; Rosa, C. A.; Linardi, V. R.; Pataro, C. and Maia, A. B. R. A. (1997), Characterization and succession of yeast populations associated with spontaneous fermentation for Brazilian sugar-cane "aguardente" production. *World J. Microbiol. Biotechnol.,* 13, 241-243.

Nascimento, E.S.P., Cardoso, D.R. and Franco, D.W. (2008) Quantitative ester analysis in cachaça and distilled spirits by gaschromatography-mass spectrometry., *J. Agric. Food Chem.* **56**:5488-5493.

Oliveira EP, Sobrinho JBS, Negreiros JC, Amazonas L, Almeida MBA, Andrade RA, Piffer TRO & Teixeira, WS (2007) *Acompanhamento da safra brasileira. Cana-de-açúcar – safra 2007/2008, terceiro levantamento.* 13p. CONAB, Brasilia, DF http://www.conab.gov.br/conabweb/download/safra/2lev-cana.pdf (accessed on 28 January 2008)

Oliveira V A, Vicente M A, Fietto L G *et al* (2008) Biochemical and molecular characterization of *Saccharomyces cerevisiae* strains obtained from sugar-cane juice fermentations and their impact in cachaça production. *Appl Environ Microbiol* 74: 693-701

Pataro C, Guerra J B, Petrillo-Peixoto M L *et al* (2000) Yeasts communities end genetic polymorphism of *Saccharomyces cerevisiae* strains associated with artisanal fermentations in Brazil. *J Appl Microbiol.* 89: 24-31

RFA (2008) Renewable Fuel Associations, *Annual world ethanol production by country*, http://www.ethanolrfa.org/industry/statistics/ (accessed on 1st February 2008)

Richard C (2006) Brazil: a world leader. *Sugar Journal* **69**(7):11-15

Rosa C A, Soares A M, Faria J B (2008). Cachaça production In: W.M. Ingledew (ed) *The alcohol Texbook.* 5th edn. Nottingham University Press, Nottingham, in press.

Schwan RF, Mendonça AT, Silva JJ, Rodrigues V and Wheals AE (2001) Microbiology and physiology of cachaça (Aguardente) fermentations. *Antonie van Leeuwenhoek* **79:** 89–96.

Silva C L C, Rosa C A, Oliveira E.S (2006) Studies on the kinetic parameters for alcoholic fermentation by flocculent *Saccharomyces cerevisiae* strains and non-hydrogen sulfide-producing strains. *World J Microbiol Biotechnol.* **22**:857-863

Valdes C (2007) Ethanol demand driving the expansion of Brazil's sugar industry. *Sugar Journal* **70**:9-11

Verdi, A.V. (2006) Dinamicas e perspectives do mercado. *Econômicas* (São Paulo, Brazil) **36**:93-98.

Wheals AE, Basso LC, Alves DMG, & Amorim HV(1999) Fuel ethanol after 25 years. *Trends in Biotech.* **17**:482-487.

Chapter 2

Going against the grain: food versus fuel uses of cereals

Charles A. Abbas
Affiliate Institute for Genomic Biology, Molecular Bioengineering of Biomass Theme, University of Illinois at Urbana-Champaign, 1206 West Gregory Drive, MC-195, Urbana, IL 61801, USA

Introduction

Processors of cereal grains and other commodities today face some of the challenges that distillers face with rising energy and feedstock costs. This paper provides an overview of developments focusing on corn and other cereal grains used for bioethanol production. In the US, corn (maize) is the primary feedstock used to produce fuel ethanol. The corn dry milling process used in the US to produce fuel ethanol is similar to that used by cereal grain distilleries worldwide. This production method is very simple and yields ethanol and animal feed. By comparison, the other major process used in the US at corn wet mills yields a range of products and co-products such as corn oil, corn gluten meal, corn gluten feed, starches, and syrups (Figure 1). Recent trends and developments in wet and dry-milling ethanol technologies have been provided in a recent newsletter by O'Brien and Woolverton (2009).

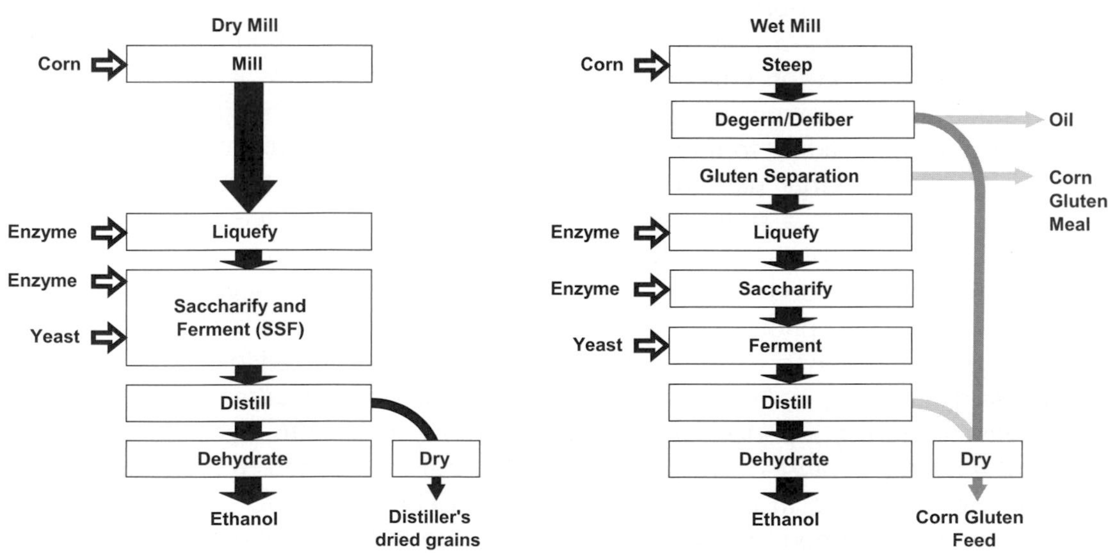

Figure 1. Comparison of ethanol production by corn dry and wet milling processes

Historic trends in commodity supply and prices

There are several historical causes of the world's agricultural commodity problems. Cycles of overproduction, trade barriers, and government price support and subsidies have had a negative impact on supplies and have destabilized the commodity markets. Growing subsidies and increased production incentives in developed countries have led to increased trade barriers by artificially dampening prices thereby creating an unfair advantage for exports from these countries over those from undeveloped countries. Trade barriers have frequently led to reduced cereal production in poor countries. Major research and development breakthroughs have led to excess production in developed countries. These countries heavily rely on liquid fossil fuels in agricultural production. Stagnated food demand in mature markets has prompted the need to look beyond food for other uses of the mounting surplus commodity crop stockpiles. Excess production has led to declining commodity prices and the idling of productive land through set-aside government-sponsored programs. Recent developments in agricultural production and higher demand and prices are beginning to reverse these trends. Today, there is greater emphasis on market-driven approaches with the adoption of freedom-to-farm policies that aim to reduce farmer reliance on government price support programs. Increased farm input costs and land values are leading to increased production costs (due in large part to high oil prices) that contribute to a steep rise in agricultural commodities prices. The above trends are coupled with increased emphasis on energy security with the adoption of policies worldwide for greater reliance on biofuels. Improved standards of living in Asia continue to increase demand during a period of tight inventories and reduced surpluses. One of the key things that we must keep in mind is that worldwide agricultural commodity supplies of oilseeds and cereal grains use are closely linked. From 1970 to 2007, production and total use rose from about 1,000 to about 2,400 million metric tons (FAPRI, 2008; USDA-ERS, 2008). In most years slight surpluses were common and as recently as 2002, commodity demand and prices were depressed. In response to the passage in the US of the Energy Independence and Security Act (EISA) in 2007, the demand for biofuels took off at a time when a drawdown in stockpiles of grains and oilseeds was occurring at a fast rate. This led to increased pressure on the market prices of these dwindling raw materials. In 2008, less than 15% of stocks remained in private and government held stockpiles as compared with a 30% surplus in 1999 (USDA-FAS, 2010).

Price pressures exerted from growing Asian economies increased demand for oil and other commodities, including food (IMF, 2008). In response to tight supplies and increased demand, prices of agricultural commodities rose in 2008 to an all time high index of 350 when measured over a starting 100 reference point index of January1992; oil prices rose sharply over the same period to an index of nearly 600, while the price of food commodities rose only slightly to an index of 175 (USDA-ERS, 2008). In spite of the rise in food and agricultural commodities, we need to keep in mind that since the 1970s, agricultural commodities have experienced normal price fluctuations with price increases often followed by periods of declining prices (FAPRI, 2008). A good example of this is the year 2000 which saw a historic low for all the major commodity crops (IMF, 2007; IMF, 2008). For this reason major agricultural commodity prices are expected to stabilize and drop from the historic high prices reached in 2008. As an example of this from highs in 2005, prices for refined and raw sugar have fallen and are leveling to levels seen back in 1996. Wheat and rice are also expected to decline to 1996 levels; other coarse grains, oilseeds and meals, will level off above their 1996 highs, but are expected to drop below the highs reached in 2008 (Figure 2; OECD-FAO, 2008).

Some of the key elements in predicting the future price of commodities are the cost of oil, land, machinery, fertilizer, seed, and taxes. In

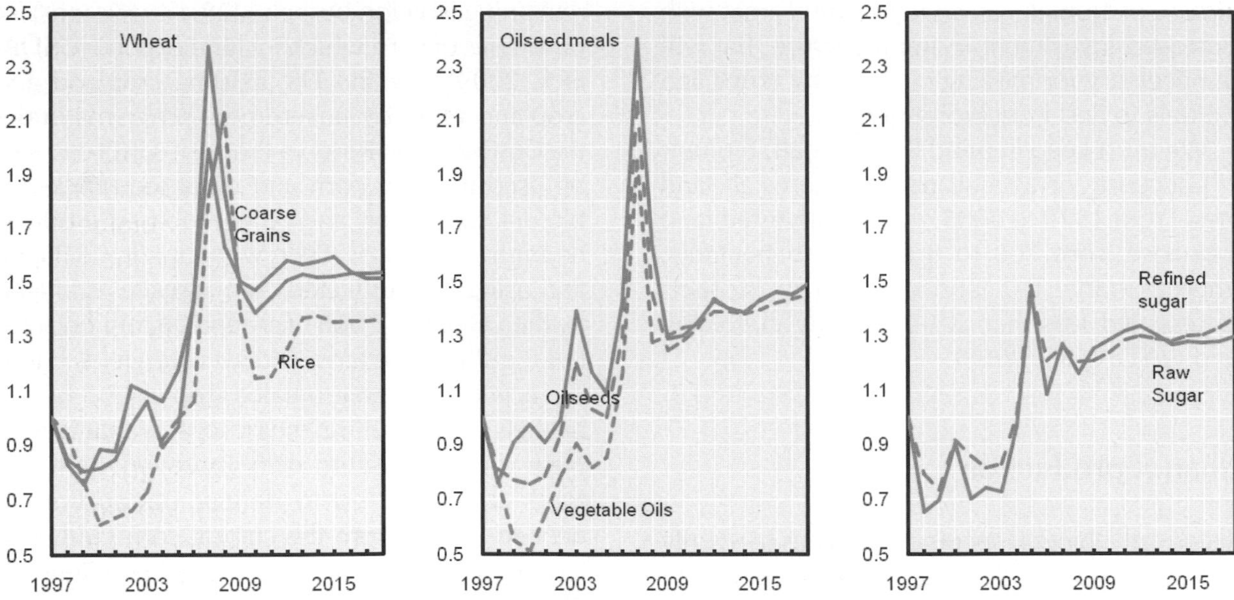

Figure 2. Outlook for world crop prices to 2018 (Index of nominal prices, 1997 = 1. Source OECD-FAO, 2008)

1996, corn traded at the commodity exchange at around $3.25 per bushel. Recent projections are consistent with corn prices to fluctuate in the range of $4.00 to $5.00 well below the highs seen in 2008 (USDA-ERS, 2009).

Worldwide ethanol production from food crops has risen from 7 billion gallons (26.5 billion liters) in 2004 to over 15 billion gallons (56.8 billion liters) in 2008. It is expected that by 2010 ethanol production from all commodity crops will be approximately 21 billion gallons (79.5 billion liters) and this figure is projected to increase in 2017 to around 25 billion gallons (94.6 billion liters) (USDA-ERS, 2008). Most of the increase in ethanol production from corn will occur in the United States (US) and for this reason the following will focus on current developments and feedstocks in North America.

Demand for biofuels

Setting the stage for increased bioethanol demand in the US is the Energy Independence and Security Act (EISA) of 2007 mandating that by 2022 36 billion gallons (136.2 billion liters) of liquid fuel must originate from renewable sources. The act also sets a ceiling of 15 billion gallons (56.8 billion liters) for the amount that can be produced from corn starch and sets a target for 21 billion gallons (79.5 billion liters) of biofuels from other conventional feedstocks, such as sugar and sweet sugar beets, as well as from non-conventional cellulosic (or, "second generation") feedstocks such as crop residues, woody material and dedicated energy crops (US-EIA, 2008).

Biofuels are attracting increased attention because of their many positive implications to energy independence, feedstock diversification, the environment, the economy, rural development, improved farm incomes, and job creation. Biofuels offer the potential for energy access in underserved areas such as the urban poor neighborhoods and rural off-grid communities. They can mitigate climate change through the reduction of greenhouse gases produced from fossil fuel uses. In developed and developing countries, biofuels can improve farm incomes and contribute to improving trade balance from reduced importation of crude oil while increasing the export of agricultural commodities that can be used for biofuel production. Finally, the increased production and use of biofuels can revitalize rural areas with increased investment in infrastructure that will be necessary for moving commodity crops and biofuels to and from biorefineries.

We must keep in mind that, overall, biofuels still account for a small percentage of all land uses. From 1970 to 2005, global harvested land area rose from 700 to 800 million hectares, whereas harvested land devoted to biofuels represented less than 3% of totally cultivated land (USDA-ERS, 2008).

Ethanol production

Historically, bioethanol production has used only a small portion of global grain production. The US consumption of corn for ethanol production represented a 7% share of the increase of the global wheat and coarse grain production from 1980/81 to 2002/03. For that same period, the total world wheat and coarse grain production increased from about 1,200 million metric tons to around 1,400 million metric tons (USDA-ERS, 2008). By comparison in 2008, in the United States corn ethanol production accounted for about 30% of the growth in global wheat and coarse grain crops from 2002/03 to 2007/08 (USDA-ERS, 2009). Note, however, that global wheat and coarse grains production has increased in the same year to 1,600 million metric tons or about a 14 % increase (USDA-FAS, 2010). Therefore, on a percentage basis the increase in bioethanol production, represents about 4.2 % in these commodity feedstocks or about 1/3 of the total increase in supplies worldwide for the 2002 to 2008 period.

Now a major ethanol biorefinery feedstock, corn is the most abundant low-cost feedstock for the production of ethanol in the United States (NCGA, 2008; USDA-ERS, 2009). Corn use for ethanol production is projected to level off at around 6 billion bushels (152.3 million metric tons) by about 2015. Given other uses of corn for feed and food uses, this level would require a total United States corn crop of around 15 billion bushels (380.7 million metric tons) with the remaining 9 billion bushels (228.4 metric tons) for other uses of corn which include exports (USDA-ERS, 2009). For the US, existing cropland and cropland idled by government programs under the Conservation Reserve Program (CRP) can also be used to grow corn and other feedstocks for biofuel, biopower, and other biobased products or animal feed uses. Even without idle CRP land and using the cultivated corn acreage estimated by the USDA for 2008 of around 86 million acres (34.8 million hectares) and average yields based on recent crops, an estimated crop of 13.5 billion bushels (342.6 million metric tons) is anticipated. New varieties of corn with improved yield and traits are projected to deliver the additional needed supply from the current corn cultivated land in the upper Midwest of the US (Edgerton, 2009).

Since 1970, the price of a barrel of crude oil has risen by over 2,000%, while in the same period corn prices per bushel rose by 300%. Over the 1998-2008 decade, corn prices rose by an estimated 283% as compared with an 804% rise in crude oil prices (NCGA, 2008). This indicates that in spite of heavy dependence of US farmers on petroleum and other fossil fuels to power their machinery and in the manufacturing of fertilizer, the impact of oil prices have been mitigated by improvements in corn yields and agronomic practices that required less input of fertilizers and chemicals.

A recent University of Illinois study estimated the current corn production costs to average about $4.00 per bushel. These production costs are based on increased farmland values and reflect increases that farmers incur from rising fossil fuel prices, higher fertilizer costs, higher seed prices, higher taxes, and higher purchase prices of farm machinery. During 2008, corn traded at the Chicago Commodity Exchange in the range of $6-8 per bushel. But over the next few months, corn traded in the range of $4 to $6 per bushel. The higher corn prices are primarily due to increased input costs for commodity grains that have been rising steadily from 2002 to 2008 (FAPRI, 2008). Reduced corn costs to farmers will have a direct impact on farm profitability and will result in better margins as well as moderate corn prices to lower levels.

Most corn in the US is grown in the Midwest, where there is relatively plentiful water as well as good fertile soil (NCGA, 2010). Five states, Iowa, Illinois, Minnesota, Nebraska and Indiana, account for over 80% of the corn grown. This distribution may change with a new focus on drought-resistant hybrids that will extend corn production to drier areas of the US (Padgette, 2008).

Corn biorefineries

Most currently operating and under-construction biorefineries are located in the Midwestern region of the US near where the corn is grown (NCGA, 2010). There are also scattered clusters of biorefineries in California's central valley, the Texas Panhandle, the Rocky Mountain States, the Southeastern region, Northwest and Northeastern states (BBI, 2010; RFA, 2010). At present (2010) in the US, there are about 211 ethanol plants operating and an additional 28 under construction (BBI, 2010). Another 200 projects have also been proposed. The processing of corn to bioethanol in the US has significantly increased since beginning at 175 million gallons in 1980. The period of 1980-2002, experienced relatively slow growth as compared with the 2003 to 2007 years, in which production doubled to over 6.0 billion gallons (22.7 billion liters). In the past three years (2008-2010), production capacity have witnessed dramatic growth with a doubling in production capacity to 12 billion gallons (45.4 billion liters) with a parallel capacity increase in plants being planned or in early phase of construction (RFA, 2010). Increased production of ethanol has been accompanied by a significant rise in corn production and the use of corn for biofuels. Since 1990, ethanol's share of the US corn crop production has increased six-fold, with the share increasing sharply from 2001 to 2008, in which it represented almost 38% of the total crop (NCGA, 2008). In spite of the increase of corn use for ethanol, in 2007 the US exported more corn than in 2005. The rise in corn exports was enabled by increased corn production from cultivated land. Increased exports and non-feed uses of corn rose from 26% in 2005 to 36% in 2007. Over the same years there was a decline in animal feed uses from 55% to 45%. As of 2009, corn uses for ethanol production have increased to 38 % (Figure 3). While USDA projections for

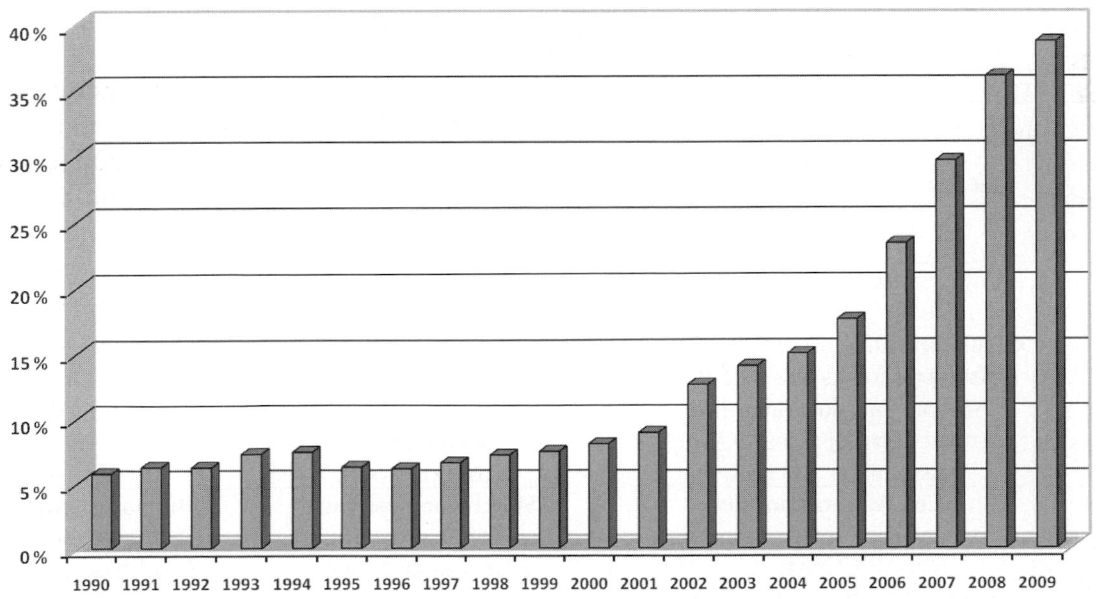

Figure 3. Ethanol share of US total corn crop 1990-2009.

2019 continue to suggest continued increase in corn uses for ethanol, these reports also indicate a modest rise in both exports and animal feed uses of corn (FAPRI, 2008; USDA-ERS, 2009).

Advances in maize biotechnology

Corn yields per acre have increased since the 1980's and are projected to continue rising at the current rate of 6% to 7%. In 2007, the United States corn crop production exceeded 13 billion bushels or 329.9 million metric tons (USDA-ERS, 2009). Projections from companies such as Monsanto and Pioneer indicate that 300 bushels per acre might be possible from new hybrids and transgenic varieties of corn developed and improved using conventional and genetic engineering approaches. If this is the case, then a 25 billion bushel corn crop (634.5 million metric tons), which in 2009 represented almost 95 % of the total world production of corn (now estimated at 668 million metric tons).

There are qualitative and quantitative approaches to improving and increasing corn starch and corn biomass through the use of traditional corn breeding and molecular biology engineering (Table 1; Moeller and Wang, 2008; Torney *et al.* 2007). Some of the genomic tools and plant engineering approaches in use for improving corn are: conventional breeding, mutagenesis and selection, molecular marker assisted breeding, genetic engineering and transgenics (Moeller and Wang, 2008). Current limitations to the use of these techniques are the limited number of genotypes to select from and the need to expand genetic pool to insure greater ability to introduce multiple traits and to improve transgene expression for the desired agronomic traits. One of the advantages of corn is the presence of complete cytological maps, sequence databases and cell lines available (Moeller and Wang, 2008). Some of the desirable plant traits and ideotypes that are current targets for improvement are: higher or modified starch, higher oil content and higher value oils such as: higher phytosterols, higher omega oils, higher Vitamin A (carotenes), higher αtocopherol and other other tocols present in natural Vitamin E, lower saturates or higher poly unsaturates, higher xanthophylls and higher protein content. Other targets are increasing bushel yield produced per acre with reduced nitrogen input, enhanced drought and pest resistant corn, reduced lignin or phenolics in the stalks, stover and cobs to lower processing cost and to improve feed and co-product value. Improving feed value requires new varieties with reduced phytate and varieties

Table 1. Breeding maize for biofuels (source: Prof. Kan Wang, Iowa State University, Ames, IA).

Summary of genetic engineering approaches and biomass yield and properties targets for improvements			
Genetic engineering	**Genetic engineering technology**:	a) Agronomical elite line transformation b) Transgene expression control c) Site specific integration and d) gene stacking	e) Plastid transformation f) Male sterility
Biomass yield	**Stress Tolerance:** - Effector genes (Super oxide dismutase-SOD, insecticidal proteins) - Transcription factors (DREB/CBF) - Signal transduction (mitogen activated protein kinase- MAPK) - Regulation (Micro RNA)	**Photosynthesis:** - Carbon dioxide (CO2) fixation (phosphoenol pyruvate carboxylase-PEPC) -Calvin cycle enzymes - Plant architecture (brassinosteroids)	**Grain Yield:** - Sink strength (ADP glucose pyrophosphorylase - AGP)
Biomass properties	**Cell wall composition:** - caffeic acid o-methyltransferase (COMT) - Specific cytochrome P450 enzymes : p-coumarate 3-hydroxylase	**Starch composition:** - Starch enzyme : Amylopullulanase	**Biomass conversion enzymes:** - Glucanase expression - Expansin

selected for higher content of the essential amino acids: lysine, tryptophan, and threonine. By engineering corn plants with segregated *in situ* enzymes it is possible to reduce cost and improve ease of processing. New varieties can be selected for higher cellulose or higher biomass (i.e. ton per hectare) and improved kernel integrity as well other enhanced corn plant physical attributes to withstand severe weather.

Substantial gains in corn yield per acre due to molecular breeding and biotechnology are predicted to double the corn crop in 2030 from 2009. By 2030, we could see yields in the neighborhood of 300 bushels per acre (18.8 metric tons /hectare), up from an average yield of 149.1 bushels per acre (9. 3 metric tons /hectare) in 2006 (Edgerton, 2009). This increase can also translate to greater corn stover biomass that would be available for as a lignocellulosic feedstock for biofuel production (Figure 4; Figure 5).

The targets set by the 2007 Energy Independence and Security Act (EISA) for the year 2022 of 36 billion gallons of liquid biofuels can readily be met from corn and/or dedicated energy crops planted on set-aside land in the USDA Conservation Reserve Program (CRP) program which is currently about 33 million acres (13.4 million hectares). A high-yield energy crop such as miscanthus grown on CRP land can be processed to produce up to 41 billion gallons (155.2 billion liters) and can alone meet the entire target. A low-yield energy crop such as switchgrass grown on CRP land can be processed to produce up to 16 billion gallons (60.6 billion

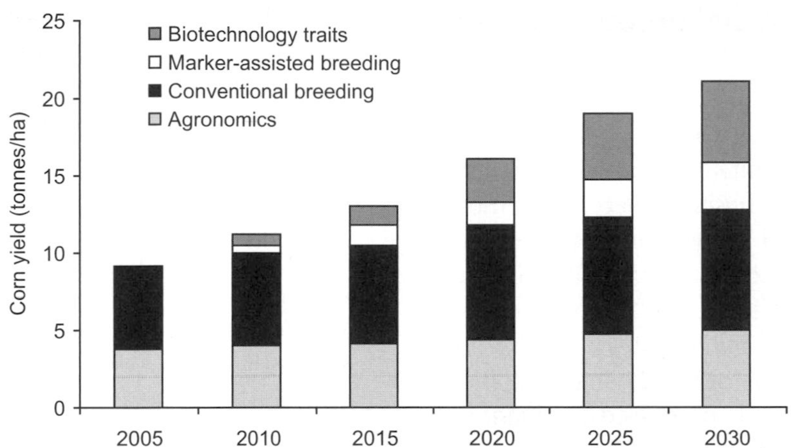

Figure 4. Long term yield potential of new technologies *(Courtesy of Michael Edgerton, Monsanto).*

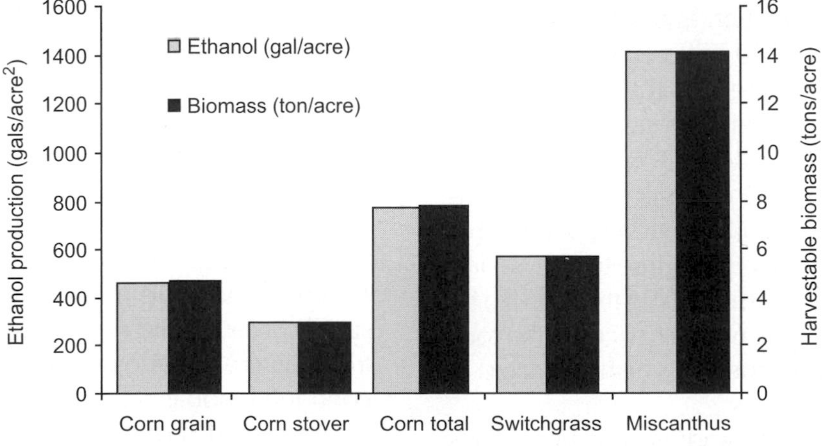

Figure 5. Comparison of ethanol production from corn and perennial grasses.

liters). The target can also be met by combining switchgrass produced on CRP with 28% corn crop of 25 billion bushels (634.5 million metric tons) or 7 billion bushels (177.7 million metric tons) as follows: 19 billion gallons (71.9 billion liters) from corn, 2.0 billion gallons (7.6 billion liters) from corn stover, 3.4 billion gallons (12.9 billion liters) from corn cobs, and 1.4 billion gallons (5.3 billion liters) from corn fibre. The projections are based on these key assumptions: a yield of 2.7 gallons of ethanol per bushel of corn; corn residues are processed to ethanol; there is 50% stover collection, theoretical conversion of sugars to ethanol, and a 25 billion bushel corn crop based on 300 bushels per acre (18.8 metric tons/hectare).

Limitations to biofuel production from corn

There are limitations to corn uses for biofuel production. These limitations can be calculated based on the 12 billion bushel (304.6 million metric tons) 2008 projected harvest and the projected future crop size for 2022 of 25 billion bushels (634.5 million metric tons). A US corn crop of 12 billion bushels (304.6 million metric tons) would produce 32 billion gallons (121.1 billion liters) if the entire corn crop is processed to ethanol. A 25 billion bushel corn crop (634.5 million metric tons) would produce a maximum of 44 billion gallons of ethanol (9 billion bushels are already in use). Total transportation liquid fuel use in the US is approximately 140 billion gallons per year (530 billion liters); therefore, total replacement of all liquid fuels derived from petroleum would require 213.4 billion gallons (808.8 billion liters) of bioethanol on an energy content basis. This is the equivalent of 79.0 billion bushels of corn that at current yields would require close to 500 million acres (200 million hectares) of land that need to be cultivated for corn. This number exceeds the total cultivated land area in the US which estimated in 2009 at 473 million acres.

One of the ways to address the limitations to the use of cereal-grain starches is to look to alternative feed stocks for biofuel production: captive fibers from cereal crop processing, cereal and non-cereal commodity crop residues, such as sugarcane bagasse, wheat chaff, and residues from soft-and hardwood processing, as well as harvesting residues from forest management programs. Future sources that can be used to expand biofuel production are dedicated energy crops: prairie perennial grasses such as miscanthus and switchgrass, and fast growing hybrids of poplar, willow, and other trees. It is clear from the above that there is a need to deploy a wide range of the existing commodity crops as well as perennial grasses and new energy crops to meet the growing demand for biofuels. This is illustrated in a comparison for the production of ethanol from corn plant to the potential ethanol from perennial crops such as switchgrass and giant miscanthus (*Miscanthus x giganteus*) on an acre basis (Figure 5, Grooms, 2008). When compared to the current cultivated land for corn grain and the reduced requirements for farming inputs, miscanthus offers an attractive alternative crop for biofuel production from poor and marginal lands (Long, 2006; Pyter et al. 2007). Further development that will reduce the barriers to economic processing of lignocellulosics and the establishment of a supply chain for dedicated perennial energy crops would be necessary to meet future biofuel needs.

Concluding remarks

In conclusion, all users of commodities (processers and consumers) will adjust to recent changes in markets. Margins will improve through early adoption of new technologies that seek to reduce water and energy uses over existing farming practices. A second green (or what is referred to today as the next wave or blue) revolution in agriculture will aid in increased production and supply of cereal and non-cereal commodity grains from the greater adoption of biotechnology. The continued global access to capital accompanied by increased farm inputs, higher production, improved yields, and gain in farm incomes will improve margins for processors, providers of seed, farm machinery and end products that will sustain growth in these important segments. Commodity prices will be stable as supply is projected to stay ahead of demand thereby insuring that increased production of biofuels have less impact on food and feed prices. There will a greater role for new technologies that aim to better manage waste effluent streams and address greenhouse gas emissions from the use of fossil fuels. Moves towards greater diversification of feedstock and a new portfolio of end products will accelerate. Over the long run, greater returns to the farming sector will ensure a continued feedstock supply with better sustainable farming practices.

References

BBI (2010). Ethanol plant list. http://www.ethanolproducer.com/plant-list.jsp

Edgerton, M.D. (2009). Increasing crop productivity to meet global needs for feed, food, and fuel. *Plant Physiology* 149:7-13

FAPRI (2008). U.S. and world agricultural outlook. FAPRI, Ames, IA

Grooms, L. (2008). Biofuels corn and beyond. Farm Industry News http://farmindustrynews.com/seed/corn/biofuels-corn-beyond/

IMF (2007). World economic outlook: spillovers and cycles in the global economy. International Monetary Fund. http://imf.org/external/pubs/ft/weo/2007/01/pdf/text.pdf (April, 2007)

IMF (2008). World economic outlook: a survey by the staff of the International Monetary Fund. IMF. http://www.imf.org/external/pubs/ft/weo/2008/01/pdf/text.pdf (November 7, 2008)

Long, S. (2006). Miscanthus --A Solution to U.S. Dependence on Foreign Oil? http://www.aces.uiuc.edu/news/stories/news3623.html

Moeller, L. and Wang, K. (2008). Engineering with precision tools for new generation of biotech crops. *Bioscience* 58:391-411

NCGA (2008). U.S. Corn growers producing food and fuel. National Corn Growers Association. http://www.ncga.com/files/pdf/FoodandFuelPaper10-08.pdf

NCGA (2010). Corn production trends 1991-2008 http://www.ncga.com/corn-production-trends

O'Brien D. and Woolverton, M. (2009). Recent Trends in U.S. Wet and Dry Corn Milling Production. AgMRC Renewable Newsletter. http://www.agmrc.org/renewable_energy/ethanol/recent_trends_in_us_wet_and_dry_corn_milling_producti on.cfm (Feb. 2009)

OECD-FAO (2008). Agricultural Outlook 2008-2017. Organisation for Economic Co-Operation and Development. OECD Publications, Paris

Padgette, S. (2008). Golden opportunities: working jointly for higher yields. Monsanto. http://www.monsanto.com/pdf/investors/2008/09-16-08.pdf (November 7, 2008)

Pyter, R; Voigt, T; Dohleman, F; Long, S.P. (2007). Growing Giant Miscanthus in Illinois. http://miscanthus.illinois.edu/wp-content/uploads/growersguide.pdf

RFA (2010). Ethanol biorefinery locations. Renewable Fuels Association. http://www.ethanolrfa.org/industry/locations

Torney, F., Moeller, L., Scrapa, A. and Wang, K. (2007). Genetic engineering approaches to improve bioethanol production from maize. Current Opinion in Biotechnology 18:193-199

USDA FAS (2010). World agricultural supply and demand (WASDE). http://usda.mannlib.cornell.edu/usda/current/wasde/wasde-03-10-2010.pdf

USDA ERS (2008). Agricultural long term projections to 2017. Economic Research Service. http://www.ers.usda.gov/Publications/OCE081/OCE20081c.pdf (February 2008)

USDA ERS (2009). The economics of food, farming, natural resources, and rural America. Economic Research Service. http://www.ers.usda.gov/Briefing/Corn/ (March 27, 2009)

US EIA (2008). Energy Information Administration. Energy Independence and Security Act (EISA) of 2007. http://www.eia.doe.gov/aeo_2008analysispapers/eisa.html

Conversion factors used

1 hectare = 2.47105 acres 1 gal of ethanol has 0.655 energy content of gasoline 1 bushel yields 2.7 gallons of ethanol

1 gallon = 3.7854 liters 1 metric ton = 39.4 million bushels (1 bushel of corn = 56 lbs)

Chapter 3

Advanced enzymatic pre-treatment for High Gravity Fermentation

Elmar Janser[1] and Erik Anker Andersen[2]
[1] *Novozymes Switzerland AG, Neumatt, CH-4243 Dittingen, Switzerland*
[2] *Novozymes A/S, Krogshoejvej 36 · DK-2880 Bagsvaerd, Denmark*

Introduction

The recent increase in energy prices and the future outlook is forcing the distilling industry towards process optimisation with a focus on energy savings. One way to save energy is to process, cook and ferment at a higher dry substance (DS) level by using enzymes and less water – this is also known as High Gravity Fermentation (HGF, see Fig 1). One of the drawbacks associated with running at a higher dry substance level is the increase in mash viscosity especially when using rye, wheat, barley or triticale. This contribution concerns the application of a new enzyme preparation and describes results on advanced pre-treatment for HGF.

HGF means processing at an increased DS level in the mash and a reduced usage of water (see Fig 2). For example, at 15% DS, 5m^3 of water is used per ton grain whereas at 35%, DS only 1.5 m^3 water is used. The grain/water ratio drops in this case from 1:5 to 1:1.5

With HGF an increased grain throughput can be realized with less water usage and using the same tank capacity. At 30-35% DS the grain

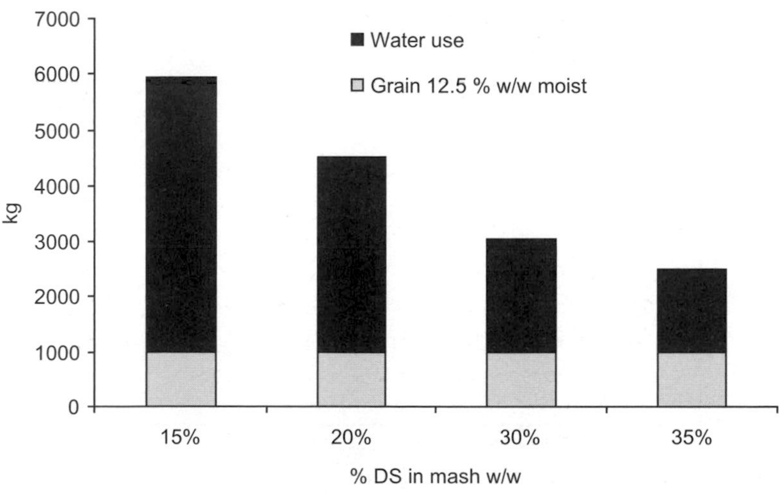

Figure 1. The concept of High Gravity Fermentation (HGF).

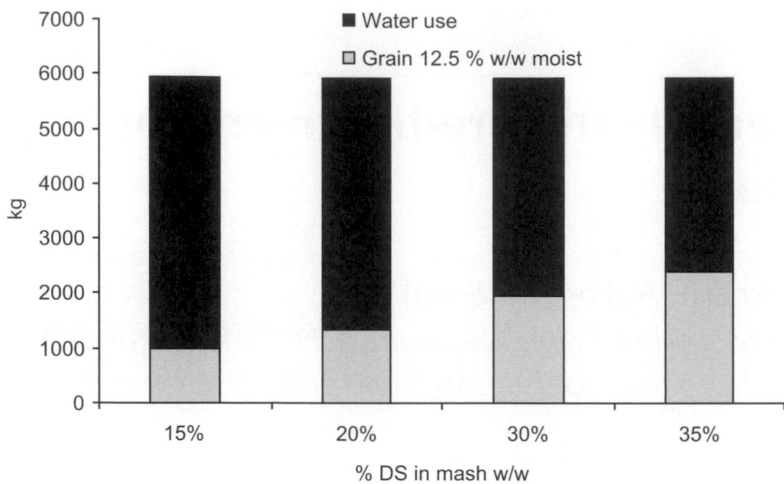

Figure 2. Water use in High Gravity Fermentation.

throughput is double or more compared to 15% DS. Compared with 15% DS, the increase in throughput is:

At 20% DS: + 32%
At 30% DS: + 95%
At 35% DS: + 138%

In North America, corn is nowadays mainly processed at 30-35% DS using a state of the art and modern alpha-amylase for liquefaction, which has also the ability to reduce the mash viscosity.

Beside water savings substantial energy savings can be realized when processing at higher DS and conducting HGF (Moelgaard 1986 – see Fig 3). It takes only one third of the energy to heat up 1 kg of grains compared to heating of 1 kg of water. Therefore, the higher the DS in the mash, the less water needs to be heated and the less overall energy is expended. Further energy savings can be realized by conducting HGF as less water needs to be evaporated during distilling following fermentation.

Table 1. Viscosity of cereals used in HGF.

	*Viscosity Pa*S*
Wheat	0.8 - 1.2
Triticale	0.8 - 1.2
Barley	3.5 - 5
Rye	6 - 10

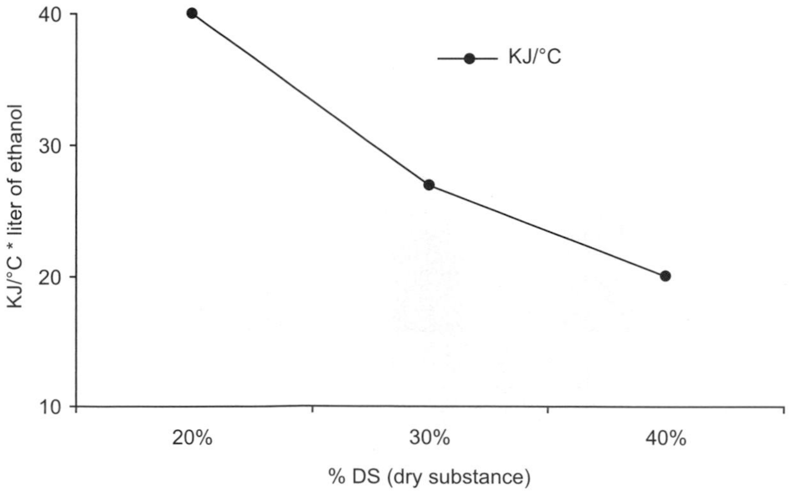

Figure 3. Energy consumption during cooking (Moelegaard et al., 1986).

Increasing the % DS concomitantly leads to increased mash viscosities in several raw materials (Table 1). We have measured viscosities in 30% DS water/flour slurries at 50°C using a Rapid Visco Analyser (RVA) and a Haake viscometer VVT 550 and found typical viscosities of: Rye (6-10 Pa*S), Barley (3.5-5 Pa*S) and wheat and triticale (0.8-1.2 Pa*S each). These values vary also from region to region and from year to year.

Table 2 shows the composition of various cereals used in HGF. Wheat, barley and rye show a much higher water soluble cell wall material content compared to corn (Mathlouthi 2002). The higher cell wall material content is the reason for the higher viscosities of these grains.

Among these cell wall materials mainly the non-starch polysaccharides, arabino-xylans and beta-glucans are found (see Fig 4).

A closer look to the compositions of various cereal cell wall components (Fig 4) shows that wheat and rye are high in water soluble pentosans, mainly arabino-xylans, whereas barley has a high soluble beta-glucan content (Olsen 2004). Corn (maize) has relatively low amounts of soluble pentosans and no soluble glucans, and this explains why high viscosity in corn is less problematic in HGF. The high non starch polysaccharides (% NSP) content in rye, barley and wheat needs to be degraded by suitable enzymes in order to lower viscosities and achieve high % DS for HGF.

Enzymes and characteristics

The microorganisms which are used for enzyme production must be non toxic and can be of bacterial or fungal origin. The enzymes are produced according to international quality standards (WHO, FAO, JECFA, FCC) for food grade enzymes. Microbial fermentations are conducted in closed submerged tanks using

Table 2. Composition of cereals used in HGF.

Component	*% content of dry matter*			
	Wheat	*Barley*	*Rye*	*Corn*
Protein	12-14	10-11	10-15	9-12
Fat	3	2.5-3	2-3	4.5
Starch	57-70	52-64	55-65	65-72
Ash	2	2.3	2	1.5
Total cell wall material[1]	11.4	14.0	14.6	9.6
Water extractable non-starchy polysaccharides (NSP):				
Arabinoxylans[1]	0.6	0.3	1.4	0.03
Beta-glucans[1]	0.14	2.4	0.8	0.05

[1] Mathlouthi (2002)

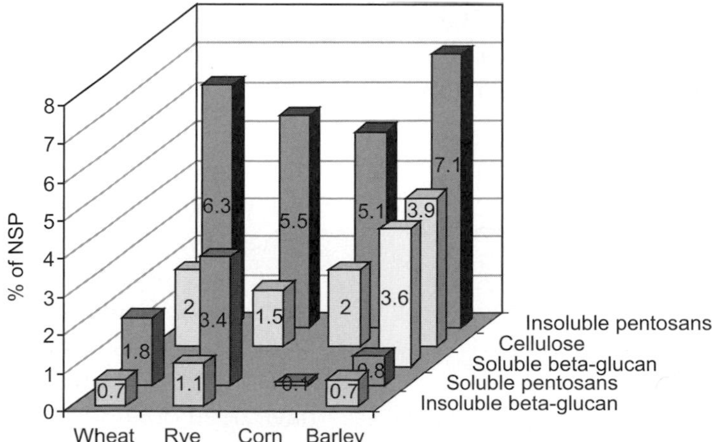

Figure 4. Non-starch polysaccharides (NSP) in various cereals.

substrates such as syrups, sugars, proteins and salts. After fermentation, the enzymes are separated from the microorganisms then standardized, filtered and sold as liquid or granules. The microorganisms are inactivated and used as fertilizer.

Industrial enzymes have several applications: in detergents, textiles, leather industry, animal feed and food processing (baking, beverages, dairy, food, nutrition, starch and ethanol). In alcohol production from grains, mainly 4 enzyme types are used:

- Alpha-amylases for liquefaction
- Amylo-glucosidases for saccharification
- Proteases for fermentation enhancement
- 1st and 2nd generation enzyme preparations of cellulases, glucanases, xylanases for viscosity reduction on rye, wheat, barley, triticale

There is now also a 3rd generation enzyme preparation, Novozymes Viscoferm® (see below).

Fig 5 shows the action of GH10 and GH11 xylanases. New developments in this sector have lead to an enzyme preparation which contains a unique endo-xylanase of the GH10 family. This enzyme is able to cleave and degrade arabino-xylan when the xylose is linked with arabinose, or in the case of xylo-glucan, when linked to glucose. Xylanases of the GH11 family, however, are only able to cleave arabino-xylan, when the xylose is not linked to arabinose or another molecule. The advantage of the GH10 endo-xylanase is that it can attack the arabino-xylan at any point and this leads to a much lower mash viscosity.

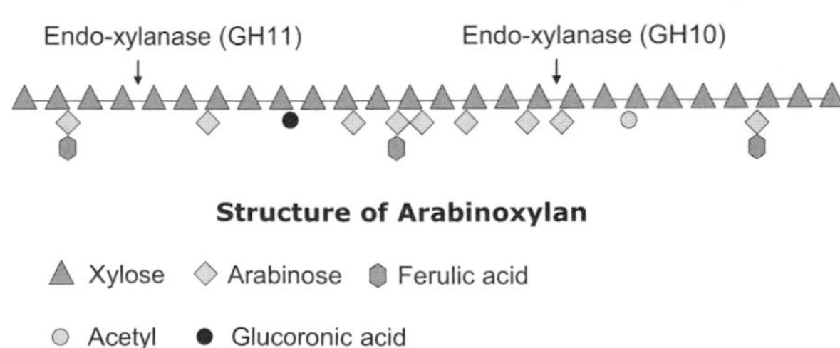

Figure 5. Action of xylanases on arabinoxylan.

A new enzyme preparation – called Viscoferm – contains, beside this unique endo-xylanase, also balanced enzyme activities of beta-glucanase, cellulase and alpha-amylase in order to cope with the different substrates compositions and raw materials.

Test results obtained with the new enzyme Viscoferm: laboratory studies

Fig 6 shows the effect of Viscoferm on viscosity reduction on 100% rye with reaction times of 0-60 minutes and different enzyme dosages (0, 0.1, 0.2 and 0.3 kg/ton DS). With rye, the initial viscosity is close to 10 Pa*S. A mash with 10 Pa*S viscosity is impossible to process, but following enzyme treatment with Viscoferm this leads to rapid viscosity reduction to below 1 Pa*S, which then can be processed.

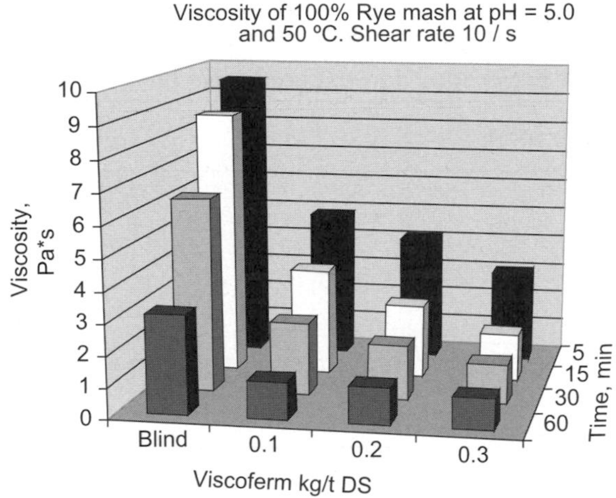

Figure 6. Influence of Viscoferm on viscosity of a rye mash.

Fig 7 shows the results with a 50/50 mix of wheat and rye mash. Wheat has a much lower viscosity with an initial value of close to 1 Pa*S. The blend has a viscosity of approx. 3.5 Pa*S due to the contribution from the rye. The enzyme treatment leads to a viscosity of below 0.5 Pa*S.

Similar tests results and enzyme performance have been obtained treating triticale and barley and are presented in Figs 8 and 9.

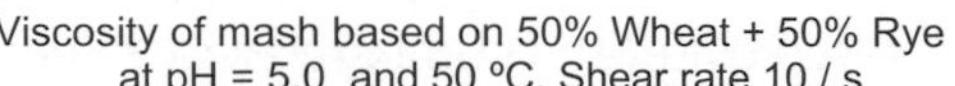

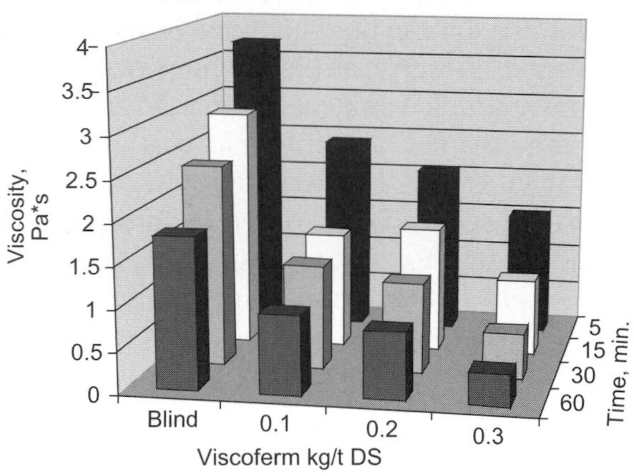

Figure 7. Influence of Viscoferm on viscosity of a wheat:rye mash.

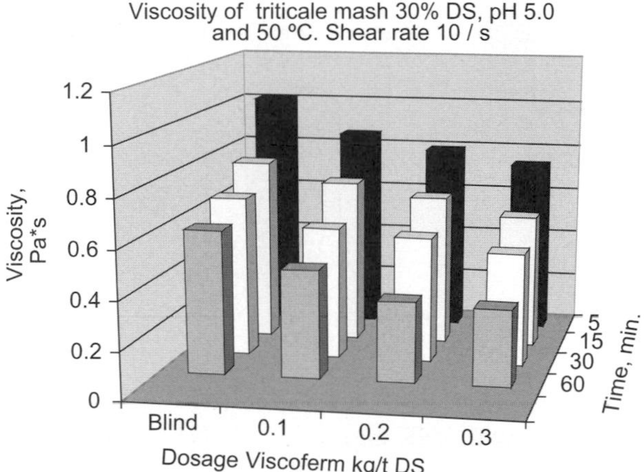

Figure 8. Influence of Viscoferm on viscosity of a triticale mash.

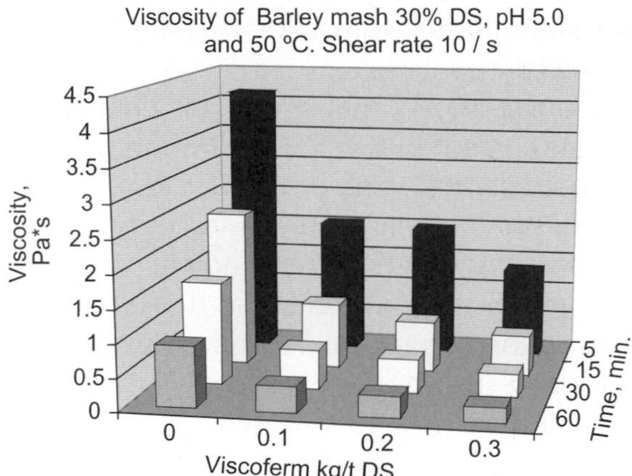

Figure 9. Influence of Viscoferm on viscosity of a barley mash.

Figure 10 shows the impact of increasing DS (28%, 30%, 32%, 36%) on viscosity of rye mash and enzyme performances over time. The determinations were done at pH 5.7 and at 50 °C. It can be seen that the enzyme treatment leads to viscosity reductions of less than 20% of the original viscosity in less than 60 minutes. In this way the rye mash slurries with as high as 36% DS can be made pumpable and processed.

Test results obtained with Viscoferm: industrial results and experience

Figure 11 outlines cereal processing on an industrial scale. The Viscoferm enzyme

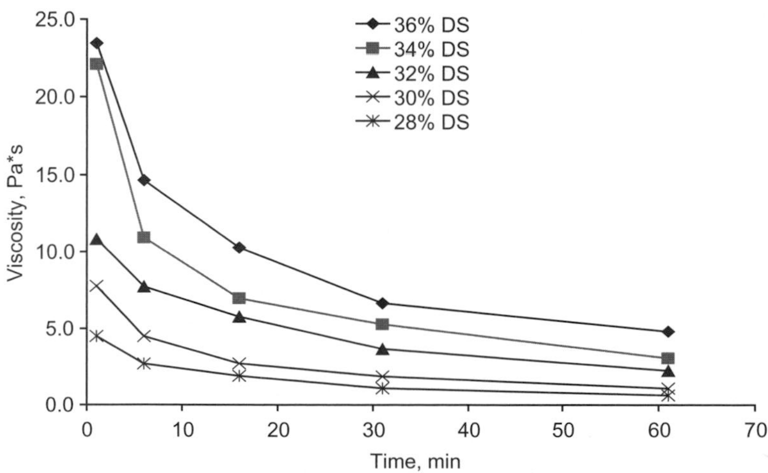

Figure 10. The impact of increasing dry substance on viscosity of a rye mash treated with Viscoferm®.

preparation was added prior to liquefaction in the slurry mix tank with a 20 – 30 minute holding at 50-55°C.

Table 3 shows that this plant obtained an alcohol content of 7-7.5% (v/v) when not using any viscosity reducing enzyme (VRE). With the use of 1st or 2nd generation VRE viscosity could be reduced and the DS correspondingly increased, leading to an alcohol content of 10.5-11.5% (v/v) following fermentation. With the use of the 3rd generation enzyme – Viscoferm – the alcohol level obtained was 13-14% (v/v).

The usage of water could be reduced significantly which can be seen from the grain/water ratio which was as low as 1:1.5 in the best case. The throughput capacities could be increased by +50% compared to a 2nd generation VRE and over 80% compared to no VRE.

In Table 4 it can be seen that this distillery got a maximal 7.5% (v/v) alcohol, when not using any viscosity reducing enzyme. With a 2nd generation VRE the obtained alcohol yield was just above 10% (v/v). Using Viscoferm, the viscosity could further be reduced and % DS maximized. The maximal alcohol output was 14.6% (v/v) in subsequent fermentation using a high alcohol tolerant yeast strain. The mash water could be reduced from 12.5m³ without VRE use down to 4.0m³ per 1.0m³ alcohol. Calculated per ton rye, the mash water use could be reduced from 4.4m³

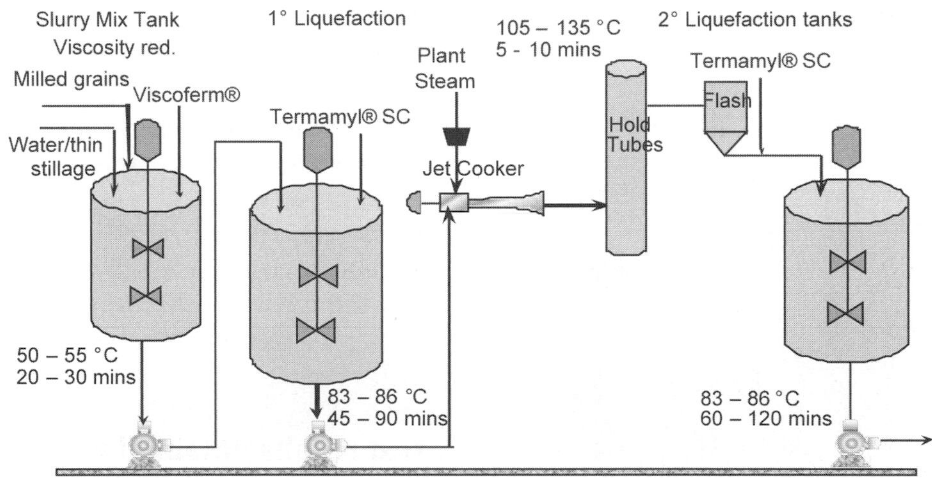

Figure 11. Common liquefaction system with VRE step.

Table 3. Example 1: 100 % rye.

100% rye	*Control No VRE*	*VRE 2nd eneration*	*Viscoferm®*
Alcohol content in mash (v/v)	7-7.5%	10.5-11.5%	13-14%
% DS achieved	17.5-18.7%	26.2-28.7%	32.5-35.0%
Rye/water ratio	1:4	1:2,2	1:1,5
Capacity increase	Benchmark	+ >30% compared to no VRE	+ >80% compared to no VRE

Table 4. Example 2: 100 % rye.

100% rye	*Control*	*VRE 2nd eneration*	*Viscoferm®*
Enzyme dosage	No VRE	0.15 kg/ton rye	0.15 kg/ton rye
DS achieved	15-18.7%	25.0%	36.5%
Alcohol content in mash (v/v)	6-7.5%	10.0%	14.6% special yeast used
Mash water use per 1m³ alcohol	12.5m³	7.2m³	4.0m³
Energy savings	Benchmark	25% steam reduction	>50% steam reduction
Capacity increase	Benchmark	+30%	+ >90%

down to 1.4m^3. The energy savings were a 50% reduction of steam for cooking and distillation.

Table 5 shows that this distillery used the best 2nd generation VRE and achieved a maximal 12% (v/v) alcohol content. Using Viscoferm, the DS could further be increased and alcohol output was over 14.5% (v/v). A yeast strain with high alcohol tolerance was used during fermentation and special attention was given to have sufficient yeast nutrients available. The steam usage could be further reduced by 25% compared to VRE use but over 50% without VRE use.

Table 6 shows tests results in a distillery with 100% wheat. In summary:

- Alcohol increased from 8% to 12.5% (v/v). The limiting factors were not the viscosity but the special distillation columns with plates which did not allow distillation of beer mashes over 12.5% alcohol.
- One of the production lines could be closed due to doubling of the other line.
- The energy savings (steam and electricity) were € 2.68/ton wheat based on a very low steam price of € 4/ton steam in this region and from 2 years ago. The energy savings split was € 1.51 for steam and € 1.17 for electricity.
- Using more realistic costs for steam of € 20/ ton or even € 40/ton, the energy savings in this case would have been over € 8 respectively over € 16 /ton wheat.
- The water savings were 1.875 m^3 per ton wheat and the steam savings were – 0.378 ton per ton wheat.

Benefits of the advanced enzymatic pre-treatment

1. Reduced costs for energy, water and operation
   - Lower energy consumption (steam, electricity, oil, gas) as less water needs to be heated, cooled and evaporated
   - Reduced water consumption
   - More flexible backset management

2. Increased output and capacity by HGF
   - Highest Gravity Fermentation with 30-35% DS levels can be realized

Table 5. Example 3: 100% wheat.

100% wheat	*Control*	*VRE 2nd generation*	*Viscoferm®*
Enzyme dosage	No VRE	0.10 l/t grain	0.10 l/t grain
Alcohol (v/v)	8-9%	10-12%	>14.5% special yeast used
% DS achieved	18.9-21.3%	23.7-28.5%	34.3%
Energy savings	Benchmark	20-25% steam reduction	>50% steam reduction
Capacity increase	Control	+30%	>70%

Table 6. Example 4: 100% wheat.

100% wheat	*Control*	*Viscoferm®*
Enzyme dosage	No VRE	0.10 kg/t wheat
Alcohol v/v	8%	12.5%
Energy costs 2005 Ru: € 4/ton steam 2005 EU: € 20/ton steam 2008 EU: € 40/ton steam	Benchmark	Energy savings (steam and electricity) at different costs per ton steam: 4 € : > 2.68 /ton wheat 20 € : > 8.73 /ton wheat 40 € : > 16.23 /ton wheat
Capacity increase	Benchmark	Only 1 production line used instead of 2 - to feed and maintain the same distillation capacity

- Thinner mash at higher solids (less water)

3. Increased efficiency in operations
   - Better mash flow and heat exchange operations
   - Improved centrifuge and evaporator efficiency
   - Reduced fouling, cleaning and wear of equipment

4. Flexibility in raw material usage
   - Cereal and raw material composition can be changed and optimised according to price and availability

5. Reduced waste and higher DDGS quality
   - More stillage can be recycled
   - DDGS has a higher protein content

Recommendations for conducting successful HGF

- Use slurry and fermentation tanks with a strong agitation system
- pH should be between 5.0 – 6.0
- Use a selected yeast with a high alcohol tolerance
- Make sure enough yeast nutrients are available
- Regularly measure the viscosity at the key points in the distillery e.g. slurry tank after liquefaction, before and after heat exchanger, in fermentation and in stillage. This ensures the benchmark values are captured when the plant is running under optimal conditions
- Pay attention to newly harvested grains

Conclusions

The development of a new enzyme product (Viscoferm) has it made feasible to drastically reduce mash viscosities in challenging raw materials such as rye, barley, wheat and triticale.

With such low viscosities, it is feasible to process these raw materials at over 30% DS, and get 14% alcohol. In terms of energy savings, 25-30% of the total energy and water can be saved compared to processing at 15-20% DS. Stillage waste can be reduced by increased recycling. Process improvements can be achieved with no extra investments or only slight adjustments. Enzymatic pre-treatments contribute to more sustainable production processes by using less energy and water. Finally, rising energy prices will make the application of novel viscosity reducing enzymes in alcohol distilleries more attractive in the future.

References

Mathlouthi, N., Saulnier L., Quemener, B. and Larbier, M. (2002). Xylanase, beta-glucanase, and other side enzymatic activities have greater effect on viscosity of several feedstuffs than xylanase and beta-glucanase alone or in combination. *Journal of Agricultural and Food Chemistry*, **50**, 5121-5127

Moelgaard et al, (1986). *Novozymes' internal work* (unpublished)

Olsen, H.S., (2004). *Novozymes' internal work* (unpublished)

Chapter 4

Growing sustainability in the wheat supply chain

James Brosnan, Tom Bringhurst and Reginald Agu
The Scotch Whisky Research Institute, Research Avenue North, Riccarton, Edinburgh, UK

Introduction

In recent years, cereal supply has become front page news around the world due to dramatic price fluctuations, local shortages and diminishing global stocks plus the controversy over end use in the food versus fuel debate. Any cereal based industry planning for the long term has to ensure that they can maintain their raw material supply at a cost and quality that keeps their business viable. The advantages of a strategic engagement with the supply chain to meet these requirements are self evident. One strand of this strategy is development of new varieties which will meet the needs of the cereal grower and end user. These varieties can only be produced by a multidisciplinary technical approach where best agronomic practice is combined with process understanding and underpinned by significant advances in crop genetics. The opportunities to be taken from this research will not only be in improved end user quality but in other key areas such as reducing the carbon footprint of the supply chain. It is likely that the latter will be of major commercial benefit to the distilling industry alongside desired increases in wheat alcohol yields. This paper describes work carried out by the UK distilling industry in collaboration with plant breeders, research institutes, farmers and other end users to provide a sustainable future for distilling wheat.

United Kingdom Cereal Supply – An "Enlightened" Supply Chain

The issues regarding sustainability of cereal supply were comprehensively covered in the 2005 Worldwide Distilled Spirits conference (Rae, 2008). This paper ended with a redefinition of sustainability as the sum of commitment and shared value. Currently in the United Kingdom, the volatility in worldwide commodity prices, as part of the general economic uncertainty, has put increased pressure on every aspect of the wheat supply chain. However, these challenging conditions just serve to emphasise the importance of an enlightened approach to supply chain management. Probably the best lesson in supply chain understanding was made by the renowned Scottish economist and enlightenment philosopher Adam Smith who made the following statement in his treatise, The Wealth of Nations:

> *It is not from the benevolence of the butcher, the brewer or the baker that we*

expect our dinner but from their regard to their own interest. We address ourselves not to their humanity but to their self-love and never talk to them of our own necessities but of their advantages.

This statement made in 1776 still has validity today but for the more progressive vision of sharing value it is useful to assess the whole supply chains' needs in order to better define the individual parts. Figure 1 shows a simplified wheat supply chain along with factors affecting sustainability for different links in the chain. Wheat production is an archetype of sustainability with the interlocking three pillars of environment, economics and social development all making a significant impact on this supply chain.

Distillers, as wheat processors, have three main areas of concern within the supply chain. Firstly, they need their raw material to be readily available from reliable sources. Secondly, they would wish to purchase wheat at a sensible cost that avoids the uncertainties of fluctuating markets. Lastly, their wheat has to perform consistently in the distillery. Similarly, each other part of the supply chain has its own perspectives on these issues of quality, price and availability and it is achieving a balance of these needs which makes the whole sustainable. In terms of the future of wheat production in the UK it is of interest to view the role of the plant breeding industry. It is plant breeders who are tasked with producing better varieties to satisfy the needs of all the other parts of the supply chain and thus who have the burden of expectation thrust upon them. However, improved varieties offer a genuine technical route for keeping wheat supplies sustainable.

Figure 2 shows a diagram of the plant breeding process. From initial crosses of parent varieties it can take a dozen years or so before a commercial variety is produced. In terms of timescales plant breeders and Scotch Whisky distillers have much in common, particularly the need to predict the marketplace years ahead. Plant breeding is very much a numbers game given the lottery like odds against achieving the commercial success and can only be played by having a huge number of initial crosses. These new varieties go through cycles of evaluation and selection, firstly within the plant breeding company and then within the official national testing system. At this stage larger amounts

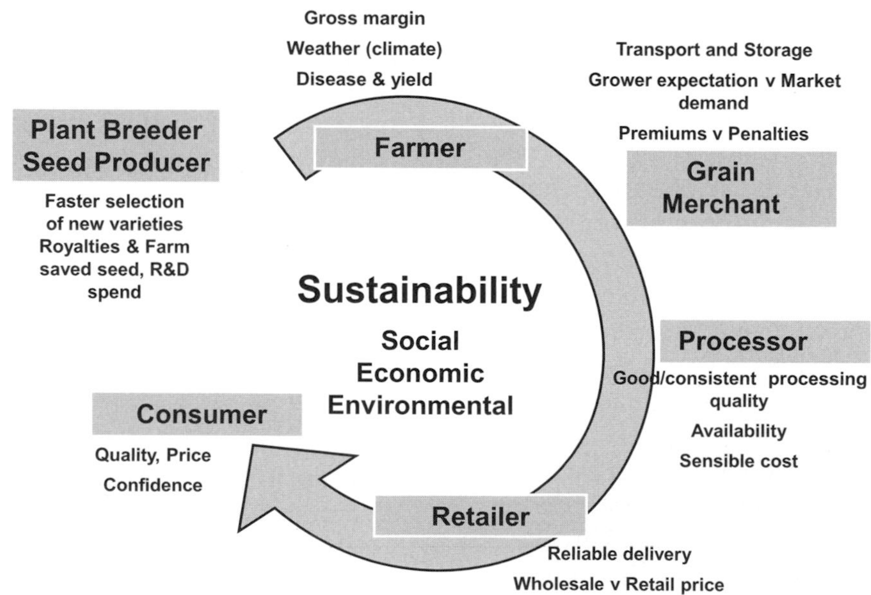

Figure 1. Diagram of a simplified wheat supply chain showing some factors affecting sustainability.

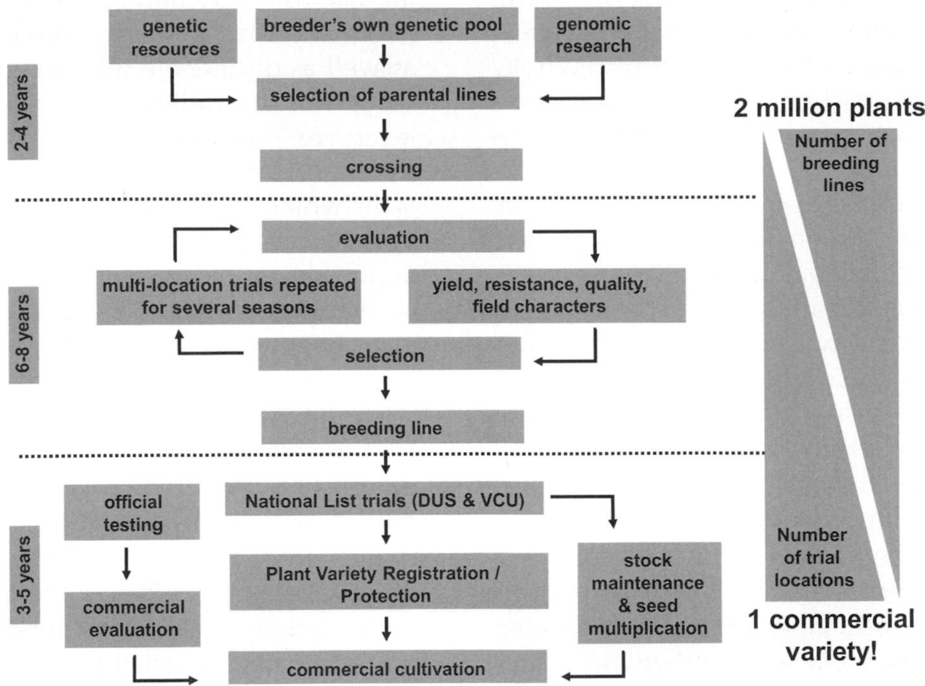

Figure 2: Diagram of the different stages in plant breeding from the original breeding line cross to generating a commercial variety. Note the odds against producing a commercial variety and the potential long timescale involved. (Diagram courtesy of the British Society of Plant Breeders.)

of seed are produced which allows processor testing to begin as well as more extensive agronomic assessment. In the UK, official testing of new wheat varieties is carried out under the auspices of the Crop Evaluation Limited (CEL) a wholly owned part of the Home Grown Cereals Authority (HGCA). CEL assessment involves all parts of the supply chain to ensure only varieties capable of strengthening the position of wheat as a UK crop are added to the Recommended List. Plant breeders accept the challenge this system involves in the hope that a successful variety will generate a commercial return in the form of seed royalties paid by the grower. However, the research and development requirements of modern plant breeding mean that this return on investment can run the risk of being marginal. It is thus in the interests of the rest of the supply chain to work with plant breeders to try and improve the odds in the quest for better varieties. To spread knowledge and understanding within the supply chain is to take a truly literal enlightened approach.

Spreading enlightenment on distilling wheat

Availability of wheat to distillers is linked into another important issue namely traceability. The UK is fortunate in that there are practical quality assurance schemes, namely Scottish Quality Cereals and Assured Combinable Crops, which ensure wheat will meet clear and agreed standards. There are obvious advantages to sourcing wheat as close as possible to the distillery in terms of transport cost, lower carbon footprint and local contacts with growers. As such the distilling industry drives wheat production in Scotland, accounting for more than 70 % of wheat produced. There are also significant tonnages sourced from the North of England for the South of Scotland grain distilleries. Of the 7 grain distilleries in Scotland, 6 run using wheat as the main raw material. The remaining distillery uses French grown maize and sometimes wheat to meet its production requirements. In total, UK distillers are currently using in the order of

800,000 tonnes of wheat. The bulk of this will be made into grain whisky for the production of blends which account for 90 % of Scotch Whisky sales. Other spirit beverages such as gin and vodka are also prepared using UK wheat at the main raw material.

Since wheat was introduced as the main cereal for grain whisky production in 1984, distillers have formed clear opinions about what makes a good distilling wheat, particularly with respect to grain hardness where soft wheat varieties were found to process better than hard wheat. A basic distillery specification will be for soft textured wheat, ideally with low nitrogen, and with moisture and specific weight within normal commercial limits. However, not all soft wheat varieties will be equally suitable for distilling as clearly shown in Figure 3 where losses of 15 litres of alcohol per tonne can be commonly seen with poor varieties that would otherwise make a basic distillery specification. Furthermore these poor varieties are often associated with higher viscosity which could give processing problems in the cereal cookers or dark grains evaporation plant resulting in increased downtime and lost production.

The Scotch Whisky Research Institute has spent many years assessing wheat varieties for their distilling potential in collaboration with plant breeders and agronomists such as the Scottish Agricultural College (SAC). This information is fed to the whole supply chain as well as distillers to influence what varieties are grown in distilling markets. Low nitrogen levels are important for distilling wheat quality as they are inversely related to starch content from which fermentable sugars are derived. Grain texture and grain shape influence distilling quality in terms of starch accumulation and accessibility. The most severe viscosity issues have been encountered with wheat varieties containing a so called 1b/1r genetic component. Interestingly other soft wheat end users also find 1b/1r varieties to give processing problems, eg poultry feed and the appropriately named sticky dropping syndrome. More detailed biochemical evaluation of distilling wheat can be found in Bringhurst et al (2008) and Agu et al (2006).

The other major requirement for distilling wheat varieties is that they must be agronomically competitive offering the grower a high and reliable yield as soft, low nitrogen wheat does not attract any premiums as would be the case with lower agronomic yielding, high nitrogen bread making varieties. For this reason, the varieties on a distiller's preferred list will not just include those capable of generating the highest alcohol yields but medium quality varieties (eg Robigus or Consort). This offers the farmer more choice to suit the particular growing conditions

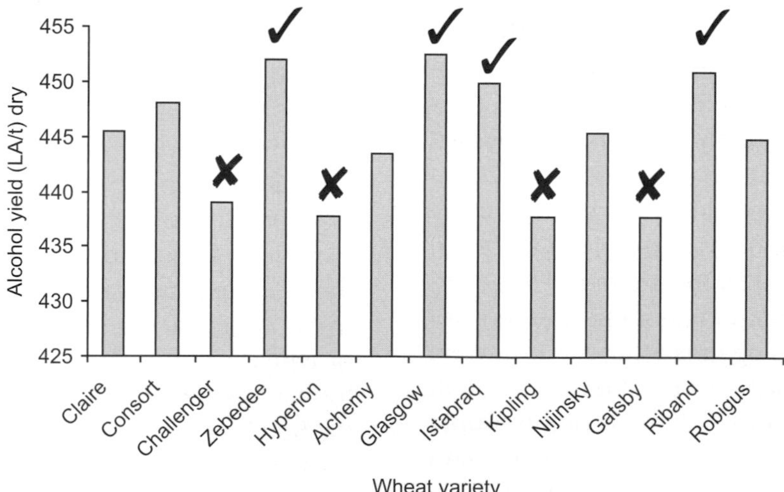

Figure 3: Wheat alcohol yields (litres of alcohol per dry tonne) showing quality differences between soft wheat varieties. Data is the average of results from 7 official trial sites from across the United Kingdom.

and unfortunately some high alcohol yielding varieties are not always suitable to be grown in Scotland. In 2008, two new varieties were added to the UK Recommended List, largely on the back of potential distilling quality. Viscount is a high alcohol yielding variety which also appears to do well in a wide variety of agronomic situations. Cassius would be classified as medium in terms of distilling quality but offers another soft wheat choice to Scottish and North of England farmers supplying the distilling market. The potential influence of new varieties remains to be seen but there is now a critical mass of distilling wheat varieties available to UK growers. These varieties have a balance of features, such as disease resistance, which should ensure that the overall distilling wheat crop is more robust and consistent in quality. An extension to having several wheat varieties grown across Scotland would be growing actual wheat mixtures rather than a single variety where it is hoped the strength of each component in the mixture balance out any weaknesses.

Seeding the future of distilling wheat

There are opportunities to improve the quality of distilling wheat but this cannot be done in isolation as the expertise of the whole supply chain is required. In addition, there is also a pivotal role for government sponsored research institutions for their advanced and specialist technical skills, particularly in the area of genetics. The UK LINK schemes, where industry funds 50 % of the project cost (often in the form of "in kind" work) which is matched by 50 % government funding, are good vehicles for establishing large, innovative and industrially relevant projects. The Genetic Reduction of Energy Use and Emission of Nitrogen through Cereal Production is a good example of such a LINK project. Known by its acronym, GREEN Grain, this project has been sponsored by UK and Scottish governments through DEFRA and SEERAD under the UK sustainable agriculture programme. The other partners are the Scotch Whisky Research Institute, the Scottish Crop Research Institute, ADAS, Syngenta Seeds, Foss UK, Green Spirit Fuels, Grampian Country Food Group and the HGCA. The aim of the GREEN Grain project is to gain a genetic and agronomic understanding of the factors that lead to high alcohol (energy) yields in wheat. The practical aspects of the project have involved extensive field trialling of around 2000 plots per year representing a diverse range of varieties and nitrogen treatments. A combination of distilling quality assessments, HPLC and NIR methods have been used to screen the grain quality produced from the plots in addition to agronomic assessments. This complex array of information has been used with genetic fingerprinting techniques to produce the first genetic maps identifying areas of wheat DNA responsible for alcohol yield. Important information surrounding environmental effects of growing wheat have also emerged in this project. In particular, the application of nitrogen fertiliser to optimise wheat agronomic yield (the standard practise) or alcohol yield. It was shown that under reduced conditions of nitrogen application a processing alcohol yield of 485 litres of alcohol per tonne (approximately 8 % better than current distillery performance) was possible but at low agronomic yield. However, more modest gains of 5-10 LA/tonne were possible which optimised the litres of alcohol produced per hectare of land used at slightly reduced nitrogen fertiliser. This latter figure is important as it represents a saving to the grower in terms of input costs and to the distiller in terms of increased alcohol yield. The genetic information on agronomy and alcohol yield offers the possibility of future varieties which will be more agronomically successful with lower inputs of nitrogen which would result in significantly higher alcohol yields. This win/win scenario for grower and processor is important in terms of sustainability of the wheat supply chain. Reducing nitrogen inputs also has the effect of reducing the greenhouse gas emissions of wheat production which benefits the broader environment. GREEN Grain is a project which has lived up to its abbreviation!

UK distilling wheat – a sustainable future?

Grain distilleries have moved from 85 % of production capacity in 2006 to nearly 100 % at the end of 2008 with further major expansions underway (Gray, 2008). This has been driven by optimistic forecasts for sales of Scotch Whisky in future years. This is a powerful message to the wheat supply chain in uncertain times. However, there is the potential that the next 2-3 years could see the beginning of a wheat based UK bioethanol industry likely to be situated in the North of England in Humberside and Teesside. This would create a market for approximately 2 million tonnes of wheat with roughly the same desired attributes as beverage distillers, ie high alcohol yield and efficient processing. Whilst a large UK bioethanol industry could create some issues for beverage alcohol distillers in terms of competing for raw materials and co-product markets there is also a benefit. It significantly increases the potential market for soft, high alcohol yielding wheat varieties which will hopefully lead to more being grown and most importantly provide the incentive for plant breeders to develop new and better varieties in the future. These future varieties will ensure distillers have a reliable and sustainable supply of UK wheat.

Acknowledgements

The authors would like to acknowledge the contribution of the following in the UK research community to improving understanding of distilling wheat: David Cranstoun (SAC), Bill Thomas (SCRI), Stuart Swanston (SCRI), Roger Sylvester Bradley (ADAS), Richard Weightman (ADAS) and Daniel Kindred (ADAS). Also members of the British Society of Plant Breeders and the CEL team of the HGCA.

References

Rae, D (2008). Sustainability in the Cereals Supply Chain. In: *Distilled Spirits: Production, Technology and Innovation*. Proceedings of the Worldwide Distilled Spirits Conference edited by Bryce, J., Piggott, J. and Stewart, G. Nottingham University Press, UK pp1-6

Bringhurst, T., Agu, R., Brosnan, J. and Fotheringham, A. (2008). Wheat for Scotch Whisky Production: Broadening the Horizon. In: *Distilled Spirits: Production, Technology and Innovation*. Proceedings of the Worldwide Distilled Spirits Conference edited by Bryce, J., Piggott, J. and Stewart, G. Nottingham University Press, UK pp 51-58

Agu, R., Bringhurst, T. and Brosnan, J. (2006). Production of Grain Whisky and Ethanol from Wheat, Maize and Other Cereals. *Journal of the Institute of Brewing*. **112(4)** 314-323

Gray, A. (2008). *The Scotch Whisky Review*. Sutherlands Edinburgh, UK pp 165

Chapter 5

Genetics of barley quality

Robbie Waugh
Genetics, Scottish Crop Research Institute, Dundee DD2 5NE, Scotland

Introduction

The barley varieties that are widely grown in the UK for malt production for the beer and whisky industries change quickly over time (see http://www.ukmalt.com/maltingbarley/maltingbarvar.asp). The primary reason for this is that barley breeders have been incredibly successful over the last century at increasing both the yield and quality of the crop. Improved yields, achieved through incremental changes in a diverse range of characters, are beneficial for the farmer, potentially increasing profit margins while an increase in quality – either in terms of malting characteristics (e.g. hot water extract, diastatic power) and/or distilling characteristics (e.g. fermentability, predicted spirit yield) directly benefit end-users in the beer and whisky industries. Other factors may also promote a shift in varietal use. For example, in 1992 the Committee on Toxicity (COT) review of naturally occurring toxicants (http://archive.food.gov.uk/maff/archive/food/bulletin/2000/no118/fac.htm) recommended that the levels ethyl carbamate, a processing contaminant formed naturally during malt whisky distillation, should be reduced to the lowest levels that are technologically achievable. The Scottish whisky industry reacted quickly by selecting barley varieties that did not produce epiheterodendrin, the major precursor of ethyl carbamate found in germinating barley grain. Increased yield, quality and other characteristics are therefore the drivers that promote a shift in the barley varieties available to the industry.

Barley improvement

Traditionally, barley improvement has been made by crossing parents that show complementary desirable characteristics to generate a large population of offspring. In subsequent generations, families derived from these offspring are then screened for a range of characteristics with the aim of identifying individuals that outperform the original parents. Improvements are possible because the original parents contain different versions of the genes, called alleles, contained in the barley genome. In total, the barley genome most likely contains between 40,000 and 50,000 different genes organised linearly along seven large chromosomes (Schulte *et al*, 2009). It is almost twice the size of the human genome. The cultivated barley varieties available today in North Western Europe contain, on average, between two and six different alleles of each gene. Alleles have subtly different DNA sequences that may ultimately be elaborated as proteins with different properties. When crossing two different varieties, at each generation a process known as 'recombination' breaks then re-joins the chromosomes of the parents. This has the effect of shuffling the allelic composition in each of the progeny and, as a result, all the offspring are different. In genetical terms, we commonly say they have a different 'genotype'. On average, each of barley's seven pairs of chromosomes recombines at two positions in each generation (once on each chromosome arm i.e. 14 recombination events in total). Breeders, when they identify superior individuals, have effectively identified new combinations of alleles that somehow outperform those found in the parents. 'Somehow' because at this point we most often don't know the genetic or physiological basis of the improvements that have been made.

Genetic analysis

The process of crossing contrasting parents and evaluating their offspring is the core of genetic analysis. Genetic analysis has the objective of identifying the location of the genes and alleles that contribute both positively and negatively to a given trait. To conduct a thorough genetic analysis it is first necessary to develop a genetic linkage map. These maps are usually constructed by following the inheritance of a large number of 'genetic markers' in a population derived from a bi-parental cross and observing the frequency of their co-inheritance. This is, of course, possible because the genes, and molecular markers, are arranged linearly along each linear chromosome. As a result, genes or markers that are closer to each other are more likely to be co-inherited than genes that are far apart. Today, genetic markers are almost exclusively based on the DNA sequence differences found at the different alleles observed in different individuals. A genetic linkage map, allows a trait phenotype to be associated with a chromosomal region by monitoring the co-inheritance of a trait phenotype with a molecular marker. When applied at increasing resolution (i.e. in larger populations) linkage mapping can facilitate the identification of the specific gene that controls the trait. Barley linkage maps have been constructed using a range of technologies (Kleinhofs *et al.*, 1993; Ramsay *et al.*, 2000, Varshney *et al.*, 2007). While these were seldom gene-based, by sharing markers across different labs, some consistency in trait analysis in terms of the underlying genetic maps has been achieved.

Modern genetic marker technologies

The generation of a high-throughput, representative and unified genotyping platform became a high priority a few years ago in the barley genetics community because it was widely recognized that such a resource would enable both integration and the investigation of novel approaches for trait analysis - such as association mapping. The 'Genomics' revolution that has occurred over the last 10 years, has provided the necessary information to allow this to happen. Based on the outputs of community gene sequencing programs, a highly parallel gene-based technology has been developed for simplifying and increasing the resolution of genetic analysis.

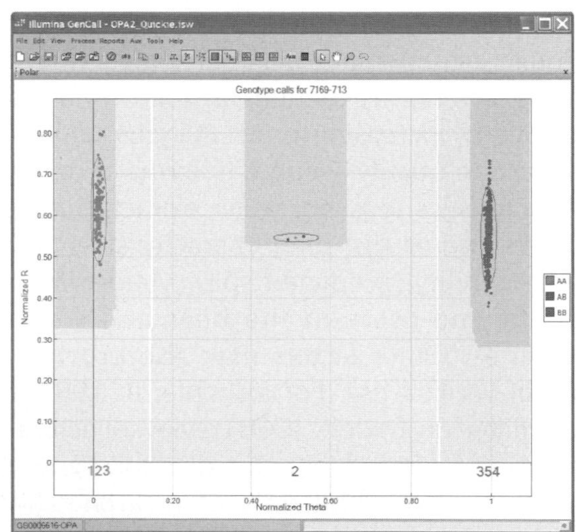

Figure 1: A screen shot from the BeadStudio software that divides a population of plants into two groups (left dots vs right dots) based on which allele they possess at the SNP marker locus 7169-713. Approximately 200 genotypes are represented on the diagram. The central dots are controls (a 1:1 mixture of two genotypes containing different alleles).

The BeadArray is a genotyping system commercialized by a company called 'Illumina' and exploits an assay known as 'GoldenGate' (Fan *et al.*, 2003). In this assay 1536 different single nucleotide polymorphisms (SNPs) (ie DNA sequence differences diagnostic of different alleles) are interrogated in parallel. The technology relies on the latest developments in laser fibre optics which provides the possibility to test so many SNPs in a single DNA sample in a single tube. Discrimination is achieved by labelling each of the alternative SNP alleles with either green or red fluorescence which can be recorded on a special instrument (a Bead Station) and analysed using dedicated software (BeadStudio). We have developed three of these (i.e. 3 x 1536 SNPs) to simplify and integrate worldwide genetics studies in barley (Rostoks *et al.*, 2006, R. Waugh, T. Close and N. Stein, unpublished results). The technology is particularly attractive because the quality of the data is so high and the markers themselves are both stable and robust (Figure 1).

Dissecting malting and distilling quality in bi-parental cross populations

Balancing good malting quality with high yield is one of the basic problems in barley breeding. High yield, often dependant on the application of nitrogenous fertilizers, is associated with high protein and beta-glucan content in the grain which are not desired for good malt. To identify loci controlling malting and yield-related traits in barley many populations have been developed over the last 15 years and each of the component individuals subjected to malt quality analysis. Genetic linkage maps of these populations have been constructed – mainly using old error prone technology – and the genetics of malting quality interrogated. From these studies a total of over 60 locations on the barley genome have been implicated in controlling malting quality (B. Thomas, unpublished).

Some specific successes have emerged from these analyses. For example, the β-amylase gene, the product of which is involved in starch breakdown and known to be highly-expressed upon germination, has been shown in several populations to be a component of malting quality. Kihara, Kaneko and Ito (1998) showed that different alleles of β-amylase exhibited different thermostability profiles and that the presence of certain alleles was correlated with malting quality. In work at the Scottish Crop Research Institute focussed on traits important to whisky distilling, Swanston *et al.* (1999) mapped and subsequently identified the gene

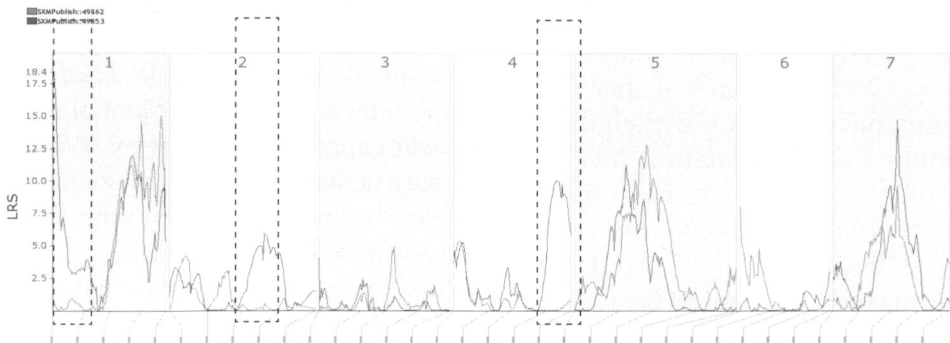

Figure 2. An example of genetic analysis of α-amylase activity (black Line) and diastatic power (grey line) in a population derived from a cross between the cultivars Steptoe and Morex. The x-axis shows each of the 7 barley chromosomes arranged 'head to tail'. They are numbered 1 to 7. The y-axis shows the likelihood ratio statistic (LRS) which is a measure of the association between a marker and the phenotype (higher value, stronger association). Because the data is continuous, it is analysed as a polygenic character. The diagram shows that - as expected - there is a correlation between alpha-amylase activity and diastatic power (DP) (i.e. there are peaks in the same places) but that DP also has significant associations with other regions on chromosomes 1H, 2H and 4H (dashed boxes).

(J. Russell, unpublished) that is responsible for the production of epiheterodendrin – a precursor of ethyl carbamate production during distillation. Epiheterodendrin is only produced in certain barley varieties. Differences in the DNA sequence between epiheterodendrin producers and non-producers (i.e. different alleles) have been used to develop a simple diagnostic assay that differentiates the two alleles. The assay is possible using DNA extracted from tiny amounts of leaf or seed material. Swanston *et al.* (1999) also showed that the region of the genome containing the β-amylase gene influenced fermentability, but the genetic control of this trait was considerably more complex. In addition to these two examples, we now know the genetic location and DNA sequences of many of the genes that specify enzymes known to be involved in malting – α-amylase, glucan synthases, limit dextrinase etc. While their genetic control frequently appears more complex that expected (see Figure 2) we expect that the application of the new genetic marker technologies outlined above will increase the resolution and quality of the genetic analysis.

Correlating quality with molecular markers in germplasm collections

Recently, there has been great interest in the use of an approach termed 'association genetics' in plants. In human and many animal species association studies have built on a tradition of studying genetics at a population level. In contrast, in plants, genetic studies have concentrated on controlled crosses often derived from inbred stocks because of their practical ease and genetical and statistical power (Jannink, Bink and Jansen, 2001; Rafalski, 2002). While its relatively easy to make bi-parental crosses with plants and generate large populations, a criticism of this approach is that it has frequently used material that limits the direct application of results (e.g. a malt vs. a feed variety) - unlike mammalian studies that have remained close to populations of medical and agricultural interest. Our recent work has shown that the elite UK barley genepool is a highly unusual population because it traces back to a limited number of recent progenitors and has undergone extensive outcrossing and recombination. This particular population history, allied to known pedigrees, offers very considerable advantages for identifying the particular regions of the genome barley that explain a major proportion of genetic variation of a wide range of traits. Because this elite population has undergone many more rounds of recombination, and the alleles shuffled many times, many more genetic markers are required for mapping than in bi-parental populations. Hence the need for the development of the genotyping platform described above.

We have been using elite cultivated UK barley material in an UK industry led project under the government SA LINK scheme (AGOUEB) to identify the regions of the barley genome controlling a wide range of barley traits, including those controlling malting quality. Because we have restricted the elite barley material to genotypes that have at least completed National List 2 trials we have been able to access a comprehensive set of phenotypic data that have been collected as part of the official trialling process. As association mapping is relatively new in plants, we have so far focussed on traits where the phenotypic data we have is robust. However, their genetic control is of varying complexity. Our initial studies (Rostoks *et al.*, 2006) gave some indication of the potential of association genetics approaches in barley. We were able to assign a putative map location for unmapped SNP alleles through association with those that had already been mapped. In addition, we were able to demonstrate a strong association with single markers in a region on barley chromosome 5 with winter/spring growth habit. Encouragingly, the region showing association coincided with the location of a major trait determining winter-hardiness locus that contains a cluster of *CBF* gene homologues that are key regulators of the cold acclimation signalling pathway (Szucs *et al.*, 2006). The accuracy of mapping Mendelian traits by association has been further confirmed by mapping the DUS character, rachilla hair length, to chromosome 5 using a panel of 192 individuals and 4600 SNPs. We are currently extending these 'proof of principle' analyses to quality traits (Figure 3).

Application of genetics in barley varietal improvement

The type of barley research described above has the objective of identifying the location of genes and alleles that affect a given trait. It does this routinely by conducting genetic analysis either of bi-parental populations by linkage analysis or collections of barley cultivars through association genetics using recently developed robust and efficient molecular markers. The desired outcome is the identification of markers that are potentially diagnostic for the trait that has been analysed (e.g. β-amylase, epiheterodendrin non-producers etc). There are a number of applications of both these diagnostics and the general molecular marker technologies in both crop improvement and in the end-user sector. Robust molecular diagnostics are exceptionally well suited to cultivar identification both in the cultivar registration process but also as a potential tool to verify the identity of grain at intake (the latter being especially important if there is a problem or dispute with a supplier). They can be used to enrich breeding genepools for desirable alleles of specific genes by selecting for the presence of the marker allele – a simple lab-based test – both in parental lines and / or in the progeny from crosses. This can avoid the need to conduct quantitative, difficult or expensive tests and reduce the number of progenies that need to be taken forward in each round of crossing in a breeding program. A good example in relation to the distilling industry is the diagnostic we have developed for epiheterodendrin producers. Its application in breeding has contributed towards the eradication of 'producers' in the spring malting barley crop improvement pipeline. At the level of detail that the elite barley genepool has now been characterised, there are possibilities to completely rethink the way breeding programs are conducted, potentially heralding an era of 'predictive breeding' where specific sets of parental lines are chosen based on their genotype at the outset and a series of crosses and progeny tests conducted, all with specific end-use markets in mind.

Finally, as more and more genes are identified and their alleles characterised in the lab, we will gain a much better understanding of the factors that influence a broad range of characteristics, including quality. This information will provide the basis of strategies that we may have to adopt to continue making improvements in the future, in the face of environmental change. In addition, we will start to understand the differences between the genetic components that influence 'yield' and 'quality' in cultivars bred and grown in our own environment and those from different locations (e.g. North America vs the UK), providing further possibilities for crop improvement.

References

Fan, J.-B., Oliphant, A., Shen, R., Kermani, B.G., Garcia, F., Gunderson, K.L., Hansen, M., Steemers, F., Butler, S.L., Deloukas, P., Galver, L., Hunt, S., Mcbride, C., Bibikova, M., Rubano, T., Chen, J., Wickham, E., Doucet, D., Chang, W., Campbell, D., Zhang, B., Kruglyak, S., Bentley, D., Haas, J., Rigault, P., Zhou, L., Stuelpnagel, J. and Chee, M.S. (2003). Highly Parallel SNP Genotyping. *Cold Spring Harbor Symposium Quantitative Biology* **68**: 69-78

Jannink, J.-L., Bink, M.C.A.M. and Jansen, R.C. (2001). Using complex plant pedigrees to map valuable genes. *Trends in Plant Science* **6**: 337-342

Kihara, M., Kaneko, T. and Ito, K. (1998). Genetic variation of Beta-amylase thermostability among varieties of barley and relation to malting quality. *Plant Breeding* **117**: 425-428

Kleinhofs, A., Kilian, A., Saghai Maroof, M.A., Biyashev, R.M., Hayes, P., Chen, F.Q., Lapitan, N., Fenwick, A., Blake, T.K., Kanazin, V., Ananiev, E., Dahleen, L., Kudrna, D., Bollinger, J., Knapp, S.J., Liu, B., Sorrells, M., Heun, M., Franckowiak, J.D., Hoffman, D., Skadsen, R. and Steffenson, B.J. (1993). A molecular, isozyme and morphological map of the barley (*Hordeum vulgare*) genome. *Theoretical and Applied Genetics* **86**: 705-712

Rafalski, J.A. (2002). Novel genetic mapping tools in plants: SNPs and LD-based approaches. *Plant Science* **162**: 329-333

Ramsay, L., Macaulay, M., degli Ivanissevich, S., MacLean, K., Cardle, L., Fuller, J., Edwards, K.J., Tuvesson, S., Morgante, M., Massari, A., Maestri, E., Marmiroli, N., Sjakste, T., Ganal, M., Powell, W., Waugh, R. (2000). A simple sequence repeat-based linkage map of barley. *Genetics* **156**: 1997-2005

Rostoks, N., Ramsay, L., MacKenzie, K., Cardle, L., Bhat, P.R., Roose, M.L., Svensson, J.T., Stein, N., Varshney, R.K., Marshall, D.F., Graner, A., Close, T.J. and Waugh, R. (2006). Recent history of artificial outcrossing facilitates whole genome association mapping in elite inbred crop varieties. *Proceedings of the National Academy of Sciences USA* **103**: 18656-18661

Schulte, D., Close, T.J., Graner, A., Langridge, P., Matsumoto, T., Muehlbauer, G., Sato, K., Schulman, A., Waugh, R., Wise, R. and Stein, N. (2009). International Barley Sequencing Consortium (IBSC) – at the transition to efficient access to the barley genome. *Plant Physiology* (in press)

Swanston, J.S., Thomas, W.T.B., Powell, W., Young, G.R., Lawrence, P.E., Ramsay, L. and Waugh, R. (1999). Using molecular markers to determine barleys most suitable for malt whisky distilling. *Molecular Breeding* **5**: 103-109

Szucs, P., Skinner, J.S., Karsai, I., Cuesta-Marcos, A., Haggard, K.G., Corey, A.E., Chen, T.H.H. and Hayes, P.M. (2007). Validation of the VRN-H2/VRN-HI epistatic model in barley reveals intro length variation in VRN-H1 may account for a continuum of vernalization sensitivity. *Molecular Genetics and Genomics* **277**: 249-261

Varshney, R.K., Marcel, T.C., Ramsay, L., Russell, J., Roder, M.S., Stein, N., Waugh, R., Langridge, P., Niks, R.E. and Graner, A. (2007). A high density barley microsatellite consensus map with 775 SSR loci. *Theoretical and Applied Genetics* **114**: 1091-1103

Chapter 6

Mobilisation of energy reserves in barley grains during imbibition of water

J. H. Bryce[1], M. B. Scott[2], K. A. McCafferty[1], A. M. Johnston[3], J. A. Raven[4], J. M. Thornton[5], P. C. Morris[1] and S. Footitt[6]

[1]International Centre for Brewing and Distilling, School of Life Sciences, Heriot-Watt University, Edinburgh, UK; [2]Reproductive and Developmental Medicine, Central Sheffield Teaching Hospitals Trust, Sheffield, UK; [3]Millipore UK, Dundee Technology Park, Dundee, UK; [4]School of Life Sciences, Division of Plant Sciences, University of Dundee at SCRI, Scottish Crop Research Institute, Invergowrie, Dundee, UK; [5]Brand Technical Centre, Diageo Global Supply, Glenochil, Menstrie, Clackmannanshire, UK; [6]Warwick HRI, University of Warwick, UK

Introduction

The production of malt that will process easily in a distillery to provide high spirit yields can only be achieved if the barley used in its production has a high percentage of viable and germinable grains (Palmer, 1989; Palmer 2006). During the mid stage of grain maturation, on the barley ear, primary dormancy develops, a mechanism which serves to prevent sprouting at the end of maturation and to disperse germination timing (Benech-Arnold and Sanchez, 2003; Hilhorst, 2007). Dormant grains are defined as those that do not germinate following imbibition of water when other factors such as temperature, light and oxygen are favourable. In the malting industry, rapid and even germination of imbibed barley is key, but germination occurs prior to endosperm mobilisation. Therefore, the reconstituted metabolic activity in grain following imbibition depends on embryo reserves. In selecting barley for malting it is therefore important to understand the factors governing the very early metabolic events following imbibition in germinable grains.

The triphasic uptake of water by dry orthodox seeds demarks germination and post-germination events. During the imbibition (phase I) of dry orthodox seeds (dormant or non-dormant), cellular components, such as membranes, organelles and associated proteins are quickly reconstituted and metabolic activities such as respiration resume. Following imbibition, seeds enter the plateau phase, phase II, during which increased metabolic activity facilitates cellular repair and maintenance (Bewley, 1997). In non-dormant seeds, events during phase II ultimately result in germination leading to the start of phase III which marks the onset of post-germinative growth. Dormant grains however remain in phase II and do not germinate.

In cereals, access to the bulk of the stored energy reserves, in this case endospermic starch, is denied to the embryo until mobilised post-germination (Botha, Potgieter and Botha, 1992). This means that until that point in time, the energy demands of dormant seed for the maintenance of cellular viability and in the non-dormant seed for the germination process are dependent on embryo reserves. Cereal embryos are energy dense containing a high percentage of stored lipid, as well as supplies of carbohydrate, for example, sucrose and the raffinose family oligosaccharides (Palmer, 1969).

Endogenous respiratory substrate oxidations can be estimated by determining the stable carbon isotope ratio of respired CO_2 by mass spectrometry. This is not confounded by non-respiratory O_2 consumption. Atmospheric CO_2, is 1.1% the heavy ^{13}C isotope, and 98.9% the lighter ^{12}C isotope (Craig, 1953). Discrimination against ^{13}C occurs during photosynthetic and other mechanisms of CO_2 fixation, while further carbon isotope fractionation occurs during subsequent metabolism (Park and Epstein, 1961). Examination of the isotopic composition of respiratory substrates in plants has revealed large differences in the $^{13}C/^{12}C$ ratio between lipids and carbohydrates. The ^{12}C enrichment of lipids is thought to result from the intramolecular $^{13}C/^{12}C$ ratios of pyruvate. Determination of the $^{13}C/^{12}C$ ratio of respired CO_2 will therefore distinguish between lipid and carbohydrate as the respiratory substrate (Jacobson, Smith, Epstein and Laties, 1970).

Respiration to generate energy requires functional mitochondria which are able to couple oxygen uptake to ATP synthesis (Douce, 1985). The adenosine triphosphate respiration (coupled respiration) of an NAD-linked respiratory substrate, such as malate, is restricted by the supply of NAD (nicotinamide adenine dinucleotide) if coupled production of ATP by mitochondria is possible. The theoretical ADP/O ratio (use of ADP to synthesise ATP relative to oxygen uptake) can be close to 3. The respiratory control ratio (RCR) is the rate of oxidation in the presence of ADP (known as state 3) divided by the rate in the absence of ADP (state 4). The ratio prior to any addition of ADP is known as state 2. Apart from succinate, mitochondrial substrates are NAD-linked. Therefore, mitochondrial malate oxidation was measured in the absence and presence of additional NAD to determine whether NAD could be a factor limiting mitochondrial respiration and hence their ability to generate energy within the cell.

In order to investigate the changes in respiratory metabolism of barley grains during their imbibition of water and early germination, we therefore carried out a time course in which we compared the respiration of a dormant and a germinable sample of barley grains. We also compared the metabolism of respiratory substrate by dormant and germinable grain. In particular, lipids and sugar levels were determined during a time course. Measurements of the $^{13}C/^{12}C$ ratio of respired carbon dioxide were also made during a time course in order to estimate the changing proportion of lipid relative to carbohydrate respired by embryos during imbibition.

Materials and methods

Plant material

Barley (*Hordeum vulgare* L. var Triumph), was used in all experiments. At harvest, dormant grain was 100% viable, with only 8% showing germination in standard tests. A non-dormant sample was produced from this population by dry after-ripening at 37°C for eight weeks; the resulting germination was in excess of 92% with no change in viability. Long-term storage of the dormant and non-dormant samples was at –40°C, otherwise the grains were kept at 4°C.

Germination and viability

For each germination assessment, replicates of 100 grains were germinated in the dark at 20°C in Petri dishes containing two 9 cm Whatman No. 1 filter papers and 5 mL water. The progression of germination was assessed at each time point as follows, splitting of the pericarp over the embryo, and emergence of the radicle through the pericarp, and chitting. Viability was determined by the 'hydrogen peroxide and peeling reference method' (Institute of Brewing, 1991).

Extraction and analysis of carbohydrate

Embryos were dissected at various intervals from imbibed grains and immediately frozen in liquid nitrogen and sugars extracted following grinding with a pellet of 1 M perchloric acid (Coombs, Hind, Leegood, Tieszen and Vonshak, 1987). Following centrifugation at 2000 *g* for 2 min, to remove protein and cell wall material, the supernatant was neutralized with 5 M K_2CO_3 and then re-centrifuged at 2000 *g* for 2 min to remove the $KClO_4$ precipitate. The supernatant was decanted and clarified by centrifugation at 10000 *g* for 15 min.

The filtrate (0.45 μm pore size) was then analysised by HPLC. Separation was achieved by HPAE and carbohydrates detected by pulsed amperometric detector. The instrumentation was as follows; a dionex PAD with a gold electrode, a Gilson 302 pump, a Gilson 305 pump, a Gilson 802 Manometric Module, a Gilson 811B dynamic mixer, a Hewlett Packard 1050 autoinjector, a Dionex eluent degas module, a Hewlett Packard Chemstation data handling system (HP3365) and a Dionex HPLC System. The Gilson HPLC system provided the gradient pumping, sample injection and column separation of components. Sugars were detected on a Dionex Carbopac PA-100 Guard column, 4 X 50 mm with a Dionex Carbopac PA-100 4 X 250 mm.

Lipid extraction

The total lipid content of barley embryos was determined after Becker, Leaver, Weir and Riezman (1978) with minor modifications. Embryos, dissected from seeds imbibed for increasing periods, were immediately frozen in liquid nitrogen, freeze-dried for 18 h in a Super Modulyo freeze dryer (Edwards Ltd, Crawley, UK), and their dry weight determined. Embryos were ground to a powder using a mortar and pestle and lipid extracted with 2 mL chloroform–methanol (2:1 v/v). The extract was placed in a centrifuge tube and the mortar rinsed with a further 1 mL of chloroform-methanol (2:1 v/v). Extract and washings were combined and centrifuged at 2000 *g* for 5 min. The supernatant was decanted and the pellet re-extracted as above. Supernatants were combined and shaken with an equal volume of 2 M KCl. Following phase separation the bottom organic phase was removed with a Pasteur pipette to a pre-weighed beaker. The remaining aqueous phase was washed three times with 2 mL chloroform-methanol (2:1 v/v) and the organic phase removed after each washing. Pooled organic phases were then evaporated to dryness at 37 °C. The amount of extracted lipid was determined by weight difference.

Respiration of embryos

After increasing periods of imbibition, 10 embryos were dissected from either dormant or non-dormant grains. Embryos were immediately placed in a Clarke-type oxygen electrode (Hansatech Ltd., UK) and oxygen uptake measured polarographically in 1 ml of reaction medium at 25°C (0.3 M mannitol; 20 mM MOPS; 10 mM KH_2PO_4 and 5 mM $MgCl_2$, pH 7.2-KOH).

Collection of carbon dioxide for $^{13}C/^{12}C$ analysis

Intact grains were imbibed in Petri-dishes on two Whatman No.1 filter papers, moistened with 5 mL water and incubated at 20°C for various intervals. Two hundred imbibed grains were placed in a glass sample tube which had been wrapped in foil. Respired CO_2 was sampled for 45 min and the grains then discarded. The carbon isotope ratio ($^{13}C/^{12}C$) of respired CO_2 was compared to the standard, Pee Dee Belemnite (PDB), the carbonate skeleton of the fossil cephalopod *Beliminitella americana* (Jacobson *et al*., 1970). The overall precision of the mass spectrometric analysis (1 SD) was 0.1% (n = 5). Data represents the mean $\pm$ SD (n = 2).

Samples of total grain carbon, starch and embryo lipid extracted from barley were placed in tin cups, combusted in an elemental analyser and the CO_2 generated was analysed on a 2020 Europa Scientific mass spectrometer for its $\delta^{13}C$ value. The overall precision of the combustion and mass spectrometric analysis (1 SD) was 0.1% (n = 5).

Isolation of mitochondria and mitochondrial oxygen uptake

Dormant and non-dormant grains were hydrated for 16 and 72 h as above. In the dormant population, any grain germinated after 72 h was discarded. Mitochondria were then isolated from embryos of these grains according to Neuberger (1985). The properties of mitochondria from the embryos of dormant grains that remained in Phase II were compared with those from embryos of nondormant grains that passed from Phase II to Phase III. Embryos (2-3 g) were excised from grains and immediately placed on ice, counted and homogenised with a cold mortar and pestle in 50 ml ice cold extraction buffer (0.3 M mannitol; 20 mM MOPS; 10 mM KH_2PO_4; 2 mM EDTA; 50 mM isoascorbate; 0.5% (w/v) cysteine; 0.5% (w/v) PVP-40 and 1% (w/v) defatted BSA, pH 7.2-KOH). All subsequent procedures were carried out at 2-4°C. The homogenate was filtered through two layers of Miracloth and centrifuged at 3000 g for five min (MSE-18 centrifuge). The pellet (starch and cell wall material) was discarded and the supernatant centrifuged at 10 000 g for 15 min. The resulting mitochondrial pellet was resuspended in wash buffer (0.3 M mannitol; 20 mM MOPS; 10 mM KH_2PO_4; 2 mM EDTA and 1% (w/v) BSA, pH 7.2-KOH), and centrifuged at 3000 g for five min to remove any remaining starch and cell wall material (Neuburger, 1985). The supernatant was again centrifuged at 10 000 g for 15 min, the pellet was resuspended with a fine Camel hair brush in wash medium (1-2 ml) and loaded onto a 0.6 M sucrose cushion before centrifuging at 10 000 g for 20 min. The final partially purified mitochondrial pellet was suspended in 250 µl of wash medium.

The protein content of each mitochondrial preparation was determined according to a modified Lowry method (Miller, 1959) with BSA as standard.

Oxygen uptake by isolated mitochondria was measured polarographically using a Clarke-type oxygen electrode in 1 ml of reaction medium at 25°C containing mitochondria (ca. 0.5 mg protein). Respiration was initiated by the addition of substrate followed by 100 nmol ADP. The following additions were also made: 10 mM glutamate with malate. Mitochondria were passed through one state 3/4 transition before measurement of state 3 and 4 rates.

Results

Germination and respiration during imbibition

Dormant and non-dormant barley samples were imbibed with water as described in the 'Materials and methods'. Their germinability and oxygen uptake were then determined.

In non-dormant barley grain, the first visible sign of the onset of germination is splitting of the pericarp which was seen after 12 h, this was followed by emergence of the radicle through the pericarp at 16 h (Figure 1). Germination (emergence of the radicle from the palea and lemma, chitting) was also first observed at 16 h. Very few grains germinated in the dormant sample (see 'Materials and methods'). Dormancy in a sample is rarely 100% because in any population of grains there is a spectrum of germinability.

Respiration of embryos isolated from intact dormant and non-dormant grain increased in a linear fashion for the first 12 h of imbibition (Figure 2). Respiration then remained on a plateau until 18 h. After this, respiration in embryos isolated from non-dormant grain increased above that seen in those from dormant grain. This was coincident with the first visible signs of germination.

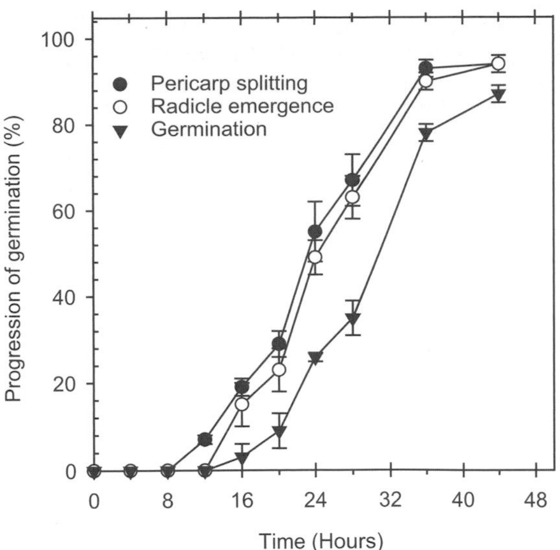

Figure 1. The progression of germination in nondormant intact barley seeds incubated in the dark at 20°C. Progression of germination was recorded as splitting of the pericarp followed by emergence of the radicle through the pericarp and germination as protrusion of the radicle from the palea and lemma. Data presented are means ± SE (n = 3). No error bar indicates SE is smaller than symbol.

Embryo mitochondrial properties

Malate is a mitochondrial TCA cycle acid and its oxidation will reflect the membrane integrity of the mitochondia and their ability to generate ATP (energy). The first point for isolation was chosen as 16 h because this is the point at which grains were first seen to chit. NAD was added to the mitochondrial preparation to determine if the mitochondria were NAD deficient, a stimulation of respiration in the presence of NAD would indicate NAD deficiency and the need for NAD synthesis.

The data in Table 1 show the state 3 and state 4 respiration of mitochondria isolated after 16 h and 72 h from dormant and germinable grain, both in the presence and absence of NAD. At 16 h, mitochondria from non-dormant grain were uncoupled in the absence of NAD, but coupled in the presence of NAD. Mitochondria from the dormant sample of grain were only coupled with NAD in one sample. ADP/O ratios were just above 1 which is significantly below the potential value of 3. At 72 h, mitochondria from both dormant and non-dormant samples were coupled and ADP/O ratios were above 2. Mitochondria from both samples showed a stimulation of respiration due to NAD. However, state 3 and state 4 respiration were significantly higher in the mitochondria from germinable grain.

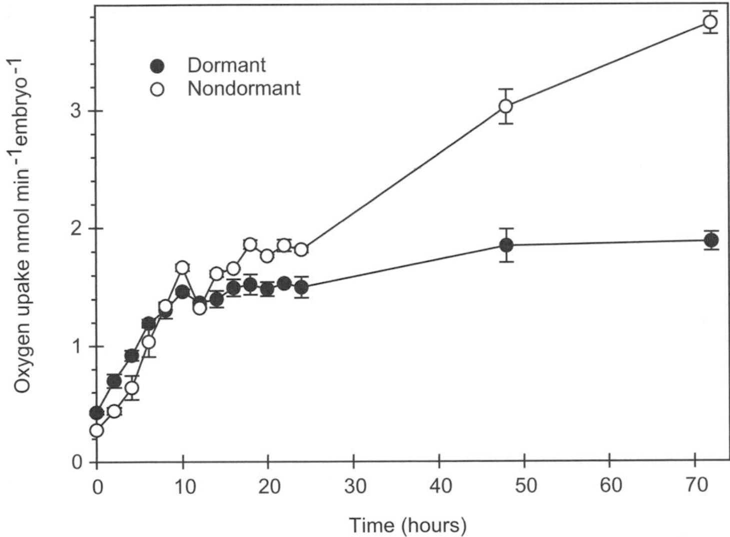

Figure 2. Oxygen uptake at 25°C by barley embryos isolated from dormant and nondormant seeds incubated as for germination tests at 20°C in the dark at increasing times after the onset on imbibition. Data presented are means ± SD (n = 3). No error bar indicates SD is smaller than symbol.

Table 1. Malate oxidation by mitochondria isolated from the embryos of dormant and non-dormant barley grain after 16 h (A) and 72 h (B) of imbibition. Oxygen consumption (nmol O_2 min^{-1} mg $protein^{-1}$). All values are means ± SE of three mitochondrial extractions. * Indicates that one sample was coupled.

	Substrate	*Oxygen consumption (nmol O_2 min^{-1} mg $protein^{-1}$)* State 2	*State 3*	*State 4*	*RCR*	*ADP/O*
A. 16h						
Dormant	Malate (10mM)	6.16 ± 0.63	10.9 ± 1.52	UC	-	-
	Malate + NAD (1mM)		20.2 ± 4.34	16.4*	1.51*	1.30*
Non-Dormant	Malate (10mM)	6.17 ± 1.30	8.7 ± 0.89	UC	-	-
	Malate + NAD (1mM)		22.6 ± 1.33	13.9 ± 1.30	1.55 ± 0.05	1.13 ± 0.03
B. 72h						
Dormant	Malate (10mM)	8.3 ± 1.24	14.0 ± 1.12	7.01 ± 0.63	2.01 ± 0.07	2.12 ± 0.11
	Malate + NAD (1mM)		29.0 ± 2.51	17.0 ± 1.43	1.77 ± 0.03	2.11 ± 0.16
Non-Dormant	Malate (10mM)	23.6 ± 0.64	45.1 ± 1.05	21.2 ± 0.74	2.14 ± 0.03	2.57 ± 0.15
	Malate + NAD (1mM)		55.9 ± 1.12	30.9 ± 0.63	1.81 ± 0.02	2.10 ± 0.17

Changes in soluble sugars during imbibition

Important storage sugars in cereal grain embryos are sucrose, raffinose and stachyose. The raffinose family oligosaccharides are alpha-galactosyl derivitives of sucrose. Thus raffinose can be degraded by alpha-galactosidase to galactose and sucrose, or by invertase to melibiose and sucrose.

The soluble sugar and lipid content of embryos was determined during the first 48 h of imbibition in both germinable and dormant grain. In dormant grain, all these sugar levels remained relatively constant over 48 hours. Whereas in germinable grain, during the first 18 h of imbibition, the sugars stachyose and melibiose showed a sharp decline in the embryo. Initial stachyose and melibiose levels were just below 0.09 μmol/g dry wt and 0.06 μmol/g dry wt respectively at the start of imbibition. These sugars declined by over 80% within the first 16 h of imbibition with the most rapid decline being in the first 10 h. Raffinose showed a slow decline in the first 18 h of imbibition from 1.8 μmol/g dry wt to 1.2 μmol/g dry wt and then a sharp decline in the following period so that raffinose was not detected after 30 h (Figure 3). Sucrose levels increased steadily from about 3 μmol/g

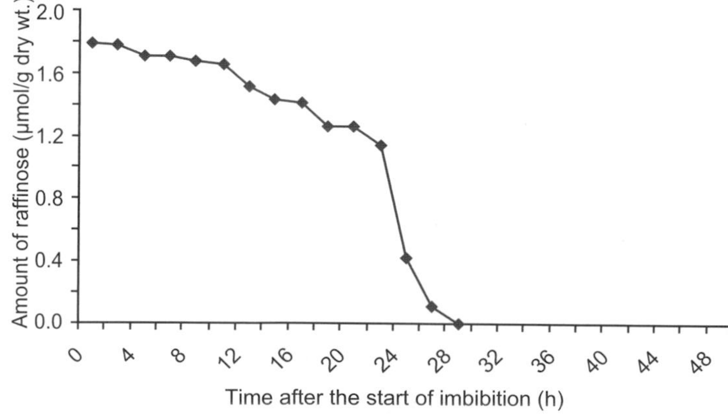

Figure 3. The raffinose levels in embryos of germinable grain during imbibition. Embryos were dissected from non-dormant barley grains during the first 48 h after the start of imbibition. Intact barley was incubated in the dark at 20°C, embryos were dissected and raffinose extracted and assayed as described in the 'Materials and methods'.

dry wt to 18 μmol/g dry wt during imbibition. While sucrose could have been sythesised from endosperm sugars, it could also have come from lipid via gluconeogenesis. Lipid levels are over an order of magnitude higher in barley embryos at maturity. Overall, lipids showed a marginal decline in the embryos of germinable grain followed by a marginal increase back to their initial levels during phase III , changes that were very similar in dormant grain.

Source of respiratory substrate

Mass spectrometery was used to measure the $^{13}C/^{12}C$ ratio of CO_2 and this was compared to the standard, Pee Dee Belemnite (PDB), which is the carbonate skeleton of the fossil cephalopod *Beliminitella americana* from the Pee Dee formation in South Carolina. The results are expressed as a (delta) $\delta^{13}C$ value in units per mil (‰):

$$\delta^{13}C = \left[\frac{^{13}C/^{12}C(sample)}{^{13}C/^{12}C(PDB)} - 1 \right] \times 1000$$

As already stated, during lipid biosynthesis, plants discriminate against the heavy carbon isotope ^{13}C resulting in lipids having a lower $^{13}C/^{12}C$ ratio than starch. Lipid and starch were isolated from barley grains (dormant and germinable), combusted and the $^{13}C/^{12}C$ ratios determined by mass spectrometry as –31.3 and –27.3‰, respectively (see Table 2).

Table 2. The $\delta^{13}C$ values in units per mil (‰), of starch and embryo lipid extracted from dormant and non-dormant barley grains as described in 'Materials and methods'. Values followed by the same letter are not significantly different at the 95% level (n = 3).

	$\delta^{13}C$(‰)	
Carbon source	*Dormant*	*Non-dormant*
Starch	-27.38 ± 0.04[a]	-27.31 ± 0.02[a]
Lipid	-31.24 ± 0.05[b]	-31.47 ± 0.05[b]

The isotopic composition of evolved carbon dioxide collected from imbibed grains was also determined by mass spectrometry (Figure 4). Thus, the initial $^{13}C/^{12}C$ ratio of respired CO_2 (~ -31.0‰) showed that lipid is the likely respiratory substrate in both dormant and non-dormant grain in the early stages of imbibition.

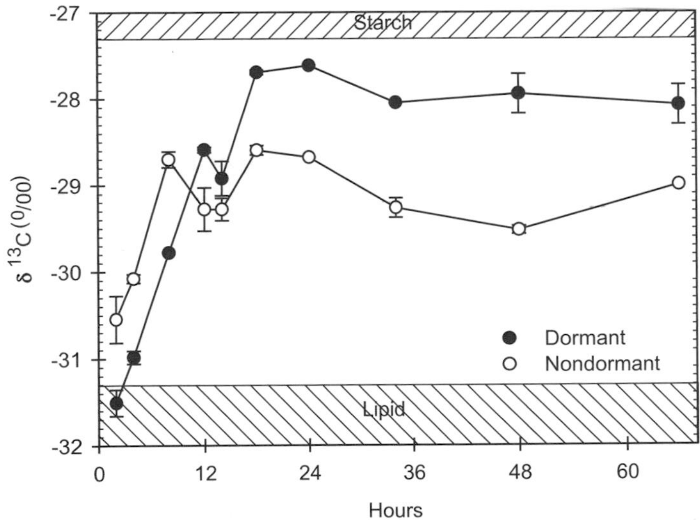

Figure 4. The $\delta^{13}C$ values of respired CO_2 collected over 45 minutes from dormant and non-dormant barley seeds at intervals after the start of imbibition. Dormant and non-dormant barley seeds were imbibed as described in material and methods for 2 – 66 h prior to the collection of respired CO_2. Shaded areas represented the measured $\delta^{13}C$ values of barley starch and lipid. Data presented are means ± SD (n = 2). No error bar indicates SE is smaller than symbol.

In dormant grain, the $\delta^{13}C$ values for respired CO_2 became steadily less negative from 2 to 18 hours of imbibition. After 18 hours, the $\delta^{13}C$ ratio reached -27.6‰ at which point it stopped changing and remained at a plateau of approximately -28‰. In non-dormant grain, the respired CO_2 $\delta^{13}C$ values became less negative during the period 2-14 h, increasing from –30.5‰ to stabilise at –28.6‰. After 24 hours the $\delta^{13}C$ values declined to -29.0‰ and then to -29.5‰ at 48 hours before increasing again. This shows that in dormant grain, carbohydrate was the predominant source of carbon substrate during phase II of respiration. Whereas in germinable grain, there was a rapid initial switch from lipid towards carbohydrate, but respiration then settled down as a fairly even mix of lipid and carbohydrate.

Conclusions

The respiration of non-dormant grain increased above that of dormant grain after 16 h, beyond its initial plateau (Figure 1). This was coincident with visible signs of germination. The mitochondria from both dormant and germinable barley were NAD deficient during imbibition. The isolated mitochondria from germinable grain were able to couple their respiration to ATP synthesis on addition of NAD at 16 h, whereas those from dormant grain were not always able to do so (Table 1). Following 72 h of imbibition, mitochondria were coupled in both germinable and dormant grain, although mitochondria were NAD deficient. Overall, this suggests that the ability of grains to germinate was associated with a more rapid reconstitution of mitochondrial activity so that they had the potential for coupled respiration at the point of chitting.

During imbibition of water in dormant grain, when the fractional contribution of lipid and starch to the carbon isotope ratio of respired CO_2 was taken into account, lipid was initially the predominant respiratory substrate, but by phase II there was a switch to respiration that was predominantly of carbohydrate. In non-dormant grain, lipid was the initial major contributor of respiratory substrate. However, by 12 hours the decline had halted and both lipid and carbohydrate made equivalent contributions to the isotope ratio of the respired CO_2.

As grains entered phase III, the embryo respiration of the grains increases, they have to a large extent consumed their initial supply of soluble sugars, their mitochondria have the potential for coupled respiration and sucrose levels begin to rise. The source of this sucrose could either be via gluconeogenesis from lipid or from metabolism of hexoses passed from the endosperm into the scutellum. The grain thus enters a phase where the respiratory energy for its embryo is from a mixture of stored lipid and sucrose. This implies that germination is dependant on embryos maintaining their ability to mobilise lipid for early seedling growth. Thus an understanding of lipid metabolism in barley embryos is essential to understand the transition from a dormant to a germinable grain.

Acknowledgements

K. A. M^c^Cafferty. received financial support from Suntory Ltd, Japan and Highland Distillers. We wish to thank Charlie Scrimgeour, Winnie Stein and Calum M^c^Cafferty for technical assistance.

References

Becker, W. M., Leaver, C. J., Weir, E. M. and Riezman, H. (1978). Regulation of glyoxysomal enzymes during germination of cucumber. 1. Developmental-changes in cotyledonary protein, RNA, and enzyme-activities during germination. *Plant Physiology* **62**: 542-549.

Benech-Arnold, R.L. and Sánchez, R.A. (2003). Preharvest sprouting. In *Encyclopaedia of Applied Plant Sciences, Vol. 3*, edited by B. Thomas, D. J. Murphy and B. G. Murray, Elsevier Academic Press, London, pp. 1333–1339.

Bewley, J. D. (1997). Seed germination and dormancy. *Plant Cell* **9**: 1055-1066.

Botha, F. C., Potgieter, G. P. and Botha, A. M. (1992). Respiratory metabolism and gene-xpression during seed-germination. *Plant Growth Regulation* **11**: 211-224.

Coombs, J., Hind, G., Leegood, R. C., Tieszen, L. L. and Vonshak, A. (1987). Analytical techniques. In *Techniques in Bioproductivity and Photosynthesis,* edited by J. Coombs, D. O. Hall, S. P. Long and M. O. Scurlock, Pergamon Press, Oxford, pp. 219-228.

Craig, H. (1953). The geochemistry of the stable carbon isotopes. *Geochimica et Cosmochimica Acta* **3**: 53-92.

Douce, R. (1985). Mitochondria in Higher plants: Structure, Function, and Biogenesis. Academic Press, New York.

Hilhorst, H.W.M. (2007). Definitions and hypotheses of seed dormancy. In: *Seed Development Dormancy and Germination,* edited by K. Bradford and H. Nonogaki, Blackwell Publishing Ltd., Oxford, pp. 50-71.

Institute of Brewing (1991). Recommended Methods of Analysis, Institute of Brewing, London.

Jacobson, B. S., Smith, B. N., Epstein, S. and Laties, G. G. (1970). Prevalence of C-13 in respiratory carbon dioxide as an indicator of type of endogenous substrate. Change from lipid to carbohydrate during respiratory rise in potato slices. *Journal of General Physiology* **55**: 1-17.

Miller, G.L. (1959). Protein determination for large numbers of samples. *Analytical Chemistry* **31**: 964.

Neuburger, M. (1985) Preparation of plant mitochondria, criteria for assessment of mitochondrial integrity and purity, survival in vitro. In *Higher Plant Cell Respiration*, edited by R. Douce and D.A. Day, Springer-Verlag, Berlin, pp. 7-24.

Palmer, G. H. (1969). Surcrose and raffinose utilization during early stages of barley germination. *Journal of the Institute of Brewing* **75**: 505-508.

Palmer, G. H. (1989). Cereals in malting and brewing. In: *Cereal Science and Technology,* edited by G. H. Palmer, Aberdeen University Press, Aberdeen, pp. 61-242.

Palmer, G.H. (2006). Barley and malt. In: *Handbook of Brewing, 2nd Edition*, edited by F. G. Priest, and G. G. Stewart, CRC Press, Taylor and Francis, Boca Raton, U.S.A., pp. 139-160.

Park, R. and Epstein, S. (1961). Metabolic Fractionation of C13 and C12 in Plants. *Plant Physiology* **36**: 133-138.

Chapter 7

The effects of lactic acid bacteria on the sensory characteristics of new-make Scotch whisky

N. R. Wilson[1], F. Jack[2], I. Takise[3], and F. G. Priest[1]
[1]*International Centre for Brewing and Distilling, Heriot-Watt University, Riccarton, Edinburgh, UK*
[2]*Scotch Whisky Research Institute, Riccarton, Edinburgh, UK*
[3]*Nikka Whisky Distilling Company Ltd., Sendai, Miyagi, Japan*

Introduction

Lactic acid bacteria (LAB) are present during malt whisky fermentations, which are essentially mixed fermentations of yeast and LAB. They constitute a small part of the natural microflora of barley grain (Booysena *et al.*, 2002), and due to their heat tolerance, are able to survive the malting and mashing stages of whisky production to become the dominant bacterial flora in the fermentation. Their tolerance of acidic pH and micoraerophilic conditions, ensure that they dominate the later stages of the malt whisky fermentation (Van Beek and Priest, 2000).

Of the LAB present in malt whisky fermentations, those belonging to the genus *Lactobacillus* are dominant, although the presence of *Bacillus coagulans, Leuconostoc mesenteroides, Saccharococcus thermophilus, and Streptococcus thermophilus* has been reported. The range of LAB present in the distillery is typically stable, but is subject to fluctuations in malt supply and distillery hygiene practices (Simpson *et al.*, 2001).

There are a wide variety of flavour compounds found in malt whisky, of which the major classes are higher alcohols, esters, organic acids, phenolics, and lactones (Palmer, 1997; Wanikawa *et al.*, 2000a). LAB are thought to influence the production of gamma (γ)-lactones, specifically γ-decalactone and γ-dodecalactone, through the hydroxylation of unsaturated fatty acids, specifically palmitoleic acid and oleic acid, which are precursors to γ-lactone production. These lactones are believed to contribute desirable "sweet and fatty" notes in malt whisky; their low sensory threshold meaning that only a small amount of the substance is required to impart a notable flavour characteristic (Wanikawa *et al*, 2000b). It is proposed that LAB are responsible for the production of hydroxylated fatty acids, 10-hydroxypalmitic acid (10-HPA) and 10-hydroxystearic acid (10-HSA), which are then converted by yeasts into γ-decalactone and γ-dodecalactone respectively. Both *Saccharomyces cerevisiae* and "wild" yeasts such as *Torulaspora delbrueckii* are able to perform this reaction (Neri, 2006).

During this study, we screened various species of *Lactobacillus* for the synthesis of hydroxylated fatty acids from palmitoleic acid and oleic acid. Strains with high activity were used in laboratory-scale fermentations and distillations to determine their effects on the sensory characteristics of the new-make spirits.

Methods

LAB were recovered from samples of late fermentation wash obtained from various distilleries throughout Scotland by plating 100 μl of serial diluted wash, treated with cycloheximide to inhibit yeast growth, on to de Man, Rogosa, Sharpe (MRS) agar plates. Different colony morphologies, as a result of incubation at 30°C, were further isolated and purified, then subjected to characterisation by Random Amplification of Polymorphic DNA – Polymerase Chain Reaction (RAPD-PCR) (Simpson *et al.*, 2001). Isolates with different RAPD patterns were retained and assayed for the ability to produce hydroxylated fatty acids from palmitoleic and oleic acids.

These bioconversions were carried out in 0.5 M phosphate buffer (pH 6.5) with palmitoleic and oleic acids as substrates. Fatty acids were extracted using ethyl acetate/methanol (9:1 v/v), dried using sodium sulphate, and resuspended in benzene/methanol (7:2 v/v). Samples were treated with trimethylsilyldiazomethane and analysed using Gas Chromatography – Mass Spectrometry (GC-MS) using a DB-1 column 30 m x 0.25 mm. Heptadecanoic acid was used as an internal standard (Wanikawa *et al.*, 2000a).

Five LAB isolates were selected for laboratory-scale fermentations and distillations, and were subsequently identified by 16S rRNA gene sequencing. One species of LAB was pitched into each fermentation at a rate of $5x10^5$-$1x10^6$ cells/ml with 8 g distiller's M-yeast into 2.1 L wort. In mixed fermentations carried out with LAB plus wild yeast, M-yeast was supplemented with 10% *T. delbrueckii* in order to determine any synergistic effect between LAB that produce high levels of hydroxylated fatty acids and yeast that produce high levels of lactones. Each fermentation was carried out in duplicate, with controls consisting of fermentations pitched with M-yeast alone, and M-yeast supplemented with 10% *T. delbrueckii*. Fermentations proceeded for 96 h, at which point 2 L of fermentation wash was distilled to 700 ml low wines, which was subsequently distilled to 155 ml spirit.

Spirits were assessed using Quantitative Descriptive Analysis (Jack, 2003), which involves trained panellists scoring the intensities of a range of pre-determined characteristics, using a scale of 0 (absent) to 3 (very strong). These spirits were diluted to 20 %ABV, of which 20 ml was presented in 130 ml clear nosing glasses.

Results

The five strains of lactobacilli that were pitched into laboratory-scale fermentations were identified, by 16S rRNA gene sequencing, as a single strain of *Lactobacillus brevis*, two strains of *Lactobacillus paracasei*, and two strains *Lactobacillus plantarum*. All of these strains were shown to produce 10-HSA from oleic acid, with the following yields: *L. brevis* KD1 – 20.9%, *L. paracasei* AF4 – 8.85%, *L. paracasei* strain CY7 – 12.25%, *L. plantarum* CY8 – 62.25%, and *L. plantarum* AL3 – 25.3%. Moreover, *L. brevis* KD1 produced 10-ketostearic acid (10-KSA) at a yield of 4.4% from oleic acid. These were the five lactobacilli chosen to be tested in laboratory-scale fermentations.

Ethanol production was not adversely affected by increased LAB presence during the laboratory–scale fermentations. Most ethanol production occurred during the first 24 h of fermentation, coinciding with rapid yeast growth and metabolism of fermentable carbohydrates. Differences in ethanol concentration between fermentations were not of notable importance, with the highest concentration being observed in the fermentation inoculated with *L. paracasei* AF4 at 8.2% ABV, and the lowest being 7.8% ABV in the *L. plantarum* AL3 fermentation. The only divergence can be observed at 48 h, with the ethanol concentration in the control fermentation being 6.8% ABV, while those fermentations inoculated with LAB had an average ethanol concentration at 48 h of 7.4% ABV. However, this difference was not evident at the conclusion of fermentation, with the ethanol concentration in the control fermentation finishing at 7.85% ABV.

Sensory analysis of the new-make spirits revealed significant in perceived sweet and green/grassy notes. Regarding the sweet note, spirits derived from control, both *L. paracasei* strains, both *L. plantarum* fermentations had very similar intensities of sweet notes, with an average score of 0.42 being attributed. However, the score given for the *L. brevis* KD1 spirit was nearly twice that of the others, at 0.79. Green/grassy notes were elevated in the spirits fermented with *L. paracasei* CY7 and *L. plantarum* AL3, with scores of 0.86 and 0.87 respectively; the control, *L. paracasei* AF4, *L. plantarum* CY8, and *L. brevis* KD1 spirits were given scores of 0.67, 0.63, 0.68, and 0.59 respectively. The three remaining sensory characteristics that exhibited statistically significant differences in the spirits were the perceived off-odours of sour, sulfury, and meaty. The range of sour scores was wide, with the *L. paracasei* CY7 spirit being given the highest score of 0.57 and the lowest score of 0.26 being attributed to the *L. plantarum* CY8 spirit, with the remaining spirits existing within a seven point range from 0.39 (control) to 0.46 (*L. brevis* KD1). The sulfury and meaty profiles of the spirits echoed the sweet profile, with the statistical significance of the differences being attributed to the scores given to the *L. brevis* KD1 spirit, since for both of these characteristics it was the *L. brevis* KD1 spirit that had the highest scores, with 0.77 and 0.47 for sulfury and meaty respectively, while the average scores for these two characteristics in the remaining spirits was 0.49 and 0.3 respectively. Including *T. delbrueckii* in fermentations pitched with LAB and M-yeast was shown to amplify the sweet note, while reducing the sulfury note of the *L. brevis* KD1 spirit, with scores of 0.99 and 0.48.

Conclusions

γ-Decalactone and γ-dodecalactone, compounds known to impart desirable sweet notes and flavours, are typically formed by yeasts through either *de novo* synthesis (Endrizzi *et al.*, 1996), or through the biotransfomation of hydroxy fatty acid precursors (Endrizzi et *al.*, 1996; Wanikawa *et al.*, 2000a). In malt whisky fermentations it is the LAB that are believed to be the primary producers of hydroxy and keto fatty acids, and as such it was hypothesised that the increased presence of LAB during fermentation would result in increased yields of γ-decalactone and γ-dodecalactone through increased accumulation of 10-HSA and 10-KSA (Wanikawa *et al.*, 2000b, 2002).

In this study, *L. brevis* KD1 was shown to significantly increase sweet flavours in new-make spirit, compared to spirits fermented without additional LAB or with other species of lactobacilli. It is believed that this is due to increased lactone content in these spirits. Pitching *L. brevis* KD1 with M-yeast that had been supplemented with 10% *T. delbrueckii* further increased the sweet characteristic observed in the new-make spirit, while simultaneously reducing the undesirable meaty and sulfury notes. This further suggests that increased lactone concentration is responsible, due to the high lactone producing ability of *T. delbrueckii* (Neri, 2006).

References

Booysena, C., Dicks, L.M., Meijering, I and Ackermann, A. 2002. Isolation, identification and changes in the lactic acid bacteria during the malting of two different barley cultures. *Int J Food Microbiol.* **76**(1-2): 63-73.

Endrizzi, A., Pagot, Y, le Clainche, A, Nicaud, J-M and J-M. Belin, J-M. 1996. Production of Lactones and Peroxisomal Beta-Oxidation in Yeasts. *Critical Reviews in Biotechnology.* **16**(4): 301-329.

Jack. F. 2003. Development of Guidelines for the Preparation and Handling of Sensory Samples in the Scotch Whisky Industry. *J. Inst. Brew.* **109**(2): 114-119.

Neri, L. 2006. The involvement of wild yeast in malt whisky fermentations. Thesis. Heriot-Watt University, Edinburgh.

Palmer, G.H. 1997. Scientific Review of Scotch Malt Whisky. *Ferment.* **10**: 367-379.

Simpson, K.L., Pettersson, B and Priest, F.G. 2001. Characterization of lactobacilli from Scotch malt whisky distilleries and description of *Lactobacillus ferintoshensis* sp. nov., a new species isolated from malt whisky fermentations. *Microbiology.* **147**: 1007-1016.

Van Beek, S., and Priest, F.G. 2000. Decarboxylation of Substituted Cinnamic Acids by Lactic acid Bacteria Isolated during Malt Whisky Fermentation. *Applied and Environmental Microbiology.* **66**(12): 5322-5328.

Wanikawa, A., Hosoi, K and Kato, T. 2000a. Conversion of Unsaturated Fatty Acids to Precursors of γ-Lactones by Lactic Acid Bacteria During the Production of Malt Whisky. *J. Am. Soc. Brew. Chem.* **58**(2): 51-56.

Wanikawa, A., Hosoi, K, Takise, I and Kato, T. 2000b. Detection of γ-Lactones in Malt Whisky. *J. Inst. Brew.* **106**(1): 39-43.

Wanikawa, A., Shoji, H, Hosoi, K and Nakagawa, K-I. 2002. Stereospecificity of 10-Hydroxystearic Acid and Formation of 10-Ketostearic Acid by Lactic Acid Bacteria. *J. Am. Soc. Brew. Chem.* **60**(1): 14-20.

Chapter 8

Developments in vodka production

Matti Korhola
Alkomohr Biotech Ltd, Lehtotie 8, FIN-00630 Helsinki, Finland

Introduction

Vodka is a relatively pure solution of ethanol (~40%v/v) in water. The ethanol is traditionally produced from starch contained in grains or potatoes, mashed to fermentable sugars, fermented by yeast, distilled to raw spirits, rectified and often filtered after diluting to about 55 % alcohol by volume. Harrison and Graham (1970) listed only 10 chemical compounds reported to be present in vodka whereas grain and potato spirit and whisky contained over 110 compounds and brandy almost 90 compounds. Since that time the analytical methods have developed greatly and today it is possible to detect hundreds of compounds in distilled alcoholic beverages. However, vodka still is the ´pure´ drink, consumed as such or diluted with mixers or flavoured with different berries, fruits, herbs or spices. Flavoured vodkas can be aged but in practice are not aged like brandy or whisky.

Vodka markets

Vodka is mostly consumed where its origins are claimed to be: Russia, Poland, and the former Soviet states (Table 1). The exceptions are the USA and the UK, together with emerging markets in the populous countries of Brazil and China (Smith, 2007).

Table 1. Vodka markets in 2006. Adapted from the IWSR Drinks Record (Smith 2007)

Market	*Million 9-litre cases*	*% of total*
Russian Federation	280.4	54.6
Ukraine	52.5	10.2
USA	49.7	9.7
Poland	27.8	5.4
Kazakhstan	10.6	2.1
Belarus	9.5	1.9
UK	7.2	1.4
Uzbekistan	6.6	1.3
Romania	5.2	1.0
Brazil	4.9	1.0
Australia	0.9	0.02
China	0.3	0.006
Others	57.9	11.3
Total	513.5	100.0

The Scandinavian countries Finland and Sweden are major producers of vodka but due to their sparse population of 5.3 and 9.2 million, respectively, they do not qualify for high ranking positions in vodka markets. In Finland, a major proportion of spirits consumption is vodka or flavoured vodka, e.g. Koskenkorva Viina, at 1.59 litres per capita, compares with other spirits at 0.71 litres per capita (and total consumption of alcohol being 8.17 litres per capita in 2004 – see: Yearbook of Alcohol and Drug Statistics, 2005). In addition, it is estimated that tourist-imported and illegal alcohol adds about 2 litres per capita to the overall consumption in Finland.

The world's leading premium vodka brands in 2007 were Smirnoff with annual sales of 218.7 million litres, Absolut 96.3, Grey Goose 32.4, Stolichnaya 27.0, Skyy 26.1, and Finlandia 24.3 million litres (Hertsi, 2008).

European and Russian regulations on vodka

The European Union (EU) passed the Regulation (EC) No 110/2008 of 15 January 2008 on the definition, description, presentation, labelling and protection of geographical indications of spirit drinks and repealing Council Regulation (EEC) No 1576/1989. This new Regulation 110/2008 is a comprehensive package and is expected to profoundly change vodka production practices in Europe. When the regulation was under consideration it raised several concerns (Atkinson, 2004). The main opposition came from the traditional vodka producers in Finland, Poland and Sweden – the biggest fear being that when the raw materials base was extended from grains and potatoes into any agricultural raw material, for instance, distillates from surplus wine, would flood the vodka market. However, in this case the vodka shall bear the labelling ´Vodka produced from grapes´.

The definition of vodka in Regulation EC110/2008 is the following:

(a) Vodka is a spirit drink produced from ethyl alcohol of agricultural origin obtained following fermentation with yeast from either: (i) potatoes and/or cereals, or (ii) other agricultural raw materials, distilled and/or rectified so that the organoleptic characteristics of the raw materials used and by-products formed in fermentation are selectively reduced. This process may be followed by redistillation and/or treatment with appropriate processing aids, including treatment with activated charcoal, to give it special organoleptic characteristics. Maximum levels of residue for ethyl alcohol of agricultural origin shall meet those laid down in Annex I, except that the methanol content shall not exceed 10 grams per hectolitre of 100 % vol. alcohol.

(b) The minimum alcoholic strength by volume of vodka shall be 37,5 %.

(c) The only flavourings which may be added are natural flavouring compounds present in distillate obtained from the fermented raw materials. In addition, the product may be given special organoleptic characteristics, other than a predominant flavour.

(d) The description, presentation or labelling of vodka not produced exclusively from the raw material(s) listed in paragraph (a)(i) shall bear the indication ´produced from ...´, supplemented by the name of the raw material(s) used to produce the ethyl alcohol of agricultural origin. Labelling shall be in accordance with Article 13(2) of Directive 2000/13/EC.

Flavoured vodka is defined by Regulation EC110/2008 as:

(a) Flavoured vodka is vodka which has been given a predominant flavour other than that of the raw materials.

(b) The minimum alcoholic strength by volume of flavoured vodka shall be 37,5 %.

(c) Flavoured vodka may be sweetened, blended, flavoured, matured or coloured.

(d) Flavoured vodka may also be sold under the name of any predominant flavour with the word ´vodka´.

The geographical indications in Regulation

EC110/2008 are: Svensk Vodka/Swedish Vodka; Suomalainen Vodka/Finsk Vodka/Vodka of Finland; Polska Wódka/Polish Vodka; Laugaricio vodka (from Slovakia); Originali lietuviska degtine/Original Lithuanian vodka; Herbal vodka from the North Podlasie Lowland aromatised with an extract of bison grass/Wódka zielova z Niziny Pólnocnopodlaskiej aromatyzowana ekstraktem z trawy zubrowej (from Poland); Latvijas Dzidrais; Rigas Degvins (from Latvia); Estonian vodka.

Russian vodkas are defined in the State Standards of the Russian Federation (GOST) GOST R 51355-99 and in an amendment Order No 290-ST by the Ministry of Industry and Energetics of the Russian Federation, Federal Agency of Technical Regulation and Metrology. Also of relevance is the standard GOST R 51652-2000 on Rectified ethyl alcohol of food raw material specifications.

Russian vodkas are defined in GOST R 51355-99 as follows:

- vodka: alcoholic beverage constituting a colourless water-alcohol liquid 40.0, 45.0, 50.0 or 56.0% proof with typical taste and scent.
- special vodka: high quality vodka 40.0-45.0% proof with deliberately peculiar scent and taste due to addition of aromatic components.

The amendment Order No 290-ST provides, in addition to specifications and norms for impurities for vodkas and special vodkas, also a permission clause: "It is allowed to manufacture vodka and special vodka for export purposes whose strength will conform to contractual terms and conditions but will be not less than 37.5%".

In the EU Regulation 110/2008 there is no upper limit of alcoholic strength for spirit drinks – they have to have a minimum alcoholic strength of 15 % by volume. Of course, there are some very strong vodkas and other spirits drinks in the market.

Production of vodka

Vodka and gin are usually dealt with simultaneously with very limited information regarding vodka production in the scientific literature (Suomalainen, *et al.* 1968; Harrison and Graham, 1970; Simpson, 1977; Clutton, 1979; Murtagh, 1999; Aylott, 2003). Currently, a lot of information is available from the internet – but some websites may not be regarded as reliable. Some of the better sites are those maintained by the Gin and Vodka Association (http://www.ginvodka.org) and the Beverage Tasting Institute (http://www.tastings.com).

The raw materials for producing vodka have traditionally been cereals such as rye, wheat, and barley, or potatoes. High quality water is also employed (Fig. 1). Recently, EU Regulation 110/2008 expanded the raw materials to those of agricultural origin as described earlier.

- Traditional: potato (12-22 % starch); grains - rye, wheat, barley (corn, rice, sorghum; 60-77 % starch)
- Other agricultural raw materials: beet, cane, molasses, fruits, grapes, sugar, whey
- Water: artesian or industrial – treated to make it "soft" (demineralization/deionization, reverse osmosis, filtration)
- Flavourings: berries, fruits, herbs, spices

Figure 1. Raw materials for making vodka

In Finland, vodka is made from barley. Altia Ltd (formerly Alko Ltd.) is the manufacturer of Finlandia and Koskenkorva vodkas (the Finlandia brand is currently owned by Brown-Forman Inc.) and has its primary production site in the municipality of Ilmajoki in the village of Koskenkorva in central western Finland. The bottling plant is located about 50 km North of Helsinki in the municipality of Nurmijärvi in the village of Rajamäki where high quality ground water is abundant, a yeast factory was founded there in 1888 – the predecessor of Alko Ltd, and the current production company Altia Plc.

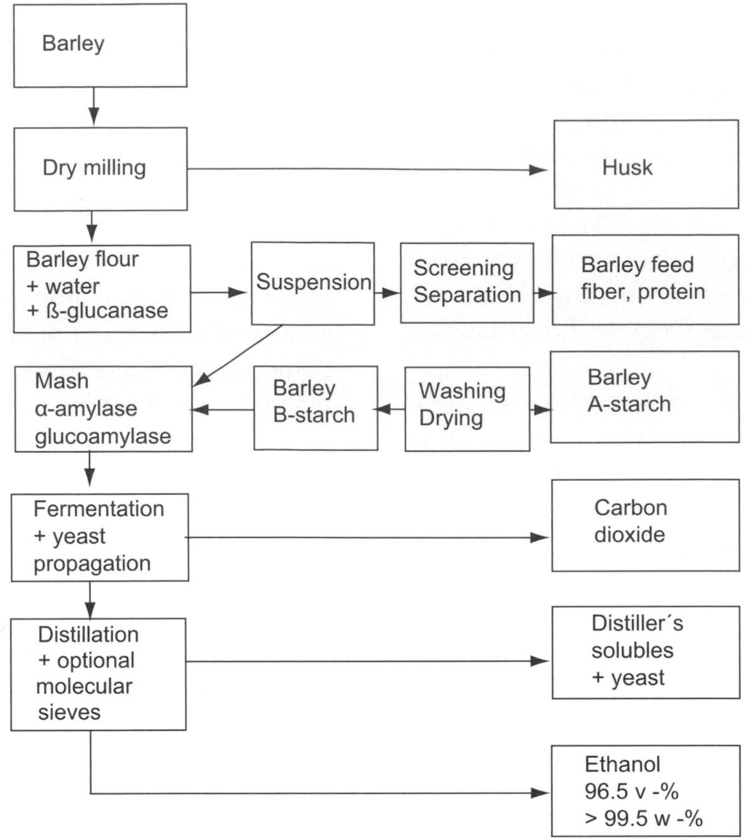

Figure 2. The Koskenkorva plant barley ethanol/starch integrality flow scheme

The starch-to-ethanol integrated production is based on patents (Lehmussaari and van der Ham, 1990). This facilitates increased product value and allows flexibility to generate higher value added products when raw material costs are favourable.

The Koskenkorva plant uses annually about 190 000 tons of barley and produces about 65 million kg (dry weight) of protein feeds, about 50 million kg of barley starch, about 26 million litres of ethanol (purified 19000 tons, technical 1500 tons), and about 20 million kg of carbon dioxide almost 17 million kg of which is recovered and sold, plus barley husks for energy production (A. Kivi personal communication; Pöyry Environment, 2006). The plant uses about 1.3 million tons of water and 2300 tons of chemicals annually. The waste water volume in 2005 was over 400,000 m^3. The average effluent flow of 2003 and 2005 was 1125 m^3/day and COD_{Cr} 1506 kg/d to the municipal waste water treatment plant and purified water had COD_{Cr} 317 kg/d, total nitrogen 23 kg/d, total phosphorus 8.6 kg/d, and total solids 210 kg/d (Pöyry Environment, 2006).

Vodka fermentations

For vodka production, continuous or cascade fermentation, as opposed to traditional batch fermentation (Suomalainen *et al*, 1968), offers higher fermenter productivity due to long term operation under optimal fermentation conditions and reduced emptying, cleaning, and refilling times. However, the main challenges of continuous operation are microbiological contamination of the fermentation by especially due to lactic acid bacteria or wild yeasts which reduce the yield of ethanol by consuming fermentable sugars more avidly than the distiller´s yeast, having shorter lag and generation times,

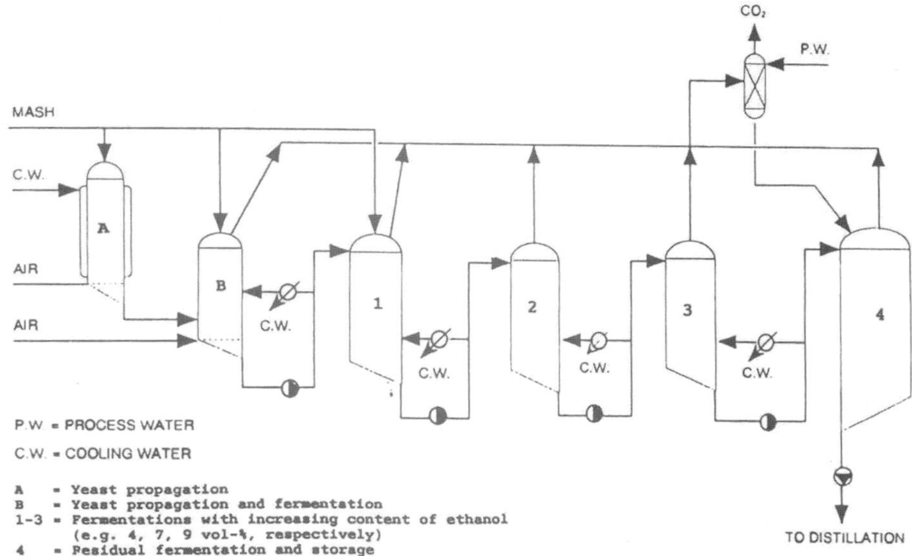

Figure 3. Cascade fermentation for milled grains (reprinted from Korhola 1994)

and resistance to stress conditions (Butcher *et al.* 1992).

The cascade fermentation process (Fig. 3) was implemented because yeast fermentation optimisation studies showed that yeast growth (Fig. 4A) was much more inhibited than alcoholic fermentation (Fig. 4B,C) reflecting that the maximum feeding rate became very low at higher sugar concentrations (Fig. 4D). The total cell mass increased at higher sugar concentrations but this did not compensate for the slow yeast growth rate. In order to increase yeast biomass sufficiently the two first vessels are aerated, the first one being dedicated to yeast propagation and the second one to propagation and fermentation. Cascade fermentation eliminates inhibitory effects of high substrate osmotic pressure (compared with batch fermentation) during early stages of fermentation allowing higher feeding rates.

The inhibitory effect of ethanol on yeast growth becomes very significant at alcohol concentrations above 6 % (w/v, Fig. 5). Of course, this depends on the strain of yeast (Korhola et al. 1986).

The continuous cascade fermentation with several fermentation vessels means that with a fixed feed rate the ethanol content in the first vessel may rise up to 4-6 %, in the second to 5-8 %, in the third to 8-10 % and in the residual fermentation and storage tank up to 12 %. Similar systems have become very common in fuel alcohol production (Madson and Monceaux, 1999).

Distillation/purification of ethanol and vodka is outlined in Fig. 6, and has been described by Clutton (1979), Murtagh (1999) and Piggot (2003). Russian Federation Standard GOST R 51355-99 states that "This standard applies to vodkas and special vodkas constituting alcoholic beverages 40.0-45.0 and 50.0-56.0% proof, respectively, produced by special adsorbing agent treatment of alcohol aqueous solution with or without addition of ingredients with subsequent filtering". A leading vodka producer in the Baltic states has described some of the stages in vodka purification (http://www.stumbras.eu), the ethanol emanating from an external outside source (http://www.biofuture.lt).

In some cases it is possible to deduce from product analyses what kind of distillation apparatus has been used: copper pot stills or stainless steel columns (Reche *et al*, 2007).

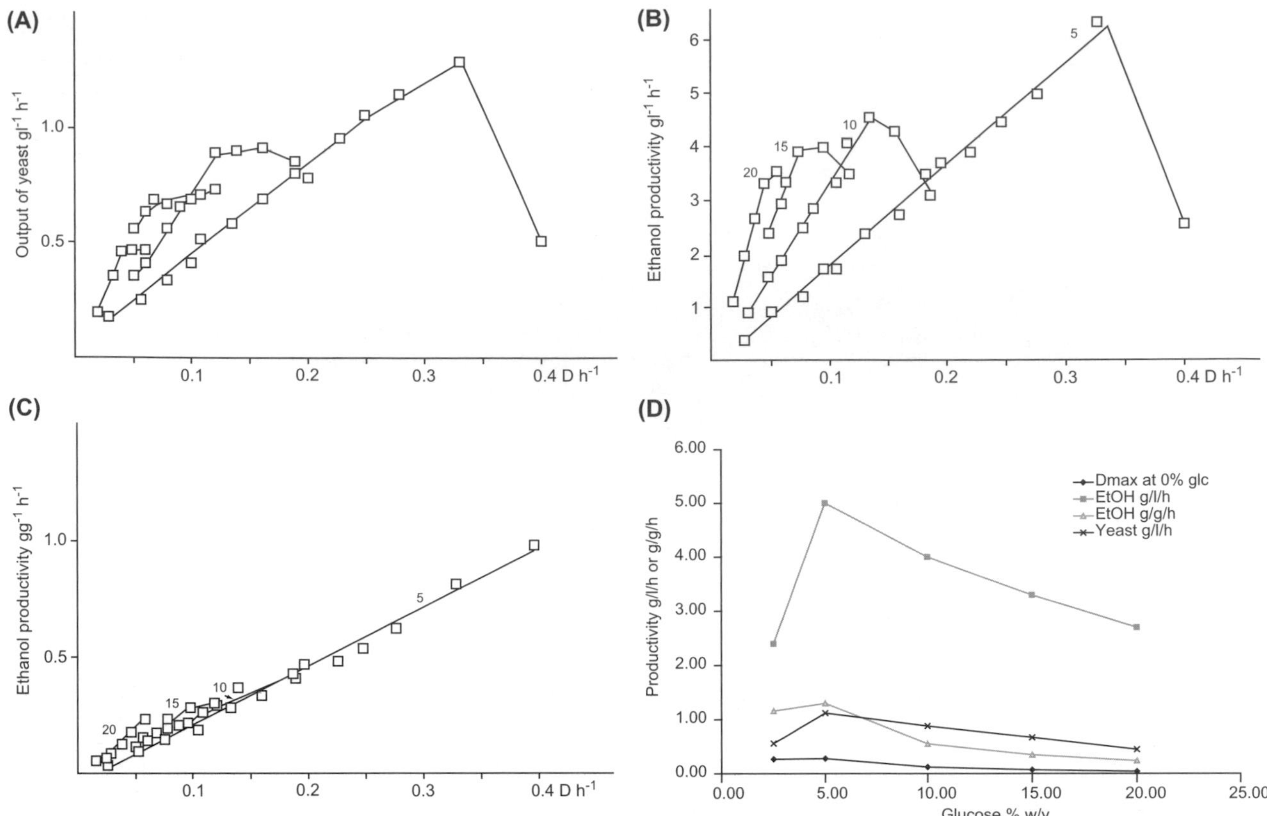

Figure 4. Determination of parameters for continuous fermentation at different glucose concentrations by the industrial yeast MK 270. (A) Output of yeast dry matter (B) Volumetric productivity of ethanol (C) Specific productivity of ethanol (D) Summary of productivity curves at maximum dilution (feed) rate allowing complete utilization of sugar

Quality and authenticity of vodka

According to the European Union Regulation 110/2008 and the Russian Federation Standard GOST R 51355-99 plus the Order 290-ST, the quality of vodka can be defined (Table 2).

From a commercial point of view, to protect the brand value the authenticity of the particular vodka is of prime importance. Since water is the main or at least the second biggest component of vodka, and the manufacturers of vodka use specific water sources or specific treatments for

Table 2. Quality requirements for alcohol for making vodka in the European Union and in the Russian Federation

Component	*EU 110/2008 g/hl (100% EtOH)*	*Russia GOST R 51355-99 Amend. No 1 Mg/dm3 of anhydrous alcohol*
Alkalescence		2.0-3.0 cm3/100 cm3 vodka of 0.1M HCl
Total acidity (acetic acid)	1.5	not more than 0.4 g/dm3 of vodka
Esters (ethyl-acetate)	1.3	10-13
Aldehydes (acetaldehyde)	0.5	3-8
Higher alcohols (methyl2 propanol1)	0.5	5-6
Methanol	30, for vodka 10	0.003-0.03 % of anhydrous ethanol
Dry Extract	1.5	
Volatile bases containing nitrogen	0.1	
Furfural	not detectable	

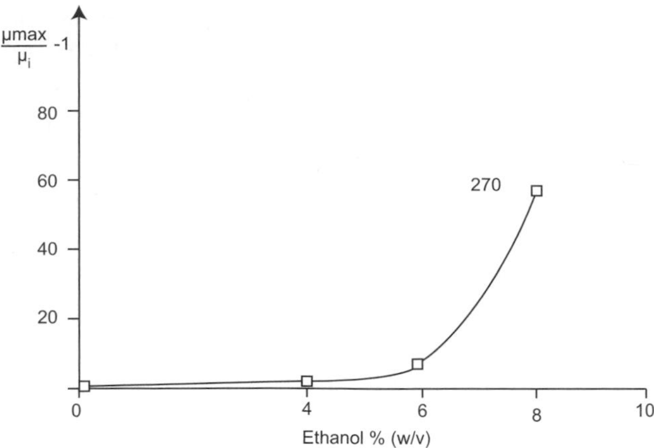

Figure 5. Inhibition of yeast growth by added ethanol

- Pot still – batch (3-6x) distillation for flavours
- Column still – continuous (2-8 columns; pre-stripper/ beer stripper/ mash column; concentrator/fusel oil concentrating column; extractive distillation column; rectifier; demethylizer/methanol column – EtOH can be very pure
- Filtration (1-10x) – EtOH diluted before to ~55 % ABV
- Filtration not mandatory, except in Russia, but widely used
- Quartz, activated hard-wood charcoal, cloth, paper, freeze-filtration, even silver filter mentioned

Figure 6. Distillation/purification of vodka

their water, it offers excellent opportunities for simple product authentication.

The anionic constituents in water have provided a useful test by simple conductivity measurements (Lachenmeier *et al,* 2008). For example, Finlandia Vodka posseses a conductivity of about 17 microSiemens/cm compared to much lower values of 3-5 for French, Polish, and Swedish vodkas and very high values of about 60-80 for two German discount vodkas. The low conductivity values probably reflect the extensive water softening procedures required and used in other parts of Europe compared to Finland where water is naturally soft. The Rajamäki bottling plant uses natural ground water. The discount vodkas may have used any commercial water source. Spirit conductivity appears to be directly proportional to the anionic content of the vodkas (Lachenmeier *et al*, 2003). Water hardness due to cations has been used to study clarity and stability of vodka (Krosnijs and Kuka, 2003).

Russian researchers have reported the ionic contents of different vodkas (Savchuk *et al*, 2001; Arbuzov and Savchuk, 2002). A particular occasional problem is that synthetic alcohol may be used to make counterfeit vodka. Acetone, 2-butanol, and crotonaldehyde have been used as marker compounds for synthetic ethanol, since they are difficult to remove by rectification distillation (Savchuk and Kolesov, 2005). Clutton (1979) has reported that in the UK, vodka has been positively marked by compounding in small amounts of a colourless, odourless substance such as glycerol, sugar syrup or a polyhydric alcohol which can be analytically detected.

Conclusions

EU regulation EC110/2008 is the most important recent development in vodka production and business in Europe. The traditional raw materials for vodka production – grains and potatoes – have been expanded to ethanol made by fermentation from any agricultural raw material. Thus, for example, surplus wine or sugar beet and sugar cane-derived spirits are currently acceptable and lawful components of vodka. The EU and the biggest vodka market in the world, the Russian Federation, have in effect practically harmonised their vodka regulations to allow commercial competition to decide which vodkas are produced.

Worldwide commercial brands dominate the global vodka market. At least one traditional vodka producer which earlier mastered the whole chain from raw materials to final product and including sales and marketing have recently sold the brand – fifth in premium brand worldwide ranking – to a global company, retaining only the actual production process themselves. Another example is a regional vodka market leader having outsourced its spirits production.

Because water comprises a major component in vodka, and water is always a locally-sourced raw material, analytical determinants of water can quite easily be used to authenticate vodka. The simplest method for vodka authentication is a conductivity measurement which reflects the inorganic anion concentration of water used for diluting spirits to final vodka strength.

Acknowledgements

I thank Mrs. Irmeli Mustonen of the Finnish Food and Drink Industries Federation for supplying the EU and Russian regulatory materials and Mr. Arttu Kivi for providing up-to-date production figures of the Koskenkorva plant of Altia Plc and both for useful comments.

References

Arbuzov, V.N. and Savchuk, S.A. (2002). Identification of vodkas by ion chromatography and gas chromatography. *Journal of Analytical Chemistry* **57**: 428-433

Atkinson, E. (2004). Gin and vodka: problems and prospects. In: *Distilled Spirits, Tradition and Innovation*, Edited by Bryce, J.H. and Stewart, G.G., Nottingham University Press, Bath, pp. 47-51

Aylott, R.I. (2003). Vodka, gin and other flavoured spirits. In: *Fermented Beverage Production, 2nd Edition*, Edited by Lea, A.G.H. and Piggot, J.R., Kluwer Academic / Plenum Publishers, New York, pp. 289-308

The Beverage Tasting Institute. All about vodka. Http://www.tastings.com read 24.7.2008

Biofuture. Manufacturing technology. Http://www.biofuture.lt read 30.7.2008

Butcher, S., Koistinen, T. and Väisänen, E. (1992). The growth of contaminating lactobacilli and alcohol or baker´s yeast production organisms under inhibitory conditions. In: *Proceedings of the COMETT Course on Microbial Contaminants*, Helsinki 1992, Edited by Korhola, M. and Backström, V. Foundation for Biotechnical and Industrial Fermentation Research **7**: 99-130

Clutton, D. (1979). The production of gin and vodka. *Brewers´ Guardian* **108** (10): 25-30

The Gin and Vodka Association. The production of vodka. Http://www.ginvodka.org read 24.7.2008

Harrison, J.S. and Graham, J.C.J. (1970). Yeasts in distillery practice. In: *The Yeasts, Volume 3*, Edited by Rose, A.H. and Harrison, J.S., Academic Press, London and New York, pp. 283-348

Hertsi, A. (2008). Finlandia Vodka lähti kiitoon. Source: Impact 02-2008, *Kauppalehti* 5.8.2008, pp. 1-3

Korhola, M. (1994). New biotechnology in distilling. *Ferment* **7**: 235-239

Korhola, M., Suomalainen, I., Väisänen, E. and Tuompo, H. (1986). Distiller´s yeast. In: *Proceedings of the Seventh Conference on Global Impacts of Applied Microbiology: Symposia on Alcohol Fermentation and Plant Cell Culture*, Helsinki 1985, Edited by Korhola, M., Tuompo, H. and Kauppinen, V., Foundation for Biotechnical and Industrial Fermentation Research **4**: 29-61

Krosnijs, I. and Kuka, P. (2003). Influence of water hardness on the clearness and stability of vodka. *Polish Journal of Food and Nutrition Sciences* **12**: 58-60

Lachenmeier, D.W., Attig, R., Frank, W. and Athanasakis, C. (2003). The use of ion chromatography to detect adulteration of vodka and rum. *European Food Research and Technology* **218**: 105-110

Lachenmeier, D.W., Schmidt, B. and Bretschneider, T. (2008). Rapid and mobile brand authentication of vodka using conductivity measurement. *Microchimica Acta* **160**: 283-289

Lehmussaari, A. and van der Ham, W. (1990). Process for producing starch from cereals. US Patent 4,957,565 (also FI 874386, EP 0267637, NL 8602850, MX 163493)

Madson, P.W. and Monceaux, D.A. (1999). Fuel ethanol production. In: *The Alcohol Textbook, 3rd Edition*, Edited by Murtagh, J.E., Nottingham University Press, Bath, pp. 257-267

Ministry of Industry and Energetics of the Russian Federation, Federal Agency on Technical Regulation and Metrology. Order No 290-ST, On the approval of amendments to national standard, 17.11.2005

Murtagh, J.E. (1999). Production of neutral spirits and preparation of gin and vodka. In: *The Alcohol Textbook, 3rd Edition*, Edited by Murtagh, J.E., Nottingham University Press, Bath, pp. 195-210

Piggot, R. (2003). From pot stills to continuous stills: flavour modification by distillation. In: *The Alcohol Text Book, 4th Edition*, Edited by Jacques, K.A., Lyons, T.P. and Kelsall, D.R., Nottingham University Press, Bath, pp. 255-266

Pöyry Environment Oyj (2006). Altia corporation. Koskenkorvan tehtaan laajennus. Ympäristövaikutusten arviointiselostus. Report 67060271EC, 120 pp. http://www.ymparisto.fi/download.asp?contentid=58167&lan=fi , read 15.6.2008

Reche, R.V., Neto, A.F.L., Da Silva, A.A., Galinaro, C.A., De Osti, R.Z. and Franco, D.W. (2007). Influence of type of distillation apparatus on chemical profiles of Brazilian cachacas. *Agricultural and Food Chemistry* **55**: 6603-6608

Regulation (EC) No 110/2008 of the European Parliament and of the Council of 15 January 2008 on the definition, description, presentation, labelling and the protection of geographical indications of spirit drinks and repealing Council Regulation (EEC) No 1576/89. Official Journal of the European Union L 39/16, EN, 13.2.2008

Savchuk, S.A. and Kolesov, G.M. (2005). Markers of the nature of ethyl alcohol: Chromatographic techniques for their detection. *Journal of Analytical Chemistry* **60**: 1102-1113

Savchuk, S.A., Vlasov, V.N., Appolonova, S.A., Arbuzov, V.N., Vedenin, A.N., Mezinov, A.B. and Grigoryan, B.R. (2001). Application of chromatography and spectrometry to the authentication of alcoholic beverages. *Journal of Analytical Chemistry* **56**: 214-231

Simpson, A.C. (1977). Gin and vodka. In: *Economic Microbiology, Volume 1, Alcoholic Beverages*, Edited by Rose, A.H., Academic Press, London, New York, San Francisco, pp. 537-593

Smith, A. (2007). Vodka meets with growing global appeal. *IWSR Spirit Review* September 2007, pp. 6-11

State Standards of the Russian Federation (GOST) GOST R 51355-99. Vodkas and special vodkas. General specifications.

State Standards of the Russian Federation (GOST) GOST R 51652-2000. Rectified ethyl alcohol of food raw material. Specifications.

Stumbras. Vodka. Http://www.stumbras.eu read 24.7.2008

Suomalainen, H., Kauppila, O., Nykänen, L. Peltonen, R.J. (1968). Branntweine. In: *Handbuch der Lebensmittelchemie, Band 7 Alkoholische Genussmittel*, Edited by Diemair, W., Springer-Verlag, Berlin, Heidelberg, New York, pp. 496-653

Yearbook of Alcohol and Drug Statistics 2005. National Research and Development Centre for Welfare and Health, STAKES, Helsinki, Finland, p. 67

Chapter 9

Use of terpene-producing yeasts in brandy production

Benoît Colonna-Ceccaldi
Pernod Ricard Research Centre, 120, avenue du Maréchal Foch, 94015 Créteil Cedex, France

The Muscat flavour

Since the Egyptian civilisation, some grape varieties have been identified as particularly aromatic, with a strong flower/fruity flavour. They were firstly cultivated around the Mediterranean Sea by the Greeks and Romans, and are now utilised throughout the world. Most of these varieties are known under the generic name of Muscat, with names like Muscat à petits grains, Muscat d'Alexandrie in France and Italy, Muller-Thurgau in Germany, Torrontes or Torontel in Spain and South America. Bronner (2003) describes 4400 grapes varieties and variants related to Muscat.

The chemical compounds responsible for this specific aroma are mainly geraniol, nerol, α-terpineol, linalool, and ß-citronellol. These monoterpenes are part of a large family of molecules obtained by association of isoprene units. The total free terpene concentration varies from 0.6 to 1.5 mg/l, depending on the grape variety and cultural parameters, with important variations of the respective proportions of terpenes (Agosin, Belancic, Ibacache, Baumes, Bordeu, Crawford, and Bayonove, 2000). In the grape berry, an important part of the terpenes is linked to glycoside residues which are more or less hydrolysed during subsequent processing (fermentation, distillation and aging,- see Agosin *et al.*, 2000). The sensorial characteristics are described as: rose flower (geraniol, nerol), rosewood (linalool) and geranium flower (geraniol, cironellol, terpineol).

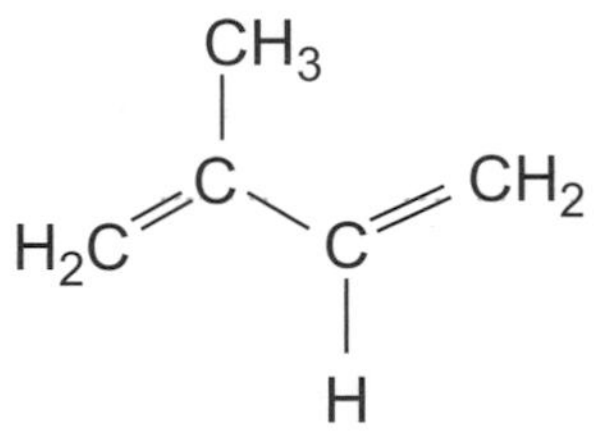

CH_3
H_2C C C CH_2
H

Figure 1: Structure of the isoprene unit

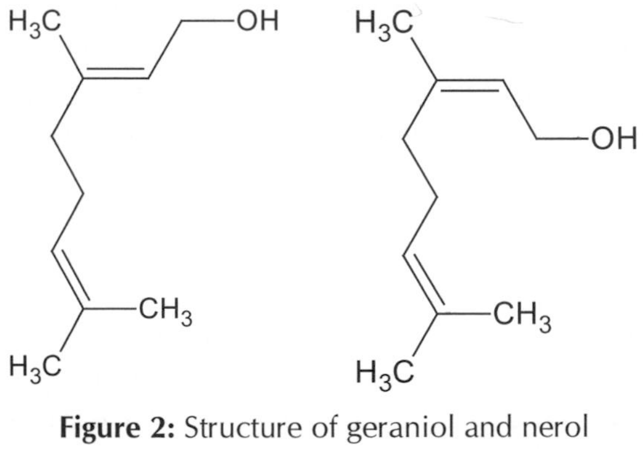

H_3C OH H_3C
OH
CH_3 CH_3
H_3C H_3C

Figure 2: Structure of geraniol and nerol

The main use of these grapes is for the production of sweet still wine, obtained either by partial fermentation, "passerillage" (drying of the grape prior to fermentation), addition of alcohol to block the fermentation ("mutage") or any other traditional technique. Best known of such products are: Muscat de Samos (Greece), Muscat de Frontignan, Cap Corse or Muscat de Rivesaltes (France), Tokaji (Hungary), and Frontignac (Australia). Some famous Muscat sparkling sweet wines are produced in Italy (Asti Spumante) and France (Clairette de Die). Dry still wines like Joao Pires (Portugal) or Muller-Thurgau (Germany) are much less common. The only Muscat-based brandy produced in significant quantities is Pisco in Chile and Peru (Colonna-Ceccaldi, 2008), while some production occurs also in Moldavia and Bulgaria.

Construction of a terpene-producing yeast strain

Due to the scarcity and higher price of Muscat grape juice, and the necessity in some countries to valorise grape juice obtained from neutral varieties, we proposed to modify a yeast strain by non-GMO techniques to obtain a strain able to produce terpenes during the course of alcoholic fermentation.

Ergosterol is the compound responsible for the mechanical resistance of the yeast plasma membrane and is a major component of yeast by weight, up to 10% of the dry matter. The ergosterol metabolic pathway starts from general carbohydrate metabolism (via acetyl-CoA) and goes through intermediates, one of them being the phosphorylated form of geraniol (Daum, Lees, Bard, and Dickson, 1998; Lamarti, Badoc, Deffieux, and Carde, 1994; Veen, and Lang, 2005). While the yeast *Saccharomyces cerevisiae* is not able to excrete this molecule under normal conditions, we have obtained a mutant partially blocked in 2 steps of this metabolic pathway, erg 9 (squalene synthase) and erg 20-2 (farnesyl PP synthase), auxotrophic for ergosterol (Chambon, Ladeveze, Servouse, Blanchard, Javelot, Vladescu and Karst, 1991; Javelot, Karst, Ladeveze, Chambon, and Vladescu, 1990; Javelot, Girard, Colonna-Ceccaldi and Vladescu, 1991).

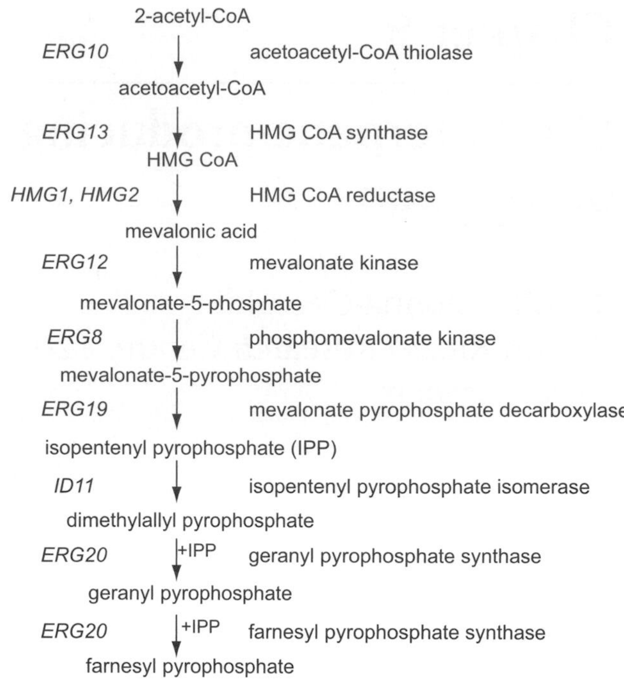

Figure 3: Farnesol synthesis pathway in *Saccharomyces cerevisiae* (after Veen, and Lang, 2005)

As the fermentative capacity and alcohol resistance of this haploid laboratory yeast were very poor, it was back-crossed with an oenological strain to obtain a genetically stable yeast able to produce high levels of ethanol, but still producing terpenes. The concentration of terpenes obtained during the fermentation can reach up to 5-10 times the level observed in a regular Muscat wine. Terpene synthesis occurred mainly during the growth phase and was increased by aeration, as sterol synthesis is an aerobic process. Despite the back-cross, and due to mutations in sterol production, the vigour of this strain was still low compared to wild yeast, hence the necessity to reduce the natural flora of the grape juice to a minimum, either by pasteurisation, filtration or centrifugation. By changing operating conditions like temperature, CO_2 pressure, aeration etc, it was possible to modify the total level of terpenes and in some cases to alter the ratio between geraniol, linalool and citronellol, thus giving a whole range of products from the same raw material.

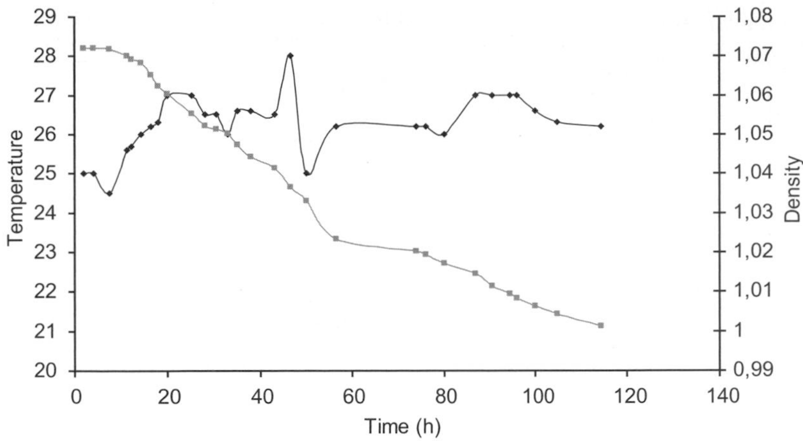

Figure 4: Wine fermentation kinetics with terpene-producing yeast strain

Industrial trials

This yeast has been used in large scale brandy production, using pasteurised grape juice obtained form very neutral varieties. For easy utilisation in an industrial situation, it has been produced as an Active Dry Yeast, a common form of commercial oenological yeast.

Fermentation was fast and complete, the wine was then distilled by a traditional "Cognac-style" process (double pot-still with cuts on the second distillate). The distillate was aged in new oak wood cask for 18 months, and used successfully as a building block to bring some freshness to neutral brandies.

The total level of terpenes in the aged distillate reached 25 mg/l, almost 250 times the perception threshold. In this case, the distillation yield was around 75%, with some conversion of geraniol to terpineol and citronellol; few changes occurred during aging.

Terpenes chiral analysis

The aromatic wine, the corresponding brandy and a commercial Muscat de Frontignan have been analysed by GC after solvent extraction on two different chiral capillary columns (Megadex DETTBS ß and Megadex DETTBS ß), to enable discrimination of all optic isomers of terpenes. Among the 5 terpenes analysed, only 3 of them contained an asymmetric carbon and thus 2 enantiomers: linalool, citronellol and terpineol.

The same result was obtained on the wine, the brandy and the commercial product: linalool and terpineol were racemic, while citronellol was 98% pure as an R-(+) form. This raises the question of the origin of the terpenes, as the metabolic pathway previously described only goes trough geraniol. By adding pure geraniol and yeast to a synthetic medium, some transformations occurred as described in Figure 7.

Table 1: Terpenes concentration in wine and distillate obtained at industrial scale

	Control wine	*Trial wine*	*Control distillate*	*Trial distillate*	*Trial after aging*
ABV %	12.35	11.5	68.5	68.5	68
Linalool µg/l	187	2040	1040	6380	5825
α-terpineol µg/l	38	520	350	7560	7200
β-citronellol µg/l	38	1510	100	8550	8680
Nerol µg/l	0	70	0	230	261
Geraniol µg/l	29	1260	60	730	761
Total terpenes	292	5400	1550	23450	22727

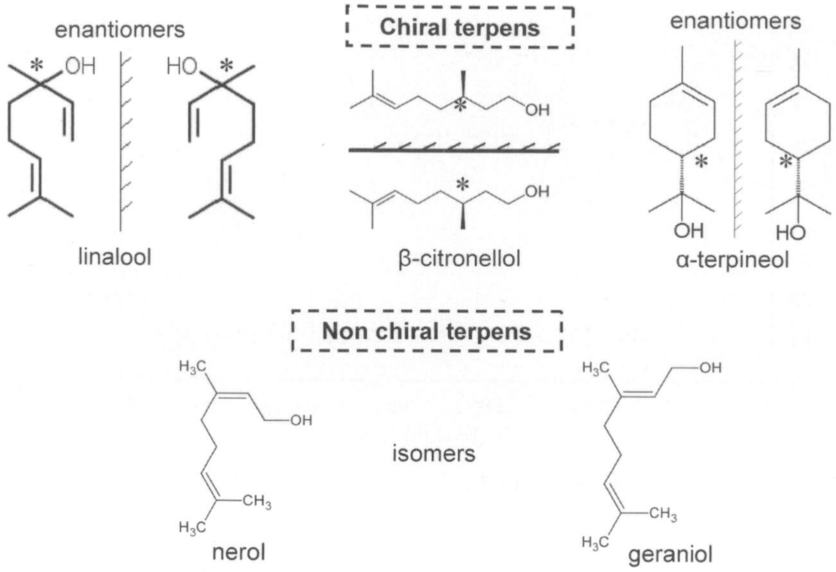

enantiomers

Chiral terpens

enantiomers

linalool

β-citronellol

α-terpineol

Non chiral terpens

nerol

isomers

geraniol

Figure 5: Chiral structure of the terpenes studied

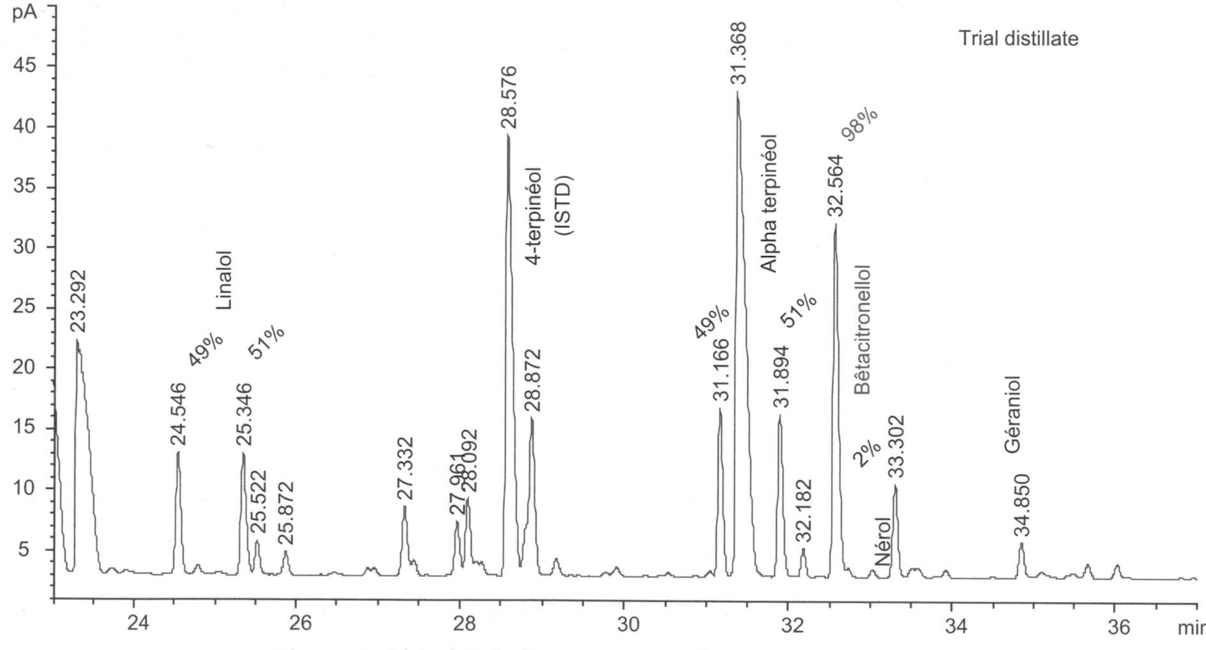

Figure 6: Chiral GC chromatogram of the aromatic brandy

Chiral analysis indicated that the pathway to citronellol is probably biologic (enzymatic transformation) while linalool and terpineol are obtained by spontaneous transformation in an acidic medium. The same mechanisms of terpene conversion have been described during the fermentation of regular Muscat grape juice (Vaudano, Garcia Moruno and DiStefano, 2004).

Conclusion

The objective of this work was the construction of a non-GMO yeast strain able to produce Muscat flavours during alcoholic fermentation, by mutation in the pathway of sterol synthesis, leading to accumulation of terpenes in the wine. This yeast has been utilised on an industrial scale

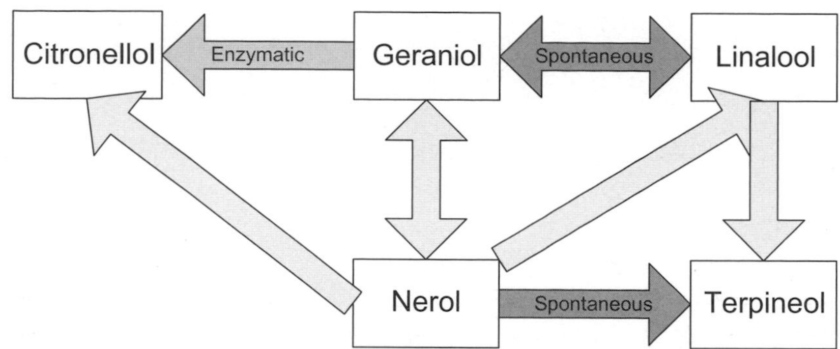

Figure 7: Transformation of monoterpenes during alcoholic fermentation

for Brandy base wine production, with a view to bringing some freshness to spirits obtained from neutral grape varieties. Chiral analysis indicates that mechanisms of geraniol transformation and the range of product obtained are the same as in regular Muscat wine.

Acknowledgements

The microbiological work (strain selection and characterisation) was performed by: Pr Karst, Poitiers University, now part of INRA Colmar/ Strasbourg University and Catherine Javelot, Barbu Vladescu, Patrick Girard and Eric Degryse in Pernod Ricard Center of Research

The terpene analysis (dosage, chirality) was done by Armand Rozenblum, Pernod Ricard, laboratory of Chemistry.

References

Agosin, E., Belancic, A., Ibacache, A., Baumes, R., Bordeu, E., Crawford, A. and Bayonove, C. (2000). Aromatic potential of certain Muscat grape varieties important for Pisco production in Chile. *American Journal of Enology and Viticulture* **51 (4)**: 404-408

Bronner, A. (2003). *Muscats et variétés muscatées.* INRA Editions/Oenoplurimedia, France.

Chambon, C., Ladeveze, V., Servouse, M., Blanchard, L., Javelot, C., Vladescu, B. and Karst, F., (1991). Sterol pathway in yeast. Identification and properties of mutant strains defective in mevalonate disphosphate decarboxylase and farnesyl diphosphate synthetase. *Lipids* **26**: 633-636

Colonna-Ceccaldi, B. (2008). *Impact of brandy production processes on flavour.* In: Distilled Spirits - Production, Technology and Innovation, Edited by Bryce, J.H., Piggott, J.R., Stewart, G.G., Nottingham University Press, Nottingham, UK, pp 229-236

Daum, G., Lees, N.D., Bard, M. and Dickson, R., (1998). Biochemistry, cell biology and molecular biology of lipids of *Saccharomyces cerevisiae*. *Yeast* **14**: 1471-510

Javelot, C., Karst, F., Ladeveze, V., Chambon, C. and Vladescu, B., (1990). Production of monoterpenes by yeast mutants defective in sterol biosynthesis. In: Microbiology Applications in Food Biotechnology, edited by Nga, B.H. and Lee, Y.K., pp 101-122

Javelot, C.; Girard P.; Colonna-Ceccaldi B. and Vladescu B., (1991). Introduction of terpene-producing ability in a wine strain of *Saccharomyces cerevisiae*. *Journal of Biotechnology* **21 (3)**: 239-252

Lamarti, A., Badoc, A., Deffieux, G. and Carde, J.P., (1994). Biogénèse des monoterpènes II – la chaîne isoprénique. *Bulletin de la société pharmaceutique de Bordeaux* **133**: 79-99

Veen, M. and Lang, C. (2005). Interactions of the ergosterol biosynthetic pathway with other lipid pathways. *Biochemical Society Transactions* **33 (5)**: 1178-1181

Vaudano, E., Garcia Moruno, E and DiStefano, R. (2004). Modulation of geraniol metabolism during alcohol fermentation. *Journal of the Institute of Brewing* **110 (3)**: 213-219

Chapter 10

Management of yeast issues in Cognac region

Ferrari G., Galy B., Roulland C., Lurton L.
B.N.I.C. (Bureau National Interprofessionnel du Cognac), Station Viticole, 69, rue de Bellefonds, 16100 Cognac, France

Abstract

Considering that the fermentation stage is of utmost importance for Cognac quality, BNIC Station Viticole has conducted several in-depth studies during the past 20years on the control of fermentation kinetics and the synthesis of volatile compounds produced during alcoholic fermentation. Grape must composition (acidity, nitrogen, sugars) and temperature, which influence both fermentation kinetics and analytical composition of wine (higher alcohols, esters) have been thoroughly studied. The results have lead to the following recommendations concerning the control of alcoholic fermentation of wines intended for Cognac distillation:

- Determination of harvest date, in order to optimize the equilibrium between sugars, acidity and nitrogen
- Management of must nitrogen content
- Reduction of solid matter suspended in the must, and temperature control

Inoculation with selected yeasts and choice of a suitable yeast strain are also important tools for fermentation control. Ecological and biochemical studies have clearly highlighted the risks linked to spontaneous fermentation and motivated a selection program for *Saccharomyces cerevisiae* strains, originating from Cognac vineyards, and suitable for Cognac base wines fermentation.

Today, must inoculation is a widespread and well-managed practise. A qualification process of selected dry yeasts, based on an assessment of physiological criteria, analytical requirements and sensory validation is being developed by BNIC. These criteria are being evaluated at pilot and industrial scales. A survey of yeast strains' behaviour in different wineries has also been implemented during several years after their qualification. Five yeast strains (two issued from the regional selection program) are recommended by BNIC for Cognac winemaking, and are mostly being used by winemakers. It is apparent that must inoculation by selected yeasts has contributed during the past 20 years to the improvement of the quality of freshly distilled spirits.

Introduction

The BNIC (Bureau National Interprofessionnel du Cognac) Station Viticole has conducted several in depth studies on the control of fermentation kinetics and the synthesis of volatile compounds produced during alcoholic fermentation for

Cognac production. The use of sulphites is forbidden in the elaboration of wine spirits for Cognac, therefore, to prevent microbiological spoilage, alcoholic fermentation has to start quickly, be regular and take place in less than seven days. Winemakers have to manage grape must composition and winemaking conditions to allow a good yeast development and to optimise yeast metabolic performance. Two main aspects have been studied: the kinetics of alcoholic fermentation and optimisation of wine quality for Cognac production.

Managing fermentation kinetics

Fermenting must without sulphites is a challenge: winemakers have to manage many parameters, all along the production process in order to reach the conditions for making a wine which satisfy Cognac quality requirements. The main difficulty comes from the endogenous micro-flora (wild yeasts and lactic bacteria) of the must, which represent risks of wine spoilage. Figure 1 shows the different stages and risks along the winemaking process used for Cognac production.

Endogenous micro-flora

Ecological and biochemical studies have clearly highlighted the predominance of *Kloekera apiculata,* as shown in Figure 2, which can grow until the third stage of fermentation process (Versavaud *et al.*, 1992).This species can lead to elevated levels of ethyl acetate in wine (as shown in Figure 3) and its activity must be avoided (Roulland, 1994).

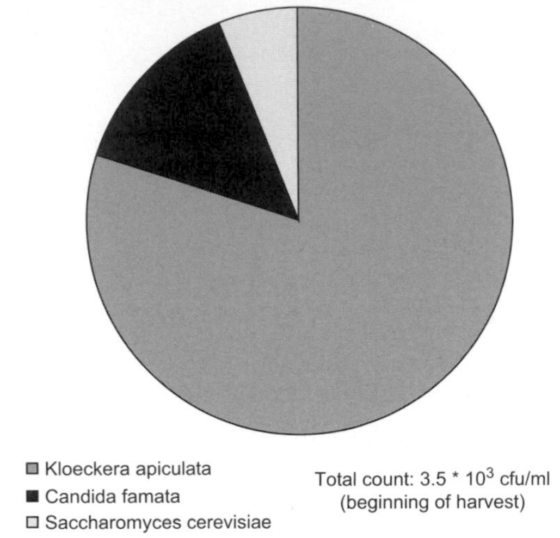

Figure 2: Micro-flora composition of must before pitching

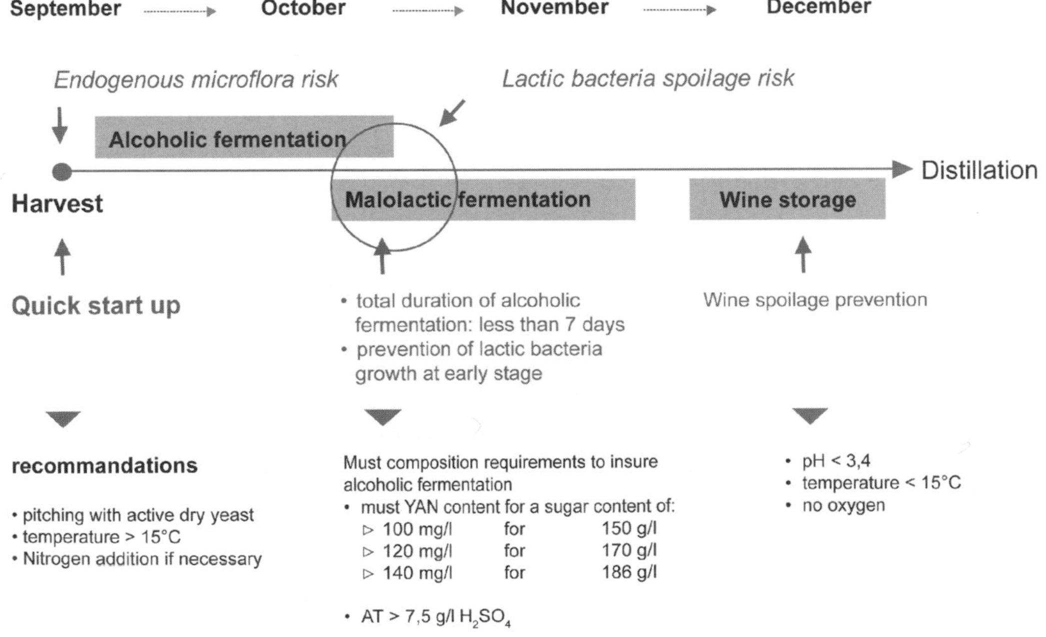

Figure 1: Managing winemaking without sulphites: risks and recommendations

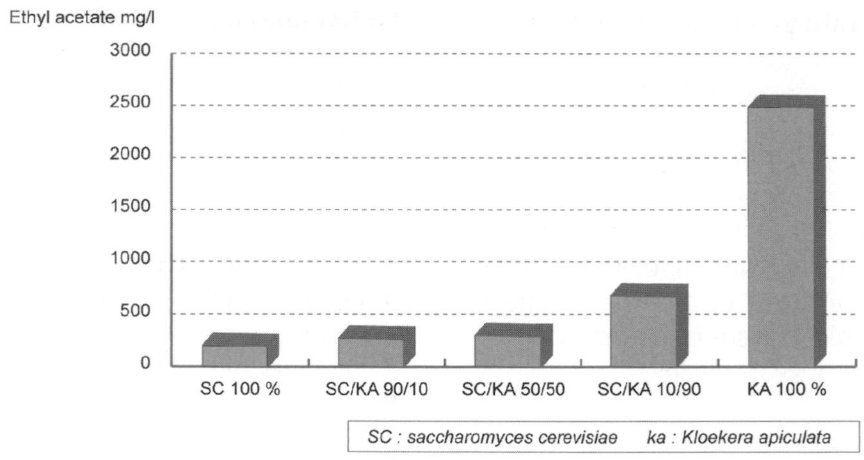

Figure 3: Effect of co-inoculation SC-KA on ethyl acetate production (Micro scale fermentation and distillation)

Lactic bacterial spoilage

Yeast assimilable nitrogen (YAN) and sugar content of must influence the total duration of fermentation, while pH determines the bacterial growth capacity. It is important to get the best conditions (must composition) to prevent malolactic bacteria developing before the end of the alcoholic fermentation. Therefore, the equilibrium between sugar, acidity and grape nitrogen content is taken into account to optimise the choice of harvest date.

Total acidity > 7.5 g/l

7.5 <Potential alcoholic strength<10.5%   YAN > 100mg/l for 9.5% alc

The risk of lactic bacteria spoilage increases with: lack of must nitrogen; high sugar content (> 9.5% as potential alcoholic strength) and low total acidity (< 7.5 g/l H_2SO_4). A potential danger zone (high risk area) for must composition during grape ripening has been defined when, at the same time, sugar content increases over 9.5% and acidity decreases under 7.5 g/l.

For example, in 2003 most of the samples from our 55 parcels maturity control network were already at risk on September 21st (Figure 4). In contrast, in 2007 only a few samples were at risk on the same date.

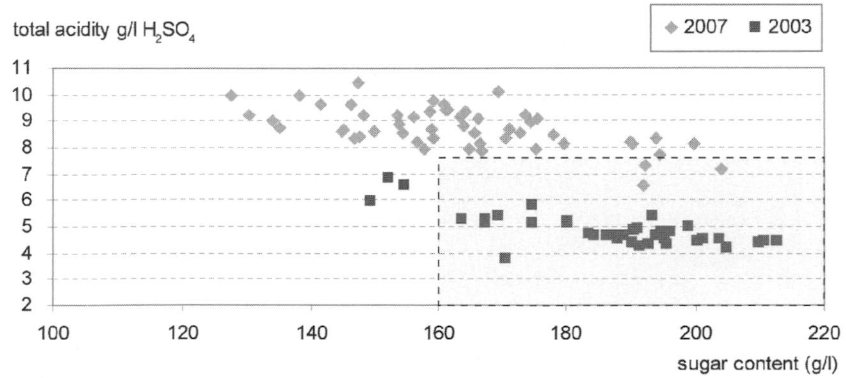

► grape must sample taken from 55 different parcels within the Cognac vineyard

Figure 4: Comparison of must composition for two vintages at the same date of grape sampling (21 st of September). "High risk" area in dotted line.

Optimising quality

Requirements

The relationship between wine spirits quality and volatile compounds, emanating from yeast metabolism has been studied and specific requirements for Cognac base wines have been defined (Cantagrel *et al.*, 2000). Those requirements (Table 1) were taken into account to select and qualify yeast strains.

Table 1: wine quality requirements for Cognac production

Wine volatile acidity:	as low as possible
Wine acidity:	at least the same as the must
Malolactic fermentation	check yeast effect on bacteria growth
Residual ethanal (acetic aldehyde) after fermentation:	low
Ethyl acetate production:	low
Higher alcohols production:	low
Aromatic profile of spirit:	no defects, fruity and flowery aroma

Optimisation

Several parameters that influence yeast metabolism and spirit quality are now known and have to be managed by winemakers (Ferrari, 2003). These include:

- fermentation temperature,
- grape must nitrogen content (Roulland, 2007),
- amount of solid matter suspended in must,
- yeast strain (Lurton, 1995).

The effect of these winemaking parameters on an industrial scale have been checked by comparing two technical itineraries (Galy, 2007): one usual, versus one with optimised parameters (see Figure 5). By choosing an appropriate selected yeast strain, temperature control, amount of solid matter and must nitrogen content, the optimised process lead to a more satisfactory balance of volatile compounds by reference to the requirements defined in Table 1 (less higher alcohols, more esters, low ethyl acetate level).

Inoculation with selected yeasts and the choice of a suitable yeast strain are very important tools for fermentation control. Nowadays, must

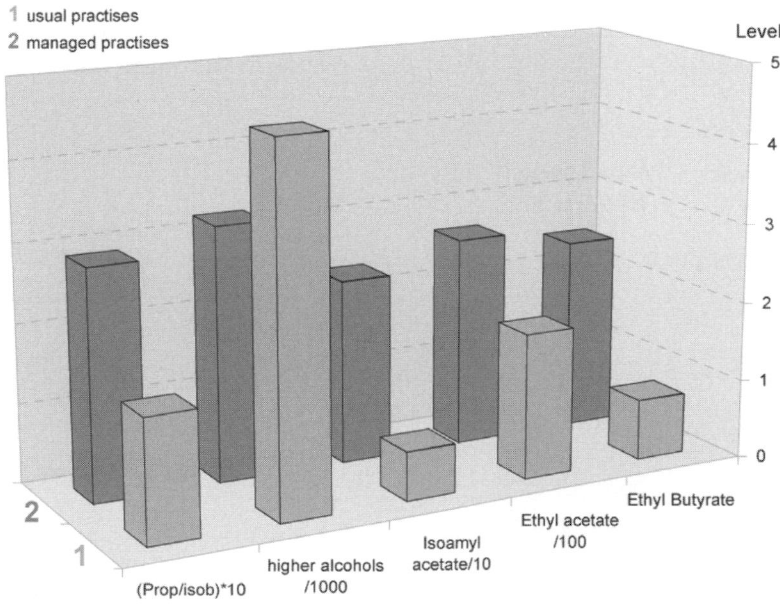

Figure 5: comparison of two different winemaking practices

inoculation is a widespread and well-managed practice for Cognac production.

Yeast qualification

In order to secure the use of selected yeast strains for Cognac production, a qualification process based on an assessment of physiological criteria, analytical requirements and sensory validation has been developed by BNIC. These criteria were evaluated at pilot and industrial scales. A survey of yeast strains behaviour in different wineries was also implemented during several years after their qualification (Roulland, 2007).

Currently, five yeast strains, two issued from a regional selection program (Roulland, 1995), have been recommended by BNIC for Cognac winemaking and are now mostly used by winemakers.

These five yeast strains all satisfy requirements defined in Table 1, but also differ slightly from one another as shown in Figure 6.

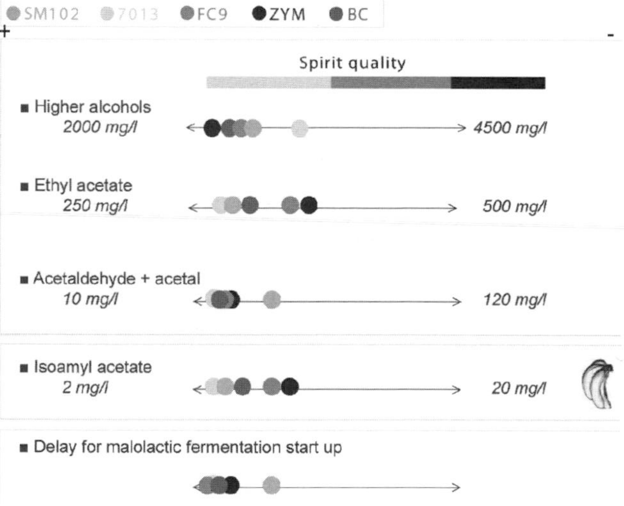

Figure 6: Recommended yeast strain classification

Conclusion

It is clear that must inoculation with active dry yeasts and selected strains has widely contributed to the improvement of freshly distilled Cognac spirits during the past twenty years. The main factors influencing fermentation progress and spirit quality have been identified and characterised.

Technical recommendations are disseminated to Cognac winemakers in order to allow them firstly to choose the best date for harvesting grapes and secondly to manage the alcoholic fermentation process.

References

Cantagrel R., Ferrari G., Galy B., Lablanquie O., Maignial L., Roulland C., Snakkers G. (2000). Maîtrise et innovation œnologiques, synthèse des connaissances sur les eaux-de-vie nouvelles. Rapport interne, Station Viticole du BNIC, Cognac France.

Ferrari G. (2003). Facteurs d'influence de la qualité des eaux-de-vie nouvelles, hiérarchisation et interactions. Journée Technique de la Station Viticole du BNIC- septembre 2003. Cognac, France.

Galy B. (2007). Maîtrise de qualité des eaux-de-vie nouvelles. Itinéraires techniques : pratiques actuelles et perspectives. Journée Technique de la Station Viticole du BNIC-6 septembre 2007. Cognac, France.

Lurton L., Snakkers G., Roulland C., Galy B., Versavaud A. (1995). Influence of the fermentation yeast strain on the composition of wine spirits. J. Inst. Food Agric., **67:** 485-491.

Roulland C. (2007). Impact de la souche de levure sur la composition des eaux-de-vie nouvelles. Journée Technique de la Station Viticole du BNIC-6 septembre 2007. Cognac, France.

Roulland C., Berty S., Galy B. (1994). *Essai de levurage mixte sur moût d'Ugni blanc : étude de l'association Saccharomyces cerevisiae – kloekera apiculata.* 9eme Colloque : gestion des populations microbiennes dans les industries agroalimentaires. Toulouse 9-10 Mars 1994.

Roulland C., Versavaud A., Galy B., Lurton L., Hallet J.N. (1995). Analyse de la biodiversité des populations levuriennes fermentaires et mise en œuvre d'une stratégie de sélection de souches pour l'élaboration du Cognac. 5eme Symposium International d'œnologie, juin 1995, Bordeaux, France.

Roulland C., Galy B., Dumot V., Lurton L. (2007). Besoins azotés des levures : cas des vinifications des vins de base Cognac. Poster, 8eme Symposium International d'œnologie, 25-27 juin 2007, Bordeaux, France.

Versavaud A., Poulard A., Roulland C., Lurton L., Lecoq M., Hallet J.N. (1992). *Etude de la microflore spontanée des vins de distillation de la région de Cognac.* 1er Symposium Scientifique International de Cognac : élaboration et connaissance des spiritueux, recherche de la qualité, tradition et innovation. 11-15 Mai 1992. BNIC ed. Cognac France.

Chapter 11

Tequila: a peculiar spirit from a peculiar source

Iván Saldaña Oyarzábal
Quality and R&D Department, Casa Pedro Domecq/Pernod Ricard México, Carr. Mexico-Puebla, Km 17.5 56400, Los Reyes La Paz, Edo. Mex., Mexico

Introduction

Tequila is one of the newest and fastest growing spirits available in the international market. While other products, such as vodka, whisk(e)y or brandy utilize raw materials available as global commodities and are being produced in many countries around the world, tequila has as a mandatory requirement the use of a specific sub-tropical lily popularly called "blue agave" or *Agave tequilana*. This plant grows only in a restricted region in Mexico and is regulated under an origin of denomination. While the main distinctiveness for other spirits are the specific production processes that transform raw materials into spirits, in tequila, its uniqueness comes from the raw material.

This paper will discuss the following: firstly, a broad introduction to commercial, historic and product definitions of tequila; secondly, an in-depth analysis of supply-demand constraints regarding raw material availability; and thirdly, the relevance of scientific research in agave to improve agriculture and utilization of this raw material. This paper provides a realistic perspective on the major challenges facing the tequila industry and the role that *Agave tequilana* research plays.

Tequila is a global spirit from very local Mexican plant

Tequila is the best known and recognized high strength alcoholic product from Mexico. For the last 200 years, Tequila has gained reputation to become the most emblematic and representative Mexican product. Its internationalization has accelerated immensely during the last 15 years, becoming the second fastest growing spirit in the global market (outwith Mexico), just after vodka. Tequila has shown an average yearly increment in volume of 8.1% over the last 5 years increasing sales from 14.1 million to 20.9 million cases between 2002 and 2007 (IWSR 08, Figure 1). Premium and ultra-premium categories are the newest and, by far, the fastest growing categories of tequila, showing 233.9% and 104.1% integrated volume increase in the 03-07 period, respectively.

Tequila is defined as: a distilled and rectified spirit obtained from the fermentation of carbohydrates obtained from *Agave tequilana* (Weber). The sugars are extracted from the false stem (also called *piña*) of this subtropical lily. The plant is also called "blue agave" due to the green-bluish coloration of their leaves. The cultivation

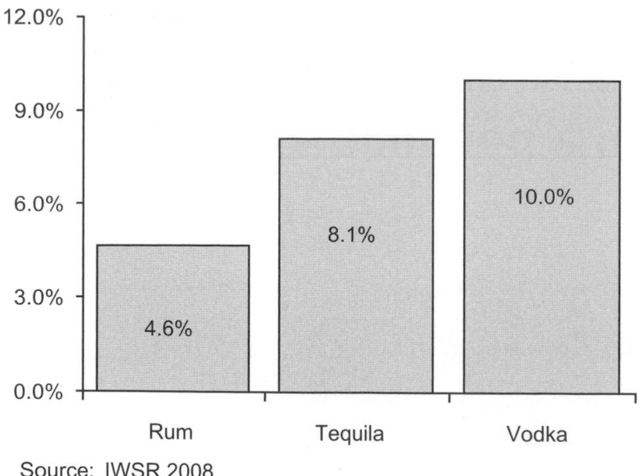

Figure 1. Integrated average annual volume growth during the period 2002-2007 of Vodka, Tequila and Rum. These three products present the highest volume growth with in the spirit market.

of blue agave is restricted to certain region of Mexico and is legally protected by an origin denomination act (see Figure 2). The DO region is very large (11,194,600 hectares) and includes 181 municipalities in 5 states (all of the state of Jalisco, plus parts of Guanajuato, Michoacán, Nayarit, and Tamaulipas) (Valenxuela).

Agave tequilana is an American native monocot plant adapted to grow in semi-arid conditions. This plant is particularly successful compared to other cultivated plants when water is limited. The long domestication of *Agave tequilana* has allowed the development of a highly productive variety that requires only seasonal rain irrigation in agriculture. Phylogenetically, it is a member of the *Agave* genus, belonging to the *Agavaceae* family, within the *Lilliaceae* order (Bogler and Simpson, 1995). The *Agave* genus natural origin is located in North America, being mostly distributed in Mexico and the southern United States, but being also present to a lesser extent in the Caribbean islands and in some other Central and South American countries. Certain Agave species (ex. *Agave americana*) can be found in the Mediterranean coast and some regions of Africa, as they were brought as ornamental flora becoming a successful exotic invader in those areas.

Although approximately 100 to 150 different species are believed to be part of this genus, the precise number is unclear, mainly due to the limited reliability of old methods of classification (García-Mendoza and Chiang, 2003), complex polyploidy variations caused by interbreeding (Palomino, Dolezel, Mendez and Rubluo, 2003), and insufficient availability of modern molecular tools for the establishment of their actual phylogeny. Historically, many species in this genus have being utilized by native North Americans for economic purposes, not only for its use in alcoholic products but for medicinal and utilitarian purposes (Gentry, 1982).

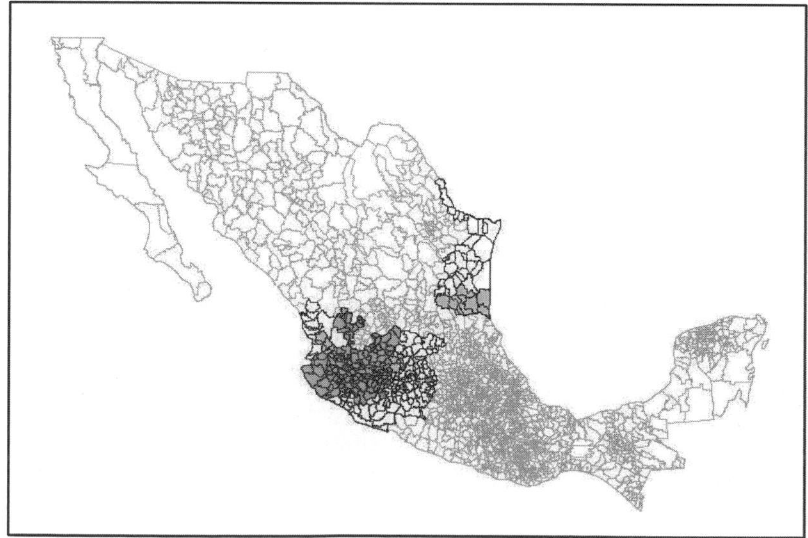

Figure 2. Areas with Origin Denomination for the establishment of ***Agave tequilana*** plantation and production sites. The OD is distributed along different districts within the states of Jalisco, Guanajuato, Michoacán and Tamaulipas (CRT 2008).

Tequila is only one of many different spirits that can be produced utilizing carbohydrates derived from other *Agave* plants. *Mezcal, Bacanora* and *Sotol*, are some examples that are produced utilizing other species different from *Agave tequilana* (ex. *Agave potatorum, Agave augustifolia*). These products have differentiated production processes and have a high organoleptic differentiation depending on the raw material utilized. These products so far, have not yet gained an important role in the Mexican or global spirit market.

All agave-derived spirits are the result of the Spanish heritage of distillation and aging technology combined with the Native American tradition of producing *pulque*, a generic name for low alcoholic content beer made from any Agave species. Due to its Spanish and pre-Hispanic heritage origin, tequila is culturally considered as a festive and unifying symbol of both traditions. Not surprisingly, tequila consumption has commonly appeared in popular Mexican films to remind nationalistic values and to materialize the national identity of modern Mexico.

Its cultural importance for Mexico and its enormous business potential were acknowledged formally in 1993, when tequila gained the status of a protected public brand that could only be conferred to products certifying certain attributes. The Tequila Regulation Council (Consejo Regulador del Tequila, CRT) was then formed, becoming responsible for enforcing producers to satisfy the rules, such as: the proper agricultural origin of the agave used, the location of the production site within de OD, and the adequate accomplishment of all quality standards in the production process and product. Today, quality standards in the raw materials, production process and final product are clearly defined, and all production plants are eligible to accreditation on a regular basis the conformity of their operations through regular audits of the CRT.

The maximum and minimum limits of the chemical composition of tequila are regulated by this authority (see Table 1), and evidence of the accomplishment of the standard is required for each product commercialised. Although official control on tequila product and process has served to gain consumer confidence and an excellent reputation worldwide in the last years, overregulation may limit the product innovation capacity of the industry and could stifle the establishment of new emerging companies in the future.

Table 1. Regulated limits for chemical compounds in tequila. Source of information: Secretaría de Economía 2006

Compound	*Limits*
Alcohol Content at 20°C (%Alc.Vol.)	35-55
Dry Extract (g/L)	0-5
Superior alcohols (g/100l A.A.)	20-500
Methanol (g/100l A.A.)	30-300
Aldehydes (g/100l A.A.)	0-40
Esters (g/100l A.A.)	2-200
Furfural (g/100l A.A.)	0-4

There is a clear classification system with defined criteria that serves to distinguish between different types of tequila in the market. Categories for tequila are properly established based on aging time and the proportion of fermentable sugars coming from the *Agave tequilana* (see Table 2). It is mandatory to label tequila products according to this classification.

Table 2. Classification of tequila by proportion of fermentable sugars and maturation in wood casks. Source of information: Secretaría de Economía 2006

By Proportion of Agave tequilana used	
Category	*Source of Sugars*
100% Agave	100% from the Agave
Tequila	At least 51% of the fermentable sugars comes from the Agave
By Aging	
Category	Maturation Time
Silver or "blanco"	No aging
Gold or "joven, abocado"	Flavored
Rested or "reposado"	2 Months to 1 year in wood
Aged	1 to 3 years aging
Extra aged	> 3 years aging

Supply-demand cycles in the tequila industry

The supply of several thousands of tons of agave each year is necessary to ensure tequila production. In 2007, approximately 500,000 tons were required for production (CRT 2008). For every liter of tequila at 100% agave between 5 to 7 Kg of agave stem is needed, depending on the efficiency of the process and the quality of the raw material. Agave plantations are restricted to an Origin of Denomination (OD) and cannot be obtained outside defined territories. The growth in sales must be accompanied by proper increments in availability of the raw material utilized. Unfortunately, while the market desire for more tequila has not stopped, since its popularity initiated 15 years ago, the stability of the supply of agave has not been effectively secured, restricting the growth.

In Figure 3, tequila production from 1997 to 2007 is analyzed. Tequila production doubled in just 4 years during 1997-2000, but this was followed by another same length period (2001-2004) of contraction. As a result, in 2004 the tequila industry was producing the same volume that it did in 1997, representing almost no integrated growth in 8 years. After 2004 and until today, new increments in volume have taken place, but this expansion is expected to end in 2008 followed with a similar decreasing trend as has occurred previously.

These eight-year cycles are not random in duration. In fact, these cycles are the result of differential availability of agave and have the same time interval that an agave plantation requires from sprout to harvest. Overproduction in the first years of cycle created an enormous surplus that was immediately followed by years of strong shortages, dramatically affecting prices. In 1998, at the middle of the production expansion stage, the price per Kg of agave was as low as US$0.05. Nevertheless, four years later the price in the market rocketed up to US$1.4 a kilo. This represents a 28 fold increase that is not seen in any other raw material utilized in the wine and spirits industry.

Agave production is partially owned by tequila producers, creating a big dependency in small farmers (Bowen and Valenzuela-Zapata, 2009). Also, the fact that agave production serves only for the tequila industry, price volatility is completely dependant on this factor, while other agricultural commodities such as grains, tend to maintain their prices due to a global and diverse demand. Farmers

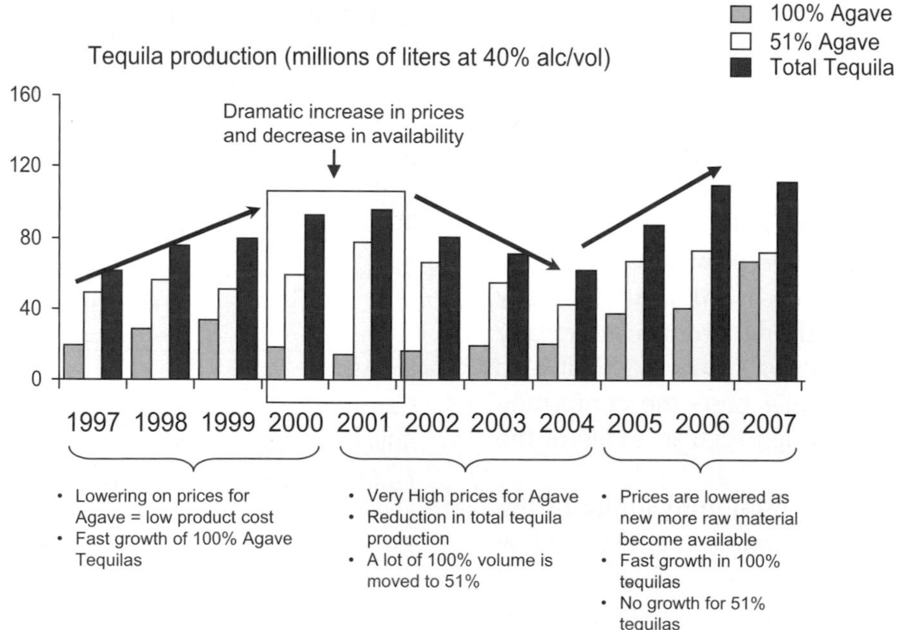

Figure 3. Trends in tequila production volumes from 1997 to 2007. Comments on factors influencing tequila production are provided. Source data: CRT 2008.

selling their agave during periods of shortage period have great gains, while during surplus conditions the price is so low that they cannot recover the investment, running out of cash to spend in establishing future plantations. The lack of new plantations has as a consequence reduced future availability of agave Global calculations estimate that between 1997 to 2000 the population of *Agave tequilana* in Jalisco decreased by 50.7% (Gonzalez, 2002). Additionally to this behavior, farmer's choice on which crop to cultivate depends on the prices they see in the market at the time of the decision. When prices are attractive they take agave as a choice, but otherwise, other alternatives such as corn are preferred. The industry suffers alike, with limited precision to establish cost of goods and strong difficulties to maintain quality and quantity of the commercialised products. A good indicator of the impact of prices in the production is the proportion of 100 and 51% category volumes manufactured (see Figure 3). At high agave costs, 51% agave tequila volumes tend to replace part of the 100% as it is too expensive to produce.

Distilleries have taken different difficult decisions to survive price and availability crises, such as removing brands permanently or temporally from the market, or downgrading 100% agave premium tequilas into the 51% tequila category, greatly damaging consumer perception in an irreversible way.

Long and medium term agricultural planning between farmers and producers has not been achieved due to lack of trust and the temptation for speculation on both parties. To guarantee a healthy future to this business, high investments over the long term in establishing plantations on a yearly basis are required. A good age balance of agave populations may be achieved, obtaining adequate harvest aligned with the demand.

Research as source for alternatives

Achieving a proper agricultural and financial supply chain for the future is not only a matter of economic and political accord but also requires a scientific approach to the limitations and opportunities that the agave offers as a crop. In the same way optimisation of production processes are crucial to ensure a successful future for the manufacture of tequila.

During the last cycle (1997-2004), biological and genetic characteristics of agave were demonstrated to play a significant role in the demand-supply problem. In 1998, approximately 22.3% of all plantations available were destroyed by epidemics of *Fusarium sp.* fungi and *Erwinia* bacteria (Rodríguez-Garay, Gutierrez-Mora, Flores-Berrios, Loera-Quezada, 2004). The speed of propagation was so high that it became unmanageable, even in industry owned plantations with no cash constraints. This loss exacerbated the supply crisis even further, enhancing the shortage from 1999 to 2003. In 2007 and 2008 prices were approximately $0.10 to $0.25 per Kg, which is considered favorable for the industry but not for farmers, so there is fear that similar epidemics will start to occur again, as the low prices reduce the farmer's ability to control agave pests adequately.

Companies have recognized the need for knowledge in order to increase gains and optimize costs. After the last crisis, research and development has increased significantly in universities, technical centers and industry. At the beginnings of 2000´s, important investments in research where made. Process optimization, cost reduction and quality improvements have being the main areas of development, taking the benefits of cross learning from affiliates of similar industries in the international scenario. Some big players such as Herradura, Allied Domecq and José Cuervo initiated more fundamental research in agave biology and its implications in agriculture, utilizing tax-reduction programs offered by the government (Casas, 2006). The most significant research program was established between Allied Domecq (today part of Pernod Ricard) and the National University of Mexico, with 13 research projects and more than 5 million dollars of investment. The program included studies never performed before, in genetics, carbohydrate chemistry, plant hormones, etc.

While some agave features may provide important agriculture advantages, others present constraints, see Tables 3a, 3b, 3c and 3d. Agave peculiarities in morphology, carbon metabolism, life span and reproduction make agave agriculture very different from any other crop utilized in the spirit industry. In fact, the agricultural model for agave is more similar to one followed by wood production than grains or fruits due to the long agricultural cycle.

Agave biology and biochemistry offer very interesting challenges and opportunities for research. In the following two sections I will share some of the work which is being performed and highlight the industrial interest.

Table 3a. Features and adaptations in Agave tequilana and their impacts on plants biology, agriculture, process and production of tequila

Category	*Biological feature*	*Role in the plant*	*Impact in agriculture, production or final product*	*Advantage /limitation*
Morphological adaptations to drought	High Leaf Succulence	Provides large water storage capacity to face prolonged drought periods	* Resistance to long periods of drought, irrigation is not mandatory	↑
	Thick cutan barrier	Keeps plants protected from bacteria and fungi	* Provides important concentrations of fatty acids that have an impact in the organoleptic characteristics of the product	↑
		Reduce water transpiration in leaves	* Increases water-use efficiency, excellent biomass productivities	↑
	Large storage stem or piña (up to 60Kg) with high concentration of sugars	Provides resources for clonally offspring and for inflorescence formation in sexual reproduction	* Harvest requires direct highly trained manpower (called jimadores) no machinery available	↓
			* Post-harvesting operations, such as transport and storage, require little infrastructure	↑

Table 3b. Features and adaptations in Agave tequilana and their impacts on plants biology, agriculture, process and production of tequila

Category	*Biological feature*	*Role in the plant*	*Impact in agriculture, production or final product*	*Advantage /limitation*
Carbohydrate metabolism	Crassulacean Acid Metabolism	Avoids gas exchange during day and allows CO_2 uptake by the leaves at night, minimizing photorespiration and water loss and maximizing carbohydrate production during water scarcity	* Increases water-use efficiency eliminating the need for irrigation and allowing excellent biomass productivities with limited rain	↑
	Fructan metabolism	Allows an efficient storage of soluble carbohydrates reserves that provides easy transportation and usability by the plant	* Carbohydrate extraction is facilitated due to the solubility of sugars, even if the extraction is performed when the agave is raw	↑

Table 3c. Features and adaptations in Agave tequilana and their impacts on plants biology, agriculture, process and production of tequila

Category	*Biological feature*	*Role in the plant*	*Impact in agriculture, production or final product*	*Advantage /limitation*
Life span	Long life span (6 to 11 years depending on natural conditions)	Allow enough accumulation of resources for reproduction and sustainability of individuals	* Very long agricultural cycles make much more complex the supply-demand forecast	↓
			* Very high productivities per hectare per year with a decent plantation	↑
			* Higher risk of plantation losses by natural conditions (epidemics, fire, etc.)	↓
			* Harvesting can be performed all year long and maturing plants may be utilized as needed	↑

Table 3d. Features and adaptations in Agave tequilana and their impacts on plants biology, agriculture, process and production of tequila

Category	*Biological feature*	*Role in the plant*	*Impact in agriculture, production or final product*	*Advantage /limitation*
Reproduction and genetic variability	Asexual reproduction by development of rhizomes from adult plants	Development of new individual allow the colonization and growth of populations	* Asexual reproduction limits genetic variability creating an strong susceptibility to epidemics	↓
			* Easy establishment of successful plantations as small fully developed plants are used instead of seeds	↑
			* New offspring requires the expenditure of adult plant resources what reduces productivity in commercial plantations	↓
	Sexual reproduction by a single flowering event in the whole life span	Allow genetic cross fertilization between genomic pools in other populations or colonies	* Crop improvement programs by artificial fertilization are almost impossible due to the duration of life cycles	↓
			* Sexual reproduction must be restricted in agriculture as it depletes sugar reserves that are used for tequila production	↓

Reproduction, genetic diversity and epidemics

The understanding of the low genetic diversity is of great importance for the industry for two reasons: 1) the high susceptibility to epidemics and 2) the generation of potential genetic improvement programs.

Agave reproduction can occur either sexually or asexually. In asexual reproduction, the establishment of clonal off-shoots or *ramets* is derived from the rhizomes of the mother plant.

This kind of reproduction is highly successful. It provides the major strategy for agriculture to establish plantations. Nevertheless, it has limitations also. For instance, new seedlings are expected to be genetically homogeneous to the mother, which implies low genetic variability that increases susceptibility to natural forces such as epidemics. Agaves can propagate sexually too, but because the flowering act involves the total consumption of the stem carbohydrates, this activity can not be allowed to happen in the productive fields (Arizaga and Ezcurra, 1995; McLaughlin, Williams, Anouti, Ravetta, and Nelson, 2000). Also, the long life span of this plant makes it very difficult to create a traditional crop improvement program based on cross fertilization of selected specimens.

The genetic diversity in *Agave tequilana* has been recently investigated by molecular fingerprinting with a method called RAPD (randomly amplified polymorphic DNA) and it was shown to be extremely low (Gil-Vega, Chavira, Martínez, Simpson and Vandemark, 2001). This has been explained as a result of the use of this asexually propagated material by the tequila farmers. Other new molecular techniques such as AFLP (Gil-Vega, Diaz, Nava-Cedillo and Simpson, 2006), and SSAP markers (sequence-specific amplification polymorphism, Bousios, Saldana-Oyarzabal, Valenzuela-Zapata, Wood and Pearce, 2007) have been developed recently to help understand the genetic variability within *Agave tequilana* varieties.

Dr. Steve Pearce's research group, in the Plant Stress Unit at the University of Sussex, has provided new tools to evaluate genetic variability in this plant, and other species in the genus. Thanks to the isolation and sequencing of specific markers it is now possible to establish the genetic distance and phylogeny between different varieties of *Agave tequilana* varieties. The isolated sequences correspond to the RNAase H gene within the *Ty-copia* familiy retrotransposons, commonly present in plants and animals. These markers are utilized to characterize the genome. From the 19 sequences isolated, 3 were capable of successfully distinguishing different varieties of *Agave tequila* plants, while AFLP – a non-specific technique – was not. These findings are helping to understand the boundaries that define the species and the variety allowed for tequila production, and indicating that other varieties different from the "azul", may be acceptable for production. Agronomists such as Ana Valenzuela, in the Universtiy of Guadalajara, are promoting that other closelye related varieties of *Agave tequilana* (Weber) var. azul should be introduced to industrial plantations, as a way to reduce the speed of disease propagation.

Another very important finding by Pearce´s group was evidence that asexually propagated plants could increase variability by internal activation of ancient retrovirus sequences present in their genome, known as retrotransposons, which could create differentiation in the DNA by multiple insertion in a relatively short period of time (Bousious *et a,* 2007). The activation of this mechanism is still being studied by this group, but preliminary data suggests that it may be triggered by plant hormones and stress. This study is of great relevance for companies that have *in-vitro* propagation programs, as hormones are used to maintain the propagation material and its genetic properties could be affected in the medium and long term, reducing the benefit expected in the fields. Still much more work is required in the area to understand this phenomenon.

Agave carbohydrates, carbon metabolism and drought stress tolerance

Carbohydrate synthesis requires CO_2 uptake which is a highly water-expensive activity in plants. During water scarcity, plants protect themselves closing stomata and reducing or stopping photosynthesis and carbon input, reducing productivity in the field. In this sense, drought tolerance is one of the most advantageous features in agave, as it can exhibit very good productivities when water is scare.

Thanks to morphological adaptations such as succulence, water storage capability and cutan isolation barrier (see Table 4) coupled with other biochemical adaptation in its metabolism, this plant can successfully grow without irrigation in semi-arid environments, and can tolerate periods of no precipitation. In fact, *Agave tequilana* exhibits one of the best water-use efficiencies (WUE, CO_2 fixated to water lost) within industrially grown plants. It's integrated daily average WUE measured expressed as the amount of CO_2 gained per H_2O lost was calculated under greenhouse conditions being 13.2 mmol CO_2/mol H_2O (Saldana-Oyarzabal, 2006). This water use efficiency is about 9 to 26 times higher than C_3, such as grape or sugar beet and 13 to 7 times higher than C_4 plants, such as grains and sugar cane.

Agaves have two central adaptations related to their carbon metabolism that provides special advantage to drought stress. First, they utilize nocturnal fixation as a clever feature that allows a considerable reduction in water losses, by avoiding water vapor escape during the hot hours of the day. This biochemical adaptation is called Crassulacean Acid Metabolism (CAM), as nocturnal CO_2 uptake is transformed into malate, and accumulated in the large cell vacuoles of the leaves. Secondly, agaves synthesize and accumulate fructans, soluble polymeric branched carbohydrates based on units of fructose. Fructans can provide physiological advantages such as a fast metabolic mobilization of reserves and the stabilization of cells membrane when abiotic stresses such as drought, heat and cold are present (Ritsema and Smekeens 2003).

Carbohydrate metabolism studies involve many processes such as the CO_2 uptake mechanism into the plant, the synthesis of simple sugars, and the transport and accumulation of these sugars into more complex carbohydrates. The area is very broad indeed, however, of great relevance for the industry as sugar is the desired material for fermentation. The interplay between CAM and fructan metabolism was investigated. The enzymology responsible for synthesis and degradation was characterized and relationships with accumulation of sugar studied (Saldana, 2006). Results showed that environmental factors can strongly affect the synthesis and degradation trends in this plant. Investigation of fructan accumulation related to agricultural conditions is vital to calculate potential impact on plantations at the level of harvest.

At the distillery, the understanding of chemical structure of agave fructan, may play an important role as hydrolyzing enzymes (as fructanases) can have industrial application in tequila, reducing energy in hydrolysis (Waleckx, Gschaedler, Colonna-Ceccaldi and Monsan 2008).

Agave fructans can also be used for the production of sweeteners with a low glycemic index, they can also be used as a prebiotic or "functional" ingredient in food or as a texturizer. Fructans have attracted the attention of health scientists in recent years due to the positive effects observed during consumption (see Roberfroid, 2002 for a review). When fructans are used as a dietary fibre they can facilitate evacuation, drive a reduction in colon cancer risk, enhance calcium assimilation and promote a better immune response. Chicory (*Cichorium intybus*) and Jerusalem artichoke are the main sources of fructan for the food industry and specific varieties have been developed for fructan production (Schittenhelm 1999) but Agave could also be a great candidate too.

Conclusion

The tequila industry needs to continue research on raw materials and processes to establish a robust knowledge capability to cope with future challenges. The supply difficulties will require better agreements between farmers and tequila industries, but also improvements in agricultural management and pest control. Multinational companies have great opportunities for performing transversal innovation information from other product processes in whisky, brandy or rum. Grey literature (unpublished information) is still the most abundant, and most advanced resource of information, yet inaccessible. Mexican research centers need to break traditional ways they innovate, getting more involved in the business and offer real applications to improve genetic diversity of agave plants and tequila productivity. The industry needs to come together to face raw material and process difficulties, not to compete against each other on a technical level. The creation of high fructose sugars and prebiotic base on *Agave tequilana* may provide opportunities to stabilize the prices and extend plantations.

Bibliography

Arizaga S, Ezcurra E (1995) Insurance against reproductive failure in a semelparous plant - bulbil formation in Agave macroacantha flowering stalks. *Oecologia* 101: 329-334

Bogler, D.J. and Simpson, B.B. 1995. A chloroplast DNA study of the Agavaceae. *Systematic Botany* 20: 191-205

Bousios, A., Saldana-Oyarzabal, I., Valenzuela-Zapata, A.G., Wood C. and Pearce, R.P. 2007. Isolation and characterization of Ty1-copia retrotransposon sequences in the blue agave (*Agave tequilana* Weber var. azul) and their development as SSAP markers for phylogenetic analysis. *Plant Science* 172: 291-298

Bowen, S. and Valenzuela-Zapata, A. 2009. Geographical indications, terroir, and socioeconomic and ecological sustainability: The case of tequila. *Journal of Rural Studies*, 25: 108-119

Casas, R. 2006. Between traditions and modernity: Technological strategies at three tequila firms. *Technology in Society*. 28:407-419

Consejo Regulador del Tequila (CRT). 2008. Producción total de tequila. Available from: http://www.crt.org.mx (verified August 7, 2008)

Garcia-Mendoza, A. and Chiang, F. 2003. The confusion of Agave vivipara L. and A. angustifolia Haw., two distinct taxa. *Brittonia* 55: 82-87

Gentry, H.S. 1982. *Agaves from Continental North America*. The University of Arizona Press, Tucson, 670p

Gil-Vega, F., Chavira, M., Martínez, G.O., Simpson, J., Vandemark, G. 2001. Analysis of genetic diversity in *Agave tequilana* var. *azul* using RAPD markers. *Euphytica* 119:335-341

Gil-Vega, F., Diaz, Nava-Cedillo and Simpson J.. 2006. AFLP analysis of *Agave tequilana* varieties. *Plant Science* **170:**904–909

González, M.A. 2002. Blue agave producers in the tequila agro-industry in Jalisco, Mexico: the beginning of production alliances in the context of the end of land reform. Doctoral thesis, University of Oxford, Oxford, UK

International Wine and Spirit Record 2008. Report on growth by category. London, UK

McLaughlin, S.P., Williams, R.R., Anouti, A.R., Ravetta, D.A. and Nelson, J.M. 2000. Allocation of resources to flowering and fruit production in *Hesperaloe funifera* (Agavaceae). *Journal Of Arid Environments* 45: 99-110

Palomino, G., Dolezel, J., Mendez, I. and Rubluo, A. 2003. Nuclear genome size analysis of *Agave tequilana* Weber. *Caryologia* 56: 37-46

Schittenhelm, S. 1999. Agronomic performance of root chicory, Jerusalem artichoke, and sugarbeet in stress and nonstress environments. *Crop Science* 39: 1815-1823

Ritsema, T. and Smeekens, S. 2003. Fructans: beneficial for plants and humans. *Current Opinion In Plant Biology* 6: 223-230

Roberfroid, M.B. 2002. Functional foods: concepts and application to inulin and oligofructose. *British Journal Of Nutrition* 87: S139-S143

Rodríguez-Garay, B., Gutierrez-Mora, A., Flores-Berrios, E.P,, Loera-Quezada, M.M. 2004. In: *Ciencia y Tecnología del Tequila: avance y perspectivas*. Ciatej, Guadalajara, Mexico, pp. 15-38

Saldaña-Oyarzábal, I. 2006. Carbohydrate metabolism in the leaves of the *Agave tequilana* (Weber) plant. Doctoral thesis, University of Sussex, East Sussex, UK

Secretaría de Economía. 2006. Norma Oficial Mexicana NOM-006-SCFI-2005, Bebidas Alcohólicas-Tequila-Especificaciones. *Diario Oficial de la Federación 6 de Enero de 2006*

Waleckx, E., Gschaedler, A., Colonna-Ceccaldi, B., Monsan, P. 2008. Hydrolysis of fructans from Agave tequilana Weber var. azul during the cooking step in a traditional tequila elaboration process. Food Chemistry, 108:40-48

Chapter 12

The microbiology and biotechnology of rum production

Graham H. Fleet and Victoria Green
Food Science Group, School of Chemical Sciences and Engineering, University of New South Wales, Sydney, New South Wales, Australia, 2052

Introduction

Rum is a distilled alcoholic beverage derived from fermented sugar cane products, principally, molasses ,sugar cane syrup or sugar cane juice. Historically, sugar cane (*Saccharum officinarum*) is thought to have originated from New Guinea some 10,000 years ago. There are reports on the consumption of a spirit style of beverage derived from sugar, in India around 2000BC. Considered as a spice, sugar eventually found its way to Europe, where the Spanish and Portuguese established sugar cane plantations in the 1400s. Christopher Columbus took plantings to the Caribbean islands and the South Americas in 1493 and, during the 1500s, sugar cane plantations flourished in these regions. Rum production from sugar cane materials soon followed, and was well established in the Caribbean region during the 1600s. Countries such as Jamaica, Barbados, Trinidad, Martinique, Haiti, Guadeloupe, Guyana, Puerto Rico and Cuba became well known for their rum distilleries. The evolution of the rum industry in this region has a colourful history that is intimately linked to trade rivalry and conflict between the then colonial powers, piracy, the development of the slave trade between Africa, Europe and the Americas, and onset of the American War of Independence (Nicol, 2003; Broom, 2003). The Caribbean countries remain the center of the modern rum industry, but rum is also produced in other countries such as Brazil, USA, Australia, and parts of Asia and Africa-wherever sugar cane is cultivated.

Microbial fermentation is a key biotechnological process in the production of all alcoholic beverages, including rum. The microorganisms that grow throughout this process have a major influence on the flavour and quality of the final product, and the efficiency of the overall process. For most alcoholic beverages such as beer, wine, cider and whisky, there is sound scientific understanding of the microbial species that conduct the fermentation and how they impact on product quality (Rose, 1977; Lea and Piggott, 2003). However, this is not the case for rum production. While some basic microbiological studies on the process were done in the early 1900s, there have been few advances since that time. This article gives an overview of current knowledge on the microbiology of rum production, indicating the gaps in understanding and directions for further research.

The process of rum production

The basic process for rum production consists of the following operations: preparation of the raw material (molasses, sugar syrup or sugar cane juice); fermentation of this material; distillation of the fermented product; collection of the distillate; maturation of the distillate in wooden barrels; packaging of the final product. Detailed descriptions of the process can be found in Lehtonen and Suomalainen (1977) and Nicol (2003)and more general overviews are given in I'Anson (1971) and Kampen (1975).

Raw materials

Molasses is the main raw material used for rum production because of its lower cost and because it can be stored in bulk, without further processing, for long periods prior to use in fermentation. In this way, the seasonal impact of sugar production on rum production is avoided. Molasses is a by-product that remains after refining sugar from cane juice and is a black, viscous liquid containing about 55%w/v total fermentable sugars, of which about 35% is sucrose and 20% is a mixture of glucose and fructose. In addition to water and these sugars, it contains small amounts of many other nitrogenous, phosphorus, metal- ion, vitamin, gum and colloidal constituents that provide essential nutrients for yeast growth during fermentation. Trace amounts of volatile alcohols, acids, esters, aldehydes, ketones, phenolics, and nitrogen compounds are also present, and may be distilled over to influence rum flavour . Many factors affect the composition and quality of molasses and these include the cultivar and cultivation of sugar cane, the sugar refining process and conditions of molasses storage (Murtagh, 1995 a,b; Bortolussi and O'Neil , 2006). Just prior to use in fermentation, molasses is clarified by chemical or physical processes, adjusted to pH values around 5.0-5.5, given a mild heat pasteurization treatment, and then diluted with water to give a final concentration of 100-150g/liter for fermentable sugars. Yeast nutrients such as ammonium sulphate and vitamin mixtures may be added to ensure complete fermentation.

In some distilleries, sugar syrup is used as the starting material. The syrup is prepared by heat evaporation of sugar cane juice after it has been partially inverted to avoid crystallization of the sucrose. It has a final sugar content of about 80%w/v and is diluted with water to 100-150 g/litre of sugar before fermentation. Some distilleries use freshly extracted sugar cane juice which has a sugar content of about 10-15%w/v. This is widely used in Brazil where the fermented, distilled product is specifically known as " cachaca" (Faria *et al.*,2003).

The literature reports widespread use of dunder in rum production. Dunder is the liquid residue obtained from the distillation vessels after distillation of the fermented product (Kampen, 1975). It is enriched in heat inactivated microbial cells, principally yeasts, and the contents extracted from them. It is acidic and rich in nutrients and, used directly, it should be sterile. It is mixed with molasses or syrup at proportions of 20-50%v/v to decrease the requirements for dilution water, to assist with acidification of the molasses or syrup, and to provide nutrients to encourage microbial growth during fermentation. If it is not used directly, and stored, it becomes contaminated with microorganisms that can impact on the fermentation. In some cases, deliberate storage and ageing of dunder has been conducted to encourage the development of a wild microbial flora. Such dunder gives a rum with a heavier flavor (I'Anson, 1971).

Fermentation

After preparation, the molasses, syrup or juice is transferred to large tanks, nowdays made of stainless steel, for fermentation. Until the early 1900s, fermentation was a spontaneous process that developed from the growth of microbial contaminants (indigenous microflora) present in the molasses, syrup or juice, and also coming from processing equipment (I'Anson, 1971; Fahrasmane and Ganou-Parfait, 1998). To encourage a faster onset of fermentation, a proportion of fermented product from a previous fermentation (back slops) was often added to the tanks. Yeasts ultimately dominated these fermentations, primarily transforming the sugars into ethanol and carbon dioxide. During the last 50- 75 years, various distilleries have isolated and identified the main yeast strains responsible for the fermentation, and have developed procedures for maintaining and propagating these strains in pure culture, and then inoculating them into the ferment . Some of these isolates have been commercialized by yeast companies, and it is now possible to purchase active dry cultures of yeasts for direct inoculation into the ferment (Fahrasmane and Ganou-Parfait, 1998). Fermentations are generally conducted at temperatures of 30-35°C and are completed within 30-48 hrs. The fermented product is transferred to a holding tank where a good proportion of the yeast and other microbial cells sediment out, after which the product is sent for distillation. Some distilleries may remove the microbial cells from the ferment by centrifugation, before distillation.

Distillation, maturation, packaging

Distillation serves to evaporate and condense the alcohol and other volatile products that become the rum distillate. It is a specialized process that is conducted using continuous distillation columns and pot stills, and has a key impact on the composition and concentration of flavour volatiles that comprise the final rum distillate. The science and technology of this process and its application to rum production are described in I'Anson (1971) and Kampen (1975), Lehtonen and Suomalainen (1977) and Nicol (2003). The distillate is stored in wooden (oak) barrels for several years where further chemical changes occur to moderate product flavor. Finally, the distillates are blended, and packaged for sale.

The microbiology of rum production

Studies on the microbiology of rum production date back to the 1890s. Despite over 100 years of research, microbiological understanding of the process is very limited and is significantly lagging compared with many other alcoholic beverages.

The key requirements of microbiological information are:

- What microbial species occur throughout the process chain?
- What are the growth kinetics of individual microbial species throughout production?
- What factors affect the growth of these species?
- What chemical and biochemical changes do these species cause to the fermentation substrate?
- How do these changes impact on the sensory properties of rum and its appeal to consumers?

There are two main points in the production chain where microorganisms impact on rum quality; the raw materials (molasses, sugar syrup and juice); and the process of fermentation. Fermentation is the main stage where microorganisms determine rum flavour and quality. The microbiological status of dunder will also be significant, depending on how it is used.

Molasses, sugar syrup, juice

Molasses and syrups may be stored in bulk quantities on site at the distilleries for many months before use in rum fermentation. During this time, microbial contaminants have the potential to grow and produce metabolic end-products that could impact on rum quality. Despite this possibility, we have not been able to find any systematic investigation of the microbiology of molasses or syrups during storage. Because of the heat processes involved, freshly produced molasses or syrup contain few microorganisms (Owen, 1911, Browne, 1929). The high concentrations of sugars (about 60% w/v), low water activity (approx. 0.76), and relatively low pH (5.0-5.5), make these raw materials unfavourable environments for the growth and survival of microorganisms. Nevertheless, the literature contains sporadic reports of the isolation of yeasts and bacteria from these materials. The main yeasts found tend to be osmotolerant species of *Zygosaccharomyces*. *Schizosaccharomyces*, *Torulospora* and *Saccharomyces* (Hall *et al*., 1935; Owen, 1949; Tilbury, 1980; Tokuoka,1993; Bonilla- Salinas *et al*., 1995; Fahrasmane and Ganou-Parfait, 1998). Information on the presence of bacteria in molasses and syrups is scant and inconsistent. Bacterial populations are generally low (10^2-10^3 cfu/ml) and reflect a diversity of species within *Bacillus, Clostridium, Zymomonas, Lactobacillus* and *Propionibacterium* (Hall et *al*., 1935; Murtagh, 1995a,b; Fahrasmane and Ganou-Parfait, 1998; Todorov and Dicks, 2005). In our observations, *Bacillus* species (e.g. *B. subtilis*) are most prevalent. Because molasses and syrups present most stressful, inhospitable and unique environments for the survival and growth of microorganisms, it is very likely that they will harbor a diversity of species in a stressed physiological state that will escape detection by cultural methods normally used for microbiological analyses. Novel culture methods as well as specialized, culture- independent molecular methods may be required for their analysis and detection (Ercolini, 2004; Giraffa, 2004). The impact of such microbial populations on the quality of the molasses or syrups used in rum production requires investigation.

Freshly extracted sugar cane juice contains significant populations (10^4-10^6 cfu/ml) of yeasts and bacteria, depending on the quality of the cane and hygiene of the crushing process (Fahrasmane and Ganou-Parfait, 1998). The yeasts represent a mixture of *Candida, Hanseniaspora, Pichia, Kluyveromyces, Saccharomyces* and *Schizosaccharomyces* species (Shehata, 1960; Morais et *al*., 1997; Pataro et *al*., 2000; Schwan et *al*., 2001; Gomes et *al*., 2002), and the bacteria are represented by a diversity of lactic acid bacteria , acetic acid bacteria and *Bacillus* species (Fahrasmane and Ganou-Parfait, 1998; Schwan *et al*., 2001). The juice is microbiologically unstable and will start to ferment within several hours. Consequently, it cannot be stored and must be used immediately.

Fermentation

Fermentation is a microbiological process and, as mentioned already, is a key operation in rum production. The microbial species that conduct the fermentation determine process efficiency, ethanol yield, and rum flavor and quality. Essentially, sugars within the molasses, syrup or juice are metabolized into primarily ethanol and carbon dioxide, and a vast array of secondary end-products (e.g. higher alcohols, organic acids, esters, aldehydes, ketones, nitrogen volatiles, sulphur volatiles, phenolic volatiles) that have flavour impact. The relative amounts of these secondary products determine final rum flavour and vary according to the conditions of fermentation and the species and strains of yeasts and bacteria that grow during fermentation (Lehtonen and Suomalainen, 1977; Watson, 1993; Berry and Slaughter, 2003).

Yeasts

Early microbiological studies on rum produced by spontaneous fermentation of molasses revealed that two yeast species predominated during the process. These were identified as strains of *Schizosaccharomyces pombe* and *Saccharomyces cerevisiae*. Fermentations with *Schiz. pombe* generally gave rums with stronger aromas, but were much slower and required 3-4 days or more for completion. In contrast, fermentations with *S.cerevisiae* were faster, being completed within 36-48 hours, and gave a lighter style of rum. *Schizosaccharomyces pombe* was more likely to occur in fermentations with higher initial sugar concentration and where a good proportion of slops or dunder was added to the molasses or syrup, thereby decreasing its pH to below 5.0 (Ashby, 1907; Pech *et al.*,1984; Fahrasmane, Ganou-Parfait and Parfait, 1988; Watson, 1993; Fahrasmane and Ganou-Parfait, 1998). Very little research has been done to understand the kinetics of growth of these yeasts during molasses or syrup fermentation and to understand how they impact on rum flavor. Fermentation with *Schiz. pombe* generally give rums with lesser amounts of higher alcohols and short chain fatty acids, but greater quantities of esters, compared with those conducted with *S.cerevisiae* (Fahrasmane et *al.*, 1985). Modern rum production is largely focused on the use of strains of *S.cerevisiae* that have been isolated from particular distilleries, and then propagated in- house for inoculation into the molasses as starter cultures. Various yeast companies sell distiller's strains of *S.cerevisiae* that may be used, thereby avoiding the demands of in-house propagation (Watson, 1993). With regard to non-*Saccharomyces* yeasts, some species of *Zygosaccharomyces* and *Dekkera*, in addition to *Schiz. pombe* have the potential to grow in molasses and sugar syrups, and may represent novel yeasts for exploitation in rum production.

In contrast to molasses or syrup fermentations, significant research has been done on the growth of yeasts during sugar cane juice fermentation for *cachaca* production. The early stages of fermentation are characterized by the growth of various species of *Hanseniaspora, Kloeckera, Pichia, Kluyveromyces* and *Candida*, but they are soon overgrown by strains of *S.cerevisiae* which eventually dominate and complete the fermentation. In some cases, strains of *Schiz. pombe* were observed to dominate these fermentations (Morais et *al.*,1997; Pataro et *al.*, 2000; Schwan et *al.*,2001). With this knowledge, a program of yeast strain selection and evaluation is being conducted to develop starter cultures that give optimized fermentation and a cachaca product with defined quality (Dato, Junior and Mutton, 2004; Oliviera et *al.*, 2004; Vicente et *al.*, 2006)

Bacteria

Early literature (Allan, 1906: Ashby, 1907; Hall *et al.*, 1935) as well as more recent literature (Ganou-Parfait, Fahrasmane and Parfait , 1987; Fahrasmane and Ganou-Parfait, 1998) report the contribution of bacteria to rum fermentations. However, there appears to be no detailed studies of their growth during fermentation, how they interact with the growth of yeasts and how they impact on rum quality. Species of *Clostridium, Bacillus, Zymomonas*, lactic acid bacteria and propionic acid bacteria have been reported to be involved. It is expected that the extent of their growth will be moderated by their tolerance of ethanol produced by the yeasts, the acidity of the medium, and their requirement for nutrients. Possibly, their contribution will be greater in slower developing ferments, such as those conducted by *Schiz. pombe*, where the production of ethanol is slower, and in those where the medium is enriched in micronutrients by the addition of dunder. Fermentations conducted at higher pH values (e.g. greater than 5.5) are, also, more likely to have a stronger contribution from bacteria. If they grow to significant populations in the early stages of the fermentation, they are likely to produce acids and other metabolites that could inhibit or retard the growth of yeasts. Also, they would utilize sugars, so that less would be available for conversion to ethanol by the yeasts. Consequently, by these mechanisms they could decrease the efficiency of the fermentation process (Kampen, 1975; Lehtonen and Suomalainen, 1977). Their growth will be accompanied by the production of metabolites that impact on rum flavor, and this could be detrimental or beneficial, depending on the species which grow (Fahrasmane and Ganou-Parfait, 1998). According to Hall *et al.* (1935) the growth of *Clostridium saccharolyticum* was necessary for the development of characteristic rum flavor, possibly through its production of butyric acid. The microaerophilic conditions of molasses fermentation are conducive to the growth of species of *Lactobacillus* and *Propionibacterim*, the latter contributing desirable propionic acid flavor to rum (Fahrasmane and Ganou-Parfait, 1998). *Lactobacillus* species have recently been found to be significant in the alcoholic fermentation of malted barley mash for whisky production (van Beek and Priest, 2003; Priest, 2004), so it is not unexpected that they may grow in conjunction with yeasts during rum fermentations and have subtle influences on rum flavour.

Dunder

As mentioned already, dunder is often used in rum production and this can have important microbiological significance that seems to have escaped scientific study. Although it should be microbiologically sterile immediately after coming from distillation vessels, it may be stored to encourage contamination and microbial (bacterial) growth that impacts on rum fermentation and product flavor(Kampen, 1975). In this context, the microbial ecology of dunder requires detailed study. Its chemical composition can impact on microbial growth during rum fermentation, through acidification of the fermentation medium and enrichment of the medium in micro-nutrients. However, details of its chemical composition are not evident from the literature, and remain another important direction for research.

Conclusions

Microorganisms produce the ethanol and other flavour volatiles that are essential to the character and quality of rum. The key reaction is the alcoholic fermentation of molasses, sugar syrup or sugar cane juice by yeasts. Although strains of *S.cerevisiae* dominate this fermentation, other yeasts such as *Schiz. pombe* can be significant and contribute different flavours to the final product. More research is needed to understand and exploit the impact of different yeast species and strains on the individuality of rum flavour. Depending on the distillery and the subtleties of the process, such as the use of dunder, bacteria may contribute to the fermentation, in association with yeasts. Further research is required to understand the occurrence and growth of bacterial species associated with these fermentations, how they influence rum quality and process efficiency, and the significance of dunder in contributing to their role. Microorganisms also determine the quality of the raw materials (molasses, sugar syrup and cane juice) used for rum fermentation, and specific investigations are needed to better define this influence.

References

Allan, C. (1906). The manufacture of Jamaica rum. *West Indian Bulletin* **7 :** 141-142.

Ashby, S.F. (1907). The study of fermentations in the manufacture of Jamaica rum. *International Sugar Journal* **11 :** 243-251.

Berry, D.R. and Slaughter, J.C. (2003). Alcoholic beverage fermentations. In: *Fermented Beverage Production*, second edition, Edited by Lea, A.G.H. and Piggott, J.R., Kluwer Academic/ Plenum Publishers, New York, pp. 25-40.

Bonilla-Salinas, M., Lappe, P., Ulloa, M., Garcia-Garibay, M. and Gomez-Ruiz, L. (1995). Isolation and identification of killer yeasts from sugar cane molasses. *Letters in Applied Microbiology* **21:**115-116.

Bortolussi,G. and O"Neill, C.J.O. (2006). Variation in molasses composition from eastern Australian sugar mills. *Australian Journal of Experimental Agriculture* **46:** 1455-1463.

Broom, D. (2003). Rum. Octopus Publishing Group, London

Browne, C.A. (1929). The spontaneous decomposition of molasses. *Industrial Engineering and Chemistry* **21:** 600-606.

Dato, M.C.F., Junior, J.M.P. and Mutton, M.J.R. (2005). Analysis of the secondary compounds produced by *Saccharomyces cerevisiae* and wild yeast strains during the production of " cachaca". *Brazilian Journal of Microbiology* **36:** 70-74.

Ercolini, D. (2004). PCR-DGGE fingerprinting: novel strategies for detection of microbes in food. *Journal of Microbiological Methods* **56:** 297-314.

Fahrasmane, L. and Ganou-Parfait, B. (1998). Microbial flora of rum fermentation media. *Journal of Applied Microbiology* **84:** 921-928.

Fahrasmane,L., Ganou-Parfait, B. and Parfait, A. (1988). Yeast flora of Haitian rum distilleries. *MIRCEN Journal* **4:** 239-241.

Fahrasmane,L., Parfait, A., Jouret, C. and Galzy, P. (1985). Production of higher alcohols and short chain fatty acids by different yeasts used in rum fermentation. *Journal of Food Science* **50:**1427-1430.

Faria,J.B., Loyola, E., Lopez, M.G. and Dufour, J.P. (2003). Cachaca, pisco and tequila. In: *Fermented Beverage Production*, second edition, Edited by Lea, A.G.H.and Piggott, J.R., Kluwer Academic, New York, pp.355-363.

Ganou-Parfait,B., Fahrasmane,L. and Parfait, A. (1987). *Bacillus* spp in sugar cane fermentation media. *Belgian Journal of Food Chemistry and Biotechnology* **42:** 192-194.

Giraffa, G. (2004). Studying the dynamics of microbial populations during food fermentation. *FEMS Microbiology Reviews* **28 :** 251-260.

Gomes, F.C.O., Pataro, C., Guerra, J.B., Neves,M.J., Correa, S.R., Moreira, E.S.A. and Rosa, C.A. (2002). Physiological diversity and trehalose accumulation in *Schizosaccharomyces pombe* strains from spontaneous fermentation during the production of the artisanal Brazilian cachaca. *Canadian Journal of Microbiology* ***48*** **:** 399-406.

Hall, H.H., James, L.H. and Nelson, E.K. (1935). Microorganisms causing fermentation flavours in cane syrups, especially Barbados "molasses". *Journal of Bacteriology* **33:** 577-585.

I'Anson, J.A.P. (1971). Rum manufacture. *Process Biochemistry* **July**: 35-39.

Kampen, W.H. (1975). Technology of the rum industry. *SUGAR y AZUCAR*, **July**, 36-43.

Lea, A.G.H. and Piggott, J.R. (2003). *Fermented Beverage Production*, second edition. Kluwer Academic, New York .

Lehtonen, M. and Suomalainen,H.(1977). Rum. In: *Economic Microbiology*, Edited by Rose, A.H., Academic Press, London, pp. 595-633.

Morais, P.B., Rosa, C.A., Linardi, V.R., Pataro,C. and Maia, A.B.R.A. (1997). Characterization and succession of yeast populations associated with spontaneous fermentations during the production of Brazillian sugar cane *aguardente*. *World Journal of Microbiology and Biotechnology* **13:** 241-243.

Murtagh, J.E. (1995a). Molasses as a feedstock for alcohol production. In: *The alcohol text book; a reference for the beverage, fuel and industrial alcohol production industries,* Edited by Jaques, K.A., Lyons, T.P. and Kelsall, D.R., Nottingham University Press, Nottingham, pp. 89-96.

Murtagh, J.E. (1995b). Feedstocks, fermentation and distillation for production of heavy and light rums. In: *The alcohol textbook; a reference for the beverage, fuel, and industrial alcohol production industries,* Edited by Jaques, K.A., Lyons, T.P. and Kelsall, D.R., Nottingham University Press, Nottingham, pp.243-255.

Nicol, D.A. (2003). Rum. In: *Fermented Beverage Production*, second edition, Edited by Lea, A.G.H. and Piggott, J.R., Kluwer Academic, New York, pp.263-287.

Oliveira, E.S., Rosa, C.A., Morgano, M.A. and Serra, G.I. (2004). Fermentation characteristics as criteria for selection of cachaca yeast. *World Journal of Microbiology and Biotechnology* **20:**19-24.

Owen, W.L. (1911). Recently discovered bacterial decomposition of sucrose. *Journal of Industrial and Engineering Chemistry* **July :** 481-486.

Owen, W.L. (1949). *The Microbiology of Sugars, Syrups and Molasses.* Barr-Owen research Enterprises, Baton Rouge.

Pataro,C., Guerra,G.B., Petrillo-Peixoto,M.L., Mendonca-Hagler, L., Linardi, V.R. and Rosa, C.A. (2000). Yeast communities and genetic polymorphism of *Saccharomyces cerevisiae* strains associated with artisanal fermentation in Brazil. *Journal of Applied Microbiology* **89:** 24-31.

Pech, B., Lavoue, G., Parfait, A. and Belin. J.M. (1984) Fermentations rhumieres: aptitude des souches de *Schizosaccharomyces pombe* Lindner. *Science des Aliments* **4:** 67-72.

Priest, F. (2004). Lactic acid bacteria- the uninvited but generally welcome participants in malt whisky fermentation. *Microbiology Today* **31:** 16-18.

Rose, A.H. (1977). Economic Microbiology, volume Academic Press, London.

Schwan, R.F., Mendonca,A.T., daSilva, J.J., Rodrigues, V. and Wheals, A.(2001). Microbiology and physiology of *Cachaca* (*Aguardente*) fermentations. *Antonie van Leeuwenhoek* **79:** 89-96.

Shehata, A.E.E. (1960). Yeasts isolated from sugar cane and its juice during the production of Aguardente de Cana. *Applied Microbiology* **8:** 73-75.

Tilbury, R.H. (1980). Xerotolerant (osmophilic) yeasts. In: *Biology and Activities of Yeasts*, Edited by Skinner,F.A., Passmore, S.M. and Davenport, R.R., Academic Press, London, pp.153-179.

Todorov, S.D. and Dicks, L.M.T. (2005). *Lactobacillus plantarum* isolated from molasses produces bacteriocins active against gram negative bacteria. *Enzyme and Microbial Technology* **36:** 318-326.

Tokuoka, K. (1993). Sugar-and salt tolerant yeasts. *Journal of Applied Bacteriology* **74:** 101-110.

Van Beek, S. and Priest, F. (2002). Evolution of the lactic acid bacterial community during malt whisky fermentation: a polyphasic study. *Applied and Environmental Microbiology* **68:** 297-305.

Vicente, M., Fietto, L.G., Castro I., dos Santos, A. N. G., Coutrim, M. X. and Brandao, R.L. (2006). Isolation of *Saccharomyces cerevisiae* strains producing higher levels of flavoring compounds for production of " cachaca" the Brazilian sugar cane spirit. *International Journal of Food Microbiology* **108:** 51-59.

Watson, D.C. (1993). Yeasts in distilled alcoholic beverage production. In: *The Yeasts*, second edition, Edited by Rose, A.H. and Harrison, J.S., Academic Press, London, pp. 215-244.

Acknowledgements

This project was supported by an Australian Research Council (ARC) Linkage grant between the University of New South Wales and Bundaberg Distillery, Diageo (Australia)

Chapter 13

Potential of Blanquilla pear variety to produce pear spirits: influence of the raw material on the final quality of the spirits

Laura García-Llobodanin*, Carme Güell, Montse Ferrando, Francisco López
Departament d'Enginyeria Química, Facultat d'Enologia, University Rovira i Virgili, Av. Països Catalans 26, 43007, Tarragona, Spain

Introduction

In Spain there is an important pear production industry, with the *Blanquilla* variety being the favourite among consumers. This typical Spanish variety has an important economic influence and, therefore, the idea of using the surplus to produce a pear-based spirit is of great interest for the Spanish pear growing areas. The use of pear juice concentrate as the raw material for the process has two logistic advantages compared to the raw fruit or juice: the storage space needed is smaller, and it is less prone to spoilage. However, the concentration process can cause aroma losses, so its use for spirit production must be carefully studied. In the present work, we compared the aromatic profile of pear spirits produced with concentrated pear juice, natural pear juice and pear mash from *Blanquilla* variety under the same fermentation and distillation conditions.

Materials and methods

Pear juice preparation

Pear mash, natural pear juice, and pear juice concentrate from the *Blanquilla* variety, were produced and donated by Nufri S.A. (Lleida, Spain). They were all obtained from the same production batch, in order to assure comparable results. The concentrated juice, of 71 °Brix, was diluted with water until a juice of 12.5° Brix was obtained. The dilution was done prior to the fermentation process. To characterise the raw materials, total sugars were measured using a GAB kit for sugar analysis (GAB Sistemática Analítica S.L., Spain), and the pH was monitored with a Crison Basic 20 pH meter.

Fermentation process

The pear mash, natural pear juice and diluted juice concentrate from *Blanquilla* pear, were separately fermented in 20 L plastic tanks under semi-anaerobic conditions. A volume of 15 L was used for each fermentation. The tanks were inoculated with a dose of 20 g/hL of yeast, according to the instructions provided by the supplier. The yeast used was a commercial strain of *Saccharomyces cerevisiae* (BDX, ENOFERM, France). Fermentations were performed in triplicate. After the fermentations finished (total sugars concentration lower than 4 g/L), the tanks were kept closed at room temperature for some days before distillation (in order to enhance the aromatic profile of the ferments).

The final concentration of total sugars in the ferments was determined with a GAB kit (GAB Sistemática Analítica S.L.). The ethanol and acetic acid concentrations before distillation were determined by high performance liquid chromatography (HPLC), following the method described by García-Llobodanin et. al. (2007).

Distillation process

The pear distillates were obtained by double batch distillation of the fermented raw materials in presence of their lees, in a 20 L copper alembic. The operation conditions were the same in the three cases: 14 L of the fermented raw materials were distilled using water as the refrigerant and an electric heater as the still heat source. The distillations were performed in triplicate. The fractions collected during the first distillation were: the first 60 mL (corresponding to the head, which was discarded), the following 3.5 L (heart fraction), and finally 600 mL (the tail fraction, which was also discarded). The heart fraction was second distilled using the same equipment. In this case, the head fraction was defined as the first 35 mL and the heart fraction volume was adjusted in each case to obtain an ethanol concentration between 25% (v/v) and 30 % (v/v). Samples from the heart fractions were analyzed by gas chromatography (GC), according to the method described by Garcia-Llobodanin et al. (2007).

Statistical analysis

One-way analysis of variance (ANOVA) was applied to ascertain if there were significant differences (at 5% level) between the different *Blanquilla* pear distillates obtained.

Principal components analysis (PCA) was performed to the pear spirits, to determine the degree of differentiation caused by the variation of the raw material used.

All the statistical analyses were performed by means of SPSS statistical package (version 15.0).

Sensory evaluation

The pear distillates were diluted with demineralised water to an ethanol content of 20% (v/v), according to the guidelines proposed by Jack (Jack, 2003) for the preparation of sensory samples of whisky. Then, they were tested for their flavour quality using order-of-precedence tests. Sensory evaluation was conducted with a panel of 24 consumers, whom were asked to evaluate separately the smell and the taste of the spirits. The results were analyzed using the Friedmann statistic test, described by Jellinek (1981).

Results and discussion

The characterisation of the raw materials employed can be seen in Table 1.

Table 1. Characterisation of the raw materials used for the fermentations.

Parameter	*Pear concentrate (diluted)*	*Pear mash*	*Pear juice*
Total sugars (g/L)	103.6 ± 1.7	69.4 ± 8.9	83.3 ± 9.3
° Brix	12.5	-	12.5
pH	4.10	3.77	3.96

After four days of fermentation, the total sugar concentration was below 4 g/L in all of the fermentation tanks. After twelve days of fermentation, superficial growth of microorganisms was observed in all of the tanks. Immediately after, the tanks were put in a cool room until distillation. Table 2 shows the sugar content, the ethanol, and the acetic acid concentrations of the fermented raw materials before starting the distillation. These results suggest that the contamination observed in the tanks was due to acetic acid bacteria, which oxidised part of the ethanol present to acetic acid. Some of the pear mashes were the most affected by this contamination.

Table 2. Concentrations (g/L) of total sugars, ethanol and acetic acid in the fermented raw materials.

g/L	*Pear concentrate*	*Pear mash*	*Pear juice*
Total sugars	3.3 ± 0.2	2.9 ± 0.3	3.6 ± 0.2
Ethanol	39.7 ± 1.4	19.3 ± 8.1	24.5 ± 5.6
Acetic acid	6.7 ± 1.7	12.5 ± 6.9	4.1 ± 0.7

Table 3 shows the volatile composition and ethanol content of the different pear spirits obtained by double distillation of the fermented raw materials. The equipment had a failure during one of the distillations from pear juice concentrate and during one of the distillations from pear mash, so these two samples were discarded.

The pear mash spirits presented the highest concentration of ethyl acetate (which is mainly produced by bacterial spoilage), furfural (highly toxic compound) and methyl acetate (also produced by spoilage of the raw material) (Soufleros, Mygdalia and Natskoulis, 2005).

On the other hand, the natural juice spirits had a very high concentration of methanol, exceeding the limit of 1000 g/hL a.a. (grams per hectolitre of absolute alcohol) imposed by the European Council Regulation 1576/89. Methanol is a highly toxic compound, which can even prove fatal if present in high concentrations (Cortés, Gil and Fernández, 2005). It is produced by enzymatic degradation of pectic substances present mainly in the skin of the fruits (Da Porto, 2002). The pressing of the raw material influences the methanol content by releasing a higher amount of pectolytic enzymes (Cortés-Diéguez , Gil de la Peña and Fernández-Gómez, 2000; Cortés et. al., 2005). Therefore, a strong pressing process could be the reason for the high methanol concentration found in the natural juices.

The total higher alcohols impart a positive flavour to the spirits, being the limit fixed by the European Council Regulation 1576/89 for fruit spirits of 150 g/hL a.a. All the pear distillates fulfilled this requirement.

On the contrary, the minimum ethanol content in fruit spirits according to the same regulation (37.5°) was not obtained in our pear

Table 3. Concentrations (g/hL a.a.) of the main volatile compounds present in the pear spirits from pear juice concentrate, pear mash and pear natural juice.

Compound	*Pear concentrate*	*Pear mash*	*Pear natural juice*
Acetaldehyde	7.4 ± 3.4[a]	53.8 ± 18.6[b]	5.8 ± 1.8[a]
Acetal	1.2 ± 0.5[a]	0.8 ± 1.0[a,b]	0.1 ± 0.2[b]
Furfural	6.8 ± 2.5[a]	35.4 ± 16.0[b]	5.3 ± 1.6[a]
Methanol	38.6 ± 18.8[a]	350.4 ± 155.3[a]	1253.6 ± 453.8[b]
Ethanol (% v/v)	31.8	27.4	26.1
1-propanol	0.0 ± 0.0[a]	41.1 ± 4.7[a]	214.7 ± 97.6[b]
2-methyl-1-propanol	77.0 ± 4.0[a,b]	98.2 ± 44.0[a]	53.1 ± 21.9[b]
1-butanol	2.1 ± 0.3[a]	7.7 ± 0.6[b]	6.3 ± 0.6[c]
2-butanol	0.0 ± 0.0[a]	2.3 ± 0.4[a]	253.3 ± 75.6[b]
2-methyl-1-butanol	22.4 ± 1.2[a]	49.0 ± 22.1[b]	20.5 ± 10.7[a]
3-methyl-1-butanol	95.1 ± 4.5[a]	178.1 ± 77.7[b]	90.1 ± 26.6[a]
1-hexanol	79.3 ± 32.1[a]	85.0 ± 11.7[a]	209.5 ± 33.2[b]
Phenethyl alcohol	3.2 ± 0.2[a]	13.8 ± 7.5[b]	7.8 ± 5.3[a,b]
Total higher alcohols	**279.1 ± 42.3**	**475.2 ± 168.7**	**855.3 ± 271.5**
Methyl acetate	0.5 ± 0.0[a]	20.5 ± 12.0[b]	8.5 ± 3.0[a]
Ethyl acetate	300.9 ± 14.0[a]	1144.0 ± 286.3[b]	141.3 ± 44.4[a]
Ethyl hexanoate	0.3 ± 0.1[a]	0.0 ± 0.0[a]	0.2 ± 0.4[a]
Total esters	**301.7 ± 14.1**	**1164.5 ± 298.3**	**150.0 ± 47.8**

Different superscripts within the same row indicate significant differences ($P<0.05$) between parameter values.

spirits. The present experiments were performed only with the aim of comparing the raw materials employed. Nevertheless, the ethanol content should be taken into account in future work, in order to fulfil this regulation.

The principal components analysis (PCA), separated the compounds in three main components. PC2 was composed by 2-butanol, methanol, 1-propanol, 1-hexanol and acetal. It differentiated the natural pear juice spirits from the rest. PC3 was composed by ethyl hexanoate and 1-butanol. It differentiated the pear juice concentrate spirits from the others. PC1 was composed by 2-methyl-1-butanol, 3-methyl-1-butanol, phenethyl alcohol, methyl acetate, furfural, 2-methyl-1-propanol, acetaldehyde and ethyl acetate. In this case, the principal component (PC1) did not differentiate any of the raw materials used. Figure 1 plots the principal component 2 (PC2) versus the principal component 3 (PC3).

The sensory evaluation showed that for both the smell and the taste, the spirits from natural pear juice were the preferred ones. They were followed by the spirits of pear juice concentrate. The spirits from pear mash had a very negative evaluation, probably because of their high concentration in ethyl acetate (Soufleros et al., 2005).

In conclusion, the *Blanquilla* variety of pear was a suitable raw material for the production of pear spirits. However, the processing of the raw material should be carefully controlled to avoid bacterial contamination and methanol formation. The pear juice concentrate, because of its production process, was less affected by these problems. Nevertheless, part of the volatile composition is lost during the process. Therefore, some improvement should be made in the future (i.e. the addition of the extracted aroma compounds to the pear concentrate before fermentation), if the pear juice concentrate is to be used.

References

Cortés-Diéguez, S.M., Gil de la Peña, M.L., Fernández-Gómez, E. (2000). Influencia del nivel de prensado y del estado de conservación del bagazo en el contenido en metanol, acetato de etilo, 2-butanol y alcohol alílico de aguardientes de orujo. Alimentaria **316**: 133-138.

Cortés, S., Gil, M.L., Fernández, E. (2005). Volatile composition of traditional and industrial Orujo spirits. Food Control **16**: 383-388.

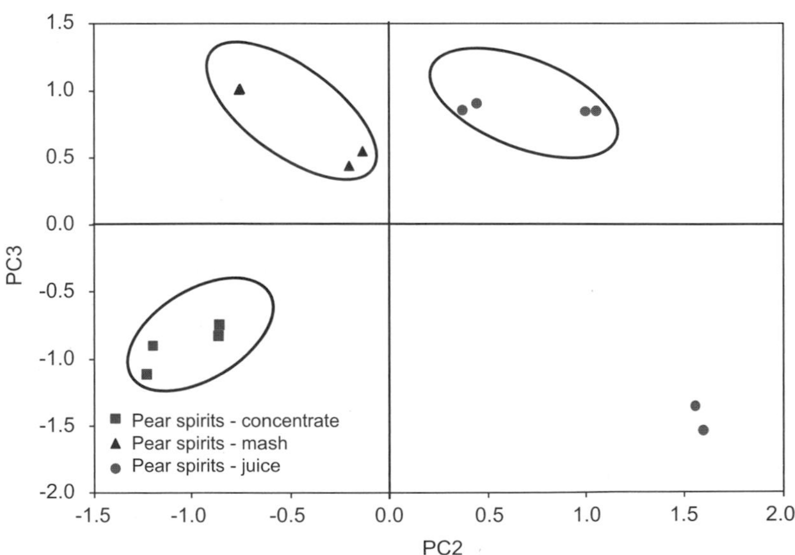

Figure 1. Principal components analysis (PCA) of the main volatile compounds in the pear spirits.

Da Porto, C. (2002). Volatile composition of 'grappa low wines' using different methods and conditions of storage on an industrial scale. International Journal of Food Science and Technology **37**: 395-402.

Garcia-Llobodanin, L., Achaerandio, I., Ferrando, M., Güell, C, López, F. (2007). Pear distillates from pear juice concentrate: effect of lees in the aromatic composition. Journal of Agricultural and Food Chemistry **55**: 3462-3468.

Jack, F. (2003). Development of guidelines for the preparation and handling of sensory samples in the Scotch Whiskey industry. Journal of the Institute of Brewing **109**: 114-119.

Jellinek, G. (1981). Sensorische Lebensmittelprüfung. Verlag D&PS, Germany.

Soufleros, E.H., Mygdalia, S.A., Natskoulis, P. (2005). Production process and characterization of the traditional Greek fruit distillate 'Koumaro' by aromatic and mineral composition. Journal of Food Composition and Analysis **18**: 699-716.

Chapter 14

Distller's Yeast Discussion Forum

Reporter: G M Walker

Forum panel members: Katherine Smart (Nottingham University, UK)
Graham Fleet (University of New South Wales, Australia)
Derek Jamieson (Heriot-Watt University, UK)
Robert Piggot (Ethanol Technology, Canada)
Tony Balzan (AB Mauri, Australia)
Yves Gosselin (Fermentis, France)

Chair: Graeme Walker (University of Abertay Dundee, UK)

Academic type questions

Will distillers need to consider GM-yeasts to meet sustainability targets (energy savings, reduced water usage)?

(Tom Bringhurst – SWRI)

The panel was of the impression that although sustainability targets could indeed exert novel pressures on distillery yeast strains this did not necessarily mean distillers would have to embrace genetically modified yeasts. In fact they believed that it is highly unlikely that distillers will move to adopt GM yeasts in the foreseeable future. The main reasons cited being that it is entirely feasible to produce the traits required by sustainability targets within existing yeast strains, using classical breeding techniques. The panel highlighted that desired traits, such as thermal or osmotic tolerance, have already been shown as an obtainable outcome from classical yeast breeding programs, and by paying close attention to yeast nutritional physiology.

How do you see possibilities for constructing by genetic engineering or by breeding highly tolerant (resistant) distillers yeast?

(Matti Korhola – Allcomohr Biotech)

In general the panel agreed that GM technology provides good possibilities for the development of resistant yeast strains. However, it was also of the view that this does not mean classical breeding techniques should be ruled out. Public acceptance was again highlighted as a major barrier to the successful implementation of GM technology within conventional distilleries.

There is a move to get shorter and shorter fermentation times but does this mean missing out on flavours that develop later in fermentation?

(Anonymous)

The general consensus among panel members was that the answer to this question depends entirely on the product being manufactured. It was suggested that faster fermentation times would result in a reduction of volatile end products observed at the cessation of longer fermentations. It was also noted that many alcoholic beverages derive important flavour compounds from bacteria present at the end of fermentation. Considering this along with the fact that shorter fermentation times are likely to reduce the amount of bacterial growth observed in longer fermentations it was concluded that shorter fermentation times could indeed alter the flavour profile of the end product. The panel believed that shorter fermentation times could affect the wine industry in particular considering the current drive for unique wine products.

What would be the fastest way to introduce maltotriose utilisation into bioethanol yeast?
(James Brosnan – SWRI)

The panel suggested that the fastest way to introduce maltotriose utilisation into a non-utilising yeast strain would be through GM techniques (i.e. the insertion of genes encoding maltotriose utilisation into the genome of the targeted yeast strain). However, upon expanding the idea, the discussion concluded that it would far easier, quicker and more cost effective to simply select a yeast strain that already exhibits maltotriose utilisation. As a side issue it was argued that this would be especially pertinent if flavour compounds were important in the end product.

Ways to improve oligosaccharide utilisation?
(Benoit Colonna – Pernod Ricard)

The panel suggested that the answer to this particular question is twofold depending on whether the yeast strain in question is a GM or a "standard" strain. If the latter was true then the most effective way to improve oligosaccharide utilisation would be through modification of the strain in question through standard GM techniques. If the strain in question is already a GM yeast then it was agreed the best way would be through conventional mutagenesis. Additionally, it was considered that the use of non-*Saccharomyces* yeasts and/or mixed yeast species have future potential to improve substrate utilisation and to enhance flavour of distilled spirits.

Are there opportunities in the foreseeable future for the production of ethanol from polysaccharides without the use of yeast?
(Paul Hughes – Heriot Watt University)

After discussing the well documented examples of ethanol production the panel concluded that ethanol from non yeast sources is a viable method of non-potable ethanol production. The main example cited by the panel was bioethanol production from bacterial fermentation of ligno-cellulosic hydrolysate feedstocks.

Industrial type questions

Given the greater freedoms in the bioethanol industry, when or will GM yeast become dominant and what will they be capable of?

(J. Brosnan – SWRI)

First-generation bioethanol: The panel did not foresee the implementation of GM yeast as becoming a dominant factor within the biofuel industry for first generation bioethanol. The main reason for this was the use of yeast from the fermentation in the production of animal feeds. With this in mind it was envisaged that with public acceptance for GMO's being somewhat limited a wider discussion with the populace would be required in order to convince them that GMO's are a valid and morally acceptable tool at our disposable. Without this it was thought to be almost impossible for GM yeast to become the dominant strain within the biofuel industry. The panel proposed that current limitations with biofuel programs implemented by major players in the industry (eg. USA, Brazil) are not centred on yeast but more to do with limitations within feedstock supply and process techniques.

Second-generation bioethanol: It was agreed that GM yeast could prove to be a vitally important factor within production of bioethanol from ligno-cellulosic feed stocks. In this case, however, alternative uses of spent yeast from the fermentation would need to be identified.

Knowing the limitations what can the yeast industry bring to the Scotch whisky industry?

(Anonymous)

The panel began by outlining what it saw as the major limiting factors of innovation within the Scotch whisky industry. These were considered to be twofold; firstly that whisky production is inextricably linked to a specific raw material and secondly that it is bound by a defined legal framework. Although these factors hold the potential to limit innovation it was concluded that specific research areas within the yeast industry give rise to chances to innovate with regard to Scotch whisky production. It was agreed that the major areas for innovation could centre on selecting novel yeast strains for whisky fermentation and process optimisation. Specific examples mentioned included yeasts with the ability to utilise maltotetrose and novel yeasts flavour profiles (e.g. less sulphury notes). Examples of process optimisation included high gravity fermentations and the possibility of supplementing commercial whisky fermentations with zinc. It was felt that by working together, the yeast suppliers and Scotch whisky industry can find novel approaches to innovating within the production process of Scotch whisky.

We often hear about thermo-tolerant yeast. Do we have one? It will be a great boon for tropical countries.

(P. Sriram – United Spirits Ltd India)

The notion was put forward that when discussing tolerant yeasts in the context of potable alcohol production one has to be careful about labelling a particular yeast strain as being tolerant to one specific parameter. In that there is a lot more to the perfect beverage yeast than just exhibiting tolerance to one specific parameter. Whilst it was agreed that thermotolerant yeast strains do exist it was envisaged that, at present, there was no reason to believe that they would be utilised by the alcoholic beverage industry. Reasons given for this centred heavily on the fact that fermentations carried out above 40°C are highly inefficient in terms of ethanol production and yeast growth.

Will one yeast serve all or will we be looking at different strains for different mash bills?

(M. Spandern – Agrobusiness Consulting)

Upon discussing this question the panel argued that as the alcoholic beverage industry possesses a wide variety of products all with different process techniques, the situation differs depending on the type of alcoholic beverage being produced. Examples cited highlighted the differences between two specific products. Namely, Scotch Whisky and neutral spirits (e.g. Vodka). It was agreed that one yeast strain serves the Whisky industry well as the sugars present within both grain and malt are similar. For this reason one particular yeast strain has little difficulty in utilising the sugars at its disposal. On the contrary it was agreed that with neutral spirit production the situation is more complex. The main reason for this surrounds the fact that increased enzyme use in this sector broadens the range of sugars that the yeast strain being used is expected to utilise. This ultimately exerts significantly greater pressures on the yeast strain in question when compared to the situation observed in Scotch Whisky production.

What is a good vitality test for dried distillers yeast?

(Anonymous)

The panel believed that a well established standard vitality test does not exist within the industry. It was argued that a variety of different "application tests" are carried out by both brewers and distillers, with small scale fermentation efficiency tests being utilised the most.

Are there any opportunities in exploring synergies between a particular yeast strain and a particular barley variety (or malting regime) to improve potential distillery yield during fermentations?

(M. Kinsman – Bairds Malt)

The panel did not appear convinced about the viability of pursuing such avenues of research. However, it was also felt that this type of research could present potential opportunities and as such would be worth discussing. It was noted that research carried out in the United States has highlighted that certain grain types release more fermentable sugars than others.

We currently use bagged yeast in our malt distilleries, should we move to liquid yeast, dried yeast or stay with bags?

(Anonymous)

It was agreed that although the variety of yeast formats available to malt distilleries all exhibit advantages and disadvantages, dry yeast has longer shelf, is easier to transport and is available in more varieties. It may be a good choice for remote distillers but utilizing fresh yeast is the preferred option. The main reason being that dried yeast exhibits a reduction in cell vitality when compared to fresh yeast.

Chapter 15

New build distilleries – challenges of sustainability

Mike Jappy
Diageo Global Supply, 1 Trinity House, Elgin, Moray

Background

In February 2007, Diageo announced a £100m investment in its Scotch whisky operations. This investment, responding to increasing sales in both mature and emerging markets, comprised 3 main elements:

- £40m to increase Grain Distillation capacity at Cameronbridge in Fife
- £40m to deliver a new malt distillery and bio-energy plant at Roseisle in Moray
- £20m expansion of warehousing and packaging capacity.

Diageo, like many other companies and organisations, have established some very challenging environmental targets and goals. We aspire to be a truly sustainable organisation, and this strongly influenced our thinking when developing plans for increasing the distillation footprint.

This paper primarily considers the challenges faced in building new distillation capacity and specifically the challenges of energy management, water management and sustainability.

Project objectives

The brief for the increase in malt distillation capacity was to:

- Deliver 10million litres of additional capacity,
- Establish new standards of environmental performance,
- Operational by the spring of 2009.

Environmental

Initially we had to define what "environment performance" meant in the context of malt distilling.

In a typical malt distillery, around 90% of the total energy consumption is related to steam generation. 10 million litres of capacity is equivalent to over 6 million litres of oil.

Distillation also requires large quantities of water, for both processing and cooling. Process water is permanently abstracted from the environment, while cooling water is generally returned after the thermal energy, which it has gained, has been removed or reduced.

As well as malt spirit, a distillery also generates large quantities of co-products from the mashing and distillation processes. These co-products, high in biological oxygen demand (BOD), are in some instances discharged directly into the environment, although more conventionally processed into animal feedstuff. Animal feeds production is itself a highly energy intensive process, and unreliable from a revenue generation perspective.

Therefore "environmental performance" in the context of this project has been defined as a reduction in fossil fuel consumption and minimisation of water abstractions, with a subsequent reduction in BOD discharges to the environment.

We set ourselves an aspiration to deliver a truly sustainable distilling operation, which would be both fossil fuel and water neutral.

Options for delivering capacity

Diageo currently operate 27 malt distilleries across Scotland and most of these are in production 5 out of 7 days. One obvious option to deliver the additional capacity would be to move to a 24/7 production cycle. However, this can only be achieved at certain distilleries as 7-day operation can adversely affect some spirit characters. Additionally the ability to flex between 5 and 7-day operation is used to cope with the normal changes in inventory demand from the baseline production.

Adding capacity to some of our existing distilleries was a viable option. This can be done at several distilleries to meet the 10mla requirement, which would also allow a suitable mix of new make spirit characters to keep the inventory of maturing spirit in balance. This option however, like the 24/7 option does not fully address the required improvement in environmental performance, especially where a "fossil fuel neutral" solution is the goal.

A new build option allows the opportunity to site a distillery at a location where all opportunities to reduce and offset the fossil fuel demand can be taken, as well as manage the water and co-products.

Location

After considering many locations available to the project team, Roseisle in Moray was chosen as the preferred option.

The site, owned by Diageo, is home to a maltings which opened in the early 1980's. The site has available space and the existing infrastructure to support a distilling operation, including water supplied from underground aquifers. The capacity of the maltings also roughly matched that of a 10mla distillery. Diageo owns another maltings facility 3km north of Roseisle, at Burghead, which also supports the choice of location.

Locating a distillery in close proximity to a malting plant provides many opportunities for synergies. Waste heat from the distillation can readily be used as a source of energy for the malt kilning process. As the main raw material for the distillery is on the same site, then transport movements can be reduced, saving road miles. Opportunities for managing the co product streams from both distillery and maltings are presented and building from new allows sustainability to be incorporated into the design.

The solution

Spirit character

It became apparent that building a new 10million litre distillery at Roseisle was the preferred solution. However, introducing 10 million litres of the same new make character into the maturing inventory each year would quickly lead to imbalance, so the distillery needed to be capable of producing more than one character.

Inventory demands dictated that any new capacity must include additional "light" spirit character. "Light" new make spirit characters, such as grassy / fruity, which require long fermentation and slow distillation, can be difficult to achieve and maintain. Therefore, the key process design criteria were influenced by the necessity to produce this "light" character. Specifically this determined the number of fermentation vessels, and size and shape of the stills.

The "heavy" new make spirit characters, "sulphury / meaty" are normally associated with distilleries which use worm tubs to condense the spirit vapour. However, previous work at Dailuaine distillery, had proved that "heavy" new make spirit character can be produced using condensers, if the copper contact is controlled.

Therefore, introducing stainless steel condensers and changing fermentation and distillation conditions, allows "heavy" character to be produced at Roseisle.

Biomass

The use of biomass to generate energy is not new technology. However, the use of spent grains in this application isn't well developed. We were aware of breweries in Europe and Africa who were conducting trials in the area, so it was decided to pursue this option to deliver the reduction in fossil fuel consumption we desired.

Again having a malting plant adjacent to the distillery was beneficial, as not only did we have the spent grains (draff) from the distillery as a source of biomass, but also the dust and culms from the maltings. Dust and culms have very low moisture content, helping to increase the dry matter content of the mixed biomass, which is essential for combustion.

Water recovery

Distillation produces 2 liquid co-product streams, pot ale from the first distillation and

Spent lees, from the second. In addition, the maltings on site produces large quantities of water from the steeping process.

We utilise both aerobic and anaerobic digestion systems, individually, at other distilleries for the treatment of pot ale and spent lees, and are well aware of their potential to reduce BOD and suspended solids prior to discharge. We decided to join both processes together, with an additional membrane bio-filtration stage to achieve recovered water suitable for re-use as steeping water.

Waste heat recovery

Another co-product of distillation process is waste energy, in the form of hot water. Most distilleries utilise as much of this waste heat source as they can, but in the majority of cases the excess heat has to be rejected, via cooling towers or surface water lagoons, before the water is either recycled or returned to the environment.

At Roseisle we are able to go one step further by utilising this waste heat as an energy source in the malting process.

Roseisle Distillery

In terms of process equipment, Roseisle is little different to any other distillery. It has a 4-roll mill, two mashtuns, fourteen washbacks (fermentation vessels) and 14 stills. A team of 10 experienced operators, who currently work at other Diageo distilleries, will operate it. There are no warehousing facilities at Roseisle; all spirit will be taken off site for maturation.

The inclusion of stainless steel condensers to deliver spirit character, while not exactly new, is quite novel as an alternative to worm tubs.

Where possible we have taken the opportunity to deploy new technologies for the control of the process: such as gravity determination by mass flow meters, in-line determination of spirit strength and the use of wireless connectivity.

Other innovations have been driven by the requirement to engineer out confined space entry. For example, we have adopted external heat exchangers in preference to more traditional steam pans or coils in the stills, and have flanged the sections of the stills to eliminate the need for entry during repairs or replacement.

In terms of security of spirit, we control access using a swipe card identification system rather than the more traditional category A and B padlocks.

Water management

Currently water for both Roseisle and Burghead maltings is abstracted from an underground aquifer on site at Roseisle. The water is pumped the 3km to Burghead via an underground pipeline. The water demand of the existing 2 sites is in the region of 650,000m3 / year, and the addition of a 10 million-litre distillery would add a further demand for water - around 300,000m3 per year.

In order to minimise this additional abstraction, the liquid co-products of both the distilling and malting operations on the Roseisle site are subject to a 3-stage treatment process. The resulting reclaimed water being used to provide steep water at Burghead maltings.

The feed streams for water recovery are pot ale, spent lees and steeping water from the maltings. As yeast cells cannot be digested, the pot ale is centrifuged to remove solids, before the feed steams are balanced for volume and load. Anaerobic digestion reduces the BOD load by around 80%, by converting organic carbon into methane gas. This is collected and sent to a biogas boiler.

Aerobic digestion then removes the remaining BOD and finally membrane filtration separates the solids from the final treated water.

The quantity of water recovered is equivalent to around 95% of the water demand of the distillery, and will be sent to Burghead to be used as steep water. It is anticipated that, with optimisation, this gap can be closed to achieve a total "water neutral" solution.

Energy management

The annual energy demand, required to raise steam for Roseisle distillery is equivalent to 6,400,000 litres of heavy fuel oil. One of the main objectives of this project is to minimise the consumption of fossil fuel, and this has been achieved by a combination of using the solid co-products of the distillation and malting processes as biomass, methane production from the water recovery process, and utilising the waste heat from the distillery to offset fossil fuel consumption in the maltings.

Biomass burning

The feedstock for the biomass burner comprises: spent grains (draff), pot ale solids, and the dust and malt culms generated during the malting process.

The spent grains are mechanically dewatered, before mixing with the pot ale solids and dust and culms. To ensure combustion the mix must have a dry matter content greater than 45%, and this is achieved utilising a steam drier. The biomass is then fed into a moving grate burner for combustion.

Biogas

As described above, methane is produced by anaerobic digestion of the liquid co-products. This gas is collected and is used as fuel in a stand-alone gas fired boiler.

Heat recovery

Like most distilleries waste heat is recovered and used where possible to reduce energy consumption. The mashing liquor is preheated by the water from worts cooler, and the distillery is equipped with 2 multi pass condensers. These generate water at a higher temperature than conventional condensers, which is collected and used to preheat wash and low wine charges. It is also used as a heating medium for the accommodation area. However, the majority of the hot water will be utilised in the maltings. For most of the year, the hot water will be used to pre-heat the incoming air in the malt kilns, which will significantly reduce the amount of oil currently used in this duty. And during the harvest intake, the hot water will be used in a similar way in the barley drier on site.

Energy balance

In terms of an overall energy balance, biomass and biogas provides around 50% of the energy demand for the boilers at the distillery. The remainder is provided using conventional fossil fuel fired boilers. Waste heat recovery at the maltings offsets another 35% of the energy requirement of the distillery, and so overall the operation is almost 85% fossil fuel neutral.

It has also been assumed for the purposes of this calculation that the thermal drier in the biomass plant will be in continual use. This drier has a parasitic demand equal to around 10% of the overall energy requirement for the distillery. However, again with optimisation, it is anticipated that the use of the drier can be minimised. This and other incremental optimisation changes will get us closer to the target of "fossil fuel neutral".

Sustainable development

When considering the overall "sustainability" of the project we also took into account how we would construct the distillery building. While a building which produces and stores flammable liquid has some restrictions in materials of construction, it is possible to ensure that the development is carried out in a sustainable manner. The Building Research Establishment provided guidance and assessment methodology in the area of sustainable developments, and Roseisle distillery has been constructed with a view to achieving an "excellent" accreditation rating as assessed by their environmental assessment method. This not only considered materials of construction, but sustainability of materials used, quantity of materials send to landfill, methods of heating and ventilation etc, and one very visible feature, a sustainable urban drainage system. This flood control measure takes the form of a feature pond at the front of the distillery.

To date, a rating of "very good" has been achieved and it is anticipated that we will secure an accreditation rating of "excellent" once the project is complete.

Traffic impact

As all the malt supply and co-product management is internalised on site, traffic movements are greatly reduced compared to a more conventional distillery build, where all raw materials and co products are moved on and off site. It is estimated that this has saved around 9000 heavy goods vehicle movements per year. The operation of Roseisle distillery will actually result in a slight decrease in vehicle movements when compared to the current movements on and off site at present.

Project Forth

Project Forth at Cameronbridge Distillery in Fife, will see capacity increased from 65mla to 105 mla by 2010. Like Roseisle, this project also includes a bio-energy and water recovery plant. However, at Cameronbridge, the steam derived from the biomass will be used to drive a turbine, producing electricity, in addition to meeting the steam demand of the distillery. Overall the site will be 95% fossil fuel neutral, will recover 30% of its water requirement and the BOD load discharged into the Forth estuary will be reduced by 99%.

Challenges

There have been many challenges to overcome in the delivery of this project. Some of the most difficult and frustrating hurdles were not technical, but associated with gaining the necessary approvals for the project from both a planning and operational licensing perspective. Current European legislation fails to recognise the potential of the distilling liquid co-products as a renewable source of energy and SEPA (Scottish Environment Protection Agency) had little choice but to regard them as waste. This has brought wholly unnecessary and burdensome regulations into play, which drove design decisions around the bio-energy plant that were financially costly and achieved no environmental benefit.

The long-term sustainability of the Scotch Whisky industry will depend upon the transfer of the similar technologies to those deployed at Roseisle across the existing malt distilleries. The policy makers in Brussels, Westminster and Holyrood need to quickly update the legislative framework to provide encouragement and support to businesses moving into renewable energy. Existing regulations do neither - they are relevant to the past, not the future.

Summary

The expansion of both Malt and Grain spirit capacity can be delivered in a truly sustainable manner. At Roseisle, we delivered the biggest malt distillery in the Diageo portfolio. The building was designed, constructed and accredited to the highest environmental standard for a building of its type and the operation of the distillery is largely neutral in terms of water and fossil fuel consumption.

The distillery provides a blueprint for future developments in Diageo's distilling operations, and is something that all who have been involved in design and delivery can be justifiably proud.

Chapter 16

Anaerobic treatment of distillery and brewery wastewaters

J. C. Akunna

Urban Water Technology Centre, School of Contemporary Sciences, University of Abertay Dundee, Bell Street, Dundee, DD1 1HG, Scotland, UK

Introduction

Anaerobic treatment has preference over aerobic processes for high strength wastewaters because of comparatively low sludge production and low energy consumption. One of the main setbacks of anaerobic systems is the relatively long biomass retention time (or solids retention time, SRT) required for effective treatment, due to the relative slow growing methane-producing bacteria. In conventional anaerobic systems, hydraulic retention time (HRT) within the system has to be maintained long enough in order to ensure long SRT, thus necessitating the need for relatively large reactor systems. However, with the advent of high rate reactor systems which are capable of separating HRT and SRT, anaerobic processes are presently popular choice for the treatment of intermediate to high strength wastewaters.

A GRAnular Bed Baffled Reactor (GRABBR), shown schematically in Figure 1, is one of the high rate anaerobic wastewater treatment systems which, due to its compartmentalised design, encourages plug flow, phase separation and minimises short-circuiting (Barber and

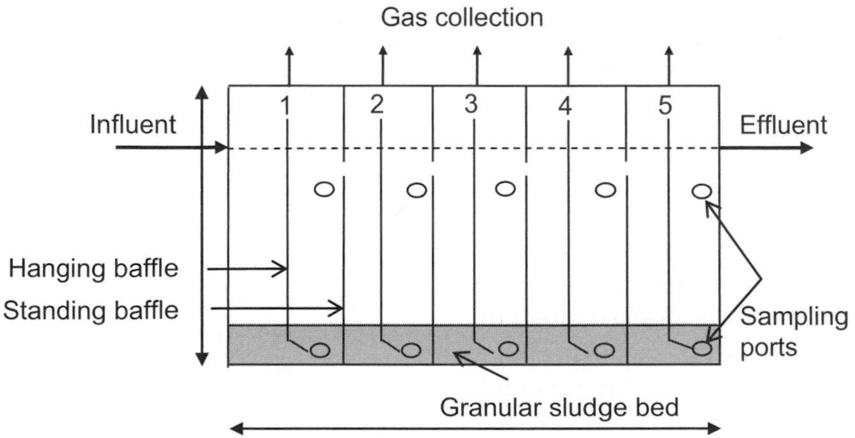

Figure 1. Schematic of a 5-compartment GRABBR

Stuckey 1999; Balch and Akunna 2003a,b). The importance of phase separation (i.e. separation of acidogenesis and methanogenesis process stages) has been found to be suitable for the treatment of complex substrates in order to ensure process stability (Pohland and Ghosh 1971; Anderson *et al.* 1994; Shin *et al.* 2001). Each compartment of the GRABBR is itself a separate treatment unit and completely mixed. This paper discusses the performance of GRABBR when used to assess the treatability of distillery and brewery wastewaters. These wastewaters are also characterised by relatively high solids content, which may limit the type of system suitable for their treatment.

Two different GRABBRs were used for the study. The aim was not to compare their relative performances but to evaluate the treatability of both wastewaters and to identify the characteristics of the GRABBR system in terms of phase separation, effects of seed sludge bed size, stability at various loading rates, COD removal and biomass washout.

Treatment of distillery wastewater

This study was carried out with a 35-litre GRABBR divided into 10 equal compartments, maintained at constant temperature of 37°C and seeded to approximately 13% of the working volume with granular sludge obtained from a mesophilic UASB reactor treating papermill wastewater. The raw wastewater composed of COD (16600-58000 mg/l), suspended solids (232-7810 mg/l), volatile suspended solids (200-7340 mg/l), Total Kjeldahl Nitrogen, TKN (500-1200 mg/l), and pH (3-4). The reactor was fed with diluted wastewater at a constant feed strength of 9500 mg/L (total) COD, at different retention times to obtain organic loading rates (OLRs) of 0.99, 1.33, 2.37 and 4.75. The raw wastewater was diluted to the desired strength with tap water and the pH was corrected to about 7.5 using 10M NaOH. Detailed experimental methodology can be found in Akunna and Clark (2000).

Up to 90% COD removal was obtained at relatively low OLR as shown in Table 1. The maximum specific gas production during the studies was approximately 0.3 $m^3CH_4/COD_{removed}$. High influent solids hindered the application of higher OLR. Raw wastewater pre-treatment for solids reduction may be necessary in order to operate at higher OLR.

Table 1. COD removal efficiencies at different organic loading rates (distillery wastewater)

OLR (kg COD/m³.d)	COD_{in} (mg/l)	*COD removal* (%)
0.99	9500	87
1.33	9500	91
2.37	9500	92
4.75	9500	80

Treatment of brewery wastewater

The laboratory study was carried out with a 10 litre capacity 5-compartment GRABBR. Two investigations were conducted, the first with mainly brewery wastewater and the other enriched with excess yeast. Table 2 shows the wastewater characteristics. Excess yeast contains relatively high amounts of sulphates which, when treated anaerobically can lead to process failure due to sulphide toxicity.

Tap water was used, when necessary, to dilute the raw wastewaters to the required strength. pH was adjusted to between 7.2 and 7.5 by adding $NaHCO_3$ and NH_4HCO_3 solutions. No correction was made when the pH values of the wastewaters were greater than 7.2. Detailed experimental set-up can be found in Baloch *et al.* (2006).

Table 3 shows the overall performance in terms of COD removal in both studies and Figure 2 shows the profile of COD concentration within the system during the first study. For both wastewaters, influent COD concentrations were variable and increases in OLR were achieved by varying both influent COD concentrations and HRT. From Table 3 it can be seen that with the brewery wastewater the GRABBR achieved

91% COD removal at a maximum OLR of 15 kgCOD/m^3.day. For the yeast enriched brewery wastewater, the GRABBR achieved 75% COD removal for the same OLR of 15 kgCOD/m^3.day. For the former, the removal efficiency fell sharply to 60% when the OLR was raised to 20 kgCOD/m^3.day.

Table 2. Types and composition brewery wastewaters used in the study

Parameter	*Concentration (mg/l)*[a]	
	Brewery effluent	*Yeast-enriched wastewater*
COD	3000 - 6000	50000-110000
Suspended solids	50 - 1000	2000 -3000
TKN	24 - 200	500-10000
SO_4^{2-}	35	160
pH	5 - 11	8.3

[a] All parameters are in mg/l except pH

Table 3. COD removal efficiencies under different loading conditions

Yeast-enriched brewery wastewater		*Brewery wastewater (Average values)*	
OLR (kg COD/ m^3.day)	*COD removal (%)*	*OLR (kg COD/ m^3.day)*	*COD removal (%)*
3	88	1	97
5	91	2.5	93
10	90	5	96
15	75	10	90
20	60	15	91

Figure 2 demonstrates some of the benefits of GRABBR – plug flow and phase separation. The stability of the system was enhanced by the fact that as the OLR was increased; downstream compartments of the reactor were put to more effective use and vice versa. Thus, the GRABBR is capable of accommodating a wide range of wastewater production rates (and thus wide variation of OLRs) without incurring increased operational difficulties and costs. Gas production rates in both studies were similar, ranging from 0.3-0.38 m^{3}CH$_4$/COD$_{removed}$.

Conclusions

This study has shown that distillery and brewery wastes are amenable to anaerobic digestion. The benefits of GRABBR have also been demonstrated by the study. At relatively low OLR, GRABBR operates as one completely mixed unit utilising only the inlet compartment of the system. More compartments within the system contribute to treatment as OLR is increased. At relatively high OLR, stability of the system is ensured by the self-creation of different phases within the reactor, with mainly acid production in the inlet compartments and methane production in the downstream compartments. The reactor is thus capable of accommodating effluents with variable production rates and characteristics.

The study also showed that the GRABBR can treat yeast-enriched wastewater. The

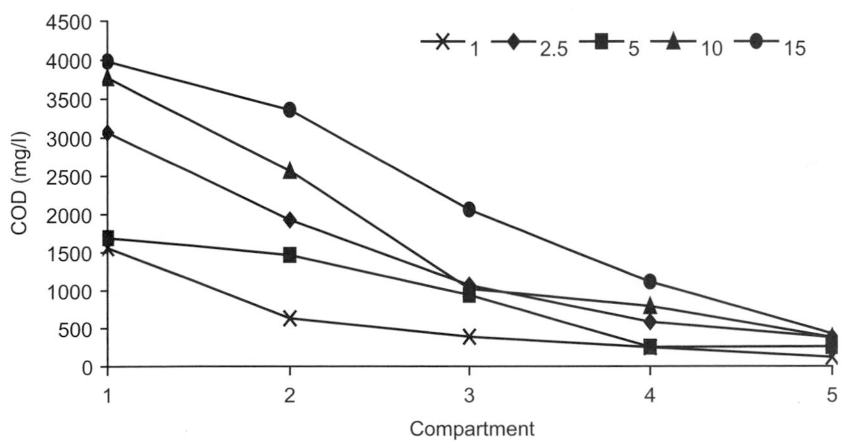

Figure 2. COD profile with the GRABBR when treating brewery wastewater

compartmentalised nature of the system enables sulphate in the yeast to be reduced to sulphide at the inlet compartments in order to reduce sulphide inhibition of methane-producing bacteria inhabiting at the outlet compartments.

Acknowledgements

The authors would like to thank the University of Abertay Dundee (UAD) for supporting this study.

References

Akunna, J. C. and Clark M. (2000) Performance of a granular-bed anaerobic baffled reactor (GRABBR) treating whisky distillery wastewater. *Bioresour. Technol.* **74**, 257-261.

Anderson, G. K., Kasapgil, B. and Ince, O. (1994) Microbiological study of two-stage anaerobic digestion during start-up. *Water Res.* **28**, 2383-2392.

Baloch, M. I. and Akunna, J. C. (2003a) Granular Bed Baffled Reactor (Grabbr): Solution to a Two-Phase Anaerobic Digestion system. *J. Environ. Eng.* ASCE, November 2003, 1015-1021.

Baloch, M. I and Akunna, J. C. (2003b) Effect of Rapid Hydraulic Shock Loads on the performance of Granular Bed Baffled Reactor. *Environ. Technol.* **24**, 361-368.

Baloch, M. I., Akunna, J. C. and Collier, P. J. (2006) The performance of a phase separated granular bed baffled reactor treating brewery wastewater. *Bioresour. Technol.* **98**, 1849-1855.

Barber, W. P. and Stuckey, D. C. (1999) The use of anaerobic baffled reactor for wastewater treatment: a review. *Water Res.* **33**, 1559-1578.

Pohland, F. G. and Ghosh, S. (1971) Developments in anaerobic treatment processes. *Biotechnol. Bioeng.* Symp., **2**, 85-106.

Chapter 17

Anaerobic treatment and biogas production from stillage at a bourbon whisky distillery: a full scale project profile of a sustainable alternative for stillage management

Robert Hickey[1] and Kevin Smith[2]
[1]*Ecovation, Inc., 50 Square Drive, Suite 200, Rochester, New York 14564, USA*
[2]*Maker's Mark Distillery, 3350 Burks Spring Road, Loretto, Kentucky 40037, USA*

Introduction and background

Production of ethanol and alcohol spirits from grain results in the production of co-products comprised of spent grains and dead yeast cells. Traditionally, these are collectively referred to as "thick slop", whole stillage or spent wash and are commonly used as animal feed supplements directly as slop, concentrated to what is referred to as wet cake or Distillers Wet Grains (DWG) or dried to produce Distillers' Dried Grains with Solubles (DDGS). Of these, only DDGS can be stored and shipped reasonable distances; the others need to be used locally. DDGS is produced by using a centrifuge to separate and partially dewater the spent grains to a cake solids concentration of ~32% solids. The remaining water phase (referred to as solubles) is sent to an evaporator and concentrated to a syrup of between 25-35 % solids. This is then added to the centrifuged grains. This material is either sold as DWG or dried to produce DDGS (90% solids content).

The production of DDGS is a capital intensive process, has a high energy demand and represents a significant cost center. A traditional dry house process for managing whole stillage can represent 30% of the energy demands of a typical bourbon distillery. In addition, the evaporation and drying steps are large gas emissions points in ethanol and spirits facilities.

Makers Mark is recognized by the Guinness Book of World Records as the world's oldest operating bourbon distillery. The distillery was named a United States National Historic Landmark in 1980. The site consists of 620 acres, most of which is treated like a nature preserve. The distillery has a longstanding tradition of environmental stewardship. The continuous environmental goals can be broadly described as:

- Water conservation;
- Energy conservation;
- Waste minimization (recycling and reuse); and
- Air emissions reduction.

Because the distillery is located in a rural, agricultural area of Kentucky, historically, Makers Mark was able to manage their whole stillage by giving it away as slop to local farmers. As production in the distillery has increased, this became a bottleneck. If the local farmers did not take the stillage, production would have to be curtailed. With a planned additional increase in production capacity of 50%, Makers Mark decided to investigate alternatives for managing their spent grains that would require less energy, reduce emissions and result in production of co-products with a value greater than the cost of co-products management.

Alternatives that were considered for management of the stillage included:

- Anaerobic digestion of whole stillage;
- Capture of the spent grains for use as animal feed using a novel approach coupled with high-rate anaerobic digestion of the filtrate stream;
- Truck to another facility with excess dry house capacity; and
- Traditional dry house approach to produce DDGS.

In their effort to incorporate a sustainable alternative for managing the spent grains (whole stillage) at their expanding bourbon distillery and to reduce operating costs, Makers Mark decided to investigate the approaches that offered the potential for energy production and minimizing the carbon footprint of the facility via a series of field pilot tests before deciding on what they would install.

Presented in this paper is a summary of the results of the treatability testing, a description of the alternate stillage management approach selected and installed and an update on the current status of the system.

Summary of preliminary testing conducted

Anaerobic digestion of whole stillage (and thin stillage)

Maker's Mark conducted a year long test to evaluate the potential to anaerobically digest the stilllage direct with no pretreatment. This testing was not considered successful because:

- Low total suspended solids (TSS) removal efficiency was achieved;
- High concentrations of suspended solids remained and these could only be used as a nutrient/soil amendment and, therefore, had much lower value than if the solids were captured for use as animal feed; and
- The digestion process demonstrated less than stable operation; high volatile fatty acids (VFA) accumulation occurred regularly.

While not specifically tested at Makers Mark, there has been some lab testing for the treatment of thin stillage (centrate from centrifugation of the whole stillage). Schaefer and Sung of Iowa State examined thermophilic digestion of thin stillage from a fuel ethanol plant as part of a United States Department of Agriculture (USDA) grant. They reported for thermophilic system between a 20 and 30 day hydraulic retention time (HRT) was needed to keep the volatile fatty acids at or below 2000 mg/L. At the 30 day HRT, they were able to achieve 58.2% TSS removal of the 27,700 mg/L in the thin stillage. The removal efficiencies for Chemical Oxygen Demand (COD) and soluble COD (sCOD) were 82% and 96.6%, respectively. This translates to 61% reduction in the particulate COD which agrees well with the TSS removal efficiency observed. This means that greater than 40% of the TSS fed to the anaerobic digester would be in the effluent and require disposal as a nutritional supplement or soil amendment to farm land or be disposed of as excess sludge.

Alternate stillage management approach and testing

The goals of the alternate approach for stillage management were to:

- Capture as much of the suspended solids as possible as modified DWG that could be used as animal feed to generate revenue;
- Produce a filtrate that was low in TSS that was suitable for treatment in a high-rate anaerobic reactor; and
- Capture of the nutritional value of the stillage and not having large quantities of Solids that needed to be disposed of while being able to generate energy in the form of biogas.

To achieve this, Ecovation proposed the following process scheme. The whole or thick stillage could be preconditioned such that a high capture efficiency of the spent grains and yeast bodies (~98%) could be achieved using a screw press. This would yield a filtrate that had low TSS but all of the sCOD which could be readily treated in a high rate anaerobic treatment system for producing biogas. The anaerobic effluent would then be further treated in an anoxic – aerobic activated sludge process to achieve reduction of the Biochemical Oxygen Demand (BOD) and ammonium to meet surface water discharge criteria in the existing permit.

Testing of elements of the proposed treatment scenario was conducted at Maker's Mark and an off-site location using whole stillage samples from the distillery

On-site testing was conducted for use of the Screw Press. Results demonstrated that with pH adjustment and the use of a generally regarded as safe for animal feed (GRAS) polymer; at concentrations of ~ 175 mg/L polymer a cake solids of 37 to 40% TS could be achieved with the high TSS capture efficiency needed.

A two-month test was conducted to determine removal efficiency, gas production and composition and acceptable applied organic loading rates (OLR) of the screw press filtrate using an anaerobic MFT[SM] (Mobilized Film Technology) reactor. The study was conducted at the treatability laboratory of Environ located in Brentwood, TN.

Testing was conducted using a 10 liter working volume bench scale MFT constructed using 4″ diameter clear polyvinyl chloride (PVC) pipe. The unit, schematically shown in Figure 2, was equipped with an influent feed pump, recycle or "pulse" pumps and micronutrient feed pump. As a result of the breakdown of the proteins in the filtrate, sufficient alkalinity is produced to maintain a reactor of pH of between 7.0 and 7.4 without alkali addition.

The system was loaded at an applied OLR of 11.2 to 23.0 kg COD/m^3-d. Results of the laboratory pilot testing demonstrated that soluble COD removal of between 94% and 96% could be consistently achieved. Removal efficiencies for total COD ranged from 88% to >90% depending on the TSS concentration in the feed. Biogas (methane) production was observed to be 99% of the theoretical value based on the total COD removal achieved.

The process selected

The alternative solution proposed by Ecovation was selected as the best option for Makers Mark. This was based on:

- The ability to achieve the highest and best use of the spent grain solids (the spent grains are worth more as a feed source in terms of revenue potential and environmental appropriateness when captured and used as an animal feed supplement); the ~98% capture efficiency of the TSS means very little solids to manage out of the anaerobic system;
- The low energy demand and carbon footprint of processing the co-products; and
- The ability to produce 15-20% of the distillery energy use can be met with the amount of biogas that could be produced.

Makers Mark teamed with Ecovation to design and install this alternate stillage management approach at its distillery.

It should be noted, however, that there was a somewhat higher biogas (methane) yield for the digestion of the whole stillage but this advantage compared to the benefits of the alternative stillage management approach was judged insufficient to justify moving ahead with this option.

Full scale treatment system design

Based on the preliminary testing conducted, and the planned production increase of 50%, the basis of design (Table 1) was developed for the full scale stillage management system.

Table 1. Basis of Design for Stillage Management system at Makers Mark, Loretto, KY

Parameter	*Thick Slop*	*Units*
Current flow	631,400	gallons per week
Future flow	970,200	gallons per week
Total COD	86,000	mg/L
Soluble COD	28,000	mg/L
TSS	38,750	mg/L
Phosphorus – P	472	mg/L
Nitrogen – TKN	3,450	mg/L
Temperature	>200	°F
pH	3.0 – 4.0	s.u.

The potential energy that can be recovered from the high-rate anaerobic treatment system (once the distillery reaches full production capacity) is presented in Table 2.

The overall processing scheme developed is presented in Figure 1 and described in detail in the following section.

Table 2. Summary of the Bioenergy Production at Makers Mark

COD:	34,000 lbs/day
Biogas (methane):	312,000 ft^3/day (172,000 ft^3/day)
Heat value:	100 -165 MMBTU/day
Distillery gas use:	625k-937k ft^3 /day
Natural gas replaced:	15-20%
Value of biogas:	\$1,000-\$1,650 per day

*assumes 90% conversion of COD, 5.61 ft^3 methane/lb/COD & \$10 MMBTU natural gas replacement value, 15 MM ft^3/mo. average natural gas use for distillery, 6-day week operation.

The first step in the process consists of recapturing some of the heat in the stillage to preheat the lake water used in the mashing process. The partially cooled stillage is then pumped back to the existing wastewater treatment site (~ a kilometer away from the distillery) to a mixed equalization (EQ) tank.

From the EQ tank, the stillage is pumped to the treatment building and preconditioned.

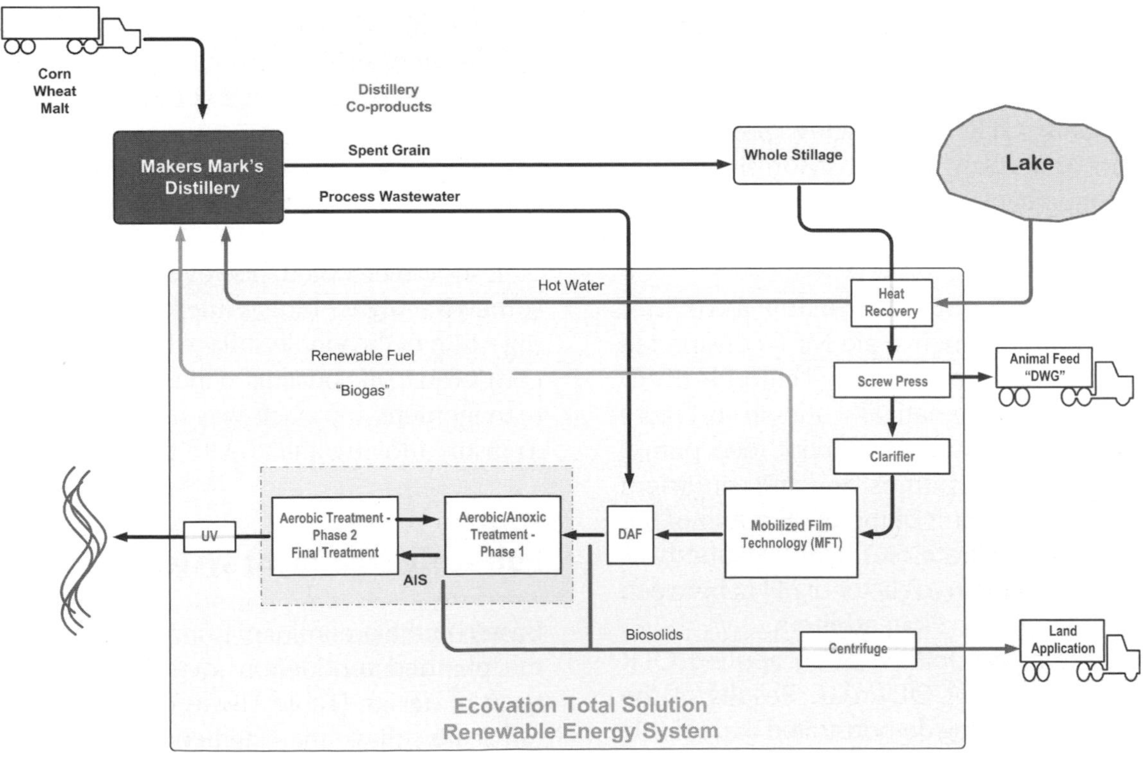

Figure 1.

The pH is adjusted via addition of lime and a GRAS polymer which is added to a flash tank that feeds by gravity into the headboxes of the screw presses. The lime addition serves the dual purpose of pH adjustment and precipitation of phosphorus (which needs to ultimately be removed down to low levels for stream discharge.

The preconditioned stillage is then processed using a screw press for dewatering. This is shown below in Figure 2.

Figure 2.

The combination of preconditioning and screw press allows capture of ~98% of the suspended solids in the stillage as DWG that is ~38 to 40% TS. The screw presses are located on a mezzanine section so that the DWG produced can be conveyed directly into the load-out trucks for delivery, as seen in Figure 3. All the DWG produced is sold to local farmers via a broker who handles all of the logistics of sale and transport.

Figure 3.

If the DWG were to be dried to produce DDGS, approximately a 30% saving in drying costs would be realized due to the lower moisture content of the wet cake from the screw press compared to a centrifuge and the need for an evaporator for thin stillage is eliminated as well.

The DWG material could also be used as fuel for a biomass boiler. The best option depends on the locale and cost of energy and electricity. For Makers Mark, production of modified DWG is the best option.

The filtrate from the screw press is collected and passed through a high-rate lamella plate separator (see Figure 4) to capture any suspended solids that are extruded through the screens during pressing. These settled solids are returned directly to the head box of the screw press for reprocessing.

Figure 4. Clarity in the outlet section of the lamella

The clarified filtrate, which has a TSS of less than 3,000 mg/L and a COD of approximately 28,000 mg/L, is fed to a high rate anaerobic system. In this case Ecovation's MFT process, as seen in Figure 5, was selected as the high rate anaerobic system due to its ability to tolerate high concentrations of suspended solids should there be any operational issues with the pretreatment and screw press system, especially during start-up.

The biogas produced from high-rate anaerobic treatment of the filtrate has relatively low concentrations of H_2S. As a precaution to avoid corrosion due to the use of the biogas, however, the biogas is treated for removal of any H_2S using an iron sponge. The biogas is dried, then compressed and sent back to the distillery where it is utilized in the boilers for steam production.

Figure 5. The MFT with the biogas treatment skid shown in the foreground

The anaerobic effluent is then commingled with the rest of the process wastewaters from the distillery and sent to a Dissolved Air Flotation (DAF) unit for TSS removal. The clarified effluent is then treated in a two stage anoxic – aerobic modified activated sludge treatment unit for removal of residual BOD/COD, ammonium and phosphorus. For the retrofit the Advent Integral System (AIS) process, shown schematically in Figure 6 was used. This is because the AIS could be readily retrofitted into existing two tank sequencing batch reactor (SBR) to provide continuous treatment, see Figure 7, and achieve the relatively stringent effluent requirements presented in Table 3.

Figure 7.

The effluent from this step is disinfected using ultra violet (UV) and discharged to surface water.

System performance during start-up

The entire system commissioned and seeded during April and May 2008. The only full month of operating performance to date is for June. The distillery was shut down for a period around the

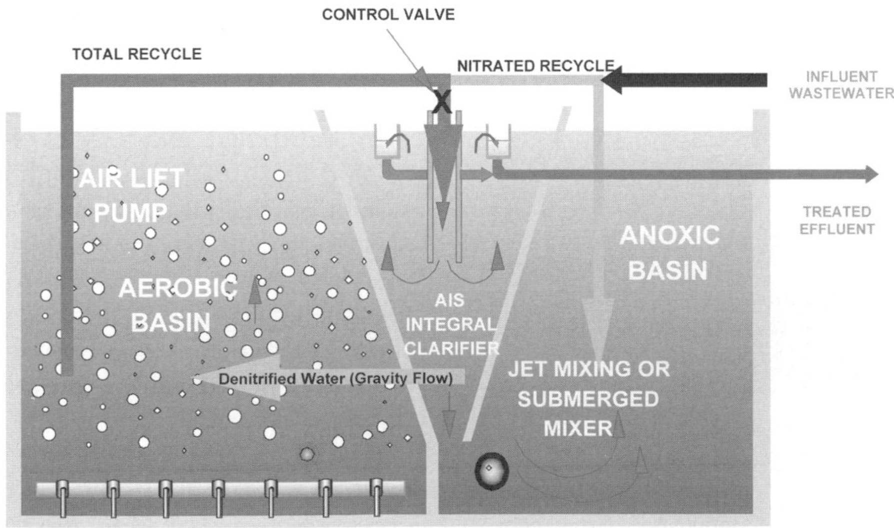

Figure 6. Schematic of the AIS

Table 3. Effluent discharge requirements for receiving stream

Parameter	*Discharge*	*Units*
Temperature	31.7 max	°C
Dissolved Oxygen (DO)	7.0 min	mg/L
pH	6.0 min / 9.0 max	s.u.
TSS	30 avg. / 60 daily max	mg/L
Nitrogen, Ammonia	4.0 mo. avg. / 8.0 daily max	mg/L
Total Phosphorus	5.0 avg.	mg/L
Oil and Grease	10.0 mo. avg. / 15 daily max	mg/L
Chlorine, Total Residual	11.0 mo. avg. / 19.0 daily max	mg/L
BOD-5	15.0 mo. avg. / 30 daily max	mg/L

July 4th holidays, then back in operation until the annual distillery summer shutdown that began the beginning of August. The system has not been loaded to the design levels at this point.

The screw presses have performed as designed consistently producing a modified DWG with a TS content of 38% to 40%. The filtrate quality in terms of TSS after the lamella separator averaged 1,350 mg/L during June, ranging from 440 to 4,190 mg/L; only one value exceed the design value of 3,000 mg/L.

The high-rate anaerobic MFT system is still seedinh but performed well given this fact. Average results for the month of June are presented in Table 4.

During the month the daily flows to the system averaged 58,600 gpd of stillage and 11,400 gpd of process wastewater. The anaerobic system averaged ~ 25 MM BTU/d to the boilers during this period.

Table 4. Summary of results for the high rate anaerobic treatment.

Parameter	*Units*	*Influent*	*Effluent*	*% Removal*
COD	mg/L	14,410	4,980	65.4
sCOD	mg/L	12,820	3,110	75.7
TSS	mg/L	1,350	1,650	

The average final effluent exiting the AIS anoxic-aerobic system during June is provided in Table 5. All the effluent criteria were met even during start-up.

Table 5. Final Effluent Quality during June 2008

COD	56 mg/L
TSS	33 mg/L
NH4-N	0.6 mg/L
PO4-P	3.4 mg/L
D.O.	7.5 mg/L

Conclusions and discussion

Whole stillage can be fractionated into a DWG equivalent material (in terms of protein, fat, and nutritional value) using a screw press when the stillage was preconditioned via pH adjustment and addition of a GRAS polymer at low doses.

The filtrate from the solids handling contains considerable dissolved organic carbon that can be converted to biogas that can be used to offset a portion of the energy demand in the distillery.

The treatment scheme does not require an evaporator, eliminating a major energy user and emissions source from within a distillery or fuel ethanol facility. Overall the proposed scheme provides a much better energy balance and sustainable operation than current practices.

The benefits to Maker's Mark of adopting this alternate stillage management approach include:

- De-bottlenecking constraints placed on production due to relying on farmers to come and take the stillage or slop away;
- Allows a scheduled 50% increase in production at the distillery to proceed;
- Was achieved at much lower capital expense and operating costs than a conventional dry house;
- Renewable energy in the form of biogas is produced ;
- We are able to redeploy existing wastewater treatment assets to achieve a stringent effluent discharge criteria;
- Additional energy savings are achieved by using the heat in the stillage to preheat the lake water used in the mashing process; and
- Overall reduction in the carbon footprint of the facility.

Chapter 18

Effective treatment of distillery wastewater using membrane bio-reactor (MBR) technology

Farid Turan
Process Consultant, Wehrle Environmental, Witney, OX28 1NH

Introduction

The characteristics of wastewater from a whisky distillery requires a very efficient biological treatment that can tolerate dissolved and particulate forms of copper, as well as providing final effluent of a reliable and consistent high quality for direct discharge.

In recent years, the use of membrane bioreactor (MBR) technology for wastewater treatment has grown dramatically. The MBR process offers many advantages and it is widely considered as the best available technology for the food and drinks sector. The MBR process is particularly suited for relatively difficult organic waste streams with a potentially toxic and recalcitrant nature, as is the case with distillery effluents.

An MBR is essentially a hybrid process in which a highly efficient biological process is coupled directly with a membrane separation process (see figure 1).

The MBR process is, in principle, based on the common activated sludge process. In the bioreactor, the activated sludge is intensively aerated while being fed with the wastewater. It is then pumped to the ultrafiltration unit, where the separation of the sludge and treated water takes place. Sludge is then returned back to the bioreactor.

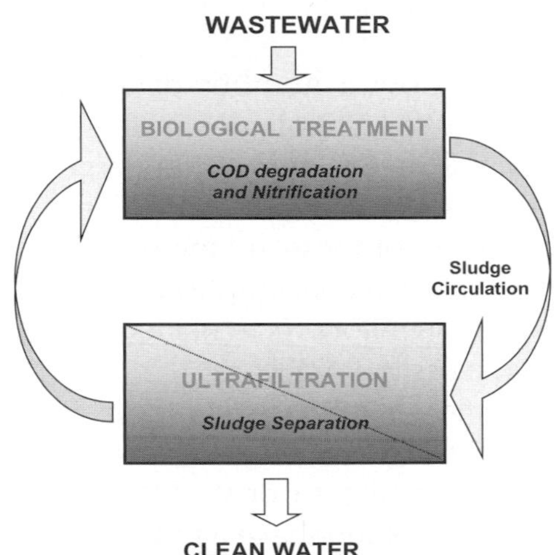

Figure 1. MBR process

Under the aerobic conditions, the dissolved and colloidal organic matter and fine suspended solids are all biodegraded or accumulated by the sludge in the bioreactor. A main feature is that MBRs tend to operate at relatively high sludge concentration. The complete retention of all biomass within the system also guarantees that any valuable and slow growing bacteria are not discharged with the treated wastewater. With very low surplus sludge production, the process operates at longer sludge age. In all, this guarantees a more stable process, but more importantly, the MBR process allows for recalcitrant COD to be also biodegraded, with excellent final water quality.

Crossflow MBR vs. submerged system

MBR systems are generally characterised by two configurations: submerged (immersed or integrated) MBRs and crossflow (external or side stream) MBRs. The main task of the membrane is to effectively separate the treated effluent from the biomass, retaining the suspended solids and bacteria. The various membranes in use today fulfil this requirement well. However, there are distinct differences between these alternative MBR technologies, in particular with regard to energy consumption, maintaining an economic permeate flux and ease of use, i.e. cleaning (see Figure 2).

There are now a number of alternative submerged MBR technologies in the market, driven by the recent growth for large scale municipal wastewater treatment plants. The main advantage of these submerged MBRs is their lower power consumption, due to the absence of a high-flow recirculation pump, as required in crossflow MBRs.

Most submerged MBRs rely on the hydrostatic pressure exerted by the sludge on the membrane or permeate suction to drive filtration. The submerged membranes have a more open pore structure, more akin to microfiltration as opposed to ultrafiltration. While this is acceptable for 'easy' waste streams such as municipal wastewater, the cocktail of chemicals found in industrial waste liquors pose a serious risk of fouling. As such, submerged MBRs are associated with relatively low permeate flux rate, thus requiring much larger membrane area and higher replacement costs. Also, they have operational issues with 'difficult' membrane cleaning, module clogging and ageing.

The crossflow or external MBR is widely considered to be more suitable for industrial wastewater streams often characterised by high temperature, high organic strength, low filterability, extreme pH, and high toxicity as in the case of distillery spent liquors.

Crossflow MBRs have been proven in industrial effluent treatment for over 20 years.

In these applications, the risk of fouling is reduced by the scouring effect created by the high flow velocity of sludge across the membrane surface (see figure 3). If fouling does occur, crossflow tubular modules can be easily cleaned in situ by CIP process.

Perhaps of greatest importance is the issue of membrane flux (permeate flow in relation to membrane area). For submerged MBRs, this is as low as 10-15 l/(m^2h) compared to typical flux of 80-150 l/(m^2h) as applied to crossflow MBR systems.

As such, up to ten times the membrane area is required for the submerged systems.

Not only does this add to the initial capital costs but also higher replacement costs. In contrast, the cost of the membranes and replacement is very low for tubular MBRs.

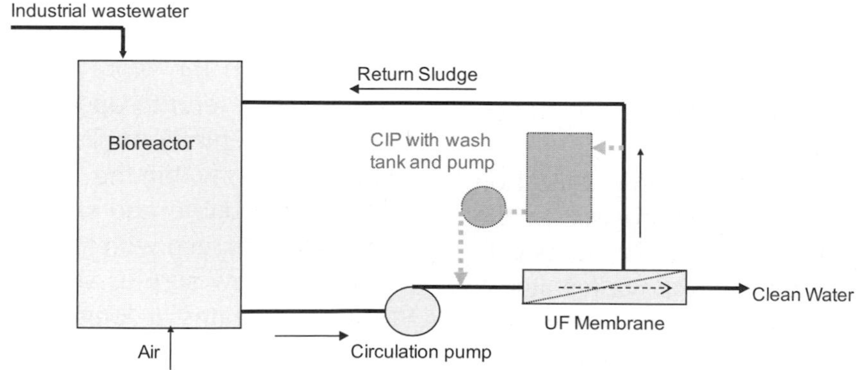

Figure 2. Crossflow MBR Schematic with Cleaning-in-place (CIP)

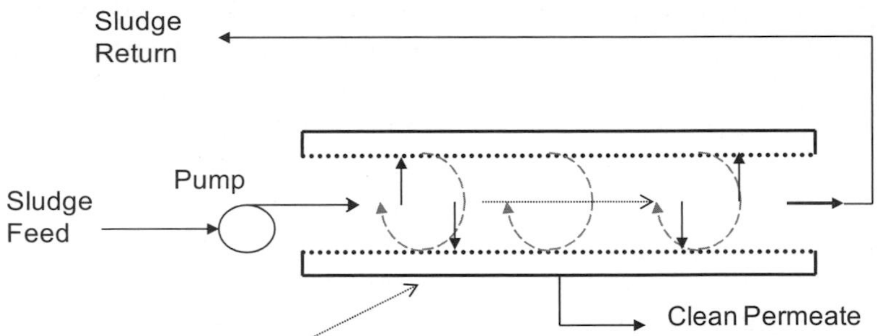

Figure 3. Self-scouring action of crossflow membranes

Membrane lifecycle cost is governed by the initial membrane costs for a new plant, the replacement cost and the membrane life. The latter is affected by the operating conditions of the total process. For example, poor membrane filtration performance leads to a higher chemical cleaning demand and accelerated aging of membranes. For most industrial effluent treatment applications with low-to-medium flow capacity, the economics is in favour of crossflow MBRs despite its higher energy consumption More recently, crossflow MBRs are justified for even much larger flow applications.

The whisky distillery sector is already familiar with crossflow membrane systems for the removal of copper. However, the tubular membranes in MBR applications tend to perform much more efficiently with high permeate flux and infrequent cleaning cycles. This is mostly due to very efficient biology that protects the membranes from fouling.

As such, membrane 'life' is greatly extended with ~5 years being typical for MBRs.

Development of low energy crossflow MBR

With increasing energy costs, the challenge for Wehrle was to develop a low energy crossflow MBR system that could demonstrate starkly reduced energy consumption whilst inheriting the advantages of high flux, minimal fouling and ease of cleaning.

The main consumer of energy in a crossflow UF process is the recirculation pump, to provide the pressure and flow velocity required to drive the filtration process and to minimise fouling. The energy required to run the recirculation pump is the product of the pressure head and the flow rate. The pressure head is proportional to the square of the velocity. This means that a small reduction in velocity will lead to a much larger reduction in the pressure head and consequently energy. To illustrate, a reduction of 50% in flow velocity will lead to an 87.5% reduction in energy consumed. Of course, such an action would result in a reduction in UF flux and an increased risk of fouling.

Wehrle developed the Bio-membrane Low Energy (LE) process, incorporating variable speed drives and back flush capability with new developments in process operation. With these changes, a good flux can be maintained at reduced crossflow velocities. Although increased membrane area is required for processing the total design flow, the cost associated in providing a few additional tubular UF modules is relatively low.

Also, by controlling the speed of the recirculation pump with a variable speed drive, it is possible to vary the flux rate to match the incoming flow. This provides a flexible mode of MBR plant operation with conservation of energy during periods of low flow. The specific energy consumption for the LE process is reduced to 1.3 – 1.5 kWh/m^3.

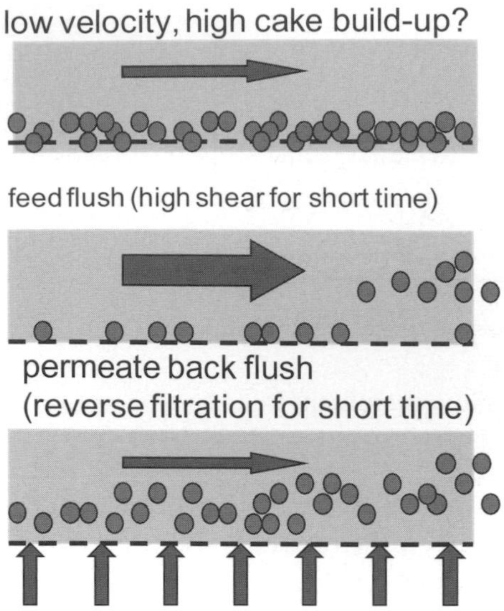

low velocity, high cake build-up?

feed flush (high shear for short time)

permeate back flush
(reverse filtration for short time)

Figure 4. Principle of 'low energy' crossflow MBR

Cross-flow MBR pilot trials at Glenallachie Distillery

Extended on-site pilot trials were performed by Chivas at their Glenallachie Distillery by using the Wehrle packaged MBR pilot plant between mid-April and July of 2007.

The specific aim was to investigate the MBR performance under 'typical' conditions with pre-treated distillery effluents, together with and without prior copper removal and also its response to shock loads, including the spiked addition of 10% pot ale.

The MBR pilot plant was seeded with some activated sludge from a local distillery. The feed to the MBR was screened, balanced and pH corrected. After a period of 2 weeks, the MBR feed was supplied with the blended nutrient (to supplement nitrogen and phosphorus), similar to the existing biological filter system, as required for healthy sludge growth.

The MBR biology adapted very quickly to the distillery influent to provide excellent UF permeate quality, with initial influent COD and copper removal efficiency of +95-99%. The MBR performance was tested in response to variable pH and shock loadings of high influent copper and COD, as well as the unexpected electrical power failure. The UF membrane performance was also tested to determine 'flux' and cleaning regime.

Despite the various shock loads, the MBR plant performance was robust and quickly recovered including after power failure and the addition of 10% by volume of pot ale. A key finding from these pilot trials was that the influent copper could be effectively retained and wasted with the sludge in its non-toxic complexed and particulate form.

The pilot trials demonstrated that crossflow MBR process is very well suited for the treatment of whisky distillery effluent, offering enhanced and reliable performance. The UF membranes flux is expected to be relatively high and require simple cleaning.

The expected treated wastewater quality from the MBR process is shown in Table 1.

Table 1. Expected distillery wastewater quality-post MBR treatment

Main parameters of MBR	*Expected final water quality*	
Final COD	mg/l	<100
Final BOD	mg/l	<10
Total suspended solids, TSS	mg/l	<2
Ammonia	mg/l	<1
Copper	mg/l	<0.25

Following the pilot investigations, Chivas have invested in the full upgrade of their wastewater treatment facilities at Glenallachie based on the crossflow MBR process.

The Wehrle MBR design provides a very compact installation with minimal impact since the main process plant is installed inside an existing building at the distillery.

The project was managed in partnership between Chivas and Wehrle Environmental. The plant has been in successful operation since October 2008 and provides very efficient performance, both in terms of excellent final quality and membrane filtration.

Future perspectives

The distillery sector is challenged for the future to further reduce its environmental impact, which includes reducing waste and energy, recycle raw materials and water.

For high strength organic wastewater from distilleries, the MBR process can also be integrated with anaerobic pre-treatment to provide the optimum plant configuration in terms of energy conservation and very reliable and efficient treatment performance. It is possible to provide a sustainable solution with biogas from the effluent for energy recovery and to discharge back to the environment what is considered 'clean' water.

Future wastewater treatment systems need to provide a compact, flexible, robust, reliable and highly cost-effective treatment, to ensure acceptance by the distilleries. The MBR technology is now available in the form of mostly pre-assembled systems.

The distinct advantages offered by crossflow MBR technology provide the distilleries with a practical and cost-effective solution to treating their problematic spent liquors.

Figure 5. Typical crossflow MBR packaged plant installations

Chapter 19

Process developments for distillery co-products

David Scheiby[a], Dr Heinz Decker[a], George Svonja[b] and Dominique Kühner[b]
[a]*GEA Wiegand GmbH; Einsteinstrasse 9-15, D-76275 Ettlingen, Germany;*
[b]*GEA Barr-Rosin Ltd; 48 Bell Street, Maidenhead, Berkshire, SL6 1BR, United Kingdom*

Abstract

The means of dispensing of co-products has long been an economic and environmental challenge to the distilled spirits and modified starch industries. Cereal based co-products have traditionally been utilised within the agricultural economy, where European and UK animal feed markets currently experience a protein supply deficit that is met by foreign imports.

This paper looks at a new generation of process technologies, where significant improvements have been made over the last decade with thermally integrated and more energy-efficient production methods. Moreover, there has been a shift in the development of higher nutritional-value products as a result of low-temperature processes, improved separation processes and enzymatic conversion of polysaccharides for wider use.

Included within the range of processes, this paper will look at modern developments in mechanical vapour recompression (MVR) evaporators, superheated steam atmosphere dryers and the recovery of latent heat from these systems as useful heating sources within a distillery complex. These technologies have far-reaching application within the context of energy reduction, environmental emissions and discharge reduction, and within emerging biomass-to-energy systems.

Introduction

This paper looks at process strategies for co-products within whisky and grain distilling against a backdrop of experience gained within similar, cereal processing industries, namely: distilled spirits, the modified starch and sweetener, and bioethanol industries. The starch and biofuels industries have, in recent years, stimulated new processing developments, whilst evidence exists to show that market demand for co-product nutrition is viable, buoyant, and itself is a driver for innovation and product development.

In setting the framework, it is necessary to be reminded of key issues faced by the distiller when handling co-products, namely:

- Significant volumes of organically loaded water as a result of fermentation and distillation operations
- Shelf life of spent grain, its variable nutritional quality and uptake
- Environmental emissions
- Costs of energy, and
- Market demand for co-products

No doubt the whisky industry has traditionally been linked to the rural economy of Scotland, where one imagines an era farmers produced barley while supplementing animal rations through the availability of a ready supply of distillery draff.

From a processing viewpoint this evolved in the decades of the 1960s and 70s, when our predecessors from Wiegand, Barr & Murphy and Rosin Engineering, were innovators of what could now be considered a conventional approach to co-product processing:

- Pot ale or spent wash – which although dilute, contains the major proportion of the co-product dry matter – was concentrated to produce syrup. A ten- to twelve-fold increase in concentration results in a volume reduction for transportation of pot ale/spent wash, whilst increasing its nutritional content and value as a saleable product.
- Dryers were introduced to produce "dark grains" from draff, extending the shelf-life and transportability of spent grain.
- Evaporation and drying operations were supplemented by effluent treatment plants, in order that waste water could be directed back into water courses in an environmentally acceptable way.

All the while, spreading pot ale to land and the discharge of effluent to sea continues as practice to the present day, within licensed consents and seasonal limitations imposed during winter.

Whilst the vast majority of plant installations in Scotland still date back to the 1980's, we hope this discussion will be enlightening as to how industry has progressed since then, while looking at new opportunities and process efficiencies. In particular:

- What "best practice" and benchmarking can be learned from industries with similar co-products?
- Is there a sustainable market for co-product?
- Ask whether we are extracting true co-product values, and look at
- Opportunities for product extension and new markets.

Then, we will look at engineering advances made in recent years, namely:

- Energy and process efficiency;
- Modern evaporator performance;
- Introduce Superheated Steam atmosphere Dryers (SSD), and at
- Opportunities for energy coupling between these operations for step efficiency gains in systems that are known and proven for their availability and reliability, year-on-year.

Is there a co-product market?

Recent data from the UN's Food and Agricultural Organisation (FAO) and International Feed Industry Federation reflect accelerating growth in meat demand as a result of population growth, economic development and increased urbanization. This has resulted in changing diets and increased meat consumption patterns globally.

In the UK, this translates to a 20 million tonne/year market for animal feed, dominated by 3 key raw materials (Figure 1):

- Feed cereals, mostly wheat (47%);
- Protein cakes and meals, most of which is imported soya (27%);
- Food and Drink industry co-products, including distillers dark grains solids (DDGS) (13%).

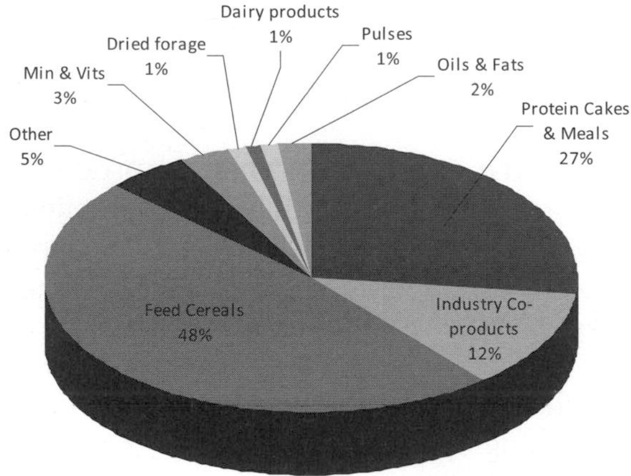

Figure 1. UK animal feed market (20 mil tonnes). Source: FEFAC 2008 / AB Agri

The most obvious demand on agricultural commodities has been from the rapid increase for cereals by the biofuels industry, and while there has been recent attention on the "food-for-fuel" debate, it is worthy to note that ethanol production simply utilises the starch component of the cereal, rendering additional protein, fibre, fats and nutrients available in the form of Dried Distiller's Grains with Solubles (DDGS). With new generation feeds becoming available, it seems likely that the Co-product segment of this chart will therefore increase, displacing the Feed cereals segment of the market where grain prices are increasingly being driven by biofuels demand.

Secondly, the growth in meat consumption drives protein imports, where the compound feed industry has seen a doubling of imported protein into Europe over the past decade. At current levels, European self-sufficiency in protein feedstuffs is estimated at below 30 %, with most protein coming into the EU as imported soya meal (Figures 2 and 3).

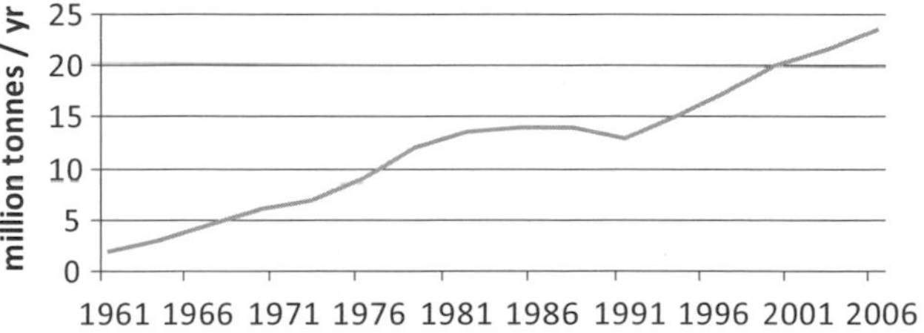

Figure 2. EU feed protein imports.
Source: AB Agri.

Are we extracting true co-product values?

Against this background, opportunities exist for feed market innovations and product extensions. For example, by moving up the value-chain from "blends" to "supplements", products of higher value, namely prebiotic and digestive aids, would increasingly be marketed. Other innovations include the addition of enzymes, such as phytase, to feedstock rations so increasing the digestibility of non-starch polysaccharides (NSP) for non-ruminant livestock.

Improved processing methods are also being practised, where for some time evaporators have been designed to operate at lower temperatures. This, we expect reduces the effects of high temperature on protein denaturing by Maillard reactions, and so improving amino acid availability and nutritional retention. Innovative marketing has resulted in the development of premium DDGS brands in the United States. Surely the time has come for us to recognise the value in prime Scottish beef, raised on a superior, home-grown, traceable, non-GMO - premium quality DDGS?

Of further significance, the fractionation of co-product streams is opening up new possibilities in animal nutrition.

The two major components of a cereal co-product can largely be split between protein and fibre (Figure 4). In terms of market values, these products can be fractionated in such a way so as to provide two, almost mutually exclusive products: One protein enriched stream, without

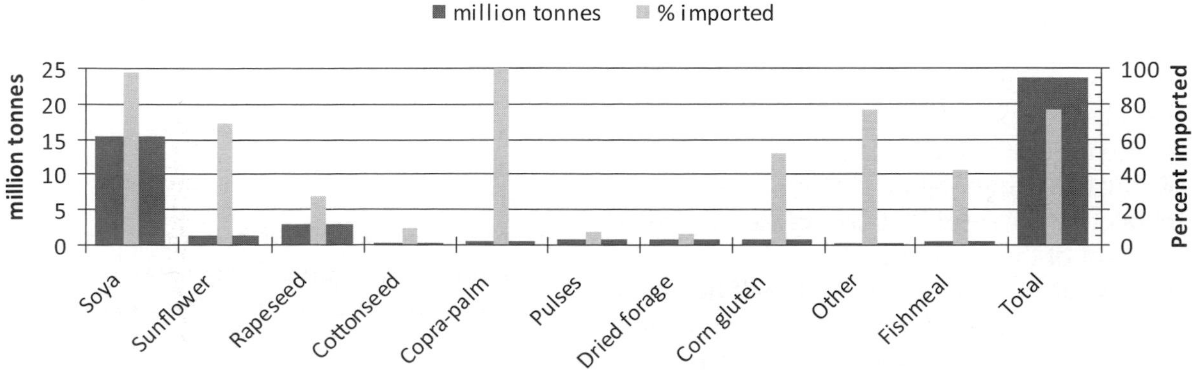

Figure 3. EU feed protein consumption and percentage of imports (2005-06). Source: after FEFAC 2008.

fibre, for use in monogastric nutrition – pigs, poultry, even fish and aquaculture; while the fibre rich stream, with a reduced amount of protein, still meets the nutritional requirements of ruminants for dairy and beef production.

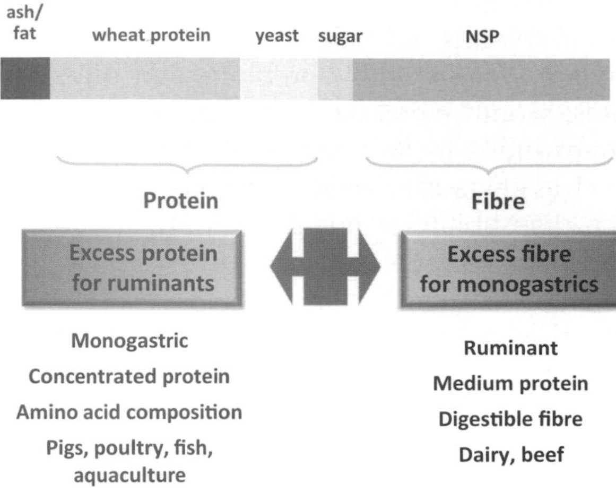

Figure 4. Co-product fractionation increases value and usefulness in new, as yet untapped applications.

Biomass energy

This discussion would be incomplete if it were not to discuss opportunities for converting biomass into energy. There is, after all, a readily available supply of homogenous product, while subsidies and grants are available in the form of renewable obligation credits amongst others.

There are however a number of pertinent issues, which include:

- The limited net heat gain of combusting/incinerating wet material;
- Significant volumes of organically loaded water still remain, often with associated sludge residues, and problematic against increasingly prevalent European landfill and effluent discharge directives;
- Relatively high NOx emissions can be expected as a result of burning the nitrogen content of the proteins;
- In view of an ongoing "food-for-fuel" debate, is the incineration of protein likely to remain an acceptable and sustainable practice?
- Economic forces will play a role. In economic speak, "Substitutes" and "Complements" will compete on the basis of supply and demand. Having created a market opportunity (or user) for biomass, the market could be expected to respond with substitutes such as crop residues – wheat straw or corn stover, which could be harvested with the cereals – or even by providing renewable energy crops such as coppice willow.

When combusting moist biomass, it can be argued from a thermal efficiency and greenhouse gas viewpoint, that co-product should be dried in order to realise the "renewable" energy portion and yield real savings in CO_2 emissions. Without drying, significant amounts of energy are lost due to the latent heat required in order to drive off moisture during (or prior to) combustion. Using new generation drying and combustion technology, the latent heat transferred to vaporise the water component of the co-product stream would be recovered as process heat, e.g. to re-use within another part of the process. Flexible solid-fuel systems may therefore have a role for both the drying and the combustion of DDGS. This gives the option of being able to switch between other fuels and DDGS, whereby one would harness seasonal supply and demand variations between protein and energy crops as a hedge. We will again return to this topic at a later stage of this discussion.

Engineering advances in evaporation and drying

We will now look at a range of process technologies that are available and discuss advances made in recent years, starting with evaporator heating:

- Mechanical vapour recompression (MVR) plants provide an efficient means of recycling the latent heat required to vaporise water, with a notable change having occurred over the past decade or so: Heavy duty fans have replaced turbo-blowers and turbo-compressors, providing a slower running, simpler and more robust means of running MVR evaporators.

- "Waste heat" evaporators are increasingly being coupled to dryer exhaust vapour lines, to recover the latent heat contained in the humid exhaust streams.
- Hot process water streams are being harnessed, with waste heat recovery, for example, from spirit condensers.
- Hybridised systems, utilizing combinations of the abovementioned heating sources.

Modern evaporator performance

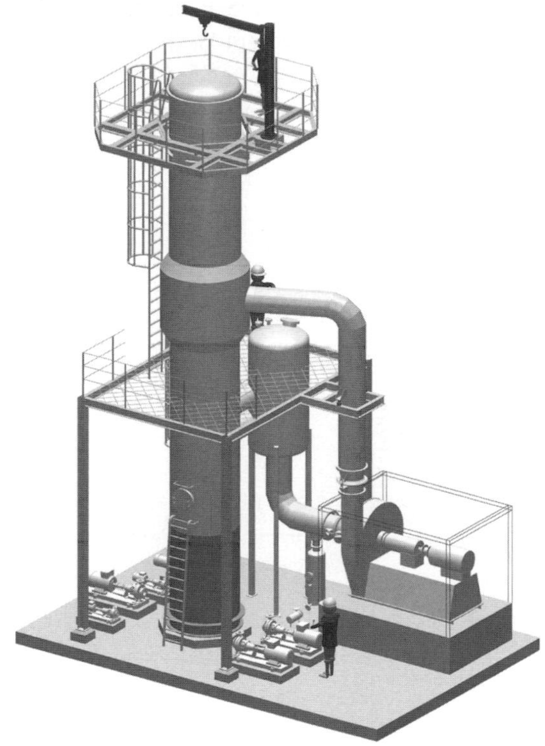

Figure 5. Schematic MVR heated falling film evaporator in single body, low temperature, multi-pass configuration.

Figure 5 schematically shows a falling film evaporator heated by a fan operated MVR. During normal production, vapour is separated from the boiling product before being recompressed and recycled through a fan. The fan provides an adiabatic temperature boost to the vapour, providing the necessary temperature differential to keep heating the evaporator and thus keep the system working. The mechanical input, or work, is a mere fraction of the latent heat being circulated within the system. This unit is representative of GEA Wiegand's MVR evaporators as used within the whisky industry – where we currently have units being installed in Speyside, the Republic of Ireland and in Northern Ireland. These units feature:

- High-efficiency, low compression Fan – MVR
- Low temperature, vacuum evaporation
- Single body, with robust tubular construction and multiple product passes
- Low specific energy consumption, typically in the range of 12 – 18 kWh/tonne evaporation
- Zero steam consumption, with no visible plume or steam venting, and little to no cooling water requirements.

Modern vapour recompressors use fans, slower running, simpler and more robust machines compared to the earlier generation of high speed turbo-blowers. Simplicity of design and construction extends to the ease of turndown and process control. Standard variable frequency drives are used, giving excellent and stable turndown capability in the range of 35 – 100 % of nominal capacity. Specific power consumption would be in the 12 – 18 kWh/tonne range at full production, less in a turndown state.

Another advance has been in the lowering of operating temperatures, where the units operate under vacuum with boiling temperatures of below 80 °C. This benefits the product, giving it a naturally more golden colour, reducing the Maillard effect on the proteins and resulting in what is widely recognised as a superior product.

Superheated steam dryer technology

Another process step change has been in the adaption of DDGS dryer technology from convective airstream drying, to drying in a superheated steam atmosphere. The goal here is to maintain the quality of the energy supplied to the dryer, keeping in mind potential for the reuse of this energy.

Dryers have generally been regarded as net energy users, emitting water vapour – and hence energy – to the atmosphere. Partial Gas Recycle Dryers (Figure 6) used direct fired, hot combustion gas as the drying medium, with vapour recycling to within stoichiometric limits on the combustion side. As a practical limitation, this restricts exhaust vapour recycling to around 70 %.

Modern steam atmosphere dryers (Figure 7) recognise that evaporative drying is a consequence of heat and mass transfer. Therefore, it is possible to evaporate moisture in a superheated steam atmosphere.

This steam can then be recycled, with the exhaust made available as a viable heat source. Energy is provided through a heat exchanger, which provides the necessary heat to the steam drying circuit. Steam generated within the dryer circuit is consequently discharged as process heat. In this example, relevant to grain distilling, there is sufficient energy available to drive a multiple-effect, pressure cascade evaporator, which again allows the latent energy to be reused several times over. Preserving quality of the energy is done primarily by reducing the amount of ingress air within the steam vapour atmosphere. This has a direct consequence on the dew-point temperature, where the higher the humidity, the higher the wet-bulb temperature.

Partial Gas Recycle (PGR) dryers operate with a wet-bulb at the exhaust of typically 82 to 84 °C, whereas a Superheated Steam Dryer (SSD) operates at wet-bulb temperatures of between 94 °C and 98 °C.

Tables 1 and 2 compare the energy recovery from PGR and SSD dryers for a 35 tonne per hour

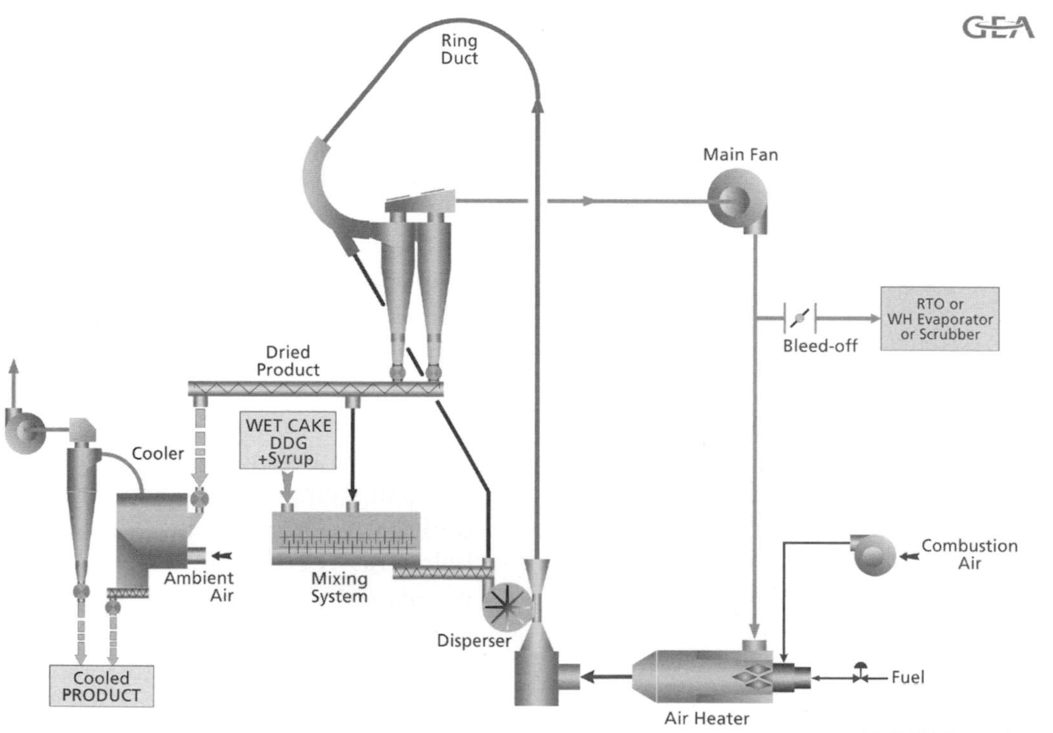

Figure 6. Process flow diagram for a direct fired, airstream type PGR dryer.

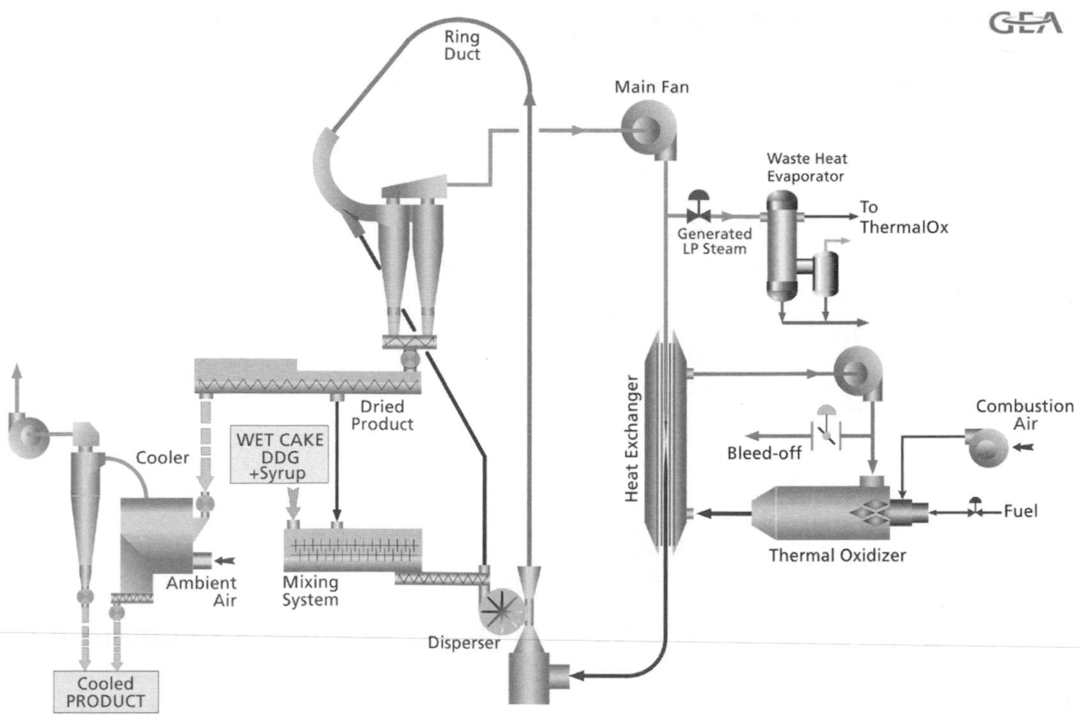

Figure 7. Process flow diagram for a superheated steam type SSD dryer. The drying circuit is indirectly heated by means of a heat exchanger, enabling the drying circuit to exhaust energy in the form of low pressure steam for use elsewhere in the process.

Table 1. Energy coupling example between a PGR dryer and exhaust heated evaporator

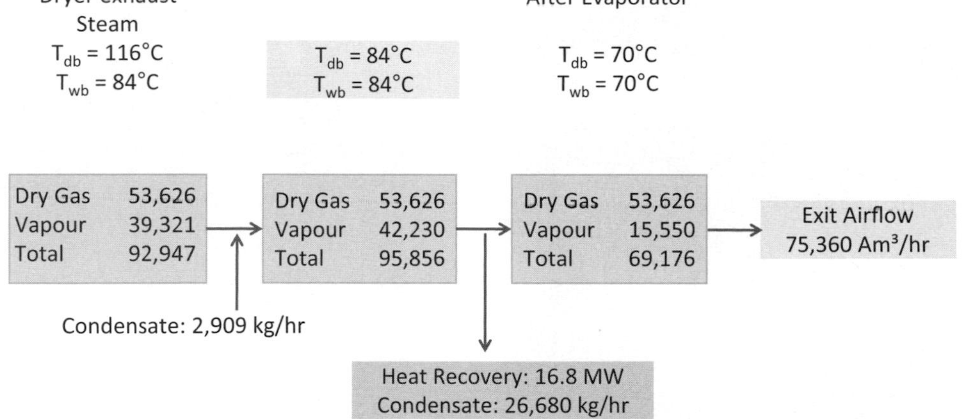

evaporative load. Exhaust temperature (wet bulb) in the PGR is 84 °C versus 98 °C in the case of the SSD unit. In the SSD's case, the result is an energy recovery of 19.8 MW against an input of 26 MW, while the higher steam temperature gives the more useful temperature for further process applications. There is also a sixfold reduction in the exhaust air volume that would require treatment from an emissions viewpoint, while the exhaust vapour plume is significantly reduced with most of the vapour being condensed on the heating side of the evaporator. Additional possibilities are thereby created for the recovery and recycling of water.

Table 2. Energy coupling example between an SSD dryer and exhaust heated evaporator

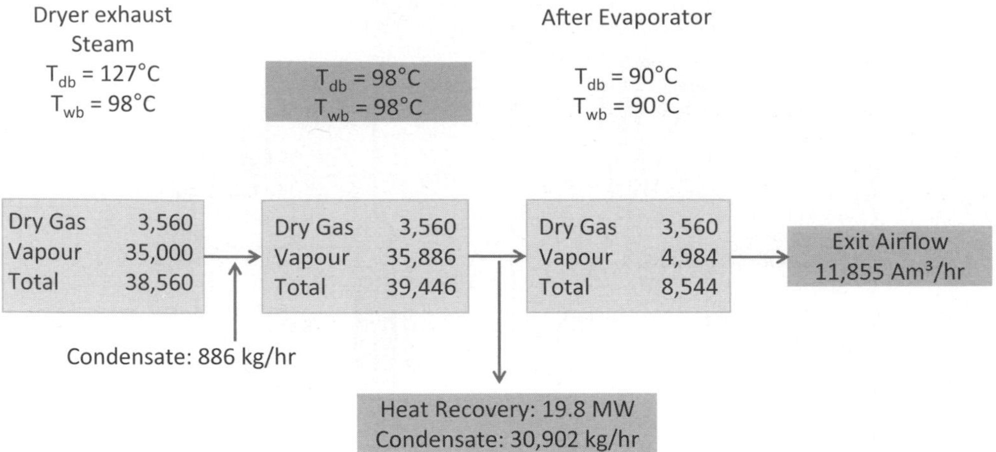

Barr-Rosin produces both Rotary and Ring type SSD dryers (Figures 8a and 8b), heated by solid, liquid or gas fuels. Figure 9 shows a 3-effect evaporator heated by vapour from the dryer unit.

DDGS and Biomass combustion

We return now to look at opportunities presented by DDGS and biomass combustion.

(a)

(b)

Figures 8a and 8b. A Barr-Rosin SSD type Ring Dryer producing DDGS and process heat as exhaust. The unit shown is solid fuel fired, with the heat exchanger passing heat from the combustion chamber to the steam drying circuit, shown on the right.

Figure 9. Example of a thermally coupled ring type dryer, where the dryer exhaust vapour heats a triple effect evaporator. Pictured is the unit during commissioning within the last 18 months, now producing DDGS.

While a new field for this industry, we believe the integration of technologies is necessary in order to realise meaningful greenhouse gas savings.

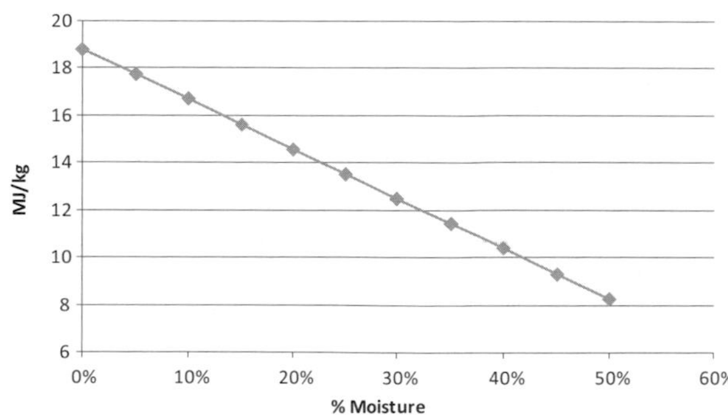

Figure 10. Combustion heat available in wet cereal co-product

The graph in Figure 10 represents the calorific value of a cereal biomass with varying degrees of moisture. Even with mechanical dewatering as much as half of the heat produced in a combustor would be spent in driving the moisture up the exhaust stack, as latent heat, without regaining such energy, and losing the potential carbon savings from burning a renewable fuel. In order to maximise the heat available in the biomass, and hence reduce the amount of CO_2 produced per net unit of heat, the biomass must be as dry as possible, and it must be dried without adding to the thermal load.

As has been demonstrated, modern SSD dryers give the ability to recover significant amounts of the energy put into drying, where effectively the SSD system has become both dryer and steam boiler. This is a key towards an improved carbon footprint and the desired reduction in greenhouse gas emissions where wet fuels are concerned.

Under DDGS firing about one third of the fuel would be used to dry the DDGS and produce steam which is then used to pre-concentrate the wastewater solids.

The concentrate would then be mixed with dewatered solids during drying. The solid fuel combustor can heat both a boiler and the SSD dryer. Under normal operating conditions the SSD dryer alone could supply up to 40 % of the

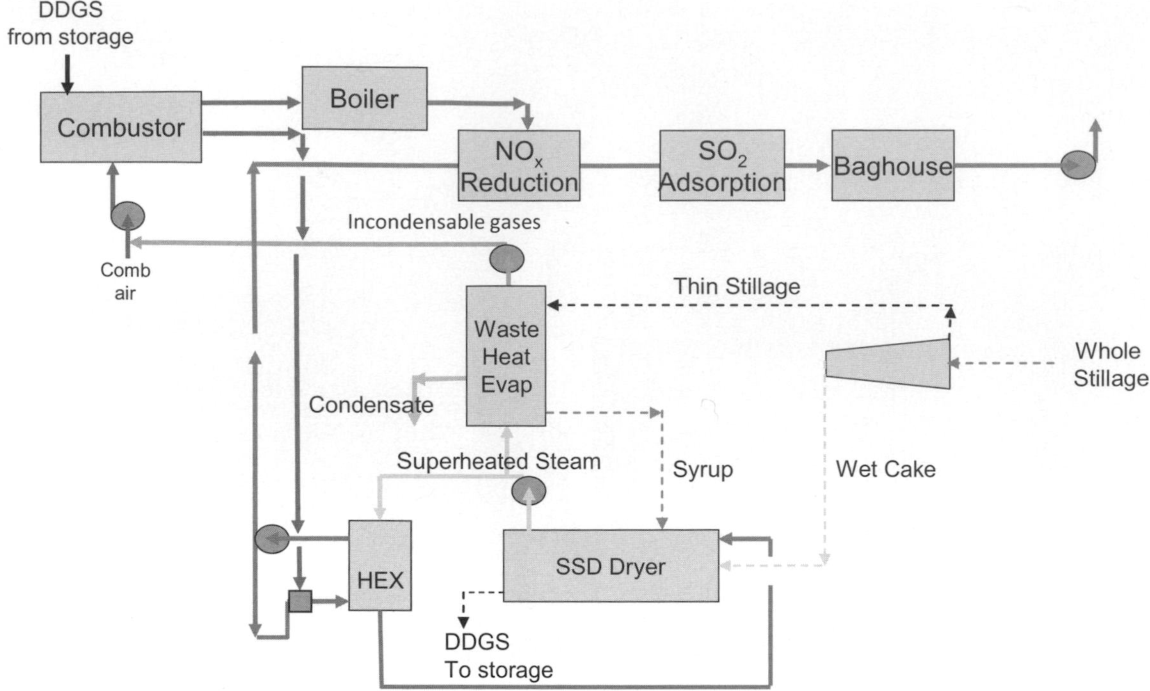

Figure 11. Block diagram of a DDGS/biomass fired SSD dryer and boiler system.

steam demand within a distillery complex while still being able to export some two thirds of the DDGS as product or energy.

This system allows the process operator to minimise risk and maximise flexibility. As the market for DDGS fluctuates, the combustor could be switched between a range of biomass and even fossil fuels.

In summary, drying biomass gives several advantages, including:

- A higher heat output and reduction in greenhouse gas for every kilogram of dry matter burnt
- Latent heat within the dryer is made available as process heat
- Dry fuel is stable and can be stored without deterioration
- Dry fuels permit flexible biomass sources, where substitutes become available
- Exhaust gas volumes are reduced, giving lower gas cleaning needs and reduced process effluent
- Exhaust plume emissions are significantly reduced.

Summary

1. Co-product demand remains buoyant and is underpinned by economic development, growing meat consumption and increased competition from non-food farming in order to meet the global demand from biofuels. More than 70 % of European feed protein is imported, indicating that opportunities exist especially since advances are being made with feed quality improvements. The creation of new fractionated protein/non-starch polysaccharide products from cereals are actively being developed, in order to enter as yet untapped markets such as pig, poultry and fish farming industries.
2. Advances made in the design of Superheated Steam atmosphere Dryers, which themselves produce high grade heat as their co-product, and the ability to thermally couple the dryer with other parts of the process, has resulted in step-change improvements in energy efficiencies and operating cost savings.
3. Evaporators continue to play an essential role by adding value to co-products and

in the treatment of organic solutions and waste water streams where environmental provisions increasingly prohibit discharge to sea or land.

4. Biomass energy has an important role to play, notably in the production of biogas as an emerging renewable energy source. However, challenges remain regarding strategies for the return of liquid and solid or sludge residues back to the environment.
5. The combustion of wet biomass is recognised as having a reduced effect on the overall carbon cycle and in reducing greenhouse gas emissions, where the heat of combustion is used to "incinerate" large volumes of water by driving the vapour up a stack or into a condensing heat sink. However, carbon neutral benefits are more readily achieved by utilising an SSD dryer which has the benefit of removing the moisture in a way that makes the "waste heat" available as process heat. Moreover, there would be sufficient calorific heat available in the dried co-product to use a portion of this to dry the total co-product component. The resulting excess could then be exported as animal feed or utilised as fuel.

With deference to this conference's themes of e*nlightenment, energy* and *environment,* it is appropriate to recognise that these factors have themselves been drivers in the pursuit of innovation and process developments for co-products. It is hoped that insight will have been given into credible solutions that are already available and feasible. With this in mind, we value opportunities to have early discussions with our customers in order to make best use of the challenges and opportunities presented by each situation.

Acknowledgements

The authors would like to thank Dr Peter Williams of AB Agri for his contributions.

References

European Feed Manufacturers' Federation (FEFAC) (2008). *Feed & Food Statistical Yearbook 2007* (Page 50) http://www.fefac.org/file.pdf?FileID = 17088

International Feed Industries Federation (IFIF). *World Feed Overview 2006*. http://www.ifif.org/files/WorldFeedOverview.ppt

Organisation for Economic Co-Operation & Development and the Food & Agriculture Organisation of the United Nations (2008): *OECD-FAO Agricultural Outlook 2008-2017. http://www.agri-outlook.org/dataoecd/54/15/40715381.pdf*

Svonja, George (2007). Drying of grain residues and sludges using biomass fuels. *The Chemical Engineer* **790**: 37-39

Chapter 20

Biological treatment of distillery effluents comprising anaerobic processes

Willie Driessen, Peter Yspeert
Paques B.V., P.O. Box 52, 8560 AB Balk, The Netherlands

Introduction

Biological effluent treatment plants are generally regarded as end-of-pipe solutions for purification of industrial effluents. Within the last 10 years effluent treatment plants, comprising anaerobic processes, have been implemented as a more integral part of the overall industrial process. Anaerobic effluent treatment technologies produce valuable energy (biogas) that can be utilised in steam boilers or CHP units. Anaerobic treatment minimizes production of waste-products (bio-solids), facilitates possible recovery of valuable resources (fertilizers) and minimizes fossil fuel consumption (reduced CO2 emissions). Recycling of biologically treated effluent offers additional benefits such as: (1) savings on effluent discharge surcharges, (2) minimization of fresh water consumption and (3) savings on thermal energy as less (cold) fresh water is required.

In the anaerobic process organic matter expressed as chemical oxygen demand (COD) is converted into biogas (mainly consisting of methane and carbon dioxide). The production of valuable energy rich biogas, the relatively small production of biological excess sludge and the recent development of more compact reactor types, such as the IC reactor, have largely contributed to the successful application of anaerobic treatment within industry (Diressen, 1994; Groot Kormelinck, 2008; Voigtlander *et al.*, 2001; Weyermann *et al.*, 1996).

Management of stillage

Stillage is an aqueous by-product from the alcohol production process. Stillage is also referred to as stillage slops, spent wash, pot ale or vinasse. Due to the high chemical oxygen demand (COD) and solids concentration waste management of stillage is a concern to the distilling industry. Figure 1 presents several alternatives of waste management methods for stillage as applied within the distillery industry.

Alternative1 describes the discharge of untreated stillage slops into the environment or effluent treatment plant. In order to return essential minerals for plant up-take, stillage in some cases is simply returned to the field (e.g. field application of sugar cane vinasse). Anaerobic treatment of the untreated stillage is possible, however requires large digesters and produces large quantities of anaerobic sludge that needs to be disposed off. Large amounts of N and P released from the solids fraction needs to be treated prior discharge into the environment.

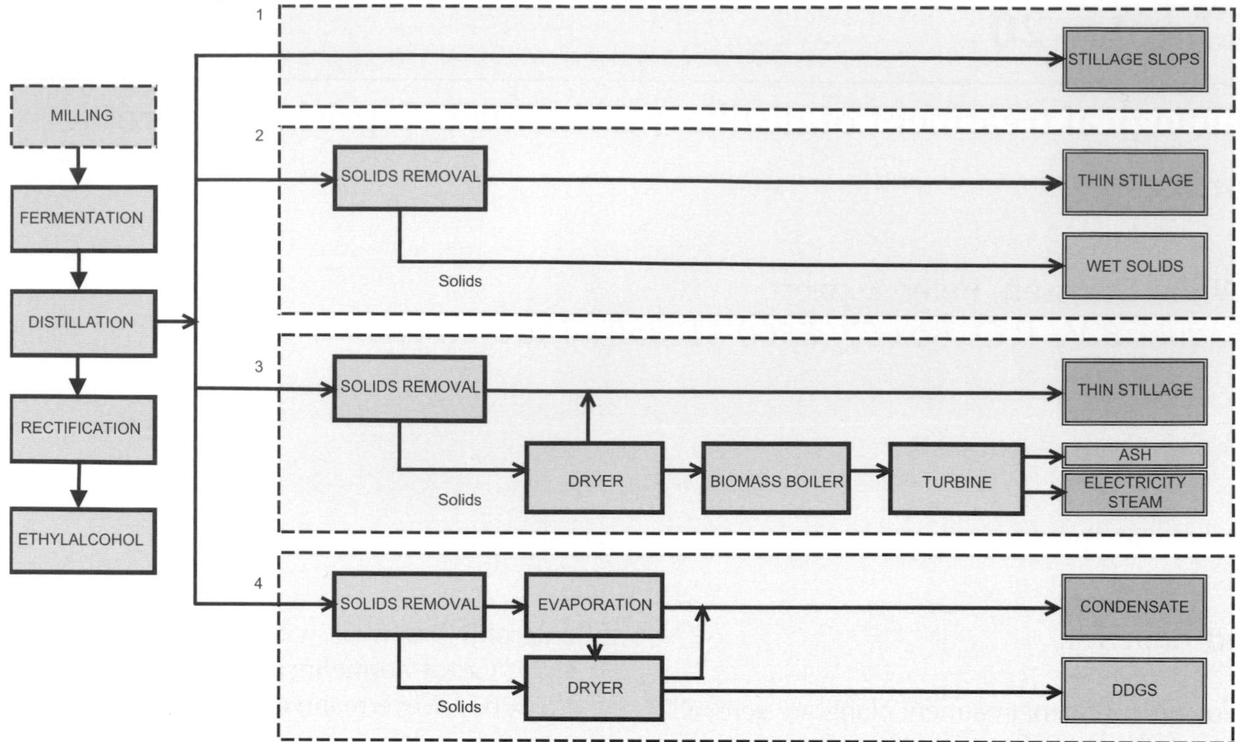

Figure 1. Alternatives of waste management of stillage

Alternative 2 involves solids removal resulting in the production of a high-strength aqueous by-product, the so-called thin-stillage. The thin-stillage is sent for purification to a treatment plant comprising anaerobic digestion. The wet solids are often mixed with other organic solids and sold as animal feed.

Alternative 3 deviates from alternative 2 as the separated solids are dried and burned in a biomass boiler to generate valuable steam. A steam turbine utilizes the steam to produce electricity that can be used in the distillery. The remaining ash is to be disposed off.

Alternative 4 is a widespread applied method involving evaporation of the aqueous fraction producing a relatively low-strength condensate. The separated solids are dried and mixed with thick syrup from the evaporation process. This blended by-product, often referred to as dried distillers grain and solubles (DDGS) is mostly sold as animal feed.

Anaerobic effluent treatment

Distilleries use various kinds of raw material for alcohol production, which results in a wide variety of effluents produced (Driessen *et al*, 1994). Table 1 presents the chemical characteristics of (thin) stillage of distilleries using different feedstock. Stillage is generally characterized by high concentrations of COD, nitrogen (N) and phosphorous (P).

Table 2 presents the composition of some evaporator condensates. Whereas stillage generally contains high concentrations of COD, macro-nutrients (N, P) and salts, condensates are characterized by relatively low COD, and low levels of nutrients and minerals.

Table 1 and table 2 show high anaerobic biodegradability for both stillage as well as evaporator condensates. The more concentrated sugar cane and sugar beet based stillage have a somewhat lower biodegradability of 65-75 % as compared to the grain and fruit based stillage showing an anaerobic biodegradability

Table 1. Characterization and anaerobic biodegradability of (thin) stillage

Parameter	*Unit*	*Sugar cane*		*Sugar beet*	*Grain*[1]	*Fruit*[2]
		Juice	*Vinasse*	*Vinasse*	*Spent wash*[3]	*Spent wash*[3]
TCOD	g/l	15-25	80-140	80-100	20-30	30-45
SCOD	g/l	12-16	-	-	15-25	25-44
BOD	g/l	10-12	25-50	25-50	10-20	10-15
TSS	g/l	2-3	2-15	2-5	2-5	2-5
pH		3-4	3-4	4-5	3-4	3-4
TN	mg/l	200-400	300-1500	300-2000	200-900	150-400
TP	mg/l	50-100	350-550	100-200	100-300	80-250
TCOD removal	%	80	60-75	65-75	80-90	85-90
SCOD removal	%	90	65-75	65-75	85-95	90-95

[1]Wheat, maize rice; [2]Grapes, apples; [3]Composition after solids removal by decanter centrifuges

of around 90 %. Specific methane (CH4) production is around 0.30-0.35 m3 CH4 per kg COD removed.

Table 2. Characterization and anaerobic biodegradability of condensates

Parameter	*Unit*	*Sugar beet*	*Grain*[1]
		Condensate[2]	*Condensate*[2]
TCOD	g/l	2-6	2-8
SCOD	g/l	2-6	2-6
BOD	g/l	1-4	1-4
TSS	g/l	<20	<100
pH		3.5-5.5	3.5-4.5
TN	mg/l	5-20	5-20
TP	mg/l	0-5	0-5
TCOD removal	%	85-95	85-90
SCOD removal	%	85-95	85-95

[1]Wheat, maize, rice
[2]Including lutter/wash water

Figure 2 and 3 present an overall process flow diagram of combined anaerobic/aerobic treatment of stillage. The process comprises solid removal, cooling, equalization/buffering, anaerobic treatment, aerobic treatment including N and P removal and a possible enhanced purification step to allow reuse of the treated water. In case of condensate treatment the flow sheet is simplified by leaving out the solids removal step as well as the removal of nitrogen and phosphorous. By-products of the treatment processes can be valorized by turning organic solids into biofuels and producing steam and/or electricity. Biogas can be utilized in CHP plants and minerals can be converted into fertilizers.

At some distilleries nitrogen and phosphorous are removed by producing magnesium ammonium phosphate (MAP) or so called struvite (Hisano *et al*, 1998). The produced struvite has the potential to be used as a slow-release fertilizer. In order to meet surface body standards extended removal of nitrogen is mostly required. Conventional nitrogen removal through nitrification/denitrification generally requires a bypass of raw effluent to add COD for the denitrification in the aerobic treatment plant. The newly developed anaerobic-ammonia-oxidation process (Anammox®) uses 50 % less aeration as compared to conventional treatment and allows removal of nitrogen without COD addition (Abma *et al.*, 2007). In such cases no bypass is needed allowing valorization of the complete raw effluent.

In certain cases purified effluent is used for in-plant activities by applying membrane filtration technologies. With membrane technology excellent water quality is achievable allowing the purified water even to be used in food industry (Driessen *et al.*, 2001)

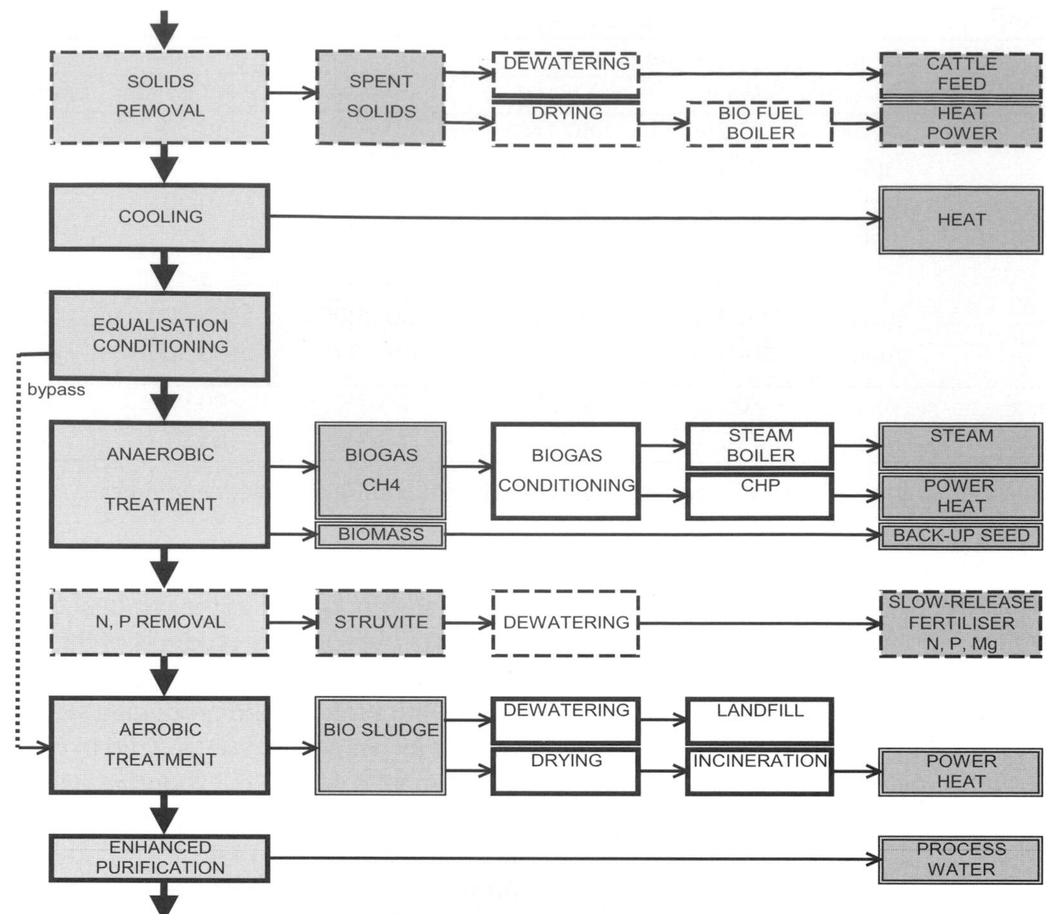

Figure 2. Simplified effluent treatment flow diagram

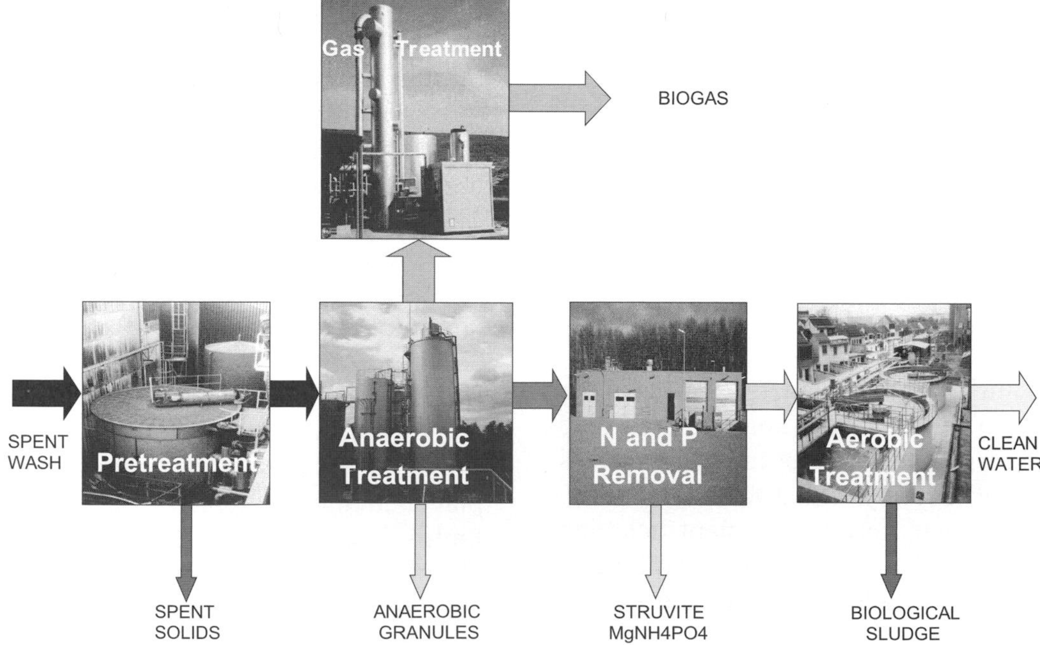

Figure 3. Simplified effluent treatment plant

Conclusions

Effluent treatment comprising anaerobic processes is a well-established sustainable solution for treatment of thin stillage and condensates.

Treatment of stillage and condensate of distilleries can offer valuable by-products as these effluents can be valorized producing biofuels and fertilizers. In such cases the effluent treatment plant becomes a more integrated part of the production process and not just an end-of-pipe solution.

References

Abma, W., Schultz, C.E., Mulder, J.W., van Loosdrecht, M.C.M., van der Star, W.R.L., Strous, M. and Tokutomi, T. (2007) The advance of anammox. *Water 21*, February, pp. 36-37.

Driessen, W.J.B.M. Tielbaard, M.H. and T.L.F.M. Vereijken (1994) Experience on anaerobic treatment of distillery effluent with the UASB process. *Water Science & Technology,* **Vol. 30, No 12**: 193-201.

Driessen, W.J.B.M., Wouters, J.W., Habets, L.H.A. and Buisman, C.J.N. (2001) New trends in anaerobic treatment: Anaerobic treatment as an integral part of industrial processes. *Proceedings of the ANAEROBIE Conference*, Klatovy, Czech Republic, pp. 43-50.

Groot Kormelinck, V. (2008) Chapter 35: Wastewater treatment and energy recovery go hand in hand in the distillery industry. In: *Proceedings of the Worldwide Distilled Spirits Conference* Edited by: Bryce, J.H., Piggot, J.R. and Stewart, G.G. Nottingham University Press, Nottingham, UK. pp. 257-264.

Hisano, T., Fukunaga, Yamashgita, M., Samenejima, Y., Kawasaki, K. Takesako, T. and P. Yspeert. (1998) Methane fermentation of wastewater from a Japanese Shochu distillery using an IC reactor, *Water Quality International*, 7 p.

Voigtländer, A., and N. Bühler (2001) Kalte Vergärung von industriellen Abwässern – Energiebilanzen und Leistungsparameter, **GWA 11**: 763-769 (in German).

Weyermann, H. Käsermann, G. and H. Dörig (1996) Anaerobe Vorbehandlung von Brennereiabwasser Schweizer *Ingenieur und Architekt,* **Nr 7**: 103-106 (In German).

Wolmarans, B. and G.H. de Villiers (2002) Start-up of a UASB effluent treatment plant on distillery wastewater. *Water SA* **Vol. 28 No. 1:** 63-68.

Chapter 21

Distiller's spent grains: a substrate for bioethanol?

Biju K. Yohannan[1], Jane S. White[2], Jason Bennett[1] and Graeme M. Walker[1]
[1]Yeast Research Group, School of Contemporary Science, University of Abertay, Dundee, Scotland, UK; [2]Edinburgh Napier University, Edinburgh, Scotland, UK

Introduction

Fuel ethanol is produced by the fermentation of sugars that are mainly produced from agricultural crops. Brazil and USA are the main bioethanol producers in the world. Maize is the main raw material for bioethanol production in North America while Brazil uses sugar cane (Wheals, Basso, Alves and Amorim, 1999; Bothast and Schlicher, 2005). This is in direct conflict with food production and to satisfy the increasing demand for alternative biofuels, biomass sources other than those used as food need to be utilised. Lignocellulose biomass such as agricultural wastes could be used as a source of fermentable sugars. This includes spent grain (SG) from distilleries and breweries. SG is the solid cereal residues remaining after extraction of wort and in Scotland, this includes spent grains from malted barley used in breweries and malt whisky distilleries and wheat or maize spent grains from grain whisky distilleries. This lignocellulose-rich biomass may provide a source of sugars for fuel ethanol fermentations and may therefore offer potentially valuable alternatives to current uses of SG as animal feed stock (Walker and White, 2007; White, Yohannan and Walker, 2008).

SGs are rich in cellulose and hemicellulose which can be converted to fermentable sugars by dilute acid and enzyme treatments followed by fermentation to produce bioethanol (White *et al*, 2008). The typical carbohydrate composition of brewing and maize distiller's spent grains are compared in Table 1. In brewing, the spent malted barley contains approximately 80% cell wall material and the rest is mainly protein (Jay, Parker, Faulks, Husband, Wilde, Smith, Faulds and Waldron, 2008) and consists of 16.8-21.9% cellulose, 28.4-29.6% hemicellulose and 21.7-23% klason (insoluble) lignin (Carvalheiro, Esteves, Parajó, Pereira and Gírio, 2004a; Carvalheiro, Duarte, Medeiros and Gírio, 2004b; Mussatto and Roberto, 2006). Pre-teatment by physiochemical and/or enzyme hydrolysis are required to convert the cellulose and hemicellulose fractions to fermentable sugars. Hydrolysis of SG mainly involves breakdown of hemicellulose for production of xylo-oligosacchrides by high temperature (up to 190°C) treatment, or to pentose by treating with dilute sulphuric acid at temperatures between 90-130°C or to pentose and hexose sugars by treating with dilute acid at 121°C for 15 min followed by enzyme incubation (Carvalheiro *et al*, 2004a; Carvalheiro, Duarte, Lopes, Parajó, Pereira and Gírio, 2005; Duarte, Carvalheiro, Lopes, Marques, Parajó and Gírio, 2004; Musatto and Roberto, 2005; White *et al*, 2008). The complex structure of lignocellulose inhibits direct hydrolysis with cellulase and hemicellulase enzymes. For complete hydrolysis physical or chemical pretreatments are required for weakening the structure of lignocellulose, followed by enzyme treatment to achieve near-complete hydrolysis (White et al, 2008; Chandra, Bura, Mabee, Berlin, Pan and Saddler, 2007).

Table 1. Carbohydrate content of spent grains

SG source	Component (g/100 g SG)		
	Glucan	Xylan	Arabinan
Brewer's malt[a]	16.8	19.9	8.5
Maize distillery[b]	18.5	14.9	5.5

[a]values for brewer's SG adapted from Mussatto and Roberto (2006).
[b]Values for maize distiller's spent grains from dry grain bioethanol plant adapted from Kim, Mosier, Hendrickson, Ezeji, Blaschek, Dien, Cotta, Dale and Ladisch (2007).

Different pre-treatments methods may be used to extract fermentable sugars from cellulose and hemicellulose with the hydrolysis products fermented together to produce bioethanol. For example, grains were subjected to steam explosion followed by bioethanol production by saccharification of liquefied grains with enzymes with simultaneous yeast fermentation using coimmobilised *S. cerevisiae* and *P. stipitis* to produce an ethanol concentration c. 48 g/L after 4 days fermentation (Shindo and Tachibana, 2006). Also, pre-treatment of brewer's SG with 0.16 N HNO_3 at 121°C for 15 min followed by enzyme incubation resulted in extraction of 40-48 g reducing sugar/100 g SG (White et al, 2008). Subsequent fermentation by *Pichia stipitis* and *Kluyveromyces marxianus* produced 8.3 and 5.9 g/l ethanol, respectively.

In the present study, pre-treatment with dilute nitric acid followed by enzyme hydrolysis was used to extract sugars from SG and to produce a fermentable hydrolysate. Conversion of SG sourced from an ale brewery, malt distillery and grain distillery to ethanol was compared. The effects of detoxification by charcoal filtration or supplementation with either yeast extract or $MgSO_4$ and $ZnSO_4$ on fermentation of hydrolysate were also investigated. Fermentation by two different yeast strains was compared; *Pichia stipitis* and *Kluyveromyces marxianus* which were previously used for fermentation of brewer's spent grain hydrolysate (White et al, 2008).

Materials and methods

Spent grain composition, source and storage

SG were provided by Belhaven brewery (BSG), Dunbar, Scotland (100% malt from ale mash, 80.02% moisture wet grains), Glenkinchie distillery (GSG), Edinburgh, Scotland (100% malt from whisky mash, 76.39% moisture wet grains) and North British Distillery (NBD), Edinburgh, (86.4% Bazilian maize, 13.6 green malt, 62.96% moisture wet grains). SG were dried at 80 °C and milled using a hammer mill fitted with a 5-mm-sized grating (Cutting Mill SM 100, Retsch GmBH, Germany) and used in all the experiments. Dried and milled BSG had 4.2% moisture, GSG had 4% moisture and NBD had 4.4% moisture.

Yeast strains and growth conditions

The yeast strains used in this study were *P. stipitis* NCYC 1540 (National Collection of Yeast Cultures, Norwich, UK) and *K. marxianus* NCYC 1425. *P. stipitis* and *K. marxianus* were maintained on 4% xylose agar slopes consisting of (g/l) yeast extract, 5; bacteriological peptone, 5; technical agar (no 3), 12; adjusted to pH 5.5 (all from Oxoid Ltd, Hampshire, UK). For experimental purposes, yeast inocula were prepared in synthetic media as described by White et al (2008) with xylose as the carbon source. Colonies from agar slopes were transferred to 100 mL synthetic media in 250 mL Erlenmyer flasks and incubated at 30°C on a rotary shaker at 100 r.p.m. (Electron incubator, Infors UK Ltd, Surrey, UK). Cells from 48 h cultures were washed three times with sterile water and used for fermentation of the spent grain hydrolysate. Viability of yeast cells was determined by staining with an equal volume of methylene violet solution (0.01% methylene violet 3RAX, 2% sodium citrate) for 5 min (Smart, Chambers, Lambert, Jenkins and Smart, 1999). Cells were counted with a haemocytometer with dead cells stained violet and live cells unstained.

Preparation of hydrolysate and yeast fermentations

Dried and hammer milled SG (20% w/v) was hydrolysed with 0.16 N HNO_3 by autoclaving at 121°C for 15 minutes (Falcon 30 autoclave, LTE Scientific, Oldham, UK). Following cooling, the pH was adjusted to pH 5-6 by stepwise addition of 10 M NaOH. A cocktail of enzymes (cellulase, ß-glucosidase, hemicellulase and xylanase), available from the Novozymes Biomass sample kit (Novozymes A/S Denmark) was then added according to the dosage used by White *et al* (2008) and incubated for 18 h at 50°C, 150 r.p.m. The hydrolysate was then separated by centrifugation at 4000 r.p.m. for 10 min and analysed for sugar content and pH.

For setting up fermentations, hydrolysate was sterilized by autoclaving and separated into 50 mL aliquots in 250 mL Erlenmyer flasks and inoculated with *P. stipitis* or *K. marxianus* from 48 h cultures to an initial density of 0.5 g/L. Cultures were incubated at 30°C, 100 r.p.m. and were sampled over a period of 2 days. Samples were centrifuged (IEC Centra-4B centrifuge) at 4000 r.p.m. for 10 min and the supernatant retained for pH, sugar and ethanol analysis. The pellets were resuspended in sterile water and the viability and concentration of the cells were determined. All fermentation experiments were performed in triplicate.

Detoxification and supplementation of the BSG and GSG hydrolysate

To optimise fermentation of the BSG and GSG hydrolysates, detoxification or supplementation with nutrients was investigated. For detoxification, the pH of the hydrolysate was increased to pH 5.5 by addition of NaOH and either fermented directly or further treated by (a) filtering through a bed of activated charcoal powder in a sterile syringe. The pH-adjusted hydrolysate was also supplemented with either (b) 0.25% w/v yeast extract or (c) 100 ppm $MgSO_4$ and 1 ppm $ZnSO_4$. The effect of detoxification or supplementation on ethanol production by *P. stipitis* was assessed.

Analysis

The dry weight of the samples was determined by drying triplicate samples for 48 h in an oven at 105°C. All percent concentrations are quoted on a dry weight basis unless stated otherwise. The reducing sugar (RS) concentration in the hydrolysate was determined using the dinitrosalicyclic RS assay (Miller, 1959) and the concentration expressed in terms of glucose equivalents by reference to glucose standards. Ethanol was analysed using a Shimadzu gas chromatography mass spectrometer GCMS-QP2010 fitted with an Agilent HP blood alcohol capillary column (ID: 0.32mm, length 7.5m, film 20 µm. All ethanol samples were analysed with a final concentration of 1% propan-1-ol as internal standard.

Results and discussion

Hydrolysate from malt and maize SG

SG sourced from an ale brewery (BSG), malt distillery (GSG) and grain distillery (NBD) were pretreated with dilute nitric acid followed by enzyme hydrolysis to produce a fermentable hydrolysate. The pH and RS concentration of the hydrolysates are presented in Table 2. It should be noted that the pH of the hydrolysates decreased by approximately 1 pH unit during enzyme hydrolysis. The pH of GSG and BSG were not adjusted prior to fermentation, whereas the reported value for NBD corresponds to the adjusted pH following NaOH addition (Table 2). NBD SG yielded the greatest amount of sugar. In all cases, the RS concentrations were greater than that reported previously for SG from an ale brewery (66.6 g/l RS, pH 5.2) as prepared under similar conditions (White *et al*, 2008). The difference in RS concentration from SG sourced from malt and maize may be due to differences in the hemicellulose composition of the two feedstocks. Incomplete hydrolysis of brewer's SG by acid and enzyme hydrolysis has been demonstrated, with the recalcitrant fraction being tentatively identified as a dilute acid/enzyme resistant xylan fraction (White *et al*, 2008). The structure of hemicellulose in brewer's SG differs from that of maize (Kabel, Carvalheiro, Garrote, Avgerinos, Koukios, Parajó, Gírio, Schols and Voragen, 2002) and as such they will have different susceptibilities to acid/enzyme hydrolysis.

Table 2. Properties of hydrolysates prepared from malt distiller's (GSG), brewer's (BSG) and maize distillery (NBD) SG by acid and enzyme hydrolysis

Source	*Malt distillery (GSG)*	*Brewery (BSG)*	*Grain distillery (NBD)*
pH	4.43	4.53	5.28[a]
Reducing sugar g/l	71.5	78.0	102.2

[a]pH adjusted prior to fermentation

Fermentability of hydrolysates from malt SG

Conversion of SG from malted barley, sourced from a malt whisky distillery (GSG) and from an ale brewery (BSG), to ethanol by acid/enzyme hydrolysis and fermentation by either *K. marxianus* or *P. stipitis* was examined (Fig 1 and Fig 2). Fermentation by *K. marxianus* for 48 h produced 14.8 and 7.5 g/l ethanol from BSG and GSG hydrolysate, respectively corresponding to cell viability of 82 and 50%. The viability of *P. stipitis* was reduced to less than 20% on both hydrolysates with no ethanol detected indicating that pH is a very important factor in determining the fermentation ability of *P. stipitis*.

Fermentation of lignocellulosic hydrolysates may be inhibited by weak acids, furan derivatives and phenolic compounds (Palmqvist and Hahn-Hägerdal, 2000) with furfural inhibiting fermentations at levels above 1g/L (Roberto, Lacis, Barbosa and de Mancilha, 1991). Acetic acid is produced from hemicellulose during the hydrolysis process and *P. stipitis* fermentation is inhibited by acetic acid with the effect being pH-dependent (Van Zyl, Prior and Du Preez, 1991; Narendranath, Thomas and Ingledew, 2001). At pH 4–5, acetic acid is largely undissociated and may pass by diffusion into the cell cytoplasm, where it may dissociate, resulting in a decrease in intracellular pH and cell toxicity. The low initial pH of the hydrolysates (less than pH 4.5) used here may have contributed to acetic acid toxicity. To investigate whether *P. stipitis* fermentation was affected by pH effects, other toxic inhibitors such as furfural in the hydrolysate or lack of nutrients, different hydrolysate treatment conditions were compared (Fig 1): the hydrolysate was adjusted to pH 5.5; (a) filtered through activated charcoal; or (b) supplemented with yeast extract or (c) Mg and Zn prior to fermentation. Increasing the pH to c.a. 5.5 prior to fermentation reduced hydrolysate toxicity with 9.06 and 13.3 g/l ethanol produced from GSG and BSG hydrolysates, respectively. The other detoxification (a) and supplementation methods (b and c) resulted in similar cell viability and ethanol yields. This indicates that the hydrolysate contained sufficient nutritional components to maintain yeast growth and fermentation, but inhibitory components remaining in hydrolysate may have a deleterious impact.

Overall, the ethanol yield from the brewery SG was greater than that from the malt distillery. This may be due to differences in composition of the SGs. The composition of malt SG depends on the operational conditions used during mashing to extract the starch. In our experience, brewer's SG contains more residual starch than distiller's SG. This would alter the glucose level of the SG hydrolysate, resulting in greater ethanol

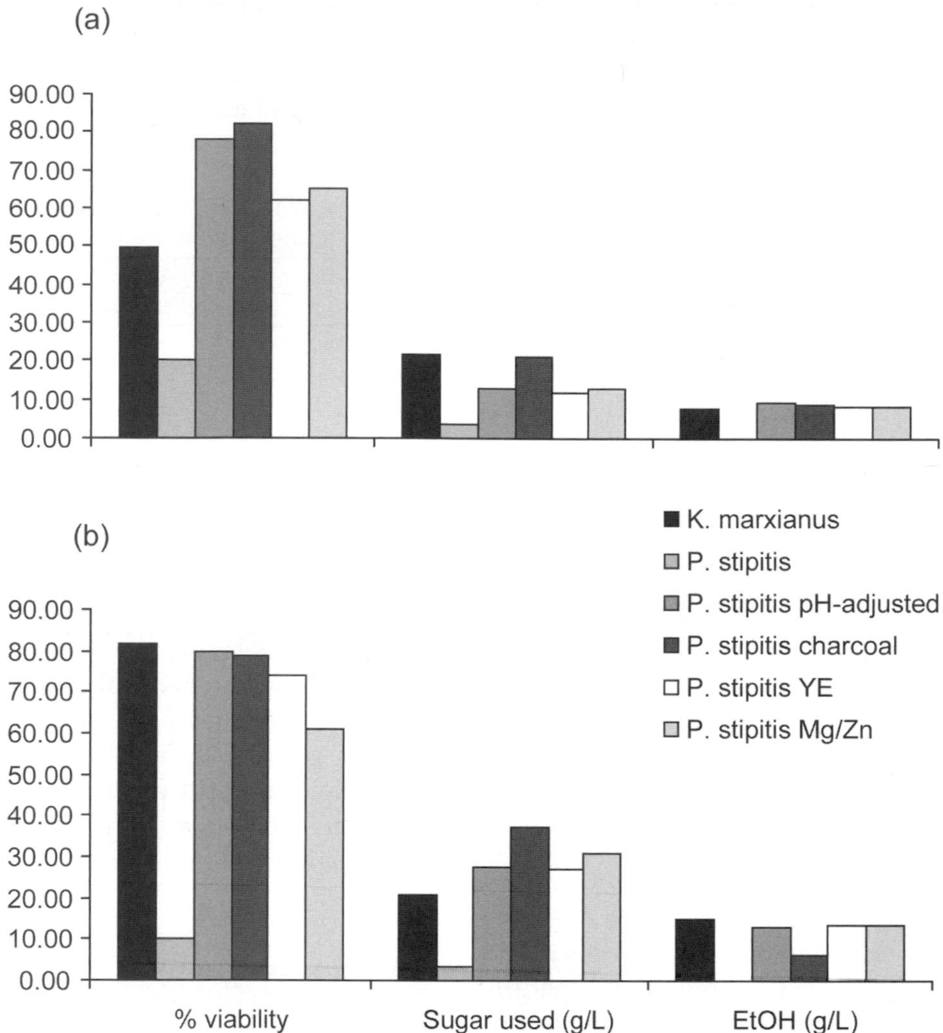

Figure 1. Comparison of yeast cell viability, sugar used and production of ethanol (g/L) of *K. marxianus* and *P. stipitis* on SG hydrolysates sourced from a malt distillery (a) Glenkinchie Spent Grain (GSG) and a brewery (b) Belhaven Spent Grain (BSG) after 48 h fermentation. The effect of hydrolysate detoxification (pH-adjustment and filtering through activated charcoal) and supplementation with either yeast extract (YE) or $MgSO_4/ZnSO_4$ (Mg/Zn) on *P. stipitis* performance is also shown.

concentrations from fermentation of the brewer's SG compared to that from distiller's.

Yield of ethanol from SG

The conversion of SG hydrolysates from brewer's, malt and maize distiller's SG is compared in Table 3. The highest ethanol yields were obtained for the brewing SG, with 7.7 and 6.9 g ethanol/100 g SG produced by *K. marxianus* and *P. stipitis* fermentation, respectively. This may be due to higher residual starch content of the BSG as discussed previously. White *et al.*, (2008) demonstrated that utilisation of xylose in spent grain hydrolysate was poor compared to synthetic media containing xylose. This may be due to the influence of inhibitory compounds (furfural, phenols, acids etc) in hydrolysates.

Interestingly, the ethanol yields are higher for the ale SG than that previously reported for SG sourced from a different ale brewery in Scotland

(White *et al*, 2008). Using the same hydrolysis conditions, fermentation by the same strains of either *K. marxianus* or *P. stipitis* produced 3.0 and 4.2 g ethanol/100 g SG, respectively. The reduced ethanol yields may be due to the lower RS content of the hydrolysate. The hydrolysate had 66.6 g/l RS compared to 78 g/l for the BSG hydrolysate in this study.

Potential to produce bioethanol from Scottish SG

In Scotland there are currently 96 malt and 7 grain whisky distilleries in operation producing approximately 187,000 and 285,000 tonnes of spent grain annually, respectively (Gray, 2008). In addition, in the United Kingdom, *c.* 644,000 tonnes of malt is used by breweries per annum (BBPA, 2006), resulting in approximately 211,000 tonnes of SG being generated annually (White *et* al, 2008). SG is traditionally used as animal feed, with the fresh SG made freely available for collection by local farmers. In some cases, where the facilities exist, distiller's SG is dried and combined with pot ale syrup to form the more nutritionally valuable dried distiller's grains with solubles (DDGS). However, the market for animal feed is limited and there is growing competition from the availability of other higher quality feeds. Another option is to directly burn the co-products, allowing the energy to be directly harnessed from the grains. However, a more logical alternative would be to convert the lignocellulosic components of the grain to ethanol, allowing further value to be extracted from it.

Under the combined acid and enzyme hydrolysis methods presented here and based on *K. marxianus* fermentation, spent grain has the potential to produce 12.1 million gallons of ethanol per annum (Table 4).

Table 4. Potential ethanol production based on SG sourced from distilleries and breweries in Scotland

Source	*Malt distillery*	*Grain distillery*	*Brewery*
Ethanol yield (gal/ton SG)[a]	11	19	22
SG (1000 t.p.a)[b]	187	285	211
Ethanol (UK gal)	2.1×10^6	5.4×10^6	4.6×10^6

[a] based on yield from *K. marxianus* fermentation (Table 3).
[b] current estimates (Gray, 2008; BBPA, 2006).

Overall this research has revealed relatively straightforward chemical and biotechnological approaches to convert brewery and distillery spent grain to bioethanol. Furthermore we believe that spent grain represents a valuable biomass resource for production of second generation biofuel.

Acknowledgements

Acknowledgement to The Scotch Whisky Research Institute and International Centre for Brewing and Distilling, Heriot-Watt University for collaboration and the Carnegie Trust for Universities in Scotland and The Institute of Brewing and Distilling for funding.

Table 3. Conversion of hydrolysate from brewer's (BSG), malt distiller's (GSG) and maize distillery (NBD) SG to ethanol. NBD hydrolysate and all those used for *P. stipitis* fermentations were adjusted to c.a. pH 5.5 prior to fermentation.

	BSG		*GSG*		*NBD*	
	Ethanol (g/l)	*Yield*[a]	*Ethanol (g/l)*	*Yield*	*Ethanol (g/l)*	*Yield*
K. marxianus	14.8	7.7	7.5	3.9	12.8	6.7
P. stipitis	13.3	6.9	9.1	4.7	ND[b]	ND[b]

[a]Yield of g ethanol per 100 g SG was calculated based on 200 g of SG originally used to prepare 1 L of hydrolysate.
[b]ND means not determined.

References

BBPA, The British Beer and Pub Association (2006). *Statistical Handbook 2006*. Brewing Publications Ltd, UK

Bothast, R.J. and Schlicher, M.A. (2005). Biotechnological processes for conversion of corn into ethanol. *Applied Microbiology and Biotechnology* **67:** 19-25

Carvalheiro, F., Esteves, M.P., Parajó, J.C., Pereira, H. and Gírio, F.M. (2004a). Production of oligosacchrides by autohydrolysis of brewers spent grain. *Bioresource Technology* **91:** 93-100

Carvalheiro, F., Duarte, L.C., Medeiros., R. and Gírio., F.M. (2004b). Optimisation of brewery spent grain dilute-acid hydrolysis for the production of pentose-rich culture media. *Applied Biochemistry and Biotechnology* **115:** 1059-1072

Carvalheiro, F., Duarte, L.C., Lopes, S., Parajó, J.C., Pereira, H. and Gírio, F.M. (2005). Evaluation of the detoxification of brewery's spent grain hydrolysate for xylitol production by *Debaromyces hansenii* CCMI 941. *Process Biochemistry* **40:** 1215-1223

Chandra, R.R., Bura, R., Mabee, W.E., Berlin, A., Pan, X. and Saddler, J.N. (2007). Substrate pre-treatment: the key to effective enzymatic hydrolysis of lignocellulosics? *Advances in Biochemical Engineering/Biotechnology* **108:** 67-93

Duarte, L.C., Carvalheiro, F., Lopes, S., Marques, S., Parajó, J.C. and Gírio, F.M. (2004). Comparison of two posthydrolysis processes of brewery's spent grain autohydrolysis liquor to produce a pentose-containing culture medium. *Applied Biochemistry and Biotechnology* **115:** 1041–1058

Gray, A.S. (2008). *The Scotch Whisky Industry Review*. Sutherlands, Edinburgh.

Jay, A.J., Parker, M.L., Faulks, R., Husband, F., Wilde, P., Smith, A.C., Faulds, C.B. and Waldron, K.W. (2008). A systematic microdissection of brewers' spent grain. *Journal of Cereal Science* **47:** 357–364

Kabel, M.A., Carvalheiro, F., Garrote, G., Avgerinos, E., Koukios, E, Parajó, J.C., Gírio, F.M, Schols, H.A. and Voragen, A.G.V. (2002). Hydrothermally treated xylan-rich by-products yield different classes of xylo-oligosacchrides. *Carbohydrate Polymers* **50:** 47-56

Kim, Y., Mosier, N.S., Hendrickson, R., Ezeji, T., Blaschek, H., Dien, B., Cotta, M., Dale, B. and Ladisch, M. (2007) Composition of corn dry-grind ethanol by-products: DDGS, wet cake, and thin stillage. Bioresource Technology **99:** 5165-5176

Miller, G.L. (1959). Use of dinitrosalicyclic reagent for reducing sugar. *Analytical Chemistry* **31:** 426–428

Mussatto, S.I. and Roberto, I.C. (2005). Acid hydrolysis and fermentation of brewer's spent grain to produce xylitol. *Journal of the Science of Food and Agriculture* **85:** 2453–2460

Mussatto, S.I. and Roberto, I.C. (2006). Chemical characterization and liberation of pentose sugars from brewer's spent grain. *Journal of Chemical Technology and Biotechnology* **81:** 268–274

Narendranath, N.V., Thomas, K.C. and Ingledew, W.M. (2001). Effects of acetic acid and lactic acid on the growth of *Saccharomyces cerevisiae* in a minimal medium. *Journal of Industrial Microbiology and Biotechnology* **26:** 171-177

Palmqvist, E. and Hahn-Hägerdal, B. (2000). Fermentation of lignocellulosic hydrolysates. II: inhibitors and mechanisms of inhibition. *Bioresource Technology* **74:** 25–33

Roberto, I.C., Lacis, L.S., Barbosa, M.F.S. and de Mancilha, I.M. (1991).Utilization of sugar cane bagasse hemicellulosic hydrolysate by *Pichia stipitis* for the production of ethanol. *Process Biochemistry* **26:** 15–21

Shindo, S. and Tachibana, T. (2006). Production of bioethanol from spent grain- a by-product of beer production. *MBAA TQ* **43:** 189-193

Smart, K.A., Chambers, K.M., Lambert, I., Jenkins, C. and Smart, C.A. (1999). Use of methylene violet staining procedure to determine yeast viability and vitality. *Journal of the American*

Society of Brewing Chemists **57:** 18–23

Van Zyl, C., Prior, B.A. and du Preez, J.C. (1991). Acetic acid inhibition of D-xylose fermentation by *Pichia stipitis*. *Enzyme and Microbial Technology* **13:** 82–86

Walker, G.M. and White, J.S. (2007). Fuelling the future: The science behind fuel alcohol yeast fermentations. *The Brewer and Distiller International* **6:** 23-27

Wheals, A.E., Basso, L.C., Alves, D.M.G. and Amorim, H.V. (1999). Fuel ethanol after 25 years. *Trends in Biotechnology* **17:** 482–487

White, J.S., Yohannan, B.K. and Walker, G.M. (2008). Bioconversion of brewer's spent grain to bioethanol. *FEMS Yeast Research* **8:** 1175-1184

Chapter 22

Energy savings using on-line multivariate distillation monitoring

K MacNamara[1], Riccardo Leardi[2], Udo Interwies[3]

[1]Irish Distillers-Pernod Ricard, Midleton, Co Cork, Ireland; [2]Department of Chemistry, Food and Pharmaceutical Technologies, via Brigate Salerno (ponte), I-16147 Genoa, Italy; [3]Iludest Destillationanlagen GmbH, Dachdeckerstr. 2, D-97297 Waldbüttelbrunn, Germany

Introduction

Production of Grain Whiskey at Irish Distillers employs a three column continuous system comprising a beer column, extractive distillation and finally rectification. In order to study this process in greater depth a pilot plant unit precisely scaled down from the production unit was constructed. The function of the beer column is simply to produce a concentrated ethanol feed for the subsequent interlinked extractive and rectification stages, and for this exercise the pilot plant is comprised of these latter two columns only and uses production plant beer column output as feed. This pilot plant and its operating software will be described together with an optimization exercise using Flowsheet Simulation. The flowsheet model was validated by comparing experimental with calculated results and with the validated model optimal settings for different operational parameters were found to allow steady state operation with minimum energy input. In order to maintain this optimum plant operation multivariate on-line process monitoring software was used to monitor steady state and immediately highlight any deviations from steady state.

The standard pilot plant software allows visualisation in trend graphs of the numerical values of 51 individual process parameters and their time traces, but without the possibility of comparing these values with any critical limits or to check if the correlations among them are preserved. Therefore a multivariate model was built from the steady state data from ten independent runs which describe the normal variability of the plant in steady state. On-line monitoring of the process is then performed using this model and specific software written in Matlab. A first screen plot shows the projection of the current data vector on the model and this indicates the current variability of the plant and the trend in variability over the last hour. If the process is detected as out of control (current data vector higher than the critical limit) further normalized contribution screen plots indicate which variables are contributing to the disturbance. An advantageous aspect of this multivariate approach is that it is much more sensitive than individual univariate monitoring of variables.

Pilot plant

The pilot plant consists of two interlinked glass columns, each equipped with 68 bubble-cap trays. With condenser and reboiler these form 70 equilibrium stages (Figure 1).

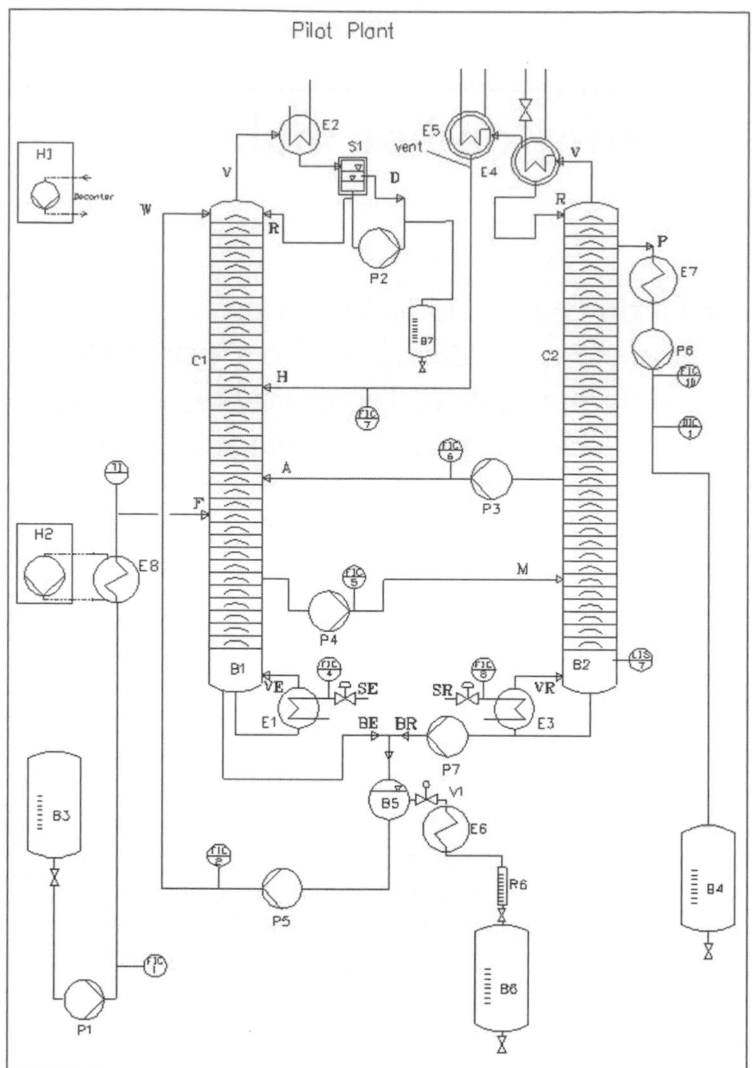

Figure 1. Pilot Plant consisting of Extractive and Rectification columns.

Using pure water (W) as extractor and feeding it at the top tray of the first column the k-values of congeners are changed resulting in the accumulation and removal (D) of higher boiling congeners at the top of this column. The lighter boiling ethanol forms a side product in the bottom section of this column and this ethanol/ water side stream (M) is fed into the second rectification column where it is concentrated close to the azeotropic value to give product (P). There are also additional heads (H) and fusel recycle (A) streams returned from the rectification to the extractive column. The bottom product overflow from both columns is collected in a buffer vessel (B5) and this serves as the dilution water stream. Feed to the system (F) is production scale beer column high wines. All operational aspects of the pilot plant are software controlled. These include steam generation and control, mass flow control and indication of all major streams and adjustment of product strength by variation of product take-off rate. The plant has 51 individual sensors and various combinations of these can be displayed as on-line trend graphs during operation of the unit. There are eight temperature sensors in the first column and thirteen in the second. Other parameters that can be displayed are column pressure drops, reflux flows, feed and side stream flows, product flow and strength etc. An in-line density meter measures the actual product strength. Figure 2 shows a typical on-line trend graph for the temperatures in both columns during a run.

Modelling and simulation

A model was constructed from the thermodynamic properties of water and ethanol, together with methanol, propanol, isobutanol and 2- and 3-methyl-1-butanol as five representative congeners. For vapour liquid equilibrium and to take into account non-ideal behaviour the UNIFAC method was applied. Input data for the model came from volume and mass flow rates, column structure, column pressure drops and concentration measurements. Raw data was processed further to determine other properties such as liquid densities and mass fractions. By flowsheet simulation, running under the same conditions and settings of plant and process parameters, the experimental data was compared with the calculated results to validate the model. The model was used for process optimization when model and experimental results coincided sufficiently. This allowed minimum reboiler duties (steam input to each column) for a given feed flow and product specification.

Multivariate process monitoring

Principal Component Analysis (PCA) is the basis for multivariate process monitoring and quality control, and is generally much more effective than the usually applied univariate approaches (Kourti and MacGregor, 1995). The previously described trend graphs display individual univariate sensor data, but it is intuitively obvious that many operational parameters during distillation are highly correlated. A temperature measurement at a certain tray is not an isolated phenomenon but will have a very high correlation with all other temperatures, which in turn will be correlated with the energy input. Reflux rates will similarly be linked to energy input and column temperature gradients.

Data in ASCII format reflecting all sources of normal system variability was collected from the steady state region of ten individual runs. From the initial available 51 sensors only 26

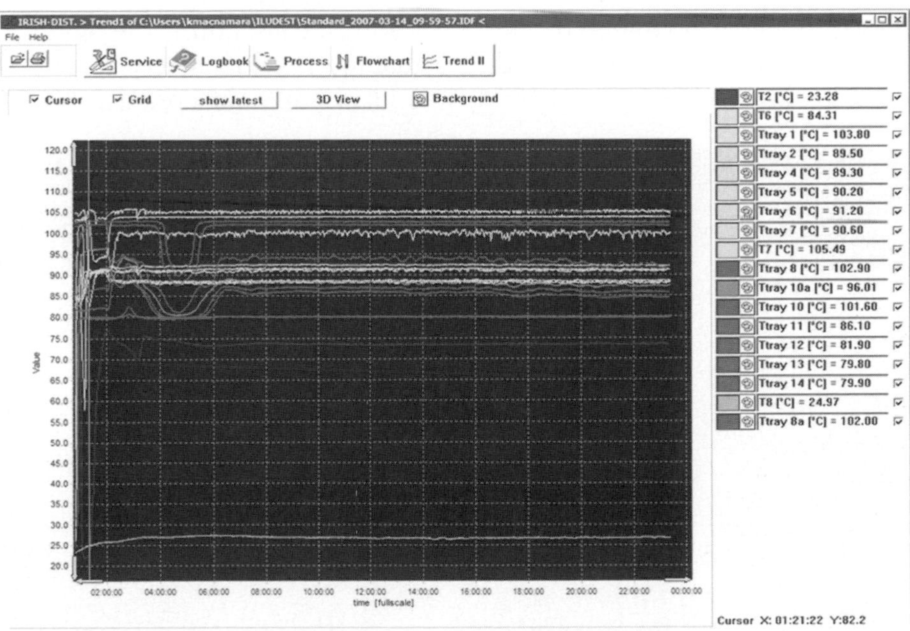

Figure 2. Trend graphs displaying temperature variations in both columns during a run.

were retained (21 column temperatures, pressure drops and reflux rates for each column and the product flow). Mass flow controlled streams and similar controlled parameters were not used. One data vector per minute for each variable was produced containing the average of the measurements in that time period. To exclude random sensor spikes, internal controls were used to check the numerical value of each variable with its possible physical range and the variation between two consecutive samplings, with a maximum possible variation defined on the basis of the physical system.

With 4551 data points collected in this way a PCA was performed with two principal components explaining 79% of the total variance. A PCA model was then constructed defining the limits inside which the process should stay. Every minute a new row or vector of data describing the process is projected onto the score plot using the loadings computed on the steady state model data delimited by the confidence ellipses corresponding to p = 0.05, 0.01 and 0.001. From the computed scores it can be estimated how far the process is from the barycentre of the model, i.e. from the ideal process. The computed residuals (indication of the difference between the measured and reconstructed values of each variable) indicate how well the process at that time is reconstructed by the PCA model, i.e. how far from the model space (in this case a plane) it lies. Additional statistical tests T^2 and Q allow the automatic detection of an outlier in both cases. With these tests it is possible to detect a fault in a process by checking just two plots, instead of as many plots as variables with a univariate approach. Further contribution plots then indicate which variables are responsible for the sample being an outlier (Conlin, Martin and Morris, 2000))

Figure 3 shows the output of the process monitoring software when the process is in an ideal condition.

The yellow star indicates the actual situation of the process and is well inside both the confidence ellipses of the PCA model (left plot) and the critical limits of the T^2 and Q statistics (right plot). The green trajectory tail indicates that the variability of the process in the last hour has been quite small. Normalised contributions plots of the diagnostics are only displayed when the current data vector is higher than the critical limit.

On the other hand Figure 4 shows that the process has now moved out of control

In the left PCA plot the yellow star is at the border of the external ellipse corresponding to p = 0.001. Also the trajectory tail shows the presence of a very clear trend which took place during the last hour. The right T^2–Q plot shows that the T^2 value is very close to the p = 0.001 critical limit. In contrast the Q value is well

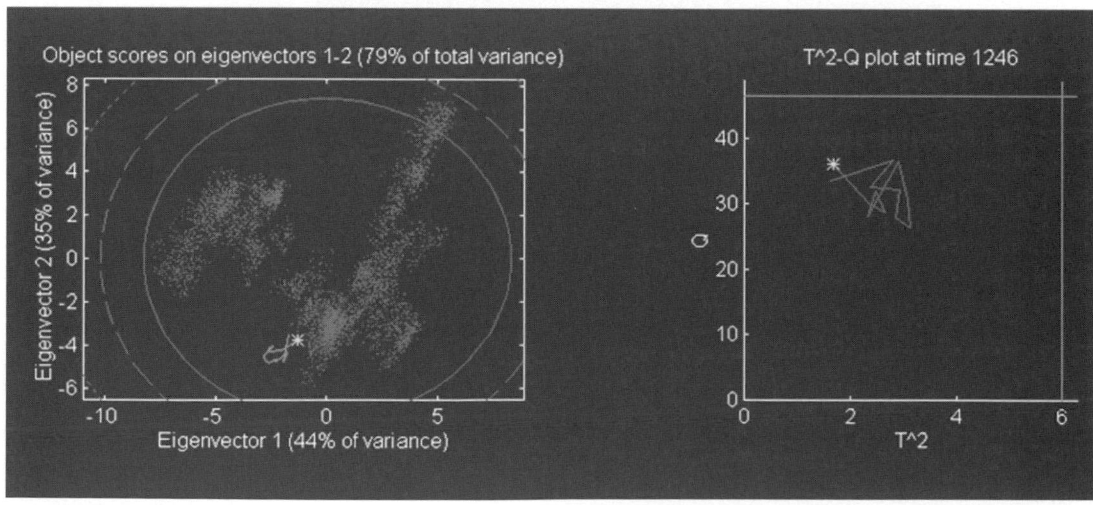

Figure 3. Output from the multivariate monitoring program for a process in steady state.

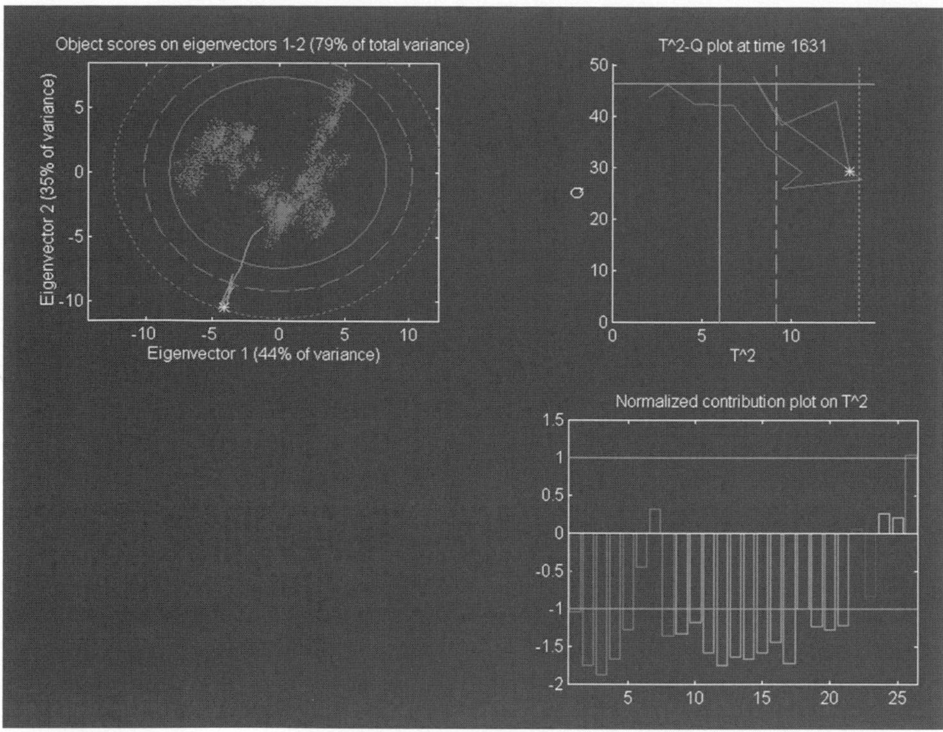

Figure 4. Output from the multivariate monitoring program for a process deviating from steady state.

below any critical limit which means that the process parameter correlations are still preserved. The T^2 normalised contribution plot now also appears and indicates that that the disturbance results from the fact that the temperatures in both columns (variables 1-21, red and green bars) are lower than they should be.

This procedure is much more robust than the standard univariate approach since it leads to a lower number of false negatives and positives. It is also much more sensitive as it allows fault detection at a much earlier stage. Energy savings can be expected as a process out of control is less energy efficient. Finally a process out of control can imply a product out of specification and therefore multivariate process monitoring data can also be linked to final product quality.

Conclusions

Multivariate Statistical Process Monitoring (MSPM) is potentially one of the most powerful applications of chemometrics. In 2003 an EU report estimated that if just 10% of the 100,000 process manufacturing plants in Europe would employ these technologies, a net benefit of the order of Euro500 million per annum to these industries would result (Morris and Martin, 2003). A contributing reason to the non-acceptance of this technology is the difficulty in convincing process engineers and technicians of the advantages. MSPM can almost always identify unusual operating periods and can usually isolate the region of the plant and the group of process variables related to the problem. Therefore they are a powerful tool for focusing the attention of process engineers to a much smaller operational area, and allow them to better use their engineering knowledge to diagnose the cause of any abnormal behaviour and thereby improve the process (Kourti, 2002).

References

Conlin, A. K., Martin, E.B., Morris, J. (2000). Confidence limits for contribution plots. *Journal of Chemometrics* 14: 725-736

Kourti, D., IEEE Control Systems Magazine, October 2002, 10-25

Kourti, T., Mac Gregor, J.F. (1995). Process analysis, monitoring and diagnosis using multivariate projection methods. *Chemometrics and Intelligent Laboratory Systems* 28: 3-21

Morris, J., Martin, E. (2003) Business Briefing: CPI Technology

Chapter 23

Fuzzy logic in the distillation process

Andrej Rotovnik
Private address: Koroška cesta 8b, SI-3320 Velenje, Slovenia
Company address: MIEL Elektronika, d.o.o., Efenkova cesta 61, SI-3320 Velenje, Slovenia

Introduction

This article presents an approach to solving the problem of and finding an optimal solution to controlling a nonlinear system in an industrial process such as distillation. The technological problems in a whisky distillery were fully described by the operators of the system, and distillate flow oscillation emerged as a basic problem. Thus we decided to set up a distillery model with a fuzzy controller supervisory system. Such a controller is able to regulate the process according to the operator's parameters and decisions, especially for control in unpredictable cases. The distillation process constitutes a relatively simple technological system, but under certain circumstances it can be very demanding to control. As a basic distillery we treat a wash and spirit still with a control loop, as shown below (Figure 1).

Real distillery model

For simulation purposes we constructed a real distillery model with a capacity of 2 x 5 litres (Figure 2, Figure 3) with a complete control system for wash and spirit still distillation.

In the development of the system we used various fluids: water, wine, beer and wash. The difference in the distillation process is seen in the different liquid froths. We used the wash from the Slovenian Institute for Hops and Brewery. When the system was set up for normal

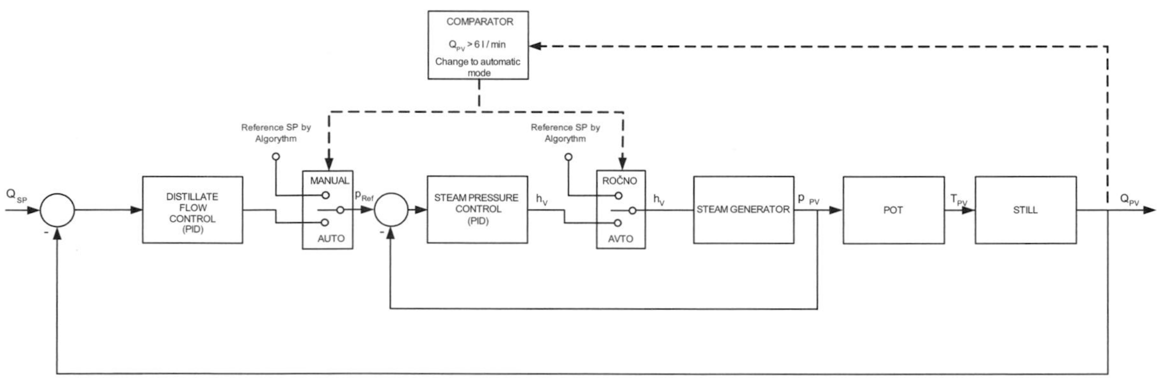

Figure 1. Control system for the distillation process.

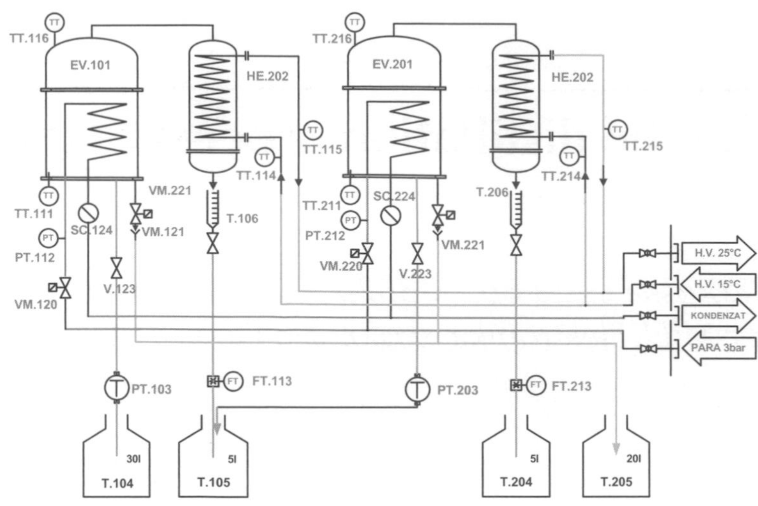

Figure 2. Technological scheme for wash and spirit still distillation.

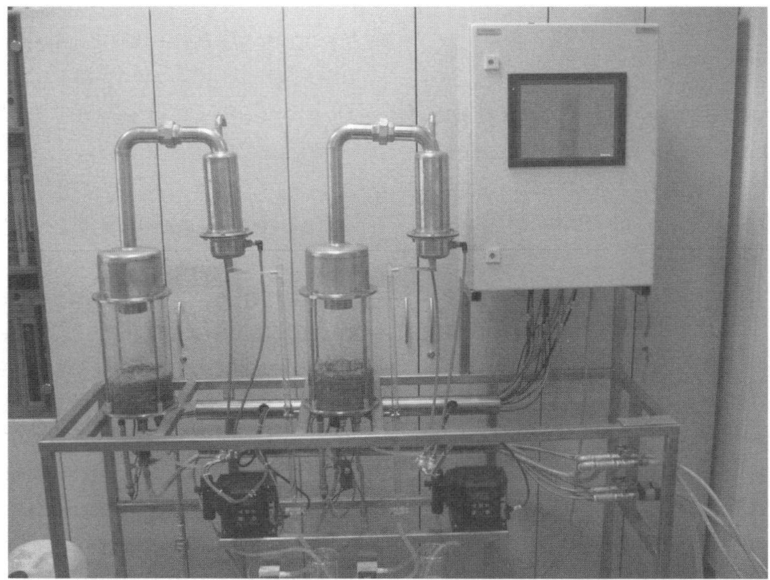

Figure 3. Real model of wash and spirit still distillation.

operation, we continued with a proportional-integral-differential (PID) steam controller design (Figure 4) for the wash and spirit still.

Steam was produced with an electric steam generator, and therefore the heating media was similar to the type used in the real distillery. Figure 5 shows the PID control responses in closed loop operation.

This control loop constituted the basis for designing a fuzzy controller, for which we consulted the operators and experts from the distillery.

Identification of the process

We investigated the distillery process and developed a mathematical model for different distillate flow rates. We perhaps could have avoided this step, as we do not strictly need a mathematical model for the nonlinear process to be controlled by a fuzzy controller. A determination was made for several set points, and we arrived at a first-order mathematical model (the ARX model that corresponds to the real model at 69.95% is shown in Figure 6).

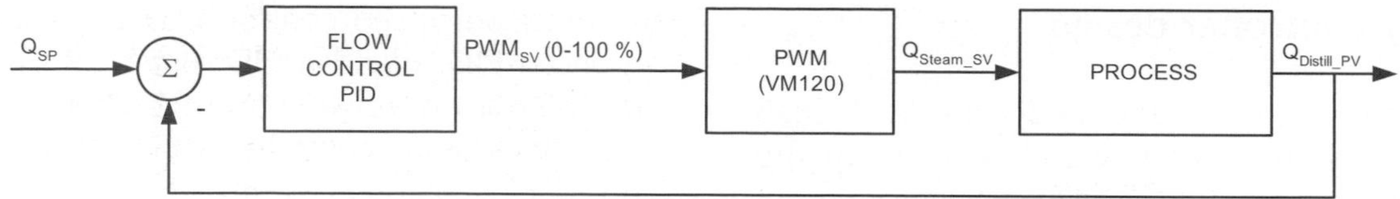

Figure 4. Steam PID in the wash (spirit) still control loop.

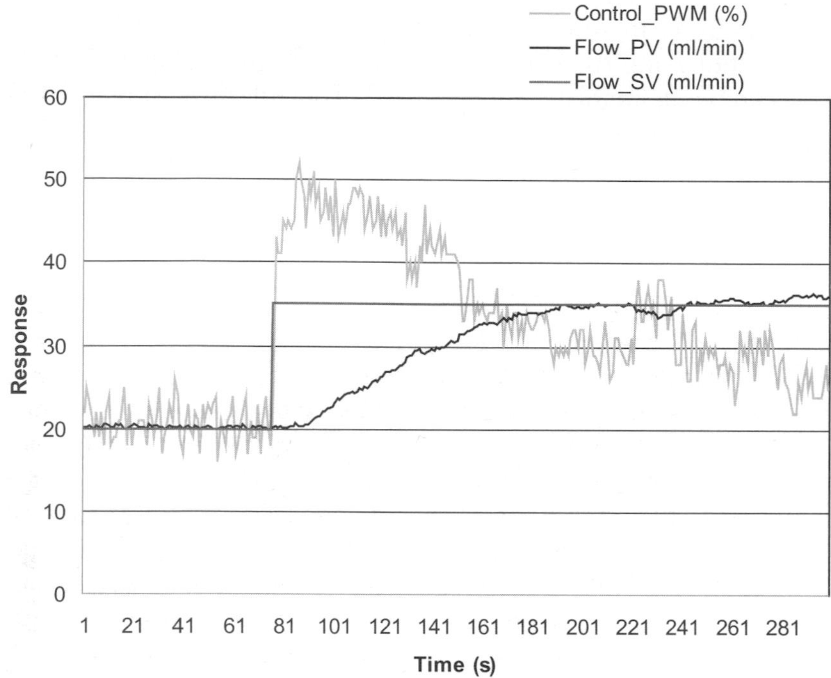

Figure 5. Developed steam PID in the closed control loop

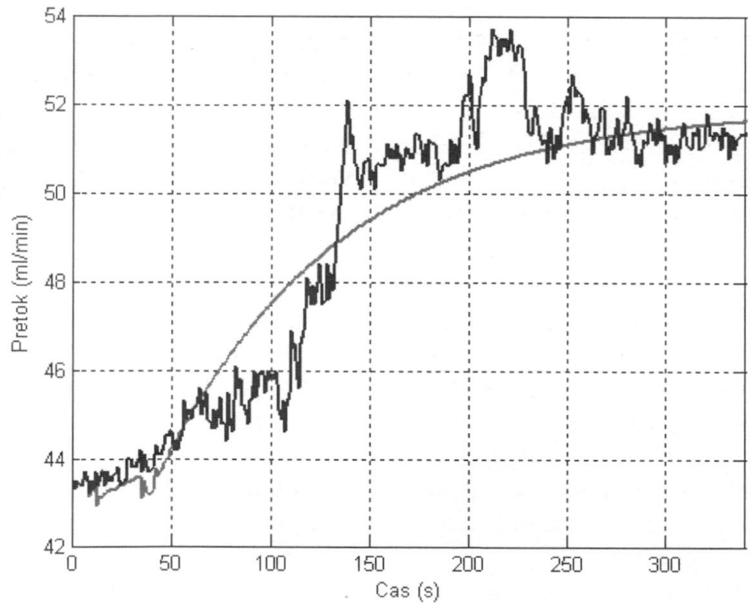

Figure 6. Step response of the real and mathematical models for a pulse-width modulation (PWM) valve change from 35% to 40%

Fuzzy controller design

The first step was performed with the Matlab development tool, in which we set up the membership functions and fuzzy rules for input and output variables. The time-based diagram of alcohols was considered (Figure 7). With many experiments and simulations in Matlab, we set up membership functions and rules for the fuzzy controller. This can be set linguistically or graphically and is shown in Figures 8a and 8b.

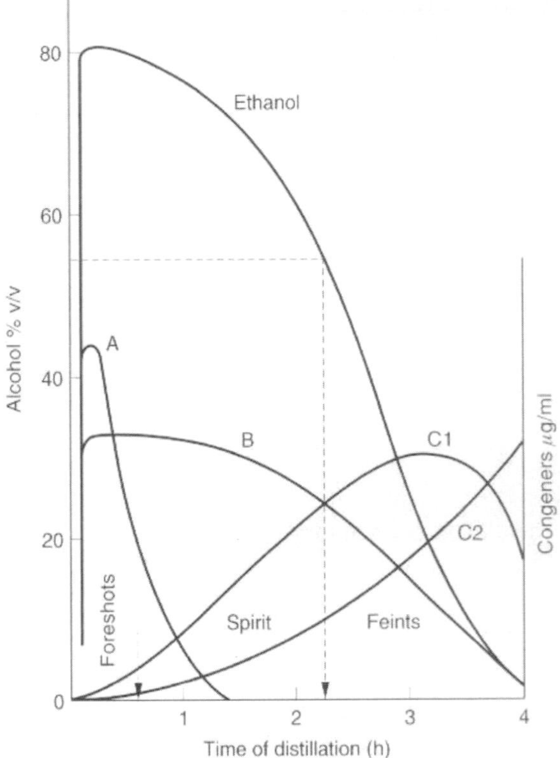

Figure 7. Relative volatility of flavour congeners (Panek and Boucher, 1989)

The fuzzy controller was primary developed in the Matlab environment, where inputs, outputs and fuzzy rules were roughly defined. The developed and simulated fuzzy controller was transferred to the programmable logic controller (PLC) control system of the real distillery model. Whilst we could not in reality simulate a full distillery, we were able to simulate basic process behaviour.

Through additional tests we optimised the PLC fuzzy controller, which is integrated in the CPU coprocessor of the industrial controller. Beside fuzzy control algorithms, we were also able to use other advanced control algorithms such as advanced PID, Blended PID, Batch FR Capture, etc. The rules were written in the Omron CJ1G-CPU43P industrial controller with the CX-Process Tool. The definition of membership functions and rules were set up in a special fuzzy control function block, and the whole algorithm then resulted in a supervisory fuzzy controller with many input and output variables (Figure 9).

The sub-programme for distillation control (measurement, scaling, HMI communication, pulse-width modulation for valve control, etc.) was made with a ladder diagram as a standard Omron PLC programme.

The supervisory fuzzy controller operates in two different modes. The process was forced to the boiling point with the maximum PID value. When the flow rate was sensed (a minimum turbine-measured distillate flow rate of 15 ml/min), the controller was switched to the second mode and continued to the end of distillation process. The nonlinear characteristic of flow rate and % ABV with acceleration of the distillate flow rate for foreshots and feints is shown in Figure 10. We could also optimise the distillation period with respect to time.

We developed a fifth order polynomial for the PLC calculation of % ABV from the Rayleigh function, as shown in Figure 11 and Table 1. We measured the vapour temperature on the top of the pot in the front of the condenser.

Table 1. % ABV percentage at different liquid and vapour temperatures

Boiling temperature	*Liquid (L) Y (EtOH)*	*Vapour (V) X (EtOH)*
°C	*% ABV (Liquid)*	*% ABV (Destillate)*
99,85	0,00	0,00
96,85	3,82	31,09
94,35	8,15	50,02
91,85	12,23	62,19
89,35	17,33	70,19
86,85	26,01	76,15
84,35	41,36	80,77
81,85	62,40	85,27
79,35	85,86	90,96
78,35	93,49	94,46
78,05	95,76	95,76

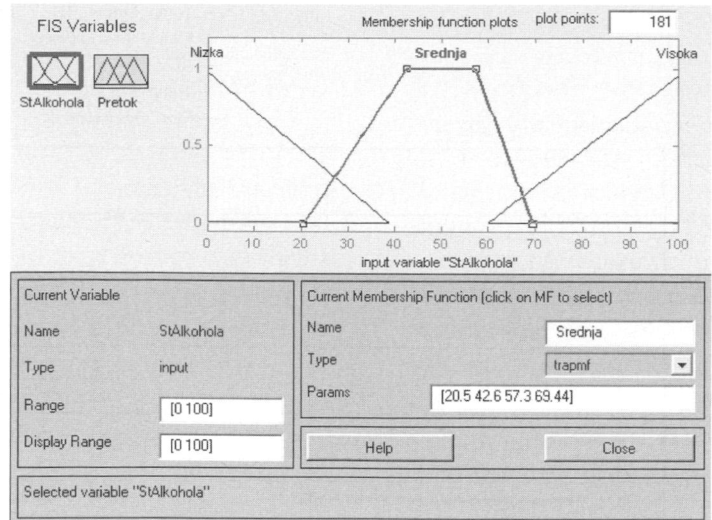

Figure 8a. Membership function for input variables, in percent alcohol by volume (% ABV).

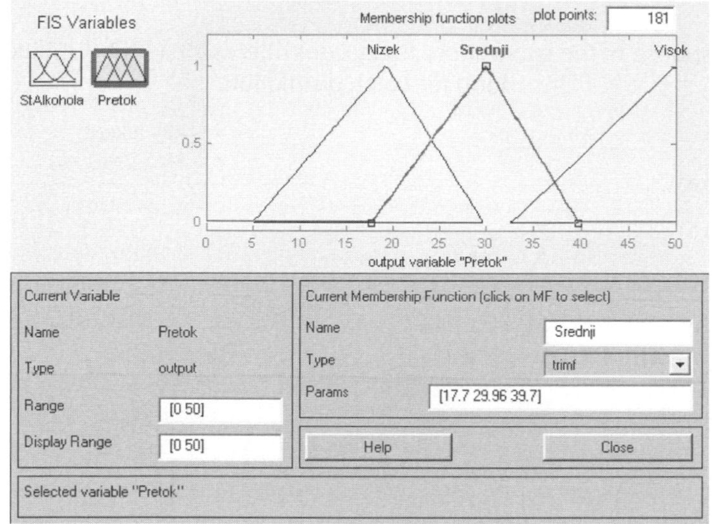

Figure 8b. Membership function for output variables – distillation flow rate (ml/min).

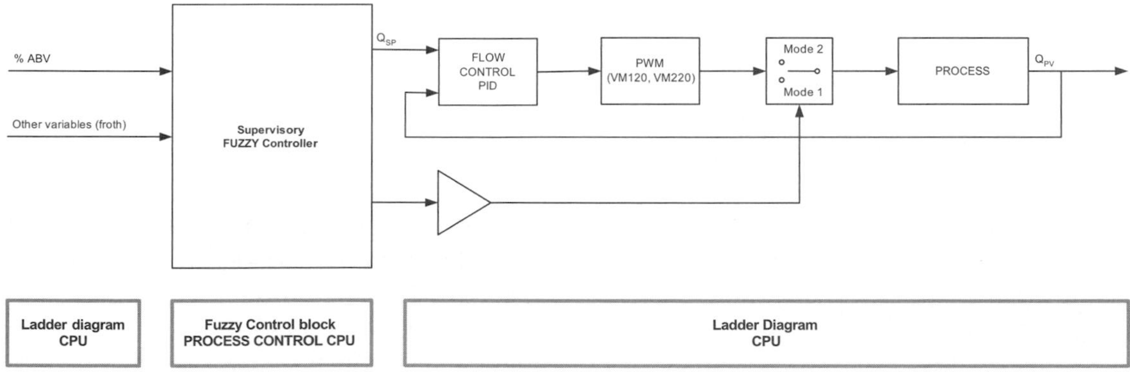

Figure 9. Supervisory fuzzy controller for a set PID value and PWM control of the on-off steam control valve

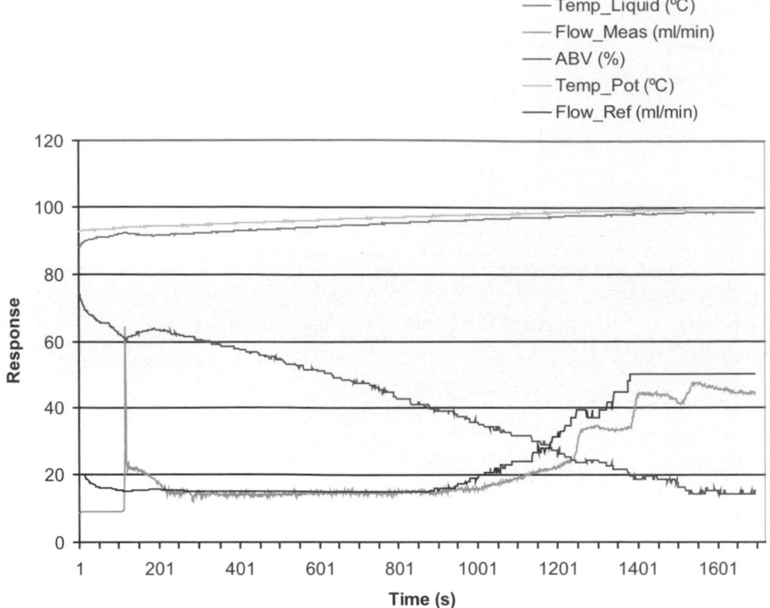

Figure 10. Response of the supervisory fuzzy controller with a PID distillate flow control loop for batch distillation.

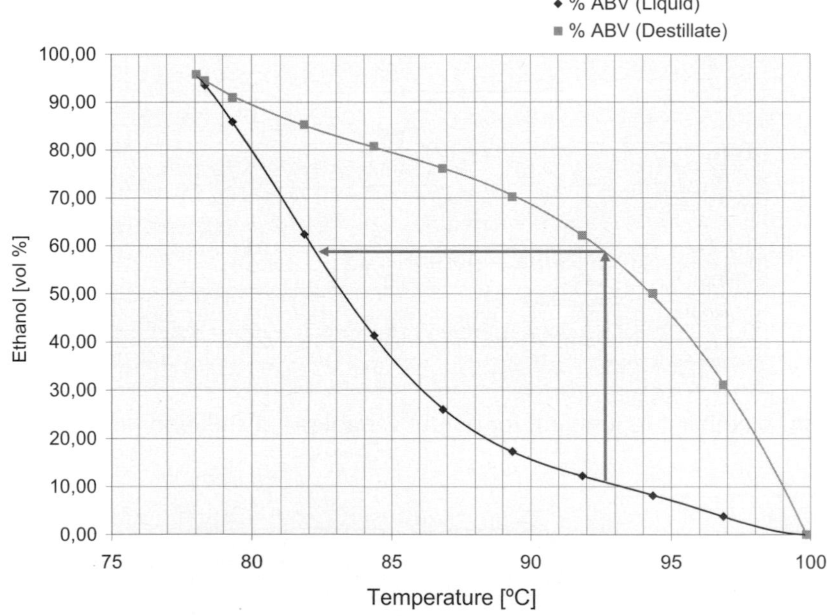

Figure 11. Rayleigh dependence of % ABV on liquid and vapour temperature.

Control system

The control system was set up with two types of visualisation. The first was based on a 12″ HMI (Human Machine Interface) touch screen and the second on a PC running a SCADA system (Supervisory Control and Data Application). A user-friendly interface was designed with the Omron CX-Designer Tool, based on the technological scheme of the distillery model (Figure 12). It contained menus with touch-screen buttons to control the system and set up various parameters.

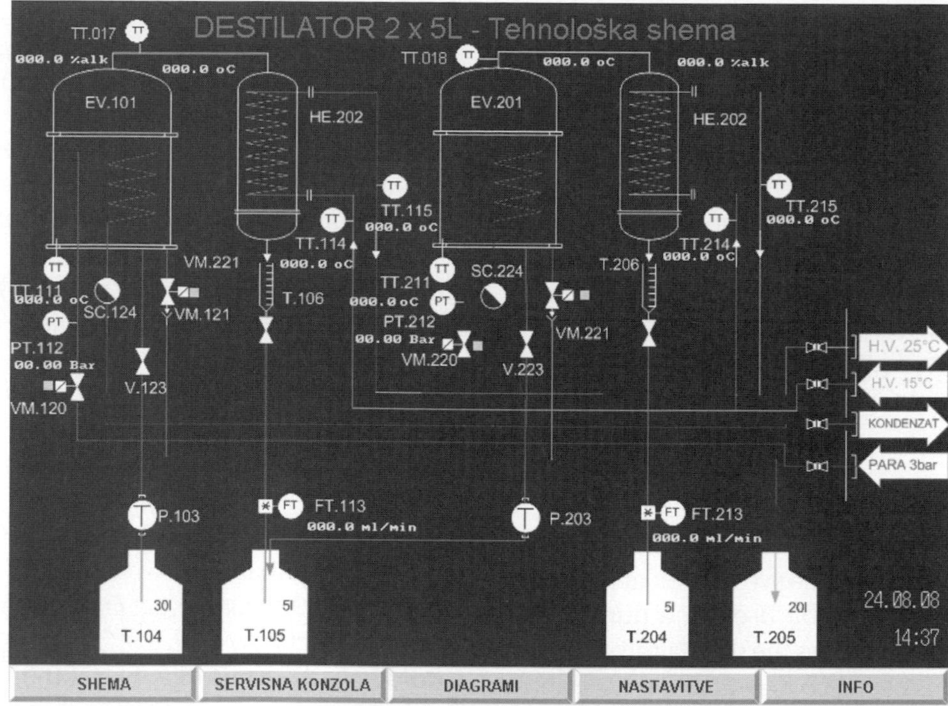

Figure 12. Touch screen for full control of the distillation process.

The SCADA system was set up using Omron CX-Supervisor software, which can be connected with other devices over an Ethernet or Internet network. Results of using the described fuzzy controller confirm that it is possible to construct a supervisory system which can satisfactorily control a nonlinear industrial process.

The maximum number of input variables to the fuzzy control block was eight, the maximum of output variables two and the maximum number of rules 64. This could imply limitations for control of a more complex system with multiple input and output variables.

The control platform described here can be used in any industrial process in which the control system cannot be realised solely through the use of conventional controllers. The wash and spirit still model developed and described in this article can be used for a variety of purposes, mainly for research in the production of whisky but also for educational purposes (students of automation and chemistry). The openness of the fuzzy controller offers a variety of possibilities to use many different parameters and variables which generally cannot be used in the distillation process.

Supervisory fuzzy controller – future development and implementation

The supervisory fuzzy controller as a generator of flow reference could be extended with a froth height sensor (camera). High boiling temperatures can cause significant problems with the froth, which can enter the condenser designed for distillate cooling. We performed several tests with a three-point sensor measuring system and analogue ultrasonic sensors, concluding that the only acceptable method would entail the use of an industrial camera system to adjust the height of the froth to the analogue value of the input variable. Implementation of this solution would be the next logical step in confirming the applicability of the developed supervisory fuzzy controller in the distillation process. It could be connected over an OPC (Object Linking and Embedding for Process Control) server with an existing control system. The measured values from the real distillery could be linked as inputs to the fuzzy controller, where decisions (outputs) would be effected by fuzzy rules. Differences in outputs between the existing control system and supervisory fuzzy control system can be eliminated with the proper setting of the fuzzy rules. In so doing, we could build a totally automated control system.

In future development, as input variables we could also consider other characteristics such as smell, viscosity, taste and colour, all of which parameters influence the final product. Additionally, we could consider maturation – a process with different input variables, such as temperature, light and wood – and set up a simulated fuzzy controller.

Conclusion

A solution such as the one we arrived at with the fuzzy controller could be used in a number of nonlinear systems, such as the distillation process. Using decisions based on fuzzy rules we are able design a controller which could be adapted to any unpredictable situation in the process. In actual processes, numerous oscillations can arise which are attenuated manually; however, with the approach described here we can deal with such eventualities completely automatically.

References

Chen, C. H. (1996). *Fuzzy Logic and Neural Network Book*. McGraw-Hill, Inc.

Donlagić, D., with coauthors. (1995). *Fuzzy Logic Control Design*. Faculty of Electrical Engineering and Computer Science Maribor, Slovenia.

Golob, M., Muškinja, N. (1994). *The basic of Fuzzy Control – Excercises*. Faculty of Electrical Engineering and Computer Science Maribor, Slovenia.

Knez, Ž., Habulin, M., Ozim, V. (1992). *Process analyses and mechanics exercises*. Univerza v Mariboru, Tehniška fakulteta kemijska tehnologija. Maribor.

Kravanja, Z. (2006). *Process Dynamics*. Fakulteta za kemijo in kemijsko tehnologijo. Maribor.

Muškinja, N. (1997). *Uporaba nadzornega regulatorja za zagotavljanje stabilnosti mehkih (Fuzzy) regulacijskih sistemov*. Doktorska disertacija. Maribor.

Omron Corporation. (1992) *Fuzzy Guide Book*. Tokyo, Japan.

Perry's. (1992). *Chemical Engineer's Handbook*. The McGraw-Hill.

Rotovnik, A., Muškinja, N. (2007). *Načrtovanje dvostopenjskega destilatorja*. Elektrotehniška in računalniška konferenca, Portorož.

Russel, I. (2003). *Whisky – Technology, Production and Marketing*, Academic Press Alsevier Ltd, London.

Škrjanc, I. (2002). *Fuzzy Modeling and Identification*. Faculty of Electrical Engineering, Ljubljana.

Vrančić D., Kandare G., Gerkšič S. (2005). *Program za samodejno nastavljanje parametrov PID regulatorjev*. Avtomatizacija v industriji in gospodarstvu, Maribor.

Chapter 24

Cachaça production through double distillation technique

P.A. Souza[1]; H.F.A. Scanavini[2]; A.J.A. Meirelles[2]; A.R. Alcarde[1*]

[1]Department of Food Technology – College of Agriculture "Luiz de Queiroz" – University of São Paulo, Caixa Postal 9, CEP 13418-900, Piracicaba, São Paulo, Brazil. 2 Department of Food Engineering, Faculty of Food Engineering, Campinas State University, Caixa Postal 6121, CEP 13083-862, Campinas, São Paulo, Brazil

Introduction

Cachaça, the Brazilian sugar cane spirit, is by definition, a distillate with alcohol content between 38 and 48°GL, obtained through distilling the sugar cane juice fermented must. Its production consists mainly of the sugar cane juice fermentation, distilling and aging. The fermentation holds the greatest influence on the final product, because in this stage, minor compounds such as superior alcohols, organic acids, esters and carbonyl compounds are formed (Lurton et al., 1995).

Ethanol is the major organic volatile constituent of alcoholic beverages, responsible for the body of alcoholic beverages. The group of superior alcohols is quantitatively the largest group that makes up the taste in alcoholic beverages (Nykänen, 1986) and is formed by the action of yeast on aminoacids. Isoamyl alcohol is the fusel alcohol of largest concentration in alcoholic beverages. The propanol level is usually high in beverages considered of low quality (Almeida and Barreto, 1972). The same occurs with acetic acid, the main compound of the cachaça acidity: lower concentrations indicate better acceptability by consumers (Boza and Horii, 1998). Methanol is an alcohol particularly undesirable in spirits, because its repeated intake, even in very small doses, can cause severe intoxication, leading to blindness and even death (Lamiable et al., 2004). The most volatile fraction of alcoholic beverages is composed of carbonyl compounds, and acetaldehyde is the largest component (over 90% of the total; Nykänen, 1986). The low acetaldehyde contents in beverages are often associated with quality improvement because its presence in alcoholic beverages is commonly associated with the known "hangover" symptoms (Nascimento et al., 1997).

Cachaça is a beverage that has great social and economic importance in our country. Its annual production is estimated at 1.3 billion litres and has remained constant in recent years. The sector generates approximately 400,000 direct jobs and presents a billing of more than US$ 600 million (PBDAC, 2008). After beer, it is the second most consumed alcoholic beverage in Brazil (ABRABE, 2007).

Cachaça has its production mainly aimed at the internal market, which has a strong popular appeal and its consumption is mainly concentrated in the low-income population. National surveys show that changes in the cachaça quality would lead to a greater acceptance, not only by the usual consumer, but also by non-consumers, and would contribute to the expansion of its exports. Therefore, the improvement of quality and standardization of the cachaça spirit should be a key goal for Brazilian distilled beverage producers.

In this context, this work investigated the cachaça production through double distillation technique. The vaporization kinetics of minor compounds is considered, and the impact that this distillation technique has on the profiles of volatiles is evaluated. Consequently, we assess the relevance of the quality of the sugar cane distillate in terms of consumers' acceptance.

Material and methods

Sugar cane juice clarified by means of boiling for 10 min and subsequently filtered for the removal of sediments was fermented by adding 3 g/L of dry yeast Y-904, under shaking, in 13-L fermenters with the temperature controlled between 28 and 32°C. After decanting of yeasts, the supernatant (yeast-free wine) submitted for distillation in laboratory distiller (Besnard-Esteves modified) of 37L of payload.

The distillations were carried out in accordance with the double distillation technique commonly used for cognac production (Léauté, 1990) using a rectifying distiller (Figure 1). In the first distillation, a small fraction of the initial distillate ("head" fraction) was withdrawn, representing 0.4% of the wine volume introduced in the distiller. The distillation process continued until the distillate in the distiller output presented 5% of alcohol, resulting in the "heart" fraction of the first distillation. The "tail" faction was also withdrawn, corresponding to the distillation after the "heart" fraction, until the distillate in the distiller output presented 0% of alcohol. The water waste (depleted wine 1) of the first distillation was discarded. Approximately 37 L of the "heart" fraction were obtained at around 42% alcohol by volume at each three batches of the first distillation, which were submitted to a second distillation (double distillation). In the double distillation process, four fractions were separated from the distillate: an initial "head" fraction (1% of the total volume that submitted for double distillation), a "heart 1" fraction (after the "head" fraction until the distillate in the distiller output dropped to 60 % alcohol by volume), a "heart 2" fraction (after the "heart 1" fraction until the distillate in the distiller output dropped to 5% alcohol by volume) and a final "tail" fraction (after the "heart 2" fraction until the distillate in the distiller output was at around 0 % alcohol by volume). The water waste of the second distillation (depleted wine 2) was also discarded. The "heart 1" fraction corresponded to the produced cachaça and was aged in 10-L oak barrels.

Figure 1.

During the distillations, distillate fractions were collected in 500 mL test tubes. Each fraction was measured for the alcohol concentration using an alcoholmeter. The temperature in the distillation body and in the boiler was also measured.

The "head", "heart" and "tail" fractions of both distillations were submitted to physical and chemical analyses, established by legislation in force in Brazil (Brazil, 2005a): alcohol content, acidity, copper, furfural, aldehydes, esters, methanol and superior alcohols.

Results and discussion

Law No 13 from the Ministry of Agriculture (Brazil, 2005b) establishes identity and quality standards for cachaça (Table 1). However, it is important to stress that a beverage that meets the standards required by legislation may not meet the quality standards demanded by consumers.

Table 1.

Component	*Limits*	
	Minimum	*Maximum*
Volatile acidity (acetic acid)	-	150
Esters (ethyl acetate)	-	200
Aldehydes (acetaldehyde)	-	30
Furfurals	-	5
High alcohols *	-	360
Congeners **	200	650
Methanol		20,0

* High alcohols = sum of alcohol iso-butyl (2-methylpropanol), isoamyl alcohols (2-methyl-1-butanol and 3-methyl-1-butanol) and alcohol n-propyl (1-propanol).
** Congeners = sum of volatile acidity, esters, aldehydes, furfurals and higher alcohols.

Table 2 shows the chemical composition of fractions obtained from distillations for the cachaça production ("heart 1" from the double distillation process). Through the analysis of profiles, the compounds have behaved as expected, that is, they vaporized according to their volatility: the most volatile compounds separated in the beginning of the distillation process such as methanol, esters and aldehydes, present in largest amounts in "head" fractions. The less volatile compounds separated at the end of distillation, such as acetic acid, whose concentration is much greater in "tail" fractions. Analyzing results for the final product ("heart 1"), it was observed that the total content of congeners is within the range set by Brazilian legislation for cachaça, which is from 200 to 650 mg/100 ml anhydrous alcohol (AA). The concentrations of all compounds separately are also according to the Brazilian legislation, except for superior alcohols (548 mg/100 ml AA), which maximum limit is 360 mg/100 ml AA.

The first distillations resulted in a "heart" containing approximately 42% alcohol by volume. In simple distillations, the first distillations performed (as reported here) normally result in "heart" fractions with approximately 28% of alcohol by volume (Léauté, 1990). This occurred because the distillations were conducted in distiller equipped with a rectifying column and also with a condenser that allow the occurrence of greater reflux. This reflux occurs naturally due to the difference of temperature between the steam formed and the external environment

	First distillations[3]			*Double distillations*			
	"Head"	*"Heart"*	*"Tail"*	*"Head"*	*"Heart 1"*[4]	*"Heart 2"*	*"Tail"*
Alcoholic graduation[1]	79,63	42,25	1,96	84,15	80,32	31,86	2,14
Volatile acidity[2]	9,16	25,11	516,69	5,93	8,88	44,75	91,16
Aldehydes[2]	107,73	10,00	0,00	88,01	9,42	0,00	0,00
Esters[2]	183,48	15,39	0,00	71,38	8,68	0,00	0,00
Methanol[2]	53,85	13,20	0,00	29,41	6,40	7,47	0,00
n-Propanol[2]	45,88	31,38	0,00	30,42	45,43	22,09	0,00
Isobutanol[2]	380,47	157,10	0,00	172,19	186,10	16,30	0,00
Isoamyl alcohol[2]	544,16	268,79	0,00	158,05	316,98	43,56	0,00
Sum high alcohols[2]	970,51	457,27	0,00	360,67	548,51	81,95	0,00
Total congeners[2]	1270,82	492,77	516,69	525,98	575,48	126,70	91,16

[1]% (v/v) 20°C; [2]mg/100 ml anhydrous alcohol (AA); [3]average referring to the 3 first batch distillations; [4]fraction considered as cachaça.

for the column, and also between the steam and water in the condenser. This reflux is responsible for a higher alcohol concentration in the distillate formed. This is why the alcohol content in the cachaça ("heart 1") was at around 80% (v/v). The first distillations were responsible for a significant reduction in the cachaça volatile acidity, measured as acetic acid. The acetic acid concentration in the "heart" fraction of the first distillation was 25 mg/100 ml AA, while in the "heart 1" fraction of the double distillation, this concentration was reduced to 8.9 mg/100 ml AA. This result is very positive because the acetic acid concentration in the distillate from the double distillation is well below the limit imposed by legislation (150 mg/100 ml AA) and also because the acidity is a quality indicator. According to Boza and Horii (1998), the lower is the cachaça acidity, the better the consumers' acceptance will be. On this basis then, double distillation improves the quality of cachaça in analytical terms.

There was also an observed decrease in methanol concentration, a highly toxic substance (Lamiable et al., 2004) and therefore undesirable in the spirit. Its concentration was reduced in cachaça due to the double distillation process, decreasing from 13 mg/100 mL AA in the "heart" of the 1st distillations to 6 mg/10 0ml AA in the "heart 1" of the double distillation.

In the case of acetalaldehyde, the influence of the double distillation was not very significant, because this compound was mainly found in the "head" fractions of distillates. Its concentration in the cachaça (9 mg/100 ml AA) is below the level permitted by the Brazilian legislation (30 mg/100 ml AA). The low acetaldehyde content in alcoholic beverages is frequently associated with an improvement in their quality. This occurs because the presence of aldehydes in alcoholic beverages is commonly associated with the known symptoms of "hangover": nausea, vomiting, restlessness, sweating, confusion, drop in blood pressure, faster heart rates and headaches (Nascimento et al., 1997).

Similarly, esters are mainly found in "head" fractions of distillates. The concentration of esters in cachaça (9 mg/100 ml AA) is far below that permitted by the Brazilian legislation (200 mg/100 ml AA).

The concentration of superior alcohols in cachaça (548 mg/100 mL AA) was above limits established by the Brazilian legislation (360 mg/100 mL AA). Perhaps the use of the rectifying distiller has contributed to a greater concentration of superior alcohols in cachaça, exactly as it did with ethanol. Yet, when a double distillation is performed, the first distillation already withdraws part of the water from the mixture to be double distilled, allowing greater concentration of ethanol and also of other alcohols in the double distillation product. Perhaps an extension of the sampling range of "heart 1" fraction could improve compliance with the cachaça legislation in relation the concentration of superior alcohols, since this concentration in "heart 2" fraction was only 82 mg/10 0mL AA. In this context, further research is needed in order to define new cutoff points between distillate fractions in the double distillation using the rectifying distiller.

Among superior alcohols, for n-propanol, there was an increase in its concentration in the "heart" fraction with double distillation, from 31 mg/100 mL AA in the "heart" fraction of the 1st distillation to 45 mg/100 ml AA in the "heart 1" fraction of the double distillation. This is a negative fact because, according to Almeida and Barreto (1972) and Boza and Horii, (1998), a lower propanol concentration in cachaça, indicates a higher quality.

The concentration of congeners in cachaça (575 mg/100 mL AA) is within the range allowed by the Brazilian legislation (200 to 650 mg/100 ml AA). Superior alcohols accounted for 95% of the total concentration of congeners of the spirit. The other 5% were represented by volatile acids, esters and aldehydes.

Although the distiller has the boiler and the inner surface of the rectifying column built in copper, the presence of copper was not detected the in the cachaça, as well as in none of the fractions analyzed. This was expected because the dragging of copper to the distillate is due to the condensation of alcoholic vapors generated during the distillation process. Since the distiller condenser is stainless steel, there was no contamination of the cachaça with copper.

Furfural and hydroxymethylfurfural (HMF) compounds were neither detected in the spirit nor in the fractions analyzed. This result was also expected because furfural and HMF mainly originate from the degradation of pentoses from sugar cane bagasse and hexoses from sugar cane juice during distillation respectively. Bagasse was not present in wine because the sugar cane juice was filtered during its purification treatment and the amount of residual sugars from fermentation was minimal because the fermentation process went by as usual until the full metabolization of fermentable sugars from the must.

Conclusions

The double distillation process contributed to the quality of the cachaça chemical composition both in legal terms, for being below the limits stipulated by the Brazilian legislation, except for the superior alcohols concentration, and in product integrity terms, since methanol and copper are toxic compounds and aldehydes are undesirable. The lower acidity suggested an improvement in the sensory quality of the final product. However, the sensory improvement of the spirit will only be proved by sensory analysis to be performed after the cachaça ageing period. This study has evaluated a new distillation technique for the improvement of the cachaça chemical and sensory quality through small changes in the production process and in the distillation equipment. In relation to the distillery configuration used (rectifying distiller), further research aimed at examining the volatilization sequence of compounds and the change in the distillate chemical composition along the distillation process could help to optimize the cutoff points in the double distillation to ensure full compliance of the resulting cachaça with the legislation currently in force.

Acknowledgements

The researchers would like to thank FAPESP, CNPq and CAPES for financial support.

References

Abrabe – Associação Brasileira de Bebidas. Available in: http://www.abrabe.org.br. Acess in: march 2008.

Almeida, M.E.W. and Barreto, H.H.C. (1972). Álcoois superiores em aguardente de cana por cromatografia gasosa. *Revista do Insituto Adolfo Lutz* **31**: 117-123.

Boza, Y. and Horii, J. (1998). Influência da destilação sobre a composição e a qualidade sensorial da aguardente de cana-de-açúcar. *Ciência e Tecnologia de Alimentos* **18**: 391-396.

Brasil. Leis, decretos, etc. (2005a). Instrução Normativa nº 24 of 8 september 2005. *Diário Oficial da União.*

Brasil. Leis, decretos, etc. (2005b). Instrução Normativa nº 13 of 29 june 2005. *Diário Oficial da União.*

Lamiable, D.; Hoizey, G.; Marty, H.and Vistelle, R. (2004). Acute methanol intoxication. *EMC Toxicology Pathology* **1**: 7-12.

Léauté, R. (1990). Distillation in alambic. *American Journal of Enology and Viticulure* **41**: 90-103.

Lurton, L.; Snakkers G.; Roulland C.; Galy, B. and Versavaud. (1995). Influence of the fermentation yeast-strain on the composition of wine spirits. *Journal of the Science of Food and Agriculture* **67**: 485.

Nascimento, R.F.; Marques, J.C.; Neto, B.S.L.; Keukeleire, D. and Franco, D.W. (1997). Qualitative and quantitative high-performance liquid chromatographic analysis of aldehydes in Brazilian sugar cane spirits and other distilled alcoholic beverages. *Journal of Chromatography A* **782**: 13-23.

Nykänen, L. (1986). Formation and occurrence of flavour compounds in wine and distilled alcoholic beverages. *American Journal of Enology and Viticulure* **37**: 84-96.

Pbdac – Programa Brasileiro de Desenvolvimento da Cachaça. Available in: http://www.cachacadobrasil.com.br/br/index.htm. Acess in: march 2008.

Chapter 25

Noise, vibration and lighting in the workplace

Dave McLaughlin
SgurrEnergy, 225 Bath Street, GLASGOW G2 4GZ, UK

Introduction

Exposure to noise or vibration, if of too high level or too long duration, causes injury. Inadequate or incorrect illumination involves risks of injury. The Noise and Vibration Group at SgurrEnergy have decades of experience in conducting assessments of risks associated with noise, vibration and ergonomic lighting. The results of these assessments assist employers in complying with statutory duties.

Noise in the workplace

Recent UK legislation (The Control of Noise at Work Regulations 2005) places statutory responsibilities on employers regarding risks associated with noise in the workplace. Similar legislation applies across Europe, under Directive 2003/10/EC of the European Parliament and of the Council (Directive on the minimum health and safety requirements regarding the exposure of workers to the risks arising from physical agents (noise)). Responsibilities are more onerous than under previous regulations. But to understand these responsibilities, one needs to understand the jargon of noise, and a little science.

Decibels

The dynamic range of the human ear is enormous. From the minimum discernable sound to the threshold of pain, the energy in a sound field can increase by a factor of a million million.

Noise and vibration are measured in decibels (dB). This is a logarithmic scale that compresses the huge range into a scale of 0 to 120, with a difference of 10 dB representing a multiplication by a factor of 10 in energy. A typical range of sound pressure levels that might be encountered in industry is shown in (Figure1).

The regulations impose two *exposure action values*, at which employers are required to take heed of a potential noise issue and take action, as well as an *exposure limit value*. However, to complicate matters further, these levels are not simple dB levels, they are weighted.

Noise weighting

The human ear is more sensitive at some frequencies (pitches) than others. When assessing the impact of noise on the ear, the noise is weighted to account for this frequency response. For continuous noise, the weighting function is

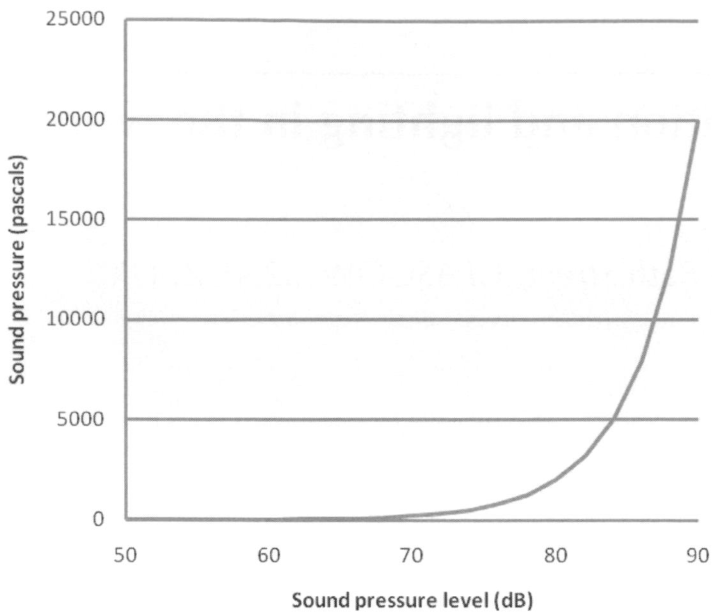

Figure 1. Sound pressure levels encountered in industry.

called "A" weighting. For transient, impulsive noise, a different, "C" weighting, function is used (Figure 2).

Where an employee is likely to be exposed to noise at or above the lower exposure action value, a competent person must make a Noise Risk Assessment (NRA). The lower exposure action value is an average level of 80 dB (A-weighted) for a 40-hour working week, or a peak level of 135 dB (C-weighted). The NRA must be used to inform working practices.

The upper exposure action value is 85 dB (A-weighted) average or 137 dB (C-weighted) peak. If this is likely to be exceeded, the employer must "reduce exposure to as low a level as is reasonably practicable by establishing and implementing a programme of organisational and technical measures, excluding the provision of personal hearing protectors, which is appropriate to the activity". The exposure limit values of 87 dB (A-weighted) average or 140 dB (C-weighted) peak must not be exceeded.

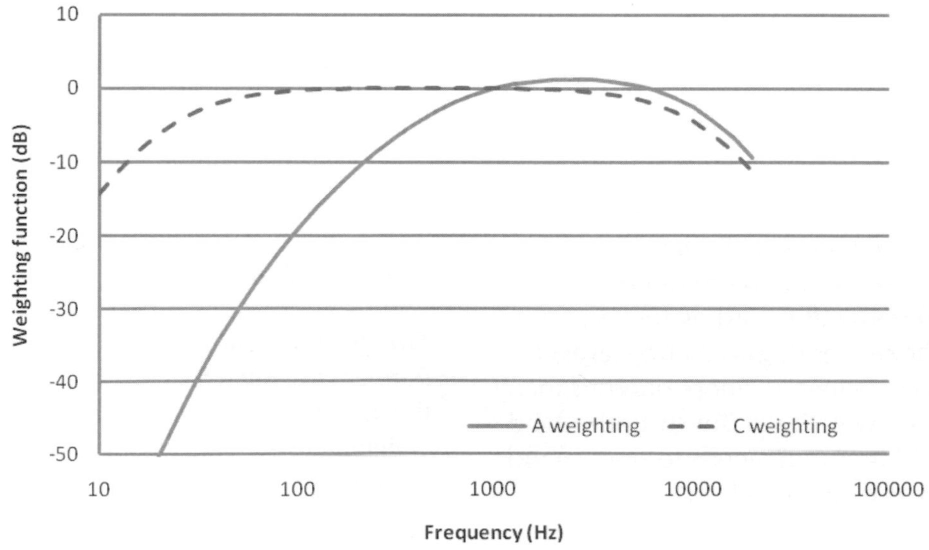

Figure 2. Noise weighting functions.

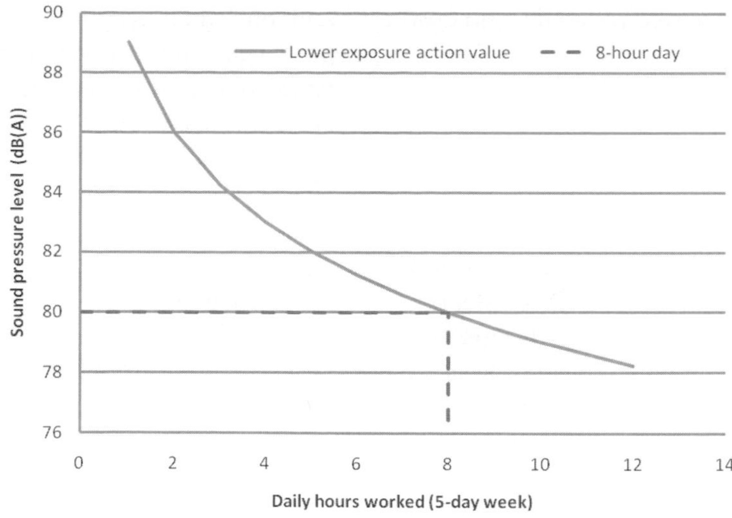

Figure 3. Lower exposure action value (dB(A)) ***v*** exposure time.

Daily personal noise exposure levels

The exposure action values and the exposure limits are specified for a working week of 5 × 8-hour days. The logarithmic nature of the decibel scale has implications for the exposure time – the permitted exposure time drops dramatically for apparently modest increases in sound pressure level (Figure 3).

Vibration in the workplace

In July 2005 the UK Parliament introduced regulations for the control of risks associated with vibration in the workplace (The Control of Vibration at Work Regulations 2005). As was the case with the noise regulations, this was driven by a European directive, namely Directive 2002/44/EC (Directive on the minimum health and safety requirements regarding the exposure of workers to the risks arising from physical agents (vibration)). These regulations are more onerous than those that applied previously.

Vibration is the most common cause of Industrial Injuries Disablement Benefit (IIDB; Health and Safety Executive 2007), and the new regulations impose exposure action values and exposure limit values analogous to those for noise.

Hand-arm vibration

Vibration White Finger (VWF) is a painful, debilitating condition caused by exposure to excessive vibration. It is required that employers have the risk associated with the use of hand held equipment assessed by a competent person. This is an area of risk assessment fraught with difficulties and it is strongly recommended that field surveys on the equipment during use are conducted rather than using manufacturers' data. Measurement of vibration on power tools is a skilled task requiring specialised equipment.

Whole body vibration

This type of vibration exposure is often associated with vehicles in which persons are seated or standing, the effect depending mainly on suspension characteristics, condition of operating surface, speed and disposition of the occupant. Such exposure can cause injury to various parts of the body, particularly the lower back.

Machinery health

Vibration levels and frequencies can also be key to machinery health monitoring and fault diagnosis, leading to improved reliability and cost savings.

Workplace lighting

Health and safety ergonomics in the workplace includes suitable lighting provision, normal and emergency. There are many sources of legislation, standards and codes of practice governing the provision of workplace lighting. These provisions depend upon the various types of area and the various tasks conducted therein and the emergency evacuation routes.

There is increasing awareness of the importance of lighting in the workspace. During normal working conditions, the lighting should be appropriate to the tasks being carried out. This is partly an issue of comfort, which affects productivity in the workplace, and partly a health and safety issue as it relates to the hazards of slips, trips and falls.

SgurrEnergy conduct surveys of normal workplace lighting in accordance with Regulation 8 of the Workplace (Health, Safety and Welfare) Regulations (1992), which requires that every workplace have suitable and sufficient lighting. This should be by natural lighting, so far as is reasonably practicable. Good lighting, whether natural or artificial, has an important role to play in promoting health and safety at work. It helps us to see hazards and it can reduce the likelihood of visual fatigue and discomfort.

Emergency lighting is subject to another set of regulations and standards, which have been significantly restructured in recent years. Employers are becoming increasingly aware of the importance of emergency escape lighting, and are taking their legal duties increasingly seriously. Emergency lighting is assessed in accordance with BS 5266-1:2005 (Emergency lighting Part 1: Code of practice for the emergency lighting of premises). Emergency lighting must continue to operate even when the normal supply is interrupted, and must be sufficient to guide a building's occupants towards fire extinguishers and escape routes.

Lighting will typically be assessed in both high and low ambient lighting conditions. In high ambient light (daylight), excessive illumination can pose a glare hazard. In darkness, reduced visibility can significantly increase the risks of slips, trips and falls as well as the hazards posed by obstructions at head height, rotating machinery and high voltage electrical equipment, among others.

Conclusions

Noise, vibration and lighting in the workplace are all areas where legislation has changed in recent years to impose significant responsibilities on employers. Employers must be aware of their responsibilities, and invest appropriate resources to ensure compliance with the law. SgurrEnergy can provide advice and specialist skills to support employers in meeting their responsibilities.

References

British Standards Institution, 2005. BS 5266-1:2005 *Emergency lighting Part 1: Code of practice for the emergency lighting of premises*. Milton Keynes: BSI.

Directive on the minimum health and safety requirements regarding the exposure of workers to the risks arising from physical agents (noise). Directive 2003/10/EC

Directive on the minimum health and safety requirements regarding the exposure of workers to the risks arising from physical agents (vibration). Directive 2002/44/EC

Health and Safety Executive 2007. Health and safety statistics 2006/07. [Online]. Health and Safety Executive. Available at: http://www.hse.gov.uk/statistics/overall/hssh0607.pdf [accessed 04 September 2008].

The Control of Noise at Work Regulations 2005. SI 2005/1643, London: HMSO.

The Control of Vibration at Work Regulations 2005. SI 2005/1093, London: HMSO.

The Workplace (Health, Safety and Welfare) Regulations 1992. SI 1992/3004, London: HMSO.

Chapter 26

The bioremediation of copper from distillery waste-water using indigenous microbes

Preeti Parikh[1], Graeme Walker[1], Phillip Collier[1] and Douglas Murray[2]
[1]Division of Biotechnology & Forensic Science, School of Contemporary Sciences, University of Abertay Dundee, Dundee DD1 1HG, UK; [2]Diageo Brand Technical Centre, Menstrie, Clackmannanshire, Scotland, UK

Abstract

Erosion of copper from the internal surface of the distillery vessels has been a major environmental concern mainly due to discharge of high concentrations of copper through drainage systems. The present study was designed to characterize the metal uptake and biosorption behaviour of indigenous microbes present and isolated from distillery environments. *Bacillus licheniformis* was isolated from distillery sump waters and identified using the API 50CH/B system. The minimum inhibitory concentration of copper against this organism ranged between 40-50mg/L. Biosorption capacities of *B.licheniformis* and a control laboratory strain *B. subtilis* 8045 for copper was determined using batch and continuous column experiments. Biosorption capacities for both strains was carried out at pH 5 and at copper concentrations of 10,50,70,90 and 200 mg/L. Immobilized bacterial studies of copper bioremediation were carried out with test and control strains using 2% calcium alginate beads to immobilize cells. Several parameters were optimized such as pH, bead size, and copper concentrations at which maximum biosorption can take place. Column bioreactor studies were done at an optimized pH and most efficient bead size and the effluent was collected at a flow rate of 1ml/min at every hour. Copper retention time in the immobilized column showed 90% removal bringing the copper levels down to below threshold levels in the first 10 hours of the column flow. The metal recovery was performed using 0.1M HCl and low pH solutions. The results of this study indicate the potential of bacterial copper bioremediation systems for distillery wastewaters.

Introduction

Water pollution has become one of the most serious problems in industrialized countries (Hameed, 2006). Regulations concerning discharge of heavy metals from distilleries (Bryce *et al.*, 2004) include trace amounts of copper. This trace element is essential for plant and animal life and is used in the electron transport chain and also forms part of oxygen transfer enzymes such as superoxide dismutase (Collier *et al.*, 1996). Copper also catalyses the synthesis of reactive oxygen species causing severe damage to the cytoplasmic constituents through the oxidation of proteins and cleavage of RNA and DNA (Crawford and Crawford, 1996). Copper also forms an important part of the cytochrome c oxidase which play a key role in the oxidative phosphorylation (Collier et al., 1996; Abrahamian (2001)).

In Scotch whisky production, copper plays an essential role in the distillation process as it is the material of choice in construction of copper stills. There are several advantages of copper in this regard including flavor to the whisky, being a good conductor of heat and also helping in removal of sulphur compounds (Lea and Piggott, 1995).

There are several conventional methods used for the removal of heavy metals from waste waters, including: precipitation, ion exchange, electrolysis, solvent extraction, evaporation, ultrafiltration and reverse osmosis (Das *et al.*, 1991). These methods are expensive and inefficient when the metal is present in low concentration (Deng *et al.*, 2006). Bioremediation is a natural process which involves the use of microorganisms and sufficient conditions of nutrients and oxygen, thus reducing decontaminants (Bhattacharyya and Banerjee, 2007). Bioremediation processes can be broadly classified into bioaccumulation, biostimulation, bioaugmentation and intrinsic bioremediation (Leung, 2004). Bacteria may be useful in heavy metal-containing effluent treatment and active uptake systems can take up both essential and non essential metal ions and hence they are important in bioremdiation. Important characteristics for metal ion removal are tolerance and uptake capacities (Boopathy, 2000). One of the most ubiquitous types of biomass available for bioremediation is bacteria (Lloyd and Lovey, 2001). Bioremediation being a natural process is widely accepted, as the microbial population declines once the contaminant decreases, leaving behind no harmful end products (Vidali, 2001). A major advantages of using this process is that it is compatible with the natural recycling methods of the earth (Agathos and Fantroussi, 2005). There are certain limitations to this process as well, when microbial metabolism may cause the microbe to release some toxic compounds. This might occur when the heavy metal is present in high concentrations and the microbe cannot degrade it (Boopathy, 2000; Vidali, 2001).

Many bacterial species have the ability to sequester metals by absorbing them on their cell surfaces or accumulating them internally (Ozdag *et al.*, 2004). Although copper is an essential element, it is toxic to bacterial cells at high concentrations leading to modification of active site of the enzyme, cell damage and decomposition of essential metabolites (Collier *et al.*, 1996; Crawford and Crawford, 1996; Deng *et al.*, 2006). Metal resistance is developed due to bioaccumulation and enzyme transformation (Leung *et al.*, 2000). When copper enters the cell it changes it ionic form from Cu^{2+} to $Cu1^{+}$, which is more toxic for the cells. This binds to certain amino acids leading to cross-linking between the proteins and hence impaired cell activity [Collier *et al.*, 1996; Lopez *et al.*, 2007]. Research has been done on metal-microbe interactions and metal uptake capacities of different organisms and it has been shown that metal binding capacity of Gram positive encapsulated bacteria is more than that of non capsulated Gram negative bacteria (Wase and Forster, 1997)]. Various factors affect the biosorption process such as temperature, pH and adsorbent concentration (Ahalya et al, 2003; Ahmad et al, 2007).

The aims of the present research were to characterize copper uptake and biosorption behaviour of indigenous microbes isolated from distillery water samples. The work has additionally investigated the ability of distillery-isolated *Bacillus licheniformis* to remove copper in both free-cell and immobilized-cell bioreactors.

Material and methods

Sample collection

Wastewater samples were collected from a distillery still sump in screw capped sterilized bottles from Cameronbridge Distillery, Scotland (courtesy of Diageo Ltd). Some physicochemical parameters of water were measured including pH and initial copper concentration.

A strain of *Bacillus subtilis* 8045 was obtained from the culture collection of University of Abertay Dundee. Pure cultures of this isolate were maintained on nutrient agar.

Isolation and identification of copper-tolerant bacteria

Preliminary analyses of a distillery sump water sample included the determination of the pH and copper concentration. The initial copper concentration was analyzed using an Atomic Absorption Spectrophotometer (Perkin Elmer). The water sample collected in sterile 500ml bottle was sampled for isolation and identification of the microbe. Initial analysis involved membrane filtration of the sample using sterile cellulose acetate filters (0.45μm, Nalgene) followed plating onto sterile nutrient agar (Oxoid) plates for further bacterial analysis. The plates were incubated at 37°C for 24 hr and resultant colonies obtained were analyzed by Gram stain. This was done with the original water sample as well as with a loopful of a representative colony obtained on the Nutrient agar plates.

Further identification methods for the indigenous bacteria in the distillery sump water included various biochemical tests. These were done by preparing agar plates for citrate utilization (Simmons Citrate Agar), specific bacterial identification (Lietch and Collier Medium), glucose utilization (Methyl Red-Vogues Proskauer), and motility testing (Motility Agar). The API 50 CH (Bio Merieux) system was additionally used for bacterial identification from the distillery water sample. This system is based on the fermentation of sugars by the isolate. The strips containing the medium were inoculated with the culture adjusted to a density of 2 McFarland (0.2ml of 1% barium chloride, 9.8ml of 1% sulphuric acid at wavelength of 600nm). The entire apparatus was incubated at 35°C for 24 hours.

Biosorption of copper and utilization by distillery-resident bacteria

Determination of minimum inhibitory concentration (MIC)

The lowest concentration of an antimicrobial agent that inhibits the visible growth of a microbe is known as the MIC. A 10ml of copper stock solution of 64mg/L was prepared using analytical grade salts of copper sulphate. Different volumes of stock solution were added to different volumes of nutrient broth to maintain a 10-fold dilution. The metal stock was filtered through a 0.45μm cellulose acetate filter. Tubes were incubated at 37°C for 24 hours. A linear MIC was also performed using different copper concentrations. A positive and negative control was maintained in each case. Results were recorded in terms of culture turbidities.

A similar MIC determination experiment was performed using nutrient agar plates, where the plates were prepared and autoclaved and different copper concentrations were incorporated in the agar. Results were recorded in terms on growth on plates after incubation of 3 days.

Biosorption

Batch experiments were performed using synthetic copper media and water samples from a distillery (courtesy of Diageo Ltd.). For experiments with synthetic copper, concentrations of 0ppm, 10ppm, 50ppm, 100ppm, 150ppm and 200ppm were prepared, by adding known amounts of copper sulphate in 10ml of 10mM MES buffer at pH 4.5. The cultures were grown in nutrient broth on a shaker incubator at 110rpm and centrifuged at 3800rpm to obtain a pellet of cells. The cells were washed with potassium phosphate buffer to adjust the density at OD 0.8 at wavelength 600nm. A viable count was done to determine the number of viable cells present.

The flasks were inoculated with the adjusted culture and incubated. The flask with 0ppm copper was set as the control. After 120 min, 10ml of the sample was removed from each flask and centrifuged. The supernatant was analyzed for copper concentration by AAS while the cell pellet was left for further analysis. Each set of flasks were set up in duplicate.

Optimization of pH and bead size (immobilised cell studies)

Biosorption was carried out with a distillery wastewater sample where several parameters were optimized. Effects of pH and bead size were optimized by immobilizing the bacteria in

2% calcium alginate and evaluating their copper uptake capabilities. The effect of pH on the sample was determined by setting up known volumes of immobilized beads in the flask with different pH. A range of pH from 1.0, 3.0, 5.0 and 9.0 were set up. Copper samples after the initial pH adjustment were measured for each flask using AAS. 4ml of beads were added to each flask. The flasks were incubated on a shaker incubator for 120 min. 10ml samples from each flask were taken after 10, 40, 70, 90, and 120 min respectively and analyzed for copper concentration.

Similarly, bead size was also optimized. Calcium alginate beads of different size; 0.45cm, 0.37cm and 0.27cm were made, respectively. The experiment was set up at pH 4.0. 5ml of beads were added into each flask and the flasks were supplemented with a glucose solution of 1% as carbon and energy source. All flasks were incubated for 4h at 35°C. Samples were collected at 2h and 4h for copper analysis. 10ml of beads were dried and the dry weight of the biomass was calculated.

Packed bed column semi-continuous flow studies

Packed bed experiments were conducted at room temperature in a 60ml sterile plastic column, packed with bed volume of 6.3ml of calcium alginate beads (biomass). The column was agitated after packing to remove the trapped air bubbles. Samples from the distillery containing approximately 5mg/L of copper were added to the column at a flow rate of 0.1ml per min. The samples were periodically added and effluent was collected every hour for copper analysis. The biosorption saturation of the packed column was reached when outlet concentration was almost equal to the inlet.

Continuous column biosorption studies

Continuous column experiments were carried out using synthetic copper as well as distillery wastewater samples. Immobilized bacterial cells were packed in a glass chromatography column of length 45cm, inner diameter of 8cm and column capacity of approximately 1.5L. The column was flushed with water to wash the beads and remove any entrapped air inside and the pH was adjusted to 5.0. A copper solution was pumped through the column of concentration 100mg/L at a flow rate of 1ml per min. the column was run until saturated. A similar column run was set up for the distillery sample.

Metal recovery

Copper was recovered from the semi continuous and continuous column by flushing the column with a fixed pH solution. Sterile water was passed through the column to remove any loosely bound copper from the bead surface. The beads were immersed into 0.1M HCl solution for extraction of the metal from the beads. Further total extractable copper was obtained by dissolving the beads into 55mM sodium citrate solution and the metal extracted was analyzed by AAS. The dissolved bead solution was centrifuged to obtain a pellet of cells. The cell pellet was further analyzed for metal extraction by glass bead homogenization.

Results

Physiochemical characteristics of distillery wastewater and indigenous microbes

The distillery wastewater had an initial pH of 4.5 and the copper concentration was 9.7ppm.

The colony characteristics of the microbes found in the water sample were small creamy white colonies that appeared on nutrient agar after incubation. On Gram staining, these colonies were found to be Gram positive endospore-forming bacilli in chains. These were observed under oil immersion using phase contrast microscopy.

Identification of the bacterial isolate

Species identification based on biochemical tests confirmed that the isolate present in the distillery wastewater sample was a Gram positive bacillus (Fig 1). A citrate utilization test carried out using Simmons citrate agar was found to be positive. This was indicated by a color change in the medium from olive green to blue due to the indicator bromothymol blue. The MR-VP medium also showed a change in color when inoculated with the bacterial colony and incubated under appropriate conditions, thus indicating the presence of Gram positive bacilli. Another test was performed by growing the isolate on nutrient agar at 55°C. The growth of the organism under high temperatures confirmed the isolate to be a Gram positive bacillus.

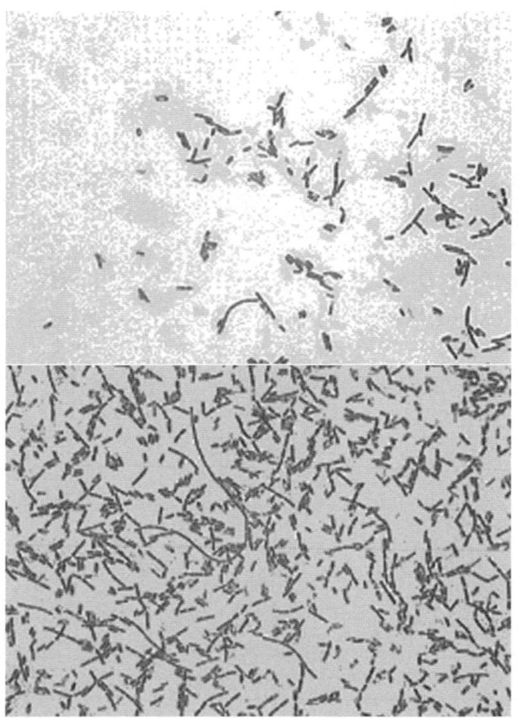

Figure1 showing the long rod shaped, Gram positive bacilli in chains with endospore.

The API 50 CH/B test was done with the lab strain of *B.subtilis* and the isolate from the distillery. A number of sugars were inoculated with both the lab and test strain and incubated under appropriate conditions. The results of the sugar fermentation of the lab strain and those of the isolate were compared with the results in the kit provided. On comparison it was found that the bacillus isolated from the distillery water sample was *B. licheniformis*. This identification was made using the Bergey's Manual of Systematic Bacteriology. A motility test was also performed to check the motile nature of the culture. The bacillus was found to be actively motile.

Minimum inhibitory concentration and copper utilization by bacteria

The MIC of copper against the test strain *B.subtilis* and the distillery isolate *B.licheniformis* was performed with different copper concentrations using the tube dilution and plate dilution methods. According to the results obtained the tolerance of the test strain was greater than that of the isolate (Tables 1 & 2). The test strain showed an MIC of almost 60mg/L, where as the isolate *Bacillus licheniformis* showed an MIC of 50mg/L.

Table 1. Twofold tube dilution method showing various concentrations of copper incorporated in nutrient agar inoculated with the test strain and isolate. The tubes were incubated at 37°C for 24h.

Tube no	*Dilution (mg/L)*	*B. subtilis*	*B. licheniformis*
1	58	+ +	-
2	56	+ +	-
3	54	+ +	-
4	52	+ +	-
5	50	+ + +	-
6	48	+ + +	+ + +
7	46	+ + +	+ + +
8	44	+ + +	+ + +
9	42	+ + +	+ + +
10	40	+ + +	+ + +
11	38	+ + +	+ + +
12	Positive control	+ + +	+ + +
13	Negative control	-	-

Table 1 shows the MIC for *B. subtilis* and *B. licheniformis* over a twofold dilution using the Tube dilution method. The copper tolerance of the test strain was more compared to the distillery isolate. The test strain *B. subtilis* showed an MIC of almost 60mg/L while *B. licheniformis* showed an MIC of 50mg/L.

Table 2. Tube dilution method in a linear range showing the MIC for test and isolate

Tube no	*Dilution (mg/L)*	*B. subtilis*	*B. licheniformis*
1	38	+ + +	+ + +
2	39	+ + +	+ + +
3	40	+ + +	+ + +
4	41	+ +	+ +
5	42	+ +	+ +
6	43	+ +	+ +
7	44	+ +	+ +
8	45	+ +	+ +
9	46	+ +	+ +
10	47	+ +	+ +
11	48	+ +	+ +
12	49	+ +	+ +
13	50	+ +	+ +
14	51	+ +	-
15	52	+ +	-
16	53	+ +	-
17	54	+ +	-
18	55	+ +	-
19	56	+ +	-
20	57	+	-

Key: + growth, - No growth

Table 2 shows the tolerance limit of the two strains over a linear range of copper concentrations. The MIC for *B .subtilis* was found to be more than 57mg/L, while the MIC for *B. licheniformis* appears to be 51mg/L.

Due to varying MIC results for *B. licheniformis*, the experiment was repeated in triplicate (not shown) and the MIC for the distillery isolate was found to be within a range of 40-50mg/L.

Removal of copper by the bacterial isolate

Biosorption studies using synthetic copper with live free cells

Batch studies using free live cells in synthetic copper solutions were carried out to determine the uptake capacity of the isolate.

Biosorption capacities of *B. subtilis* and *B. licheniformis* were studied using synthetic copper solutions of different concentrations dissolved in MES buffer. Table 3 shows the % removal of copper by the live free cells in a span of 2 hours incubation. 90% removal of copper can be seen from an initial standard concentration of 10ppm. This can be depicted from Fig 2 where flask 2 in the graph shows removal of copper from 10mg/L to 1mg/L.

Table 3. % Copper removal or uptake by *B. licheniformis*

Standard (ppm)	*Reading (ppm)*	*Copper removal (%)*
0	0	0
10	1	90
50	36.2	27.6
100	85.6	14.4
150	126.2	15.8
200	130.2	34.9

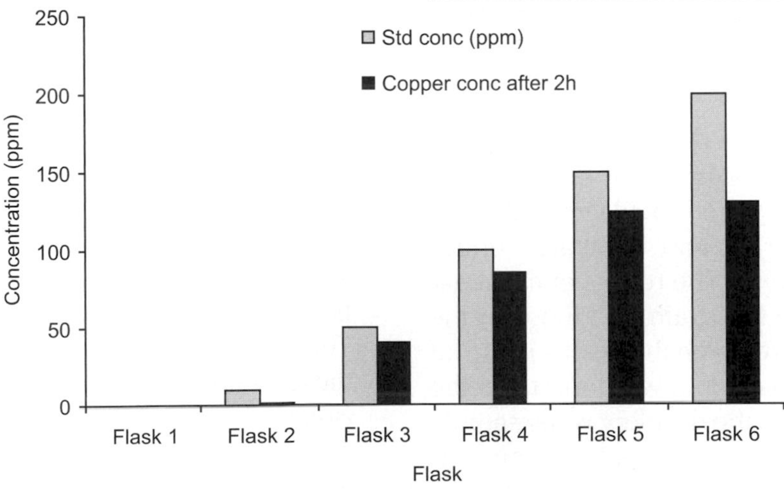

Figure 2. Biosorption capacity of *B. licheniformis* using standard copper concentrations of 0, 10, 50, 100, 150 and 200 mg/L after incubation of 2 h

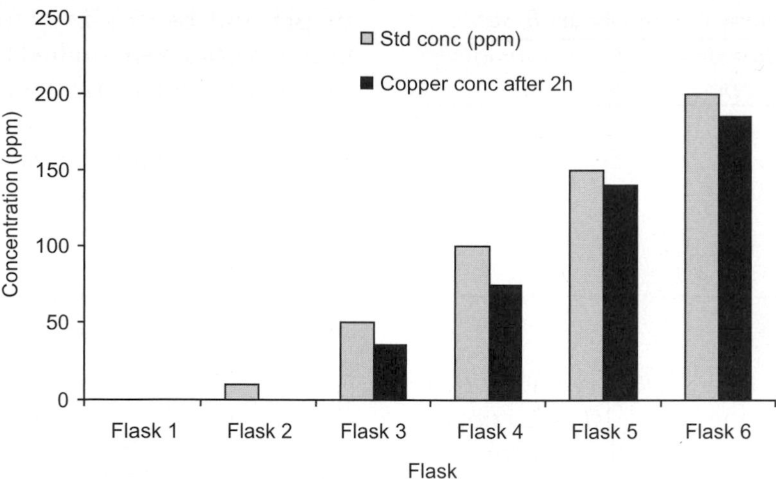

Figure 3. Biosorption capacity of *B. subtilis* using standard concentrations of 0, 10, 50,100,150 and 200 mg/L after incubation of 2h

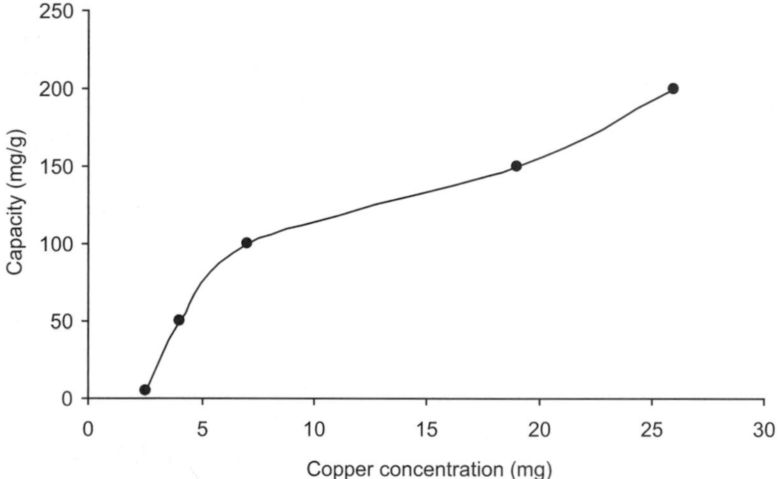

Figure 4. Effect of copper ion concentration on the biosorption capacity of *B. licheniformis* biomass. The metal ion concentration is expressed as mg of metal per g biomass.

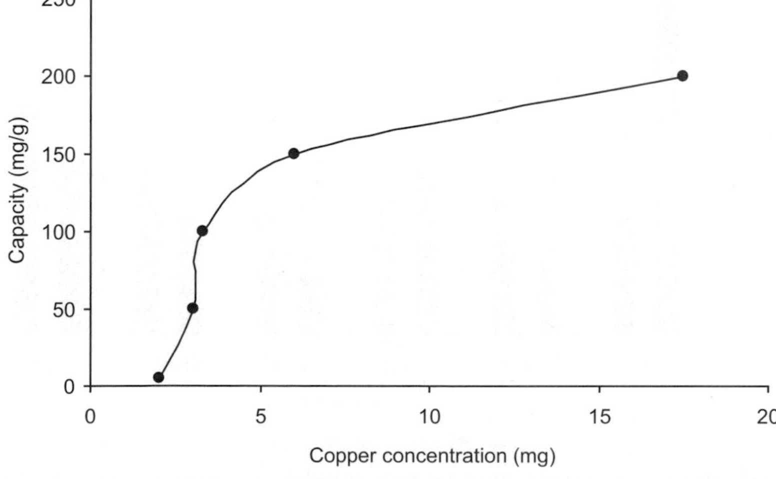

Figure 5. Effect of copper ion concentration on the biosorption capacity of *B. subtilis* biomass. The metal ion concentration is expressed as mg of metal per g biomass.

Table 4. % Copper removal or uptake by *B. subtilis*

Standard (ppm)	*Reading (ppm)*	*Copper removal (%)*
0	0	0
10	0	100
50	35.2	29.6
100	72.8	27.2
150	142.6	4.9
200	189.8	5.1

On the other hand, *B. subtilis* showed a 100% removal from the initial 10mg/L copper concentration but on comparison of results with the isolate when the concentration of copper was increased the percentage removal by *B. subtilis* decreased gradually. With 10ppm Cu, *B. subtilis* seems to have a better uptake compared with *B. licheniformis*, but when the copper concentration was increased to 200ppm, *B. licheniformis* shows greater metal uptake than the test strain. Copper at 0ppm in both experiments represented a control, without copper addition.

Biosorption with live immobilized cells

Metal uptake capacity of the isolate *B. licheniformis* was tested individually with the distillery sump water sample with optimization of pH and bead size. Effects of these two characteristics were studied to detect the changes in the metal uptake by the bacteria.

These studies involved entrapment of live cells in 2% calcium alginate beads suspended in the sample subjected to various pH and bead sizes.

Effect of pH on biosorption was studied at pH 1.0, 3.0, 5.0 and 9.0 respectively. Figure 6 shows that from an initial concentration of 6.25 ppm at time 0 min of pH 3, the copper concentration decreased to approximately 3.3 ppm at 40 min and remained so overtime. Similar results were seen for pH 5 with slight fluctuations at time 70min. Hence at pH 3, approximately 55% removal of metal was observed in relation to its initial concentration, while pH 5 showed almost 60% metal removal. On the other hand, pH 1 and 9 showed no significant contribution in the metal removal capacity of the bacteria. Hence it can be seen that metal uptake occurs best between pH 3 to 5 which corresponds to the pH of the distillery processes.

A similar result (Fig 7) gives a clear indication of copper concentration initially at time 0 min and concentration after 120 min for the various pH values as shown above. From Fig 7 it can be seen that not much contribution has been made by pH 1 and 9. Copper adsorption capacities of the bacteria work best between pH 3 and 5.

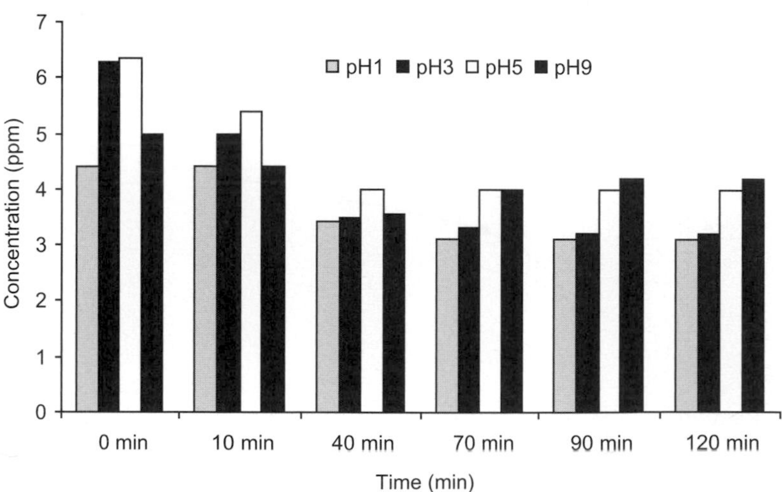

Figure 6. Effect of pH on copper uptake by the immobilized bacteria at different time intervals within a time span of 2h. Initial concentration of copper at pH 1, 3, 5 and 9 was 4.21 ppm, 6.25 ppm, 6.30 ppm and 4.88 ppm respectively.

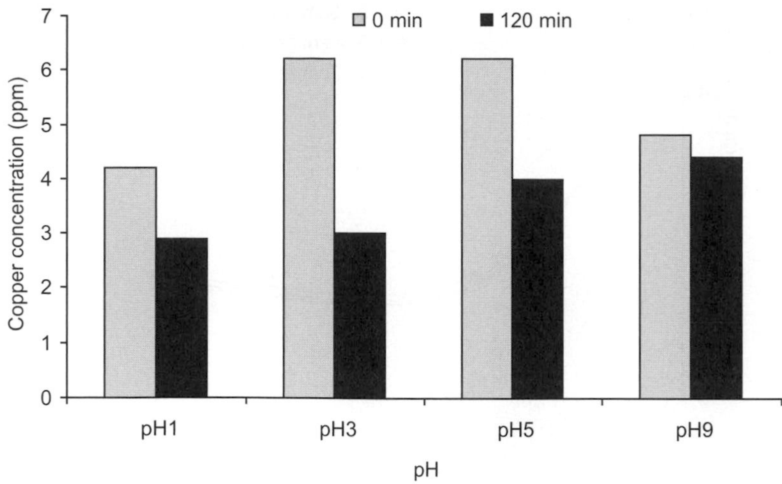

Figure 7. pH effects on copper biosorption over 2h of incubation. Initial and final copper concentration at pH 1, 3, 5 and 9 were measured at time 0min and 120min. Final concentration at 120min shows 2.94ppm, 3.24ppm, 4.02ppm and 4.24ppm respectively.

Effect of bead size on copper biosorption by immobilized bacteria

Optimization of bead size on metal uptake was studied by making beads of three different sizes and carrying out biosorption with the immobilized bacteria. Keeping other factors such as pH and temperature constant, the effect of bead size was studied.

Figs 8 and 9 represent the effect of bead size on biosorption of copper from the sample. Figure 8 shows the decrease in the metal concentration in terms of mg/L from an initial concentration of 4.85mg/L in a span of 2 hours. The results after 4 h were not significantly different than the results after 2h hence suggesting that the copper concentration did not reduce further after an equlibrium time of 2h.

From these results it is evident that all the three bead sizes removed almost 65 -67% of metal in 4h. Smaller beads were more effective (see below). Fig 9 shows the drop in concentration from the initial to final after 4hours at pH 4.0. The three lines show the metal uptake

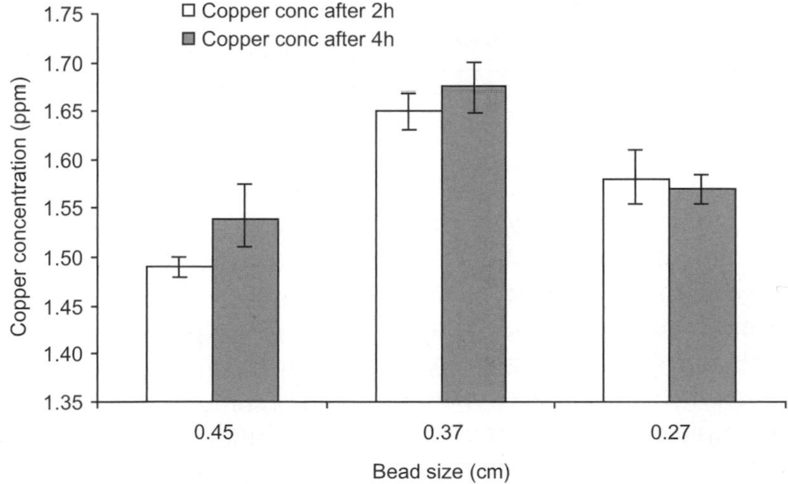

Figure 8. Effect of bead size on biosorption after 2 and 4 h incubation from the initial concentration of 4.85 mg/L at a fixed pH 4.0. The figure shows concentration of copper after 2 h and 4 h for each bead size.

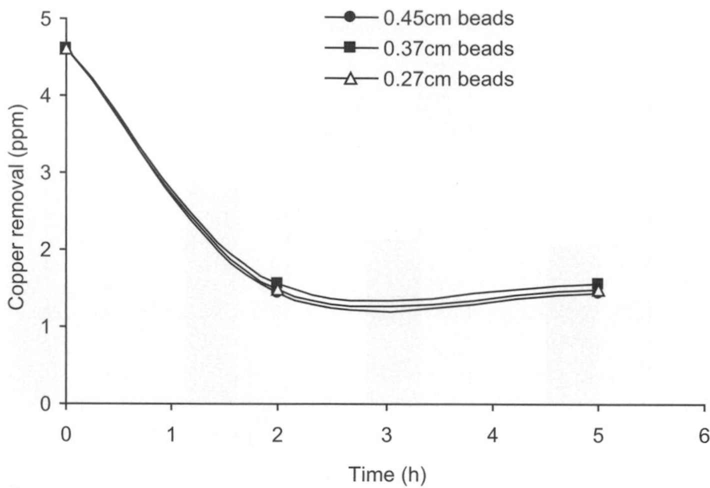

Figure 9. Effect of bead size on copper removal at pH 4.0. A drop in the copper concentration is seen from an initial concentration of 4.85ppm for all the three bead sizes at time 2 -4h

by each bead size. According to Fig 8, the samller beads have more metal uptake capacity than the bigger beads. One of the main reasons being that smaller beads have a greater surface area than the bigger beads and hence more binding sites are available for metal adsorption [25]. The actual value of metal uptake by the biosorbent shows the amount of copper adsorbed by the total biosorbent in the sample (Table 5).

Table 5. Effect of bead size on Biosorption. The table shows metal uptake by the Biosorbent in each bead size. Bead size of 0.27 shows maximum metal uptake.

Diameter (cm)	*μ Copper/g of Biosorbent*
0.45	11.0
0.37	11.21
0.27	11.70

Table 5 shows the metal binding capacity of the immobilized cells in different bead size and it is evident that the beads with smaller diameter have the maximum biosorption capacity. This fact has been depicted in Figs 8 and 9. The difference in the metal uptake is small since the initial copper concentration in the sample was only 4.85ppm. Since the experiment was performed with the distillery sample it is evident that the sample contained other metals along with copper. Hence it is possible that the binding sites of the biosorbent were taken up by other metal ions present in the sample. On an industrial scale it may not be possible to use small beads, since they are tedious to make. Further, use of small beads may lead to clogging of column due to low pressure in the column.

Packed bed column semi continuous flow studies

Column studies were carried out to determine copper adsorption by bacteria immobilized in a semi continuous column. Two columns were set up to determine the metal uptake capacity of the immobilized cells and calcium alginate alone as a control.

Fig 10 shows the adsorption isotherm of copper by the immobilized cells and the calcium alginate beads. On comparison of the two curves, it can be seen that immobilized cells take up more copper than the calcium alginate beads. When *B.licheniformis* was immobilized in the column only trace amounts of copper appeared in the effluent until 2 hours which was about 1ppm. On the other hand 1.17ppm was seen to be eluted out in the coulmn containing only calcium alginate beads in the first hour itself.

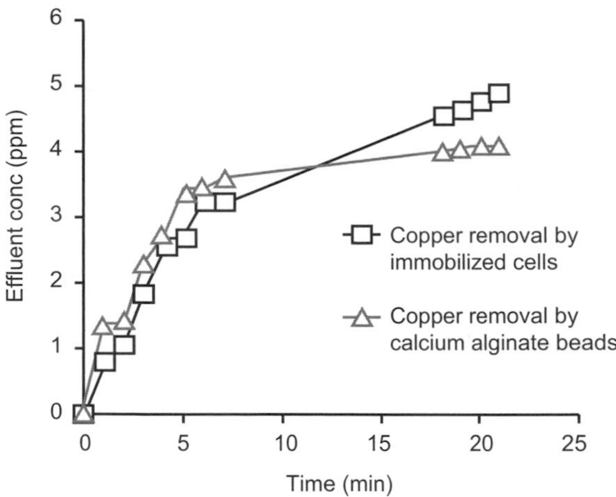

Figure 10. Semi continious column adsorption studies showing copper removal by bacteria and beads. Graph shows effleunt concentration(ppm) against time in min. Immobilized cells show higher retention time in comparison to calcium alginate beads as per the copper concentration seen in the effluent. The straight line indicates a time lag where the column flow was stopped.

Hence the first hour is taken to be crucial for copper bioremediation.

The straight line on the graph shows a time lag where the column was not supplied with the sample. Beyond a time span of 18 hours both the columns had reached saturation, where the effluent concentration was equal to the feed concentration. The graph clearly shows that immobilized cells had a greater metal uptake capacity than the beads alone, although the uptake was not markdly significant.

Copper was recovered from the immobilized cells by flushing with 45 ml of distilled water through the beads and this resulted in recovery of 0.067 mg of copper while the control beads resulted in the recovery of 0.048 mg of copper. A reason for high concentration of metal recovered from the immobilized cells could be that the metal ions attached to the outer bacterial cell wall were also flushed out along with the matrix of the beads. Further metal recovery in both cases can be achieved by dissolving the beads in 55 mM sodium citrate.

Continuous column adsorption studies

Fig 11 shows the removal of copper by the immobilized bacterial cells in a continuous column. The inlet concentration in the column was 83 ppm at the start of the column flow with a flow rate of 1ml per min. The graph shows that as time increases no copper is seen in the effluent till the 9th hour. At the 10th hour 2.47 ppm is seen to be present in the effluent collected at the bottom. This shows that the immobilized cells had the ability to retain more than 90% of the copper for 10 hours. Hence it can be seen that from an initial concentration of 83 ppm, the immobilized cells can reduce the copper levels in the inlet to permissible limits. A breakthrough point can be seen on the graph marked with the two arrows. After the breakthrough curve the column shows saturation.

On the other hand, Fig 12 shows the copper removal in a continuous column by the calcium alginate beads alone. In comparison to Fig 11, the graph shows that 1.61 ppm of copper was in the effluent at the second hour of the run. Slight fluctuations were observed in the first few hours of the adsorption graph but a steady increase can be seen until the 30th hour. If the two columns are compared it can be observed that the copper retention time in the column with immobilized cells is more than that of calcium alginate beads. The two arrows show the breakthrough points after which the column attained saturation.

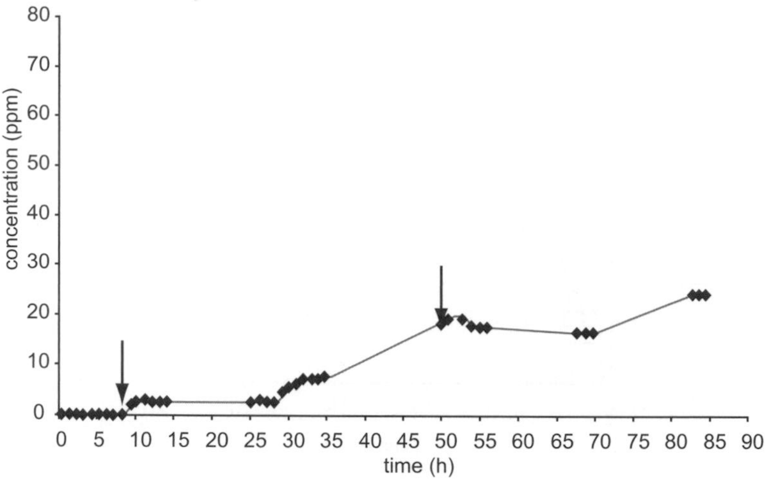

Figure 11. Continous column studies using immobilized bacteria in beads for copper removal. The inlet concentration corresponds to 83ppm. A linear increase in the elluent concentration is observed until the 80th hour after which the graph shows a straight line indicating column saturation. The two arrows indicate the important time period of 9th hour and 50th hour of column run.

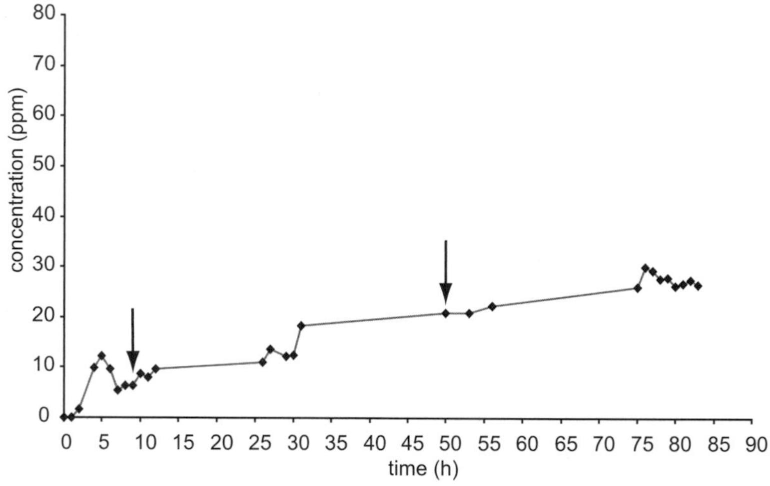

Figure 12. Continuous copper removal by calcium alginate beads in a column for metal removal. The two arrows indicate the important time period of 9th hour and 50th hour of column run. The inlet concentration corresponds to 99ppm. A steady increase in the outlet concentration is observed till the 78th hour. Column saturation can be observed thereafter where the outlet concentration remained almost constant.

Table 6. Copper concentration in mg of the two columns. A comparison of inlet and outlet concentrations is shown and the corresponding % copper removal

	Inlet	*Outlet*	*% Copper removal*
Immobilized cells	415mg	75.9mg	81.71%
Calcium alginate beads	495mg	102mg	79.39%

Table 6 shows the inlet and outlet concentration of copper in the two columns. A percentage calculation of the two column uptake shows that the immobilized cells in the beads took up 81.17% of copper from the solution, while the calcium alginate as control took up 79.39%. An increase in the metal uptake was seen in the bacteria immobilized in the beads although the increase is not very significant. A possible

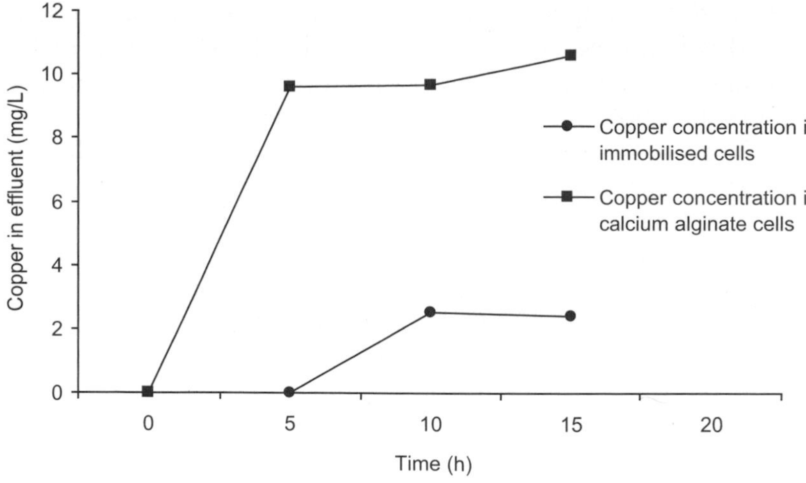

Figure 13. Copper concentration in the effluent of the two columns at 0, 5th, 10th and 15th hour. The graph shows the important time period of the column run agaisnt the effluent concentration(mg/L). A sharp increase in the effluent concentration of the calcium alginate beads is seen to 9.69ppm in the 5th hour. In comparison, the concentration in the effluent of the immobilized cells show 0ppm at the 5th hour. Graph shows that immobilized cells retained greater concentrations of copper than the control column.

reason for low uptake of metal could be the high concentration of copper in the inlet. Excess copper in the cell can lead to inactivation of cell and at times cell death. A greater uptake of metal ions is expected by the immobilized cells but this has not been the case. Although the immobilized *B. licheniformis* was successful in removal of copper ions from the sample, a reason of low metal adsorption can due to the low amount of biomass present in the column. Insufficient microbial load could have been a possible reason of fewer uptakes of copper ions from the solution. Another reason can be the removal of the metal by the column wash.

Table 7. Table showing recovery of metal from the column.

Method	*Immobilized cells*	*Calcium alginate*
Column wash	14.52mg	32.07mg
Low pH solution	22.2mg	58.98mg
0.1M HCl	7.25mg	19.47mg
55mM sodium citrate	40mg	114mg

Table 7 shows the concentration of copper recovered after the column adsorption was performed with 5l of copper solution at a flow rate of 1ml/min. From these results it can be seen that the column with the control calcium alginate beads had a greater recovery of metal in comparison to the immobilized cells. This can be interpreted in a way that the bacteria immobilized within the beads have taken up copper from the solution. Hence the ability to regenerate biosorbent beads and recovery of copper is one of the advantages of using microbial biomass to adsorb copper (Ogden and Stanely, 2003). Table 7 shows the amount of copper regenerated by dissolving the beads in sodium citrate. The control beads contributed to the recovery of 114 mg of copper, while the immobilized cells gave 40 mg of copper. The difference in the two figures suggests that 74 mg of copper was taken up by the bacteria immobilized in the beads.

For the two columns, metal recovery using 0.1M HCl was very significant, since 5l of copper solution was required to load and saturate the column at a flow rate of 1ml/min, while only 200 ml (0.2l) of HCl was needed to chelate the copper from the beads. This is an important fact to be considered, since more than 90% of copper was recovered by suspending the beads in HCl. Recovery of copper in terms of ppm was found to be 97.35 and 36.25 ppm in the control and immobilized column respectively. Hence it can be seen that the control column was able to recover more than 90% of copper. This is especially significant because it shows that copper in the influent can be concentrated almost 10 fold using this biosorption and recovery method (Leung *et al.*, 2000). To determine the amount of copper taken up by the immobilized bacteria, the bacterial cells were lysed by glass bead homogenization.

Glass bead homogenization for metal recovery from bacteria

The beads containing the immobilized bacteria were lysed to analyze the amount of copper taken up by the cellular fraction. Glass bead homogenization was done to separate the cell wall and cytoplasm from the whole cell. The immobilized cells in the beads were dissolved and re-suspended in 8ml of distilled water. 1 ml fraction was subjected to lyses by glass beads and digestion with nitric acid. The suspension was then measured in AAS for copper concentration.

The cellular fractions obtained contained the following amount of copper:

Whole cell: 8.6 ppm/ 10^7cells
Cytosol: 6.2 ppm/ 10^7cells
Cell wall: 2.3 ppm/ 10^7cells

On dissolving the beads, the pellet obtained was re-suspended in 8 ml of distilled water. The total biomass present in the immobilized cell columns corresponds to 29 g/L. In terms of ml of culture added to make the immobilized cells, 11.2 ml of bacterial suspension was added in 2 % calcium alginate to make the beads. Hence the total number of bacterial cells in the column was 11.2 x 10^7 cells. If we back calculate the value obtained for 1 ml, absorption of copper by the total bacteria in the column corresponds to 96.32 mg. According to values obtained for metal recovery from the control column, it shows that 114 mg of copper could be recovered. If we take the difference of the two values, 74 mg of copper should ideally be taken up by the bacterial cells. Glass bead homogenization shows that bacterial cells gave a contribution of 96.32 mg of copper, thus suggesting that the calcium alginate beads took up only 17.69 mg of copper. Since the immobilized column shows that calcium alginate beads contributed to 40 mg of metal, it can be clearly seen that 22. 32 mg (40 -17.68) was of the bacterial cells which could have been washed away from the cell wall on dissolving the beads. Hence it can be seen that immobilized bacterial cells have greater capacity of metal uptake as compared to calcium alginate beads alone. Thus we can conclude that immobilization of bacterial cells represent good biosorbents for metal removal.

Similar column experiments were performed with the distillery wastewater sample. Subsequent failure of the column run was seen due to clogging of the column. The distillery sample contained large amounts of sediment and heavy microbial load due to which it was difficult to perform the column experiment. Further, lab scale experiments of immobilized cells were carried out under aerobic conditions; hence a possibility of contamination was expected. Since *B. licheniformis* is an aerobic organism overgrowth of the culture is possible thus leading to clogging of the column and making it difficult for the sample to pass through.

Discussion and conclusion

Living organisms have been used as a source for heavy metal removal from industrial wastewater for a long time. Bioremediation of copper has been the interest of this study, in particular removal of copper from distillery wastewater and to reduce this to acceptable limits before discharge into the environment. Moreover, the strain *Bacillus licheniformis* isolated from the sump water of a distillery proved to be considerably better at biosorption of metal from the waters, in comparison to calcium alginate.

Immobilization studies have shown that live bacteria immobilized in the calcium alginate beads have been capable of heavy metal uptake and biosorption of copper ions.

High levels of copper tolerance were detected in the isolated strain as well as the control strain *Bacillus subtilis*. Metal tolerance was detected by performing Minimum Inhibitory Concentration using various copper concentrations. Pure cultures of both the strains were obtained by repeated isolation on nutrient agar. Identification of the indigenous (distillery-resident) microbe was performed by Gram staining, API 50CH system and biochemical test. The strain was found to be Gram positive endospore forming bacilli as per the Bergey's Manual of Systematic Bacteriology.

Metal microbe interactions were studied by performing batch experiments with synthetic copper and distillery samples. Metal uptake by *B. licheniformis* was found to be significantly greater than the control strain. Low concentrations of copper were found to have a better uptake than higher concentrations. An uptake of 90% of metal was seen by *B. licheniformis* in synthetic copper solutions. Metal removal capacity of this strain was then tested against the distillery sample, where parameters like pH and bead size were optimized. Biosorption by the strain was found best to occur at a pH range of 3.0-4.0. Immobilization studies using different bead sizes showed that smaller beads of diameter 0.27-0.37cm were more effective in metal adsorption than bigger beads due to a greater surface area for metal adsorption. Metal uptake capacity studies showed that as the copper concentration in the sample increased, the uptake by the bacteria increased till a saturation point was obtained, where no further increase in the metal uptake was seen.

Column studies were performed to investigate the metal uptake over a period of time. Effective removal of metal from synthetic copper solution was seen in case of *B. licheniformis*, where 97% of copper removal was seen within the first ten hours of the column run indicating that ten hours would be a sufficient time for reducing the metal concentration to permissible limits. On the other hand, distillery samples worked well with *B. licheniformis* as well although it was carried out as a semi continuous column. Owing to large amounts of sediments and heavy microbial load in the sample, it was difficult to perform a continuous column. Clogging of column was seen in case of experiments with big columns using distillery sample. Differences in the inlet concentration of control and isolate column with distillery sample were seen due to repeated filtration of the sample as a result of contamination and heavy microbial growth. Cell fractions obtained by glass bead homogenization showed that the *B.licheniformis* contributed to 68mg of copper from the total copper taken up by the biosorbent. On comparison of the two columns it was seen that the column with immobilized *B. licheniformis* showed a metal uptake of 82% as against the calcium alginate beads which reported an uptake of 79%. Metal recovery from biosorbent was achieved efficiently by using solutions of low pH and 0.1M HCl. Hence studies show that immobilization of bacteria in a solid matrix like 2% calcium alginate beads enhances the copper uptake from the sample.

In conclusion, immobilization of *B. licheniformis* is feasible for copper removal in batch and continuous systems. Metal uptake capacities of bacteria can be increased by increasing the concentration of biosorbent in immobilized columns. Several cycles of metal removal should be performed for better removal of copper from wastewaters. Uptake of metal ions generally occur in two phases, where first is the fast or rapid phase, where metal ions bind to the cell wall. The second phase is the slow phase, where the metal ions travel inside the cytosol (Hameed, 2006). Hence when acid digestion is done on the cell fraction, the first elution can remove the freely bound metal ions on the outer surface of the bacteria, thus providing more binding sites for the next cycle. Not so effective removal of copper was seen from the distillery sample, due to presence of other metals which generally contribute to the distillery waters.

Scaling up is essential for industrial suitability of bioremediation of copper from distillery wastewaters. Increasing the biomass load for more copper removal needs to be focused on. Studies on metabolism of copper inside the bacterial cell may also be worthwhile. Further studies are needed to increase the biosorption capacities of the biomass and to develop appropriate technologies for bioremediation of copper from distillery samples.

References

Abrahamian, J. (2001). Bio-treatment of waste streams containing organic compounds and copper. Thesis. University of Arizona.

Agathos, S. N and Fantroussi, S. El. (2005). Is bioaugmentation a feasible strategy for pollutant removal and site remediation? *Current Opinion in Microbiology*. 8:pp. 268-275.

Ahalya, N., Kanamadi, R. D and Ramachandra, T. V. (2003). Biosorption of Heavy Metals. *Energy: pp*. 1-14.

Ahmad, M. M., Saleemi, A. R and Qaiser, S. (2007). Heavy metal uptake by agro based waste materials. *Electronic Journal of Biotechnology*. 10(3):pp. 410-416.

Bhattacharyya, B. C and Banerjee, R. (2007). *Environmental Biotechnology*. India. Oxford University Press.

Boopathy, R. (2000). Factors limiting bioremediation technologies. *Bioresource Technology*. 74:pp. 63-67.

Bryce, J. H. and Stewart. G. G. (2004). *Distilled Spirits: Tradition and Innovation*. Nottingham: Nottingham University PressNottingham University Press.

Collier, P.J., Jones, G. T and Giblin, L. (1996). *The Bioremediation of Copper Containing Industrial Effluent*. University of Abertay Dundee.

Crawford, L. R and Crawford, L. D. (1996). *Bioremediation Principles and Applications*. Cambridge. Cambridge University Press.

Das, R.P., Kar, R. N and Sahoo, D. K. (1991). Bioaccumulation of Heavy Metal Ions by *Bacillus circulans*. *Bioresource Technology*. 41:pp.177-179.

Deng, L., Zhu, X., Wang, X., Su, Y and Su, H. (2006). Biosorption of Copper (II) from aqueous solution by green alga *Cladophora fascicularis*. *Biodegradation*. 18:pp.393-402.

Hameed, M. S. A. (2006). Continuous removal and recovery of lead alginate beads, free and alginate-immobilized *Chlorella vulgaris*. *African Journal of Biotechnology*. 5:pp. 1819-1823.

Lea, A.G.H and Piggott, J. R. (1995). *Fermented Beverage Production*. UK. Blackie Academic and Professional.

Leung, M. (2004). Bioremediation: Techniques for Cleaning up a mess. *Bio Teach Journal*. 4:pp. 18-22.

Leung, C. K., Yu, P. H. F., Chua, H., Wong, M-F. and Leung, W. C. (2000). Removal and recovery of heavy metal by bacteria isolated from activated sludge treating industrial effluents and municipal waste water. *Water Science and Technology*. 41(12):pp. 233-240.

Lopez, J. G., Rodelas, B., Gomez, M. A., Pozo, C and Vilchez, R. (2007). Dominance of sphingomonads in copper exposed biofilm community for groundwater treatment. *Microbiology*. 153:pp. 325-337.

Lloyd, J. R. and Lovey, D.R. (2001). Microbial detoxification of metals and radionuclieds. *Current Opinion Biotechnology*. 12:pp. 248-253.

Ogden, K., L. and Stanely, L., C. (2003). Biosorption of copper (II) from chemical mechanical planarization wastewaters. *Journal of Environmental Management*. 69:pp. 289-297.

Ozdag, H., Kilicarslan, S., Nourbakhsh, M. N and Ilhan, S. (2004). Removal of Chromium, Lead and Copper ions from Industrial Waste waters by *Staphylococcus saprophyticus*. *Turkish Electronic Journal of Biotechnology*. 2:pp. 50-57.

Vidali, M. (2001). Bioremediation. An overview.

Pure Appl. Chem. 73(7):pp. 1163-1172.

Wase, J and Forster, C. (1997). London. *Biosorbents for Metal Ions*. Taylor and Francis Ltd.

Yilmaz, E. I. (2003). Metal tolerance and biosorption capacity of Bacillus circulans strain EB1. *Research in Microbiology*. 154:pp. 409-415

.

Chapter 27

Benefits of enzymatic pre-treatment of intact yeast cells for anaerobic digestion of distillery pot ale

P. Mallick, J. C. Akunna and G. M. Walker

School of Contemporary Sciences, University of Abertay Dundee, Dundee DD1 1HG, Scotland, UK

Abstract

Potential benefits for anaerobic digestion processes of hydrolysing intact yeast cells in malt whisky distillery pot ale were investigated. Several yeast lytic enzymes, that can dissolve glucan and mannoprotein components of the cell wall, were effective. For example, anaerobic digestion of pot ale pre-treated with yeast lytic enzymes showed COD reductions of 87%, compared with only 13% without enzymes. It was therefore established that pre-hydrolysis of intact yeast cells in distillery pot ale was very beneficial for efficient anaerobic treatment of such residues for biogas production.

Introduction

Scotch malt whisky production generates pot ale and spent lees from wash and spirit stills, respectively (Goodwin and Stuart, 1994) and a typical distillery would produce 8.5-11.5L pot ale per 1L of pure alcohol (Tokuda et al, 1998). Concentrating pot ale by evaporation for animal feeds is energetically expensive and the economics of this process is directly influenced by fluctuating trends in the cattle feed market. Also, discharge of pot ale directly into watercourses is now prohibited due to environmental regulations (Tokuda et al, 1999) because of the high chemical oxygen demand (COD) and the deleterious effects on fresh water fish (Pant and Adholeya, 2007). Distillery liquid residues can be treated using aerobic biological processes but they have drawbacks including: high cost of operation, creation of other pollutants, high acidity, high oxygen demand, sludge bulking and energy consumption (Vlissidis and Zouboulis, 1993; Uzal, et al., 2003). Anaerobic treatment processes are relatively slow but they can efficiently recover biogas to be used as renewable energy for other distillery operations. Pot ale possesses chemical oxygen demand (COD) concentrations typically from 30,000-50,000 mg/l (Goodwin et al., 2001) and anaerobic digestion can not only reduce this, but also produce useful biogas. Anaerobic digestion with methane fermentation is the most suitable approach to treat distillery liquid residues and a number of reactors like the upflow anaerobic sludge blanket (UASB) reactor, upflow anaerobic filter process (UAFP) and anaerobic baffled reactor (ABR) have already been optimized and commercialized (Tokuda et al, 1999; Akunna and Clark, 2000; Baloch et al., 2006).

Undiluted pot ale comprises intact yeast cells that may deleteriously affect anaerobic digestion processes. This is due to the thick cell walls of yeast that contain tough phosphomannan, glucan, chitin and protein components (Walker, 1998). There is therefore a need to hydrolyse intact yeast cells before pot ale residues are subject to anaerobic digestion, and this study investigated the benefits of enzyme applications in this regard.

Materials and methods

Distillery liquid residues

Pot ale samples were obtained from Blair Athol malt whisky distillery (Perthshire, Scotland, UK), courtesy of Diageo Ltd. and were stored at 4°C to minimize microbial contamination.

Control yeast strain

A control yeast strain, *Saccharomyces cerevisiae* "M-type" distillers yeast strain (DCLM, obtained from Kerry Biosciences, Menstrie, Scotland) was used to study the effectiveness of various enzymes on yeast cell hydrolysis. The yeast strain was maintained on malt extract agar slopes and sub-cultured once every three weeks. To evaluate the effect of enzyme digestion on dead yeast cells, cultures were heat killed by boiling the slurry of live cells at 100°C for 60 minutes. Yeast viability was assessed using methylene blue staining (Mills, 1941).

Commercial enzymes and pre-treatment conditions

The following commercially available enzymes were initially used for enzymatic hydrolysis of the control yeast strain and pot ale samples: lyticase, alpha-amylase, cellulase, beta-glucosidase, beta-glucanase, lipase, protease, enzyme complex and papain. From the results of the preliminary studies (Mallick, 2007), the highest percentage cell lysis occurred with added beta glucanase plus protease at a dosage of 2.5 ml/g [of dry weight of the solids in the culture], pH 7.5, temperature 37°C and incubation time of 24h. Papain also showed high rates of cellular hydrolysis in pot ale samples at a dosage of 10% by volume, pH 6.0, temperature 50°C and incubation time of 22h. These enzymes and culture conditions were utilised for the pre-treatment of distillery pot ale prior to anaerobic digestion.

Anaerobic digestion

Anaerobic digestors were 10 x 1L glass bottles which were connected to 500 ml conical flasks for collection of gas. Seed inoculum was obtained from United Utilities Wastewater Treatment Plant, at Hatton, Angus, Scotland. These bottles were incubated with shaking (80rpm) at 37°C for a period of 10days. Samples were collected periodically for analysis.

Analytical methods

Aliquots from anaerobic digesters were filtered through a Whatman Type 70 mm glass microfiber filter (1.2 μm retention) and filtrates analysed for COD, ammonia, and total suspended solids (TSS) by Standard Methods (APHA, 1992). Detailed analytical methods can be obtained from Mallick (2007).

Results and discussions

Characteristics of distillery residues

Pot ale samples received from the distillery were light brown to brown turbid liquids with a dry weight of 72.7 g/L, and pH 3.5-4.5. Samples contained intact yeast cells, which stained with methylene blue dye, confirming that the cells were dead but with relatively intact cell walls. In addition to yeast cells, a lot of solid matter was observed in the samples which consisted of fibrous particles (primarily originating from spent grains) and rod shaped bacteria at approximately $1x10^8$

cells/ml that stained Gram positive (presumptive Lactobaccili).

Effect of enzyme pre-treatment on anaerobic digestion of pot ale

Anaerobic digestion trials using pot ale in 1L capacity digesters were conducted to investigate the effects of pre-treatment with beta glucanase plus protease and papain, on the digestion process. Pot ale samples were pre-treated with enzyme dosages of 2.5 ml/g [of dry weight of the solids in the culture] for beta glucanase plus protease for 24h, and 10% by volume for papain for 22h. An additional anaerobic digestor was supplemented with papain, without a pre-treatment step. This aimed to verify differences in performance between prior enzyme pre-treatment with direct enzyme treatment during the anaerobic digestion process.

Digesters were operated, with and without enzyme pre-treatment, for a total retention time of 10days at 37°C. Initial pH was adjusted to 7.5 for all digesters.

Anaerobic digestion of distillery pot ale

The physical and chemical characteristics of the Scotch malt whisky distillery pot ale sample are presented in Table 1.

Table 1. Characteristics of pot ale.

Parameters	*Value*
Total solids	17.00 g/l
Total suspended solids	8.25 g/l
Volatile suspended solids	8.10g/l
Total nitrogen	92.00 mg/l
Total COD	61,500 mg/l
pH	4.12

Figure 1 shows that microbial acidogenic activities were dominant during the initial 24h (pH decline). Thereafter pH gradually increased, indicating increased methanogenic activity. Ammonia production, attributed to protein hydrolysis, also increased during anaerobic digestion (see Fig 2).

Figure 3 shows that enzyme pre-treatments significantly reduced COD during pot ale anaerobic digestion. The slight increase in COD concentration in Day 2 may be due to increase in soluble COD resulting from intact yeast cell lysis. Beta-glucanase plus protease treatments resulted in COD reduction up to 87% compared with pot ale without enzyme pre-treatment. Pot ale pre-treated with 10% papain achieved 50 % COD reduction, but without enzyme pre-treatment showed only 13 % COD removal. Figures 1-3 show that the performance of the

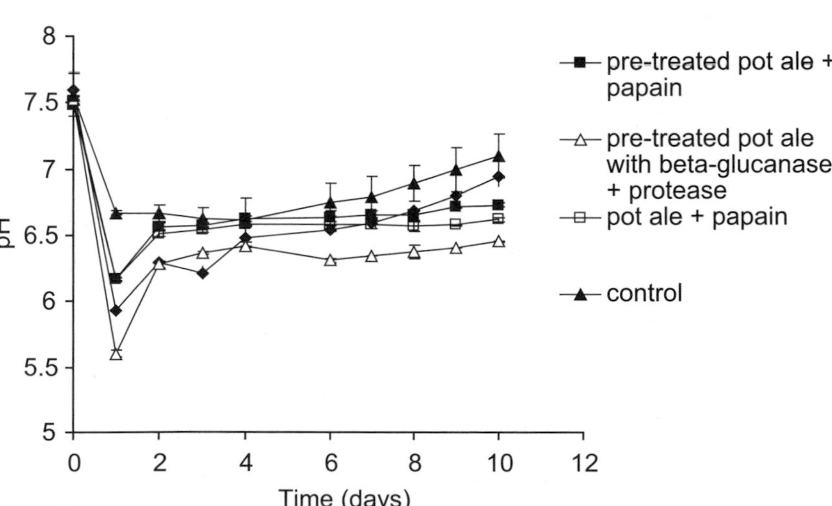

Figure 1. pH variation during anaerobic digestion of distillery pot ale

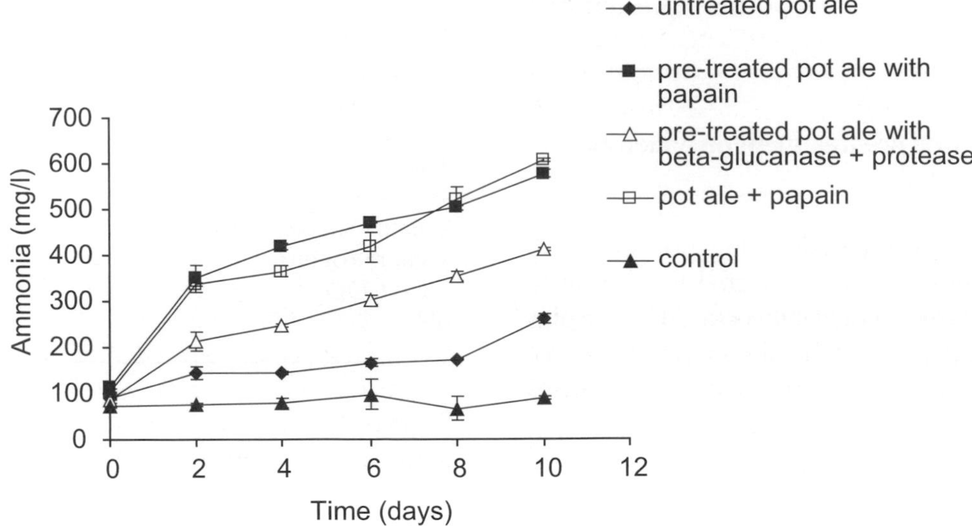

Figure 2. Ammonia variation during anaerobic digestion of distillery pot ale.

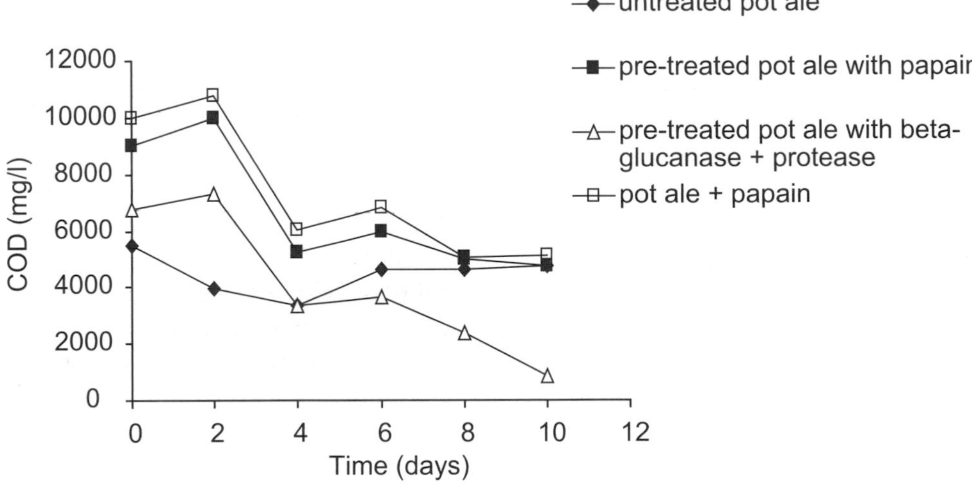

Figure 3. COD variation during anaerobic digestion of pot ale.

anaerobic digestion of pre-treated pot ale plus papain is somewhat similar to that of directly supplementing papain into digestors. Thus, in industrial applications, there may not be need for a separate pre-treatment stage prior to anaerobic digestion.

From the above results, it is apparent that enzymatic hydrolysis of intact yeast cells can greatly improve anaerobic digestion of pot ale from a malt distillery. Similar results were also obtained for yeast lytic enzymolysis during anaerobic digestion of spent wash from a grain distillery (Mallick, 2007).

Conclusions

This study has shown that enzymatic pre-treatment of pot ale was effective for increasing anaerobic digestion process efficiency. Certain commercially available enzymes were effective in digesting intact yeast cells in distillery pot ale samples. Significant improvements in COD reduction of more than 50% were achieved following enzymolysis prior to anaerobic digestion. However, in-depth studies are required to identify the most appropriate enzymes, and optimised conditions before their application. The study also showed that the hydrolysis of intact yeast cells in pot ale from Scotch whisky distilleries is a rate limiting step in the bioconversion of these residues by anaerobic processes.

Acknowledgements

We thank colleagues at Diageo Ltd for useful discussion (especially D. Murray and K. Law) and for provision of distillery samples. The provision of inoculum for anaerobic digesters from United Utilities Wastewater Treatment Plant (Hatton, Angus, Scotland) is gratefully acknowledged.

References

Akunna, J. C. and Clark, M. (2000) Performance of a granular-bed anaerobic baffled reactor (GRABBR) treating whisky distillery wastewater. *Bioresource Technology*, **73**(3), 257-261.

American Public Health Association, (APHA) (1992) Standard Method for the examination of water and wastewater, Eighteenth ed., Greenberg A.E., Clesceri, L.S., Eaton, A.D. (Eds), American Public Health Association, Washington, DC, USA

Baloch, M. I., Akunna, J. C. and Collier, P. J. (2006) The performance of a phase separated granular bed bioreactor treating brewery wastewater. *Bioresource Technology*, 98, 1849-1855.

Goodwin, J. A. J., Finlayson, J. M. and Low, E. W. (2001) A further study of the anaerobic biotreatment of malt whisky distillery pot ale using an UASB system. *Bioresource Technology*. 78, 155-160.

Goodwin, J. A. S. and Stuart, J. B. (1994) Anaerobic digestion of malt whisky distillery pot ale using upflow anaerobic sludge blanket reactors. *Bioresource Technology*. 49, 75-81.

Mallick, P. (2007) Digestion on intact yeast cells in distillery residues; pot ale and spent wash and its implication in anaerobic digestion. MSc Thesis, University of Abertay Dundee, UK.

Mills, D. R. (1941) Differential staining of living and dead yeast cells. *Food Research*, **6**, 361-371.

Pant, D. and Adholeya, A. (2007) Biological approaches for treatment of distillery wastewaster: A review. *Bioresources Technology*. 98, 2321-2334.

Tokuda, M., Ohta, N., Morimura, S. and Kida, K. (1998) Methane fermentation of pot ale from a whisky distillery after enzymatic or microbial treatment. *Journal of Fermentation and Bioengineering*. 85(5), 495-501.

Tokuda, M., Fujiwara, Y. and Kida, K. (1999) Pilot plant test for removal of organic matter, N and P from whisky pot ale. *Process Biochemistry*. 35, 267-275.

Uzal, N., Gokcay, C. F. and Demirer, G. N. (2003) Sequential (anaerobic/aerobic) biological treatment of malt whisky wastewater. *Process Biochemistry*. 39, 279-286.

Vlissidis, A. and Zouboulis, A. I. (1993) Thermophilic anaerobic digestion of alcohol distillery wastewaters. *Bioresource Technology*. 43, 131-140.

Walker, G. M. (1998) Yeast Physiology and Biotechnology. J. Wiley & Sons, Chichester, UK

Chapter 28

The microbiology and biotechnology of rum production

Graham H. Fleet and Victoria Green
Food Science Group, School of Chemical Sciences and Engineering, University of New South Wales, Sydney, New South Wales, Australia, 2052

Introduction

Rum is a distilled alcoholic beverage derived from fermented sugar cane products, principally, molasses ,sugar cane syrup or sugar cane juice. Historically, sugar cane (*Saccharum officinarum*) is thought to have originated from New Guinea some 10,000 years ago. There are reports on the consumption of a spirit style of beverage derived from sugar, in India around 2000BC. Considered as a spice, sugar eventually found its way to Europe, where the Spanish and Portuguese established sugar cane plantations in the 1400s. Christopher Columbus took plantings to the Caribbean islands and the South Americas in 1493 and, during the 1500s, sugar cane plantations flourished in these regions. Rum production from sugar cane materials soon followed, and was well established in the Caribbean region during the 1600s. Countries such as Jamaica, Barbados, Trinidad, Martinique, Haiti, Guadeloupe, Guyana, Puerto Rico and Cuba became well known for their rum distilleries. The evolution of the rum industry in this region has a colourful history that is intimately linked to trade rivalry and conflict between the then colonial powers, piracy, the development of the slave trade between Africa, Europe and the Americas, and onset of the American war of independence (Nicol, 2003; Broom, 2003). The Caribbean countries remain the center of the modern rum industry, but rum is also produced in other countries such as Brazil, USA, Australia, and parts of Asia and Africa- wherever sugar cane is cultivated.

Microbial fermentation is a key biotechnological process in the production of all alcoholic beverages, including rum. The microorganisms that grow throughout this process have a major influence on the flavour and quality of the final product, and the efficiency of the overall process. For most alcoholic beverages such as beer, wine, cider and whisky, there is sound scientific understanding of the microbial species that conduct the fermentation and how they impact on product quality (Rose, 1977; Lea and Piggott, 2003). However, this is not the case for rum production. While some basic microbiological studies on the process were done in the early 1900s, there have been few advances since that time. This article gives an overview of current knowledge on the microbiology of rum production, indicating the gaps in understanding and directions for further research.

The process of rum production

The basic process for rum production consists of the following operations: preparation of the raw material (molasses, sugar syrup or sugar cane juice); fermentation of this material; distillation of the fermented product; collection of the distillate; maturation of the distillate in wooden barrels; packaging of the final product. Detailed descriptions of the process can be found in Lehtonen and Suomalainen (1977) and Nicol (2003)and more general overviews are given in I'Anson (1971) and Kampen (1975).

Raw materials

Molasses is the main raw material used for rum production because of its lower cost and because it can be stored in bulk, without further processing, for long periods prior to use in fermentation. In this way, the seasonal impact of sugar production on rum production is avoided. Molasses is a by-product that remains after refining sugar from cane juice and is a black, viscous liquid containing about 55%w/v total fermentable sugars, of which about 35% is sucrose and 20% is a mixture of glucose and fructose. In addition to water and these sugars, it contains small amounts of many other

nitrogen, phosphorus, metal- ion, vitamin, gum and colloidal constituents that provide essential nutrients for yeast growth during fermentation. Trace amounts of volatile alcohols, acids, esters, aldehydes, ketones, phenolics, and nitrogen compounds are also present, and may be distilled over to influence rum flavour . Many factors affect the composition and quality of molasses and these include the cultivar and cultivation of sugar cane, the sugar refining process and conditions of molasses storage (Murtagh, 1995 a,b; Bortolussi and O'Neil , 2006). Just prior to use in fermentation, molasses is clarified by chemical or physical processes, adjusted to pH values around 5.0-5.5, given a mild heat pasteurization treatment, and then diluted with water to give a final concentration of 100-150g/ liter for fermentable sugars. Yeast nutrients such as ammonium sulphate and vitamin mixtures may be added to ensure complete fermentation.

In some distilleries, sugar syrup is used as the starting material. The syrup is prepared by heat evaporation of sugar cane juice after it has been partially inverted to avoid crystallization of the sucrose. It has a final sugar content of about 80%w/v and is diluted with water to 100-150 g/ liter of sugar before fermentation. Some distilleries use freshly extracted sugar cane juice which has a sugar content of about 10-15%w/v. This is widely used in Brazil where the fermented, distilled product is specifically known as " cachaca" (Faria *et al.*,2003).

The literature reports widespread use of dunder in rum production. Dunder is the liquid residue obtained from the distillation vessels after distillation of the fermented product (Kampen, 1975). It is enriched in heat inactivated microbial cells, principally yeasts, and the contents extracted from them. It is acidic and rich in nutrients and, used directly, it should be sterile. It is mixed with molasses or syrup at proportions of 20-50%v/v to decrease the requirements for dilution water, to assist with acidification of the molasses or syrup, and to provide nutrients to encourage microbial growth during fermentation. If it is not used directly, and stored, it becomes contaminated with microorganisms that can impact on the fermentation. In some cases, deliberate storage and ageing of dunder has been conducted to encourage the development of a wild microbial flora. Such dunder gives a rum with a heavier flavor (I'Anson, 1971).

Fermentation

After preparation, the molasses, syrup or juice is transferred to large tanks, nowdays made of stainless steel, for fermentation. Until the early 1900s, fermentation was a spontaneous process that developed from the growth of microbial contaminants (indigenous microflora) present in the molasses, syrup or juice, and also coming from processing equipment (I'Anson, 1971; Fahrasmane and Ganou-Parfait, 1998). To encourage a faster onset of fermentation, a proportion of fermented product from a previous fermentation (back slops) was often added to the tanks. Yeasts ultimately dominated these fermentations, primarily transforming the sugars into ethanol and carbon dioxide. During the last 50- 75 years, various distilleries have isolated and identified the main yeast strains responsible for the fermentation, and have developed procedures for maintaining and propagating these strains in pure culture, and then inoculating them into the ferment . Some of these isolates have been commercialized by yeast companies, and it is now possible to purchase active dry cultures of yeasts for direct inoculation into the ferment (Fahrasmane and Ganou-Parfait, 1998). Fermentations are generally conducted at temperatures of 30-35°C and are completed within 30-48 hrs. The fermented product is transferred to a holding tank where a good proportion of the yeast and other microbial cells sediment out, after which the product is sent for distillation. Some distilleries may remove the microbial cells from the ferment by centrifugation, before distillation.

Distillation, maturation, packaging

Distillation serves to evaporate and condense the alcohol and other volatile products that become the rum distillate. It is a specialized process that is conducted using continuous distillation columns and pot stills, and has a key impact on the composition and concentration of flavour volatiles that comprise the final rum distillate. The science and technology of this process and its application to rum production are described in I'Anson (1971) and Kampen (1975), Lehtonen and Suomalainen (1977) and Nicol (2003). The distillate is stored in wooden (oak) barrels for several years where further chemical changes occur to moderate product flavor. Finally, the distillates are blended, and packaged for sale.

The microbiology of rum production

Studies on the microbiology of rum production date back to the 1890s. Despite over 100 years of research, microbiological understanding of the process is very limited and is significantly lagging compared with many other alcoholic beverages.

The key requirements of microbiological information are:

- What microbial species occur throughout the process chain?
- What are the growth kinetics of individual microbial species throughout production?
- What factors affect the growth of these species?
- What chemical and biochemical changes do these species cause to the fermentation substrate?
- How do these changes impact on the sensory properties of rum and its appeal to consumers?

There are two main points in the production chain where microorganisms impact on rum quality. These are the raw materials (molasses, sugar syrup and juice), and the process of fermentation. Fermentation is the main stage where microorganisms determine rum flavour and quality. The microbiological status of dunder will also be significant, depending on how it is used.

Molasses, sugar syrup, juice

Molasses and syrups may be stored in bulk quantities on site at the distilleries for many months before use in rum fermentation. During this time, microbial contaminants have the potential to grow and produce metabolic end-products that could impact on rum quality. Despite this possibility, we have not been able to find any systematic investigation of the microbiology of molasses or syrups during storage. Because of the heat processes involved, freshly produced molasses or syrup contain few microorganisms (Owen, 1911, Browne, 1929). The high concentrations of sugars (about 60% w/v), low water activity (approx. 0.76), and relatively low pH (5.0-5.5), make these raw materials unfavourable environments for the growth and survival of microorganisms. Nevertheless, the literature contains sporadic reports of the isolation of yeasts and bacteria from these materials. The main yeasts found tend to be osmotolerant species of *Zygosaccharomyces*. *Schizosaccharomyces, Torulospora* and *Saccharomyces* (Hall *et al.*, 1935; Owen, 1949; Tilbury, 1980; Tokuoka,1993; Bonilla- Salinas *et al.*, 1995; Fahrasmane and Ganou-Parfait, 1998). Information on the presence of bacteria in molasses and syrups is scant and inconsistent. Bacterial populations are generally low (10^2-10^3 cfu/ml) and reflect a diversity of species within *Bacillus, Clostridium, Zymomonas, Lactobacillus* and *Propionibacterium* (Hall *et al.*, 1935; Murtagh, 1995a,b; Fahrasmane and Ganou-Parfait, 1998; Todorov and Dicks, 2005). In our observations, *Bacillus* species (e.g. *B. subtilis*) are most prevalent. Because molasses and syrups present most stressful, inhospitable and unique environments for the survival and growth of microorganisms, it is very likely that they will harbor a diversity of species in a stressed physiological state that will escape detection by cultural methods normally used for microbiological analyses. Novel culture methods as well as specialized, culture- independent molecular methods will be required for their analysis and detection (Ercolini, 2004; Giraffa, 2004). The impact of such microbial populations on the quality of the molasses or syrups used in rum production requires investigation.

Freshly extracted sugar cane juice contains significant populations (10^4-10^6 cfu/ml) of yeasts and bacteria, depending on the quality of the cane and hygiene of the crushing process (Fahrasmane and Ganou-Parfait, 1998). The yeasts represent a mixture of *Candida, Hanseniaspora, Pichia, Kluyveromyces, Saccharomyces* and *Schizosaccharomyces* species (Shehata, 1960; Morais *et al.*, 1997; Pataro *et al.*, 2000; Schwan *et al.*, 2001; Gomes *et al.*, 2002), and the bacteria are represented by a diversity of lactic acid bacteria , acetic acid bacteria and *Bacillus* species (Fahrasmane and Ganou-Parfait, 1998; Schwan *et al.*, 2001). The juice is microbiologically unstable and will start to ferment within several hours. Consequently, it cannot be stored and must be used immediately.

Fermentation

Fermentation is a microbiological process and, as mentioned already, is a key operation in rum production. The microbial species that conduct the fermentation determine process efficiency, ethanol yield, and rum flavor and quality. Essentially, sugars within the molasses, syrup or juice are metabolized into primarily ethanol and carbon dioxide, and a vast array of secondary end-products (e.g. higher alcohols, organic acids, esters, aldehydes, ketones, nitrogen volatiles, sulphur volatiles, phenolic volatiles) that have flavour impact. The relative amounts of these secondary products determine final rum flavor and vary according to the conditions of fermentation and the species and strains of yeasts and bacteria that grow during fermentation (Lehtonen and Suomalainen, 1977; Watson, 1993; Berry and Slaughter, 2003).

Yeasts

Early microbiological studies on rum produced by spontaneous fermentation of molasses revealed that two yeast species predominated during the process. These were identified as strains of *Schizosaccharomyces pombe* and *Saccharomyces cerevisiae*. Fermentations with *Schiz. pombe* generally gave rums with stronger aromas, but were much slower and required 3-4 days or more for completion. In contrast, fermentations with *S.cerevisiae* were faster, being completed within 36-48 hours, and gave a lighter style of rum. *Schizosaccharomyces pombe* was more likely to occur in fermentations with higher initial sugar concentration and where a good proportion of slops or dunder was added to the molasses or syrup, thereby decreasing its pH to below 5.0 (Ashby,1907; Pech *et al.*,1984; Fahrasmane, Ganou-Parfait and Parfait, 1988; Watson, 1993; Fahrasmane and Ganou-Parfait, 1998). Very little research has been done to understand the kinetics of growth of these yeasts during molasses or syrup fermentation and to understand how they impact on rum flavor. Fermentation with *Schiz. pombe* generally give rums with lesser amounts of higher alcohols and short chain fatty acids, but greater quantities of esters, compared with those conducted with *S.cerevisiae* (Fahrasmane *et al.*, 1985). Modern rum production is largely focused on the use of strains of *S.cerevisiae* that have been isolated from particular distilleries, and then propagated in- house for inoculation into the molasses as starter cultures. Various yeast companies sell distiller's strains of *S.cerevisiae* that may be used, thereby avoiding the demands of in-house propagation (Watson, 1993). With regard to non-*Saccharomyces* yeasts, some species of *Zygosaccharomyces* and *Dekkera*, in addition to *Schiz. pombe,* have the potential to grow in molasses and sugar syrups, and may represent novel yeasts for exploitation in rum production.

In contrast to molasses or syrup fermentations, significant research has been done on the growth of yeasts during sugar cane juice fermentation for cachaca production. The early stages of fermentation are characterized by the growth of various species of *Hanseniaspora, Kloeckera, Pichia, Kluyveromyces* and *Candida*, but they are soon overgrown by strains of *S.cerevisiae* which eventually dominate and complete the fermentation. In some cases, strains of *Schiz. pombe* were observed to dominate these fermentations (Morais *et al.*,1997; Pataro *et al.*, 2000; Schwan *et al.*,2001). With this knowledge, a program of yeast strain selection and evaluation is being conducted to develop starter cultures that give optimized fermentation and a cachaca product with defined quality (Dato, Junior and Mutton, 2005; Oliviera *et al.*, 2004; Vicente *et al.*, 2006)

Bacteria

Early literature (Allen, 1906: Ashby, 1907; Hall *et al.*, 1935) as well as more recent literature (Ganou-Parfait, Fahrasmane and Parfait , 1987; Fahrasmane and Ganou-Parfait, 1998) report the contribution of bacteria to rum fermentations. However, there appears to be no detailed studies of their growth during fermentation, how they interact with the growth of yeasts and how they impact on rum quality. Species of *Clostridium, Bacillus, Zymomonas,* lactic acid bacteria and propionic acid bacteria have been reported to be involved. It is expected that the extent of their growth will be moderated by their tolerance of ethanol produced by the yeasts, the acidity of the medium, and their requirement for nutrients. Possibly, their contribution will be greater in slower developing ferments, such as those conducted by *Schiz. pombe*, where the production of ethanol is slower, and in those where the medium is enriched in micronutrients by the addition of dunder. Fermentations conducted at higher pH values (e.g. greater than 5.5) are, also, more likely to have a stronger contribution from bacteria. If they grow to significant populations in the early stages of the fermentation, they are likely to produce acids and other metabolites that could inhibit or retard the growth of yeasts. Also, they would utilize sugars, so that less would be available for conversion to ethanol by the yeasts. Consequently, by these mechanisms they could decrease the efficiency of the fermentation process (Kampen, 1975; Lehtonen and Suomalainen, 1977). Their growth will be accompanied by the production of metabolites that impact on rum flavor, and this could be detrimental or beneficial, depending on the species which grow (Fahrasmane and Ganou-Parfait, 1998). According to Hall *et al.* (1935) the growth of *Clostridium saccharolyticum* was necessary for the development of characteristic rum flavor, possibly through its production of butyric acid. The microaerophilic conditions of molasses fermentation are conducive to the growth of species of *Lactobacillus* and *Propionibacterim*, the latter contributing desirable propionic acid flavor to rum (Fahrasmane and Ganou-Parfait, 1998). *Lactobacillus* species have recently been found to be significant in the alcoholic fermentation of malted barley mash for whisky production (van Beek and Priest, 2002; Priest, 2004), so it is not unexpected that they may grow in conjunction with yeasts during rum fermentations and have subtle influences on rum flavour.

Dunder

As mentioned already, dunder is often used in rum production and this can have important microbiological significance that seems to have escaped scientific study. Although it should be microbiologically sterile immediately after coming from distillation vessels, it may be stored to encourage contamination and microbial (bacterial) growth that impacts on rum fermentation and product flavor(Kampen, 1975). In this context, the microbial ecology of dunder requires detailed study. Its chemical composition can impact on microbial growth during rum fermentation, through acidification of the fermentation medium and enrichment of the medium in micro-nutrients. However, details of its chemical composition are not evident from the literature, and remain another important direction for research.

Conclusions

Microorganisms produce the ethanol and other flavour volatiles that are essential to the character and quality of rum. The key reaction is the alcoholic fermentation of molasses, sugar syrup or sugar cane juice by yeasts. Although strains of *S.cerevisiae* dominate this fermentation, other yeasts such as *Schiz. pombe* can be significant and contribute different flavours to the final product. More research is needed to understand and exploit the impact of different yeast species and strains on the individuality of rum flavour. Depending on the distillery and the subtleties of the process, such as the use of dunder, bacteria may contribute to the fermentation, in association with yeasts. Further research is required to understand the occurrence and growth of bacterial species associated with these fermentations, how they influence rum quality and process efficiency, and the significance of dunder in contributing to their role. Microorganisms also determine the quality of the raw materials (molasses, sugar syrup and cane juice) used for rum fermentation, and specific investigations are needed to better define this influence.

References

Allan, C. (1906). The manufacture of Jamaica rum. *West Indian Bulletin* **7 :** 141-142.

Ashby, S.F. (1907). The study of fermentations in the manufacture of Jamaica rum. *International Sugar Journal* **11 :** 243-251.

Bonilla-Salinas, M., Lappe, P., Ulloa, M., Garcia-Garibay, M. and Gomez-Ruiz, L. (1995). Isolation and identification of killer yeasts from sugar cane molasses. *Letters in Applied Microbiology* **21:**115-116.

Bortolussi,G. and O"Neill, C.J.O. (2006). Variation in molasses composition from eastern Australian sugar mills. *Australian Journal of Experimental Agriculture* **46:** 1455-1463.

Browne (1929). The spontaneous decomposition of molasses. *Industrial Engineering and Chemistry* **21**: 600-606.

Dato, M.C.F., Junior, J.M.P. and Mutton, M.J.R. (2005). Analysis of the secondary compounds produced by *Saccharomyces cerevisiae* and wild yeast strains during the production of " cachaca". *Brazilian Journal of Microbiology* **36:** 70-74.

Ercolini, D. (2004). PCR-DGGE fingerprinting: novel strategies for detection of microbes in food. *Journal of Microbiological Methods* **56:** 297-314.

Fahrasmane, L. and Ganou-Parfait, B. (1998). Microbial flora of rum fermentation media. *Journal of Applied Microbiology* **84:** 921-928.

Fahrasmane,L., Ganou-Parfait, B. and Parfait, A. (1988). Yeast flora of Haitian rum distilleries. *MIRCEN Journal* **4:** 239-241.

Fahrasmane,L., Parfait, A., Jouret, C. and Galzy, P. (1985). Production of higher alcohols and short chain fatty acids by different yeasts used in rum fermentation. *Journal of Food Science* **50:**1427-1430.

Faria,J.B., Loyola, E., Lopez, M.G. and Dufour, J.P. (2003). Cachaca, pisco and tequila. In: *Fermented Beverage Production*, second edition, Edited by Lea, A.G.H.and Piggott, J.R., Kluwer Academic, New York, pp.355-363.

Ganou-Parfait,B., Fahrasmane,L. and Parfait, A. (1987). *Bacillus* spp in sugar cane fermentation media. *Belgian Journal of Food Chemistry and Biotechnology* **42:** 192-194.

Giraffa, G. (2004). Studying the dynamics of microbial populations during food fermentation. *FEMS Microbiology Reviews* **28 :** 251-260.

Gomes, F.C.O., Pataro, C., Guerra, J.B., Neves,M.J., Correa, S.R., Moreira, E.S.A. and Rosa, C.A. (2002). Physiological diversity and trehalose accumulation in *Schizosaccharomyces pombe* strains from spontaneous fermentation during the production of the artisanal Brazilian cachaca. *Canadian Journal of Microbiology* ***48*** **:** 399-406.

Hall, H.H., James, L.H. and Nelson, E.K. (1935). Microorganisms causing fermentation flavours in cane syrups, especially Barbados "molasses". *Journal of Bacteriology* **33:** 577-585.

I'Anson, J.A.P. (1971). Rum manufacture. *Process Biochemistry* **July**: 35-39.

Kampen, W.H. (1975). Technology of the rum industry. *SUGAR y AZUCAR*, **July**, 36-43.

Lea, A.G.H. and Piggott, J.R. (2003). *Fermented Beverage Production*, second edition. Kluwer Academic, New York .

Lehtonen, M. and Suomalainen,H.(1977). Rum. In: *Economic Microbiology*, Edited by Rose, A.H., Academic Press, London, pp. 595-633.

Morais, P.B., Rosa, C.A., Linardi, V.R., Pataro,C. and Maia, A.B.R.A. (1997). Characterization and succession of yeast populations associated with spontaneous fermentations during the production of Brazillian sugar cane *aguardente*. *World Journal of Microbiology and Biotechnology* **13:** 241-243.

Murtagh, J.E. (1995a). Molasses as a feedstock for alcohol production. In: *The alcohol text book; a reference for the beverage, fuel and industrial alcohol production industries*, Edited by Jaques, K.A., Lyons, T.P. and Kelsall, D.R., Nottingham University Press, Nottingham, pp. 89-96.

Murtagh, J.E. (1995b). Feedstocks, fermentation and distillation for production of heavy and light rums. In: *The alcohol textbook; a reference for the beverage, fuel, and industrial alcohol production industries*, Edited by Jaques, K.A., Lyons, T.P. and Kelsall, D.R., Nottingham University Press, Nottingham, pp.243-255.

Nicol, D.A. (2003). Rum. In: *Fermented Beverage Production*, second edition, Edited by Lea, A.G.H. and Piggott, J.R., Kluwer Academic, New York, pp.263-287.

Oliveira, E.S., Rosa, C.A., Morgano, M.A. and Serra, G.I. (2004). Fermentation characteristics as criteria for selection of cachaca yeast. *World Journal of Microbiology and Biotechnology* **20:**19-24.

Owen, W.L. (1911). Recently discovered bacterial decomposition of sucrose. *Journal of Industrial and Engineering Chemistry* **July :** 481-486.

Owen, W.L. (1949). *The Microbiology of Sugars, Syrups and Molasses*. Barr-Owen research Enterprises, Baton Rouge.

Pataro,C., Guerra,G.B., Petrillo-Peixoto,M.L., Mendonca-Hagler, L., Linardi, V.R. and Rosa, C.A. (2000). Yeast communities and genetic polymorphism of *Saccharomyces cerevisiae* strains associated with artisanal fermentation in Brazil. *Journal of Applied Microbiology* **89:** 24-31.

Pech, B., Lavoue, G., Parfait, A. and Belin. J.M. (1984) Fermentations rhumieres: aptitude des souches de *Schizosaccharomyces pombe*

Lindner. *Science des Aliments* **4:** 67-72.

Priest, F. (2004). Lactic acid bacteria- the uninvited but generally welcome participants in malt whisky fermentation. *Microbiology Today* **31:** 16-18.

Rose, A.H. (1977). Economic Microbiology, volume Academic Press, London.

Schwan, R.F., Mendonca,A.T., daSilva, J.J., Rodrigues, V. and Wheals, A.(2001). Microbiology and physiology of *Cachaca* (*Aguardente*) fermentations. *Antonie van Leeuwenhoek* **79:** 89-96.

Shehata, A.E.E. (1960). Yeasts isolated from sugar cane and its juice during the production of Aguardente de Cana. *Applied Microbiology* **8:** 73-75.

Tilbury, R.H. (1980). Xerotolerant (osmophilic) yeasts. In: *Biology and Activities of Yeasts*, Edited by Skinner,F.A., Passmore, S.M. and Davenport, R.R., Academic Press, London, pp.153-179.

Todorov, S.D. and Dicks, L.M.T. (2005). *Lactobacillus plantarum* isolated from molasses produces bacteriocins active against gram negative bacteria. *Enzyme and Microbial Technology* **36:** 318-326.

Tokuoka, K. (1993). Sugar-and salt tolerant yeasts. *Journal of Applied Bacteriology* **74:** 101-110.

Van Beek, S. and Priest, F. (2002). Evolution of the lactic acid bacterial community during malt whisky fermentation: a polyphasic study. *Applied and Environmental Microbiology* **68:** 297-305.

Vicente, M., Fietto, L.G., Castro I., dos Santos, A. N. G., Coutrim, M. X. and Brandao, R.L. (2006). Isolation of *Saccharomyces cerevisiae* strains producing higher levels of flavoring compounds for production of " cachaca" the Brazilian sugar cane spirit. *International Journal of Food Microbiology* **108:** 51-59.

Watson, D.C. (1993). Yeasts in distilled alcoholic beverage production. In: *The Yeasts*, second edition, Edited by Rose, A.H. and Harrison, J.S., Academic Press, London, pp. 215-244.

Chapter 29

Installation and use of an environmentally controlled experimental maturation facility

Craig Owen and John Conner

The Scotch Whisky Research Institute, The Robertson Trust Building, Research Avenue North, Riccarton, EH14 4AP

Introduction

Annually, approximately 58 million litres of alcohol evaporates from maturation warehouses in Scotland. One of the main objectives for the Scotch Whisky Research Institute (SWRI) is to consider the long term sustainability of the Scotch whisky industry and identify any issues that could impact upon it. Identifying a solution or solutions that could reduce evaporation losses by a fraction of a percent would have a significant positive impact on profits and the environment.

Within the maturation research programme undertaken by the SWRI, it is often the case that studies can only be performed on full size casks, if meaningful results are to be obtained. In recent years the maturation group identified and developed maturation projects which would be of potential benefit to the industry. However, it was not possible to initiate these projects for a number of reasons. For example, if the effect of changing the environmental conditions within a warehouse is to be examined, it is not possible to undertake such a study on an industrial scale due to the high cost and risk that it would incur. Similarly, where casks are required to be monitored in 'real time', the ability to frequently access test casks and accurately monitor both external and internal cask variables becomes logistically very difficult if not impossible.

Construction and use

Construction of an environmentally controlled internal unit and an external uncontrolled unit commenced at the SWRI in 2006. This involved the modification of two existing stores at the SWRI, converting them into experimental maturation units with the capacity to hold 12 test casks each.

Figure1. The environmentally controlled maturation room.

One unit remains under ambient environmental conditions, while the other allows control of temperature, relative humidity and airflow at ranges beyond those currently seen in a warehouse. In addition, 'real time' data is obtained from inside a reference cask stored in each location. This data provides measurement of temperature, internal pressure and alcohol strength. Also, to enable the accurate prediction of evaporation losses over a short storage period, precise cask weighing equipment was installed.

Figure 2. The cask balance.

Over the past 2 years the two maturation units have been successfully commissioned and tested, and offer a range of advantages over undertaking maturation studies in full size warehouses. These include:

- Obtaining results over much shorter maturation time periods that can be used to predict alcohol losses, through accurate environmental control and precision of measurement.
- Having the ability to explore the impact of a much wider range of environmental scenarios on both evaporation losses and maturation quality.
- Examine the impact of cask orientation, design and quality on ethanol loss and spirit quality.
- Understand the effects of modifying warehouse conditions on cask wood and therefore predicting the effects of changing the environmental conditions in industry maturation facilities.

Initial trials

Two one-month tests were carried out to assess the performance of the environmentally controlled unit. The first compared losses from the ambient store with those from the controlled environment, with the temperature and humidity set to values typically experienced during the maturation of Bourbon whisky. The data recorded for temperature and humidity, along with the calculated losses of weight, ethanol and water are shown in Figure 3 and 4 and Table 1 respectively.

Table 1. Losses from casks stored in the ambient and controlled maturation units. Controlled temperature was 25°C with a relative humidity of 50%.

	% Total loss	*% Ethanol loss*	*% Water loss*
		Ambient unit	
Maximum	0.04	0.16	-0.14
Minimum	0.01	0.12	-0.23
Average	0.03	0.14	-0.20
Standard deviation	0.01	0.01	0.02
		Controlled unit	
Maximum	1.02	1.10	0.84
Minimum	0.48	0.57	0.30
Average	0.64	0.73	0.46
Standard deviation	0.17	0.16	0.17

The second trial compared losses between the two units with the controlled environment set to mimic conditions in the ambient store throughout the 28 day period. Similar losses were obtained for casks stored under these conditions suggesting the controlled environment could mimic 'normal' warehouse conditions. During all trials casks are stored in both racked and palletised orientations allowing for comparison of the losses achieved in these storage conditions.

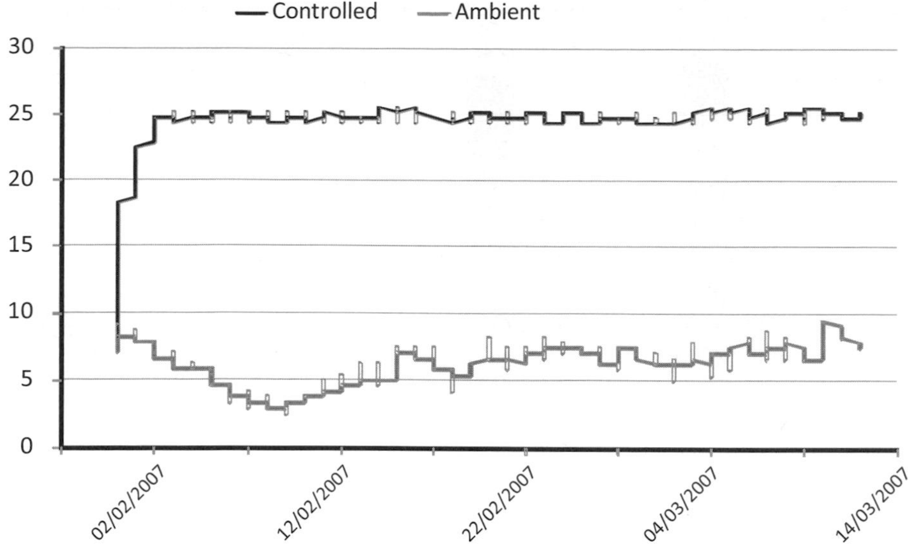

Figure 3. Temperature (°C) during the initial one month test to assess the performance of the environmentally controlled unit.

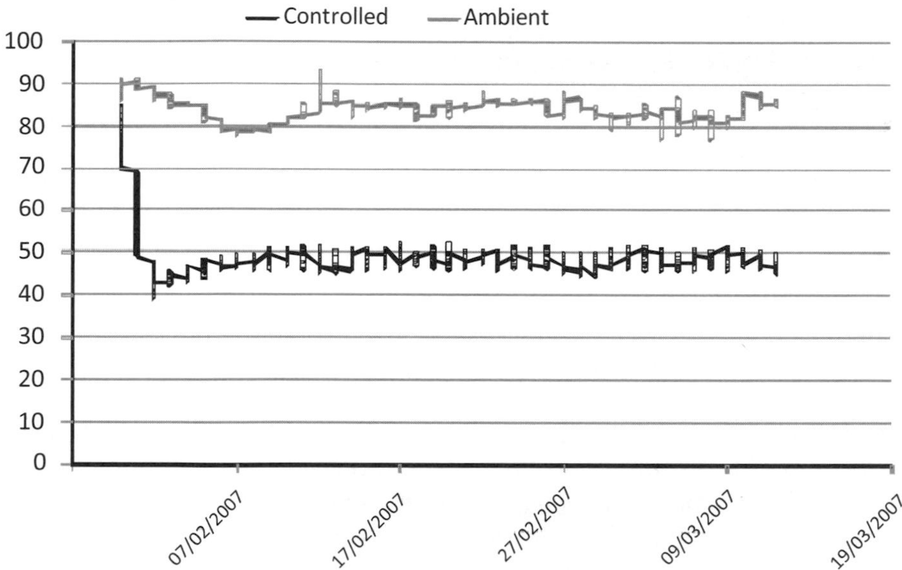

Figure 4. Relative humidity during the initial one month test to assess the performance of the environmentally controlled unit.

Current and future work

The current set of trials is underway with the controlled environment set at 10°C, 20°C and cycling between these two temperatures. All these trials were carried out at 75% relative humidity. The losses from the casks stored at the higher temperature are, not surprisingly, greater than from the lower temperature.

One interesting observation from the trials is that the spirit temperature lags behind the room temperature. This is clearly seen during the experiment cycling the room temperature between 10°C and 20°C. The temperature in the controlled environment changed over a 12 hour period between these two temperatures but the temperature of the spirit in the cask varied between 14°C and 16°C.

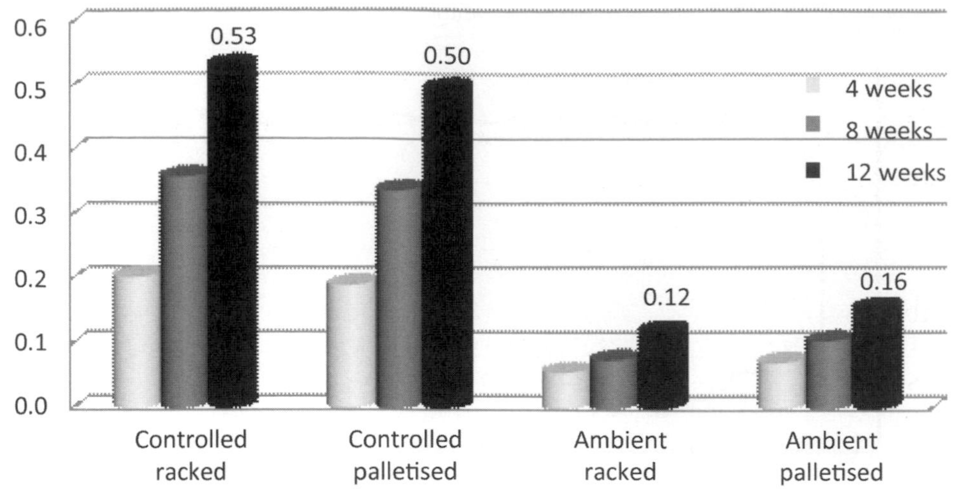

Figure 5. The average percentage weight lost by casks stored at 20°C and 75% RH.

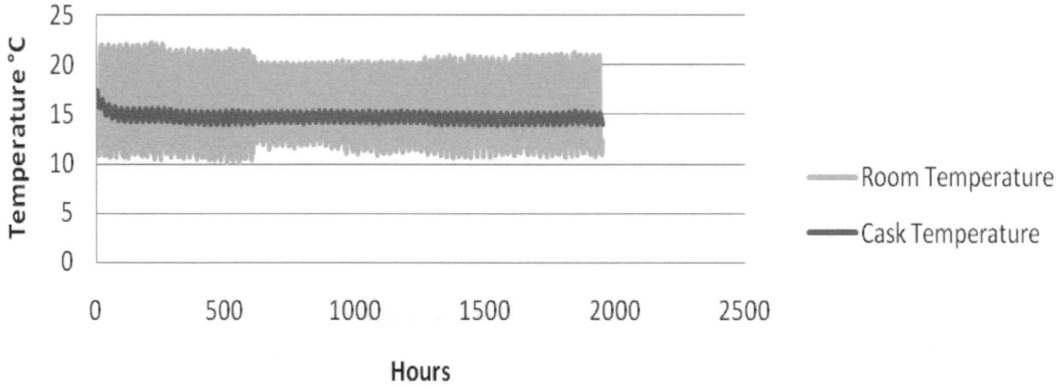

Figure 6. Cask and room temperature during the cycling trial.

The trials will continue with the introduction of higher levels of humidity in the controlled environment. This has already shown an increase in cask weight due to the uptake of water from the environment. The effect on alcohol loss in these conditions has yet to be established.

The data collected to date has shown that environmental conditions, cask orientation and cask quality all have major effects on losses and potentially spirit quality. Future work will include:

- Exploration of the impact of a much wider range of environmental scenarios on both evaporation losses and maturation quality.
- Testing the effect of high humidity conditions on reducing alcohol losses from casks.
- Exploring the impact of varying the air turnover in a warehouse on evaporation losses.
- Providing further research opportunities into the effects of predicted climate change on losses, spirit quality and emissions.
- Identify cask treatments and maturation warehouse design to reduce losses whilst maintaining spirit quality.

Chapter 30

Emerging ingredients – adding newer dimensions to alcoholic beverages

Binod K Maitin
United Spirits Limited, Technical Centre, 14 Cunningham Road, Bangalore 560 052, India

Introduction

Over the past few years, the global beverage markets have seen exponential growth, driven by ever-increasing consumer demand for newer innovative products. A large number of products, such as energy and sports drinks, enhanced waters, RTD teas etc., incorporating exotic flavours, attractive colours, exciting taste, functionality, etc. are being introduced continually. "All natural" products have shown increasing preference across all demographic segments. Additionally, the consumers are increasingly seeking a healthier lifestyle and well-being rather than only enjoyment.

Emerging ingredients offer innovative solutions to the challenges of creating new taste sensation, seeking novel ways to enhance the appearance and blends of functional ingredients working in synergy to meet the varied needs of 21st Century consumers. The trend shows excellent potential of using such ingredients also for value added creation of premium alcoholic beverages to accomplish consumer delight.

Many such ingredients have already been tested successfully in alcoholic beverages and a fabulous range of products with broad spectrum of exotic flavours have been introduced by major manufacturers and taken up by consumers worldwide.

In this paper various aspects of emerging ingredients and their applications in creating new generation alcoholic beverages is reviewed. This includes a variety of complimentary ingredients such as colours, flavours, sweeteners, acidulants, emulsifiers etc. The merits and potential uses of certain functional ingredients are described in details. Examples of popular alcoholic beverages incorporating various novelty ingredients are also included. In addition, the regulatory issues concerning use of these ingredients are highlighted.

Perceived consumer insights

Consumers are increasingly adopting a healthy lifestyle for maximizing their personal well-being and are invariably looking for newer varieties of beverages far beyond quenching thirsts. Younger consumers are driving the innovation and growth of the functionality laced beverage market to meet their aspiration of value-added premium products (Kleiner, 2008; Landi, 2008). Their perceived needs and preferred attributes are summarised below:

- Healthful & Natural products with "All Natural" & "Natural Healthier" ingredients
- Weight Management through low or no carbohydrate beverages

- Vitality and stamina for rejuvenation and longevity
- Products for Hydration, Relaxation, Enjoyment & fun
- Beauty & and anti-aging functionality for consumption by women
- Convenience to manage busy lifestyle

Meeting the above needs is an important challenge. Consequently, beverages companies are constantly introducing new products to satisfy the growing demands of these "better for you" multi-functional "smart" products.

The beverages market trend

The ever-increasing consumption of beverages and exploding introduction of newer varieties shows that "Thirst is a stronger and more stable sensation than hunger" as stated by McKiernan and co authors in a recent publication (McKiernan *et al.*, 2008).

The soft drinks industry is constantly developing innovative new products. The wide range of products has expanded far beyond colas and fruit flavours.

During the past few years, health and wellness issues have come to the forefront of people's minds and strongly reflected in changing beverage choices of the new generation of health conscious consumers.

Manufacturers are keeping pace with people's new preferences. Wide varieties of differentiated products are being created based on consumer preferences for natural ingredients and drinks with functional benefits. Most of the products include speciality ingredients such as nutraceuticals, herbs, botanicals, etc. offering unique functionality to suit the palate and the busy lifestyles of today's wellness seekers.

A wide variety of new age products such as flavoured and enhanced waters, nutritional sodas, RTD teas & coffees, premium juice beverages, etc., with exotic flavours and functional ingredients, are continually being introduced and driving the beverage market today.

In addition, energy and sport drinks consumption has continued to gain popularity among young consumers and captured the high priced premium functional beverages market that witnessed robust growth over the last decade.

Alcoholic beverages – needs to harness innovation

Innovation and introduction of newer products plays a vital role in today's highly competitive market to meet ever-changing consumer expectations.

The growth of non-alcoholic beverages with functional differentiation continues to surge and driving the trend, not least in the spirit category. But, this segment has witnessed rather limited innovative product introductions, differentiated only by flavour variants, maturity, wood finishes, alcohol strength, etc.

Exotic alcoholic beverages incorporating the perceived needs and preferred attributes similar to those of innovative alcohol free products show a great future potential to capture the share of throat of increasing new age consumers.

Emerging ingredients - the key driver for NPD

Novelty ingredients are fuelling the growth of new generation products. To share in the continued growth of the new age beverages market, the challenge for beverage manufacturer is to create appealing, nutritious and functional products.

A wide range of vibrant colours, exotic flavours, tempting herbs & spices, value added functional ingredients and other new generation novel additives such as sweeteners, acidulants, emulsifiers, etc. are continuously emerging and offering immense flexibility to incorporate the desired characteristics while creating such products to precisely suit each type of natural, functional and premium beverages.

These innovative ingredients impart subtle character, aesthetic appeal, superb mouthfeel, exhilarating taste, texture, stability, and functional benefits to the various products. Some of the commonly used and most promising ingredients are listed in Table 1 and their major characteristics are discussed below.

Colours

Colours play major role in creation of new age beverages adding visual appeal to colourless and "fun" drinks besides their requirements to enhance colours that occur naturally and offset any loss of colours during process or storage (Griffiths, 2005).

Both synthetic and natural colours are used to shape consumer preferences. However, certified synthetic colours, are the most popular, as they are brighter, more uniform, better characterized, stable and of higher tinctorial strength. They encompass a wider range of hues, and are less expensive than natural colours. The use of synthetic colorants are strictly controlled by legislation and harmonized across the European

Table 1. Beverage ingredients.

Ingredients	*Functionality*	*Examples*
Colours	Aesthetic appeal, added functionality - Antioxidant	Natural Colours: Anthocynin, Beta Carotene, Lycopene, Lutein,Turmeric oleoresin Synthetic Colours : FDA (FD & C) and EU approved colours; Brilliant Blue FCF, Fast Green FCF, Erythrosine, Tartrazine, Sunset yellow
Flavours	Character enhancement, restore taste loss, masking undesirable taste	Natural flavours : derived from fruits, herbs, botanicals etc by physical, microbiological or enzymatic processes
		Nature Identical flavours : synthesised or isolated through chemical process
		Artificial flavours : flavouring substances not identified in a natural product
	Prevents bitter taste transduction	Bitter Blocker - Adenosine Mono Phosphate - AMP (Linguagen)
Sweeteners	Compliments flavour perception, provides sweetness in "low carb" and "no carb" beverages	Artificial Sweeteners : Aspartame (NutraSweet, Equal), Acesulfame Potassium (Sunnett, Sweet One), Sucralose (Splenda)
		Functional Sweeteners : Sugar alcohols (sorbitol, mannitol, xylitol), , Isomaltulose (Xtend), Stevia
Acidulants	Taste, stability, pH control	Citric acid, lactic acid, tartaric acid, malic acid, Sodium Acid Sulphate
Emulsifiers and stabilizers	Texture appeal and stability	Gum Acacia, Cellulose Gum (Aquasorb), Lecithin
Weighting agents	Density modification, emulsion stability, Overcomes problem of ringing in beverages	Glyceryl Abietate, Glycerine, Sucrose Acetate Isobutyrate (SAIB)

Union under directive 94/36/EC [2] and by USFDA.

An increasing number of consumers are also looking for beverages with natural colours. Natural colours derived from fruits and vegetables are often perceived as being healthier because of their inherent antioxidants properties. But, due to limitations on stability, consistency, matrix effect, off-flavours and several other factors, these are less preferred by the manufacturers. Ingredient companies are, therefore, focussing on developing natural colours with enhanced stability in finished formulations. Colour plays vital role also in alcoholic beverages particularly in new age prepared cocktails and in cocktail mixers.

Flavours

Continual introduction of a large variety of exotic individual and fusion fruit flavours by most flavour manufacturers has provided greater opportunities to beverage manufacturers for introducing a wide range of beverages to fulfil the demand of consumers.

Recently "Superfruits" such as acai, pomegranate, blueberry, cranberry, goji, grape, guarana, mangosteen, noni and seabuckthorn have emerged as "the future of healthy living". With their robust nutrition profiles and high antioxidant properties these superfruits are predominately being used in juices and other beverages and enjoying growing popularity. Notable examples are "Purple", "Genesis Boost", "Zola Acai", etc.

Flavour industry innovators are increasingly inspired by these exotic superfruits and have developed a new range of superfruit flavours to embrace the consumers' ever-increasing palate aspirations with connotations of health.

Excellent taste is essential for the success of beverages. Many sweeteners, functional ingredients, herbs, botanicals etc, used in products often impart undesirable off-taste that interferes with the sensory experience. Flavours and masking ingredients are used to camouflage these unpleasant tastes.

Combating bitter taste in beverages is always a challenge for the flavour manufacturers. Specific technology is developed to improve the taste reception by neutralizing undesirable off-notes and blocking the unpleasant aftertaste from various ingredients. Linguagen discovered that adenosine monophosphate (AMP), a naturally occurring nucleotide substance, can block bitter flavours (Sheridan, 2004). It alters the perception of "bitter" by blocking the associated receptors.

The growing trend of exotic flavours has already shown significant carry over in alcoholic beverages segment particularly in vodka. There has been a wave of flavoured vodka introductions in the market by most leading manufacturers in the recent past. The popular brands such as Smirnoff, Van Gogh, Stolichnaya, Sky, Grey Goose, Burnett, etc., have introduced vodkas in multiple flavour variants. Likewise, Cruzan and Bacardi rums are available in a vast range of flavours. A few flavoured cognacs by Jacques Cardin and whiskies by Phillips Union are also known. Other flavoured spirits include a large variety of liqueurs such as 'Bols', 'Marie Brizard', 'Alize', etc., Likewise, many flavoured vodkas have been introduced also by United Spirits Limited in India.

In view of the receptiveness of the young consumers, the flavoured trend is likely to continue. This will help in introduction of prepared cocktails and provide convenience to the bartenders for making both conventional and new cocktails. Additionally, superfruit-derived flavours will offer immense potential to incorporate them in newer alcoholic beverages.

Sweeteners

The beverage market is constantly looking to introduce zero-calorie or low-calorie products (Landi, 2006). Besides commonly used artificial sugar substitutes including sucralose, the demand of sugar alcohols and natural sweeteners is also growing internationally.

There are sweeteners and sugar replacers available that provide additional benefits beyond sweetness and these ingredients can add a functional edge to beverage products which include "Xtend sucromalt", an all-natural sweetener derived from sucrose and maltose. It is 60 to 70% as sweet as sugar and delivers the full energy of sugar but is digested more slowly providing sustained energy. "Palatinose" is another sweet carbohydrate derived from beet sugar that has a very low glycemic index and provides energy over a prolonged period of time. It is reported to be suitable for sport, functional and wellness beverages and provides the same calorie value as sugars like sucrose or glucose. Nowadays 'Stevia', a natural, zero-calorie sweetener is being incorporated in many beverages and is gaining popularity. A new berry based natural sweetener "Brazzein" (500 to 2,000 times as sweet as sugar by weight) has recently emerged and is receiving attention of beverages producers.

These sweeteners offer excellent potential for development of sugar free alcoholic beverages. For instance "Island Breeze" rum is made with premium Bacardi rum infused with natural fruit flavours and sucralose.

Functional ingredients

Consumer responses to the new age beverages with innovative ingredients has been overwhelmingly favourable, particularly those beverages with added functionality (Moloughney, 2009; Pas, 2005). In the past few years, a wide variety of emerging ingredients have been utilised to capitalise on the growing "better-for-you" trend in the functional beverage market. This offers challenging opportunities to flavourists to improve the existing formulations, develop exciting line extensions and create distinctive out-of-a kind new products.

These products contain unique ingredients to provide specific health benefits, e.g. rejuvenation, free radical scavenging, energy and relaxation, and often include diet, low-calorie and no added sugar variants. The most commonly used functional ingredients are listed in Table 2.

The use of antioxidants tops the list of functional ingredients. This includes "Superfruit" extracts, EGCG from green tea, theaflavins from black tea, polyphenols from red and white teas as well as physiological antioxidants like alpha-lipoic acid, co-enzyme Q10, resveratrol, carotenoids, etc.

Tea has long been known for its rejuvenating effects and is considered to be the most widely consumed drink. A large number of tea-associated products have been launched in the market place and are gaining increasing popularity. The green tea (*Camellia sinensis*) -derived catechin flavonoid polyphenol, epigallocatechin gallate (EGCG), possess strong antioxidant properties, and is known for protection against free oxygen radicals linked to oxidative stress. Besides EGCG, L–theanine, a unique amino acid, is another recognised beneficial component of green tea which supports mental concentration and focus.

Hydroxycitric acid (HCA) extracted from Garcinia e.g. "Super CitriMax" (NutraGenesis) is a clinically proven mild herbal appetite suppressant and fat inhibitor that provides satiety and weight loss benefits.

Most of the above-mentioned ingredients are frequently used in a wide range of refreshing beverages that quench the deepest thirst of new generation consumers and complements their healthy lifestyle. Some notable examples include functional waters ('Glaceau', 'Snapple', 'Emerge', 'Skinny' etc), nutritional soda ('Hansen', 'Jones', 'GUS' 'Hanks', 'Nutrisoda' etc.) , functional teas ('Steaz', 'Zevia', 'Sweet Leaf', 'Tea's Tea', 'Piximate',etc.), energy coffees (Starbuck, Monster, Adina, etc.), premium functional drinks (Function, M13, FRS, Fuze, Vib, etc.)

These beverages are often offered in multiple variants in delicious flavour varieties and with functionality specifically targeted to the needs of the consumers. These include 'diet' with low calorie sweeteners (sucralose, stevia,etc.), 'slender' with garcinia-derived HCA, e.g., Super Citrimax (VMSRF, 2000), 'energy' with ginseng,

Table 2. Commonly used functional ingredients.

Ingredients	*Functionality*	*Manufacturers/Suppliers*
Carotenoids (carotenes, lycopene, lutein, zeaxanthin, fucoxanthin, astaxanthin xanthophylls, vitamin A, beta-carotene), isoflavones, polyphenols, vitamin C & E , ellagic acid, flavonoids (Quercetin), etc.	Antioxidants, multiple protective effects, free radical scavenger	Cognis, DSM, AIDP Inc., BASF, Polyphenolics, Cyvex
Epigallo Catchin Gallate - EGCG	Antioxidant, free radical scavenger, improves cardiovascular conditions	DSM Nutritional Products
L-Theanine	Provide relaxation. Alleviates PMS	Plantextrakt, Taiyo International
Citicoline	Protects brain aging and head trauma	Cognizin
Glucosamine & Chondroitin Sulfate	Joint pain relief, anti-inflammatory actions	Cargill, NutraSense
Coenzyme Q10 (Ubiquinone)	Antioxidant, improves cardio-vascular health	DSM Nutritional Products
Cranberry (Polyphenols)	Antioxidant, anticancer, anti-inflammatory, prevents urinary tract infection	Kaden Biochemicals GmbH, Cyvex, Ocean Spray International
Echinacea (Phenolic compounds - Cichoric & Caftaric)	"Immunity enhancer Antibiotic	Plantextrakt GmbH & Co. KG, Ecuadorian Rainforest, LLC.
Aloe vera (Polysaccharides, lectins mannans, anthraquiones)	Anti aging, Skin care	Plantextrakt GmbH & Co. KG, Ecuadorian Rainforest, LLC.
Resveratrol	Antioxidant, Anti ageing, Cardiovascular health	Kaden Biochemicals GmbH, DSM Nutritional Products
Milk Thistle (Silymarin)	Cholesterol, Protective effects on the liver	Nutra Asia Enterprises, Singapore, Naturex SA Germany
Kava Kava (Kavalactones)	Anti stress, fights against insomnia and anxiety	Naturex SA Germany Adenauerallee, Bonn
Schizandra (Lignans, schizandrin, xyschizandrin, gomisins & pergomisin)	Immuno-modulater	Ecuadorian Rainforest, LLC.
Amla (Tannins & polyphenols)	Immunity enhancer, Antioxidant	Avesthagen Inc. , DSM Nutritional Products
Kokum (Hydroxy Citric Acid)	Anti Obesity	Interhealth Neutraceuticals, DSM Nutritional Products
Hidrox (Polyphenols, hydroxytyrosol	Anti inflammatory, supports joint health, cardiovascular benefits	Organic Herb Inc.
Rosehips (Vitamin C, E, carotenoids & galactolipids	Reduces symptoms of osteoarthritis	DSM Nutritional Products, Organic Herbs Inc.

Table 2. Contd.

Ingredients	*Functionality*	*Manufacturers/Suppliers*
Ashwagandha (Essentra) (Alkaloids & Steroidal lactones)	Mood Rejuvenation Adaptogen Anti stress	Naturex SA Germany, NutraGenesis LLC USA
Valerian Root Extract (valeric acid)	Anticonvulsant, anti anxiety, muscle relaxant, remedy for insomnia, blood pressure	Alfa Chem, Beta pharma

guarana, caffeine quercetin, etc., 'relaxation' with EGCG, aswagandha, L-theanine, etc., and 'rejuvenation' with antioxidants (carotenoids, isoflavones, flavonoids,etc.).

Energy and sports drinks have shown phenomenal growth in recent times (Hein, 2007; Meadows-Oliver *et al.*, 2007). Energy drinks are designed to give a shot of energy through the combination of various natural ingredients, herbs and stimulants including caffeine. Likewise, sport drinks contains essentially purified water that is lightly flavoured and contain added vitamins, minerals and/or electrolytes, designed to replace nutrients and prevent dehydration after intense exercise.

Today's new breeds of energy drinks contain additional functional ingredients and often packed in small slender cans to tempt young consumers. The popular brands include 'NOS PowerShot X', 'Upshot', 'Snapple Element', etc. 'XS Gold Energy Drink Plus' is an another example of ultimate functional energy drink which combines exotic fruit flavours, vitamins, and Ashwagandha to help the body cope up with stress. A few relaxation shots such as "Tranquila' containing GABA and L-theanine have also been introduced. "Go Girl"

Table 3. Popular energy ingredients.

Ingredients	*Functionality*	*Manufacturers/Suppliers*
Ginseng (Ginsenosides)	Energy Booster, Anti depressant Aphrodisiac, Stress buster	Plantextrakt GmbH & Co. KG, Ecuadorian Rainforest, LLC.
Ginkgo Biloba (ginkgo-flavone, terpene lactones, glycosides)	Aphrodisiac, Antioxidant, Memory enhancer	Plantextrakt GmbH & Co. KG, Ecuadorian Rainforest, LLC.
Tongkat Ali (Glycosaponins, eurypeptides)	Testosterone enhancer Body building	Kaden Biochemicals GmbH, Nutra Asia Enterprises, Singapore Sumatra Pasak Bumi ,Indonesia Shanghai Everchem Co., Ltd., China
Guarana (Guaranine)	Physical endurance, Memory Retention	Plantextrakt GmbH & Co. KG, Ecuadorian Rainforest, LLC.
L-Carnitine	Energy nutrient, Cardiovasular health	Lonza AG
Branched Chain Amino Acid (BCAA)	Endurance, mental focus	Amino Vital
Creatine	Muscle Energy & Repair	NutraSense, ProLab
GABA (γ-Aminobutyric acid)	Relaxing, ant anxiety, anti-convulsive	Pharmline Inc, Pacific Rainbow Inc
Yerbamate (Xanthines)	Relaxant, antidepressant	Naturex SA Germany, Alfa Chem

a sugar free energy drink with 'Super Citrimax' is also available.

The most commonly used energy ingredients are listed in Table 3.

In addition to the above ingredients, several other ingredients also play a vital role in creation of new age products with increasing diversity.

A new patented sodium acid sulfate acidulant "pHase" (Jones-Hamilton Co.) effectively lowers pH without a sour taste, allowing the natural flavour of the beverage to be appreciated.

"EFICACIA" (CNI Technologies) is an all-natural product based on 100% acacia gum. It provides emulsion stability over a wide pH range and is highly compatible with most traditional weighting systems. It works well in highly coloured systems and integrates easily with the majority of artificial and natural colours.

Like soft drinks, today's health-conscious consumers have a strong liking also for unique alcoholic beverages with added functionality.

Besides a vast range of flavour variants of alcoholic beverages mentioned earlier, many herbal and spice associated vodka, gin, liqueurs, etc., are introduced in the market. 'Burnett Gin' , 'Tanqueray Rangpur Gin', 'Sonnema Herbal Vodka' and 'Marx Herbal Vodka" are a few known examples.

Garcinia containing whisky and vodka have been introduced in India by USL and is currently accepted well by consumers.

Some tea and coffee associated alcoholic beverages such as 'Charbay Tea Vodka', 'Firefly Sweet Tea Vodka', 'EspreXXO Ultimo 19/90 Coffee Vodka' are also available.

Despite regulatory and health related issues many manufacturers have even incorporated energy ingredients in alcoholic drinks, notably 'Jolt', 'Charge',' Tilt', etc.

Likewise , several spirits drinks laced with caffeine and other commonly used energy ingredients are also sold in the market place and gaining increasing popularity which include a range of 'P.I.N.K. Ultra-Premium spirits' (Tequila, Rum, White Whiskey, Gin, and Sake) with caffeine and guarana infusion and 'TIGROFF vodka' with Ginseng, Schizandra, Royal Jelly, etc.

Also, many of the emerging ingredients discussed above offer excellent potential for creation of innovative alcoholic beverages and need to be effectively explored to meet the ever increasing consumers' quest for exiting products to suit their changing lifestyle.

Regulatory issues

In common with most regulatory authorities worldwide, health claims are not permitted for alcoholic beverages. Nevertheless, the beverages containing novel specialty and functional ingredients could be developed to satisfy the ever-changing palate of new generation consumers. Manufacturers, however, have to ensure the safety of various ingredients used and compliance to the requirements of FEMA/GRAS, FDA, EU, CODEX/JECFA, etc.

The magic of "mixology" and "prepared cocktails"

Unique drink creations have become necessary to satisfy new age consumers around the world. Hence, novelty products with mixology propositions often entice the new generation adult consumers. It provides them the opportunities to explore and learn the fine craft of mixing cocktails and derive the pleasure of drinking through indulgence and creativity. The scope of mixology is being immensely expanded with the availability of new generation functional ingredients, flavours and "Superfruit' juices.

Most beverages manufacturers are now rapidly adopting the promotion of 'Mixology concepts' and 'cocktail recipes' of their products through websites and 'Mixology Talks'.

Spirits consumers are responding positively to "prepared cocktails" that offer convenience and portability. Formulating such products presents many challenges, such as navigating the legal restrictions, interactions between the ingredients, and shelf life issues. Many manufacturers, however, captured the insight and launched a number of prepared cocktails in premium and super premium segments. Noteworthy examples are 'Smirnoff Grand Cosmopolitan','Jose Cuervo Golden Margarita', 'Bacardi Hurricane', 'Bacardi Long Island Iced Tea', 'Bacardi Zombie', 'Kahlua Banana Mudslide', 'Kahlua White Russian', 'Jack Daniels Down Home Punch'.

Conclusion

The global beverage industry has undergone major developments in recent years in response to changing market dynamics and consumer trends. There has been a significant growth in the sales of non-carbonated soft drinks and, especially in recent times, functional beverages loaded with "good for you" ingredients. Sports and energy drinks have dominated the global functional beverages market, not only in terms of market share, but also in terms of increased NPD activity. The trend has encouraged alcohol beverage industry to follow the suit and develop products with exotic flavours and functionality to lure the new generation health conscious consumers, already fascinated by a rather wide range of exciting products. Emerging ingredients offer huge potential to design novel alcoholic beverages.

Acknowledgements

The author wishes to acknowledge his sincere thanks to all whose information has been included in the article and references.

References

Hein, T. (2007). Power Up. Food in Canada, September : 51- 54.

Griffiths, J.C. (2005). Colouring Foods & Beverages. Food Technology, **59**, 5: 38-44.

Kleiner, A. (2008). How to formulate innovation, Beverage World, **127**,6,1787 : 62-64.

Landi, H. (2006). The sweet stuff, Beverage World, **125**,6,1763: 57 & 60.

Landi, H. (2008). Global R & D Spotlight, Beverage World , **127**,6,1787 : 50-57.

McKiernan, F., Houchins, J.A. and Mattes, R.D. (2008). Relationships between human thirst, hunger, drinking and feeding. Physiology & Behaviour, **94**, 5 : 700–708.

Meadows-Oliver, M. and Ryan-Krause, P.(2007). Powering up with sports and energy drinks. Journal of Pediatric Health Care. **21**, 6 : 413-416.

Moloughney, S. (2009). The evaluation of antioxidants. Nutraceuticals World **12**, 2 : 36-46.

Pas, R. (2005). "Healthier" proves big driver in beverages. Stagnito's New Products Magazine. **September:** 26-32.

Sheridan,C. (2004) . A taste of the future. Nature Biotechnology **22,**10 : 1203-1205.

VMSRF (2000). Hydroxycitrisol: US Patent No. 6,160,172.

Web resources

EU Legislation : http://ec.europa.eu/food/fs/sfp/addit_flavor/flav08_en.pdf

USFDA Legislation : http://www.cfsan.fda.gov/~dms/opa-col2.html#table1A

Chapter 31

The new American craft distiller

Bill Owens
President, American Distilling Institute

The success of the 1,500 microbreweries in the U.S. is a dream come true for craft distillers, especially those making whiskey. Why? Because microbreweries produce large quantities of *wort* on a daily basis. And *wort,* or what we in the distilling industry call *wash,* is the raw source of whiskey.

Wort or *wash,* it doesn't matter what you call the sweet malted-barley water that comes out of the *mash tun* on its way to the fermentation tank. To make beer you add hops at this point (or other ingredients depending on what you're brewing) and boil it before transferring it to the fermentation take where the yeast is added (*pitched*) and fermentation begins. Making whiskey is simpler; you run the wort/wash directly from the mash tun to the fermentation tank (no hops needed) where it is cooled and yeast is pitched. One week later, the fermented wash is ready to be distilled.

As president of the American Distilling Institute, I receive enquires on a daily basis from people wanting to build a craft distillery. I always say, build your distillery next door to a microbrewery and make whiskey. Why do I push this? First and foremost, why make anything else out of grain except whiskey? Secondly, having a wash factory next door will save a *huge* capital investment, as there is no need to buy a grain silo, mash tun or fermentation tanks, let alone hire a skilled brewer to produce your wash. So why re-invent the wheel? Purchase your wash directly from a microbrewery and eliminate the capital investment. Examples of companies that have successfully done this are Stranahan's in Denver, Colorado, and Dry Fly Spirits in Spokane, Washington.

All the distiller has to do is provide the microbrewery with the grain recipe or *mash bill* for the style of whiskey he intends to make. Most breweries will produce a bright clean, high quality wash that is ideal for making whiskey. Think about it: what brewery would not want to generate some extra income by producing unhopped wash for a craft distiller? After all, we are brothers and sisters of producing handcrafted alcoholic products.

When purchasing distilling equipment, suppliers often will also offer to supply brewing systems for wash production. This adds cost. If, however, you know what you are doing, I suggest acquiring a used mono-block system with the hot liquor tank and mash tun in place. To the brewing kettle add a short column and water condenser. You now you have a whiskey still.

That said, used distilling equipment seldom comes on the market as few craft distillers have, to date, needed to liquidate assets. TThe alternative to purchasing a still is to build one yourself. Indeed, there is nothing intrinsically difficult with building your own pot still. It's somewhat common to convert beer fermentation vessels (30° cone) into kettles. By flipping the fermenter over and adding a short column and water condenser, then welding on a dish bottom, you can build a still that can be directly fired with gas. Definitive blueprints for still construction do not exist; there are so many different notions exist of what constitutes a desirable still.

The principles of how a still works are basic. Just look at old photos of stills and innovate with what you have. The technology of running a pot still is not that complicated: after all moonshiners have been building stills for generations. If a budding distiller seeks only to invest in a still, the capital investment required at this point is not great.

The renaissance in American craft distilling can be considered to have started about 30 years ago, when Jorg Rupf founded St. George Spirits in California to make eaux de vie. Today, Jorg produces over 50,000 cases of fruit-infused vodkas and hundreds of cases of whiskies, brandies and eaux de vies. This year, his distiller Lance Winter produced 6000 cases of absinthe. (Their first batch of absinthe sold out in four hours.) Jorg never dreamed that his first bottle of pear eau de vie from his German pot still, would lead to this artisan-distilling renaissance. He never dreamed that his Hangar One Vodka would be one of the nation's best selling hand-crafted vodkas. Jorg's success was no doubt helped because he was one of the first Americans distilleries to infuse vodka with real fruit. His Buddha's Hand Citron vodka took off and now distilleries from all over the world are producing flavor-infused vodkas (but most do not use real fruit). Since vodka is, by definition, colorless, flavorless, and odorless, infusing gives it character, body, mouthfeel, and a finished product that people enjoy.

Not to be overlooked is Clear Creek Distillery in Portland, Oregon, another leader in the craft industry. They produce over 30 products, ranging from Williams Pear Brandy, to McCarthy's Single Malt Whiskey (using peated malt) as well as numerous varietal brandies, grappas and liqueurs. (It is interesting to note that McCarthy's uses wash made by the nearby Widmer Brothers Brewery).

There are 156 craft distilleries listed in the 2010 American Distilling Institute's Distillers Resource Directory. Of these, just 28 are making whiskey. However, the buzz is all about whiskey, the Great American Spirit.

The typical American micro distiller operates a German pot reflux-still. He or she is often greatly influenced by the Scottish tradition of distilling malted barley wash, but propelled by American ingenuity and creativity; they are actively producing a new generation of whiskies. Only a few are arguably ill advised enough to make corn whiskey and compete with the major American bourbon distilleries, although exceptions like Tuthilltown are doing so with notable success.

American bourbon whiskey is primarily made from corn. Corn was the available grain in the early 1800s, and bourbon now is defined legally as being at least 51 percent corn aged at least two years in charred new American white oak casks. It is also required to use *backset* (a small amount of yeast from a previous distillation). As it stands, whiskies made either from barley-malt, rye or wheat own a miniscule share in the American marketplace. These styles of whiskies wait to be rediscovered by the American public and offer an arena of growth in which the craft distiller can excel. Wheat whiskey is sweet, rye has wonderful peppery notes, and many believe that single malt whiskies are the highest quality micro-distilled whiskies.

The big players in the American bourbon industry operate primarily out of nine distilleries in the State of Kentucky. Many of these were constructed in the early 1900s and most of the equipment has been in more or less continuous use since the 1950s. Today, they have started to modernize, becoming more efficient to producing products for the international market. The Scottish whisky industry exports a billion bottles a year, a lot of it to China, and American bourbon whiskey distilleries are working hard to keep up with a huge, and somewhat unanticipated international demand for Kentucky Bourbon. (Kirin, the giant Japanese brewer, purchased Four Roses distillery precisely to control bourbon supplies for their home market).

The total annual volume of the craft industry today is approaching 400,000 cases. Most major distilleries would consider a brand selling only 400,000 cases a failure. However, craft distillers focus on local markets. Only a few have brands in major markets. For most craft distillers, marketing nationally and internationally has only just beginning to appear realistic. The craft industry is less than 0.01% of spirits market but they have their eyes on the top shelf.

The big players are beginning to identify their premium brands as "small-batch, artisan-distilled, hand-crafted" with a label showing some guy in bib overalls rolling out the barrel. The reality is that these huge commercial factories are automated with nothing left to chance. They cannot create a new brand or change the formula for an existing brand for fear that the public would reject their product. (Remember New Coke?) The words artisan or handcrafted are not yet in their play book...yet. But I'll bet we'll see the marketing teams cranking up those terms sooner rather than later.

Craft distillers are not particularly fond of terms like: single barrel, double barrel, cask-strength or blended to describe their products. These are old, tired words. For example, the label of Tuthilltown's Hudson Baby Bourbon Whiskey reads "aged in a small charred American Oak cask." Tuthilltown products can be found in Paris, London and New York. High Plains Distillery, in Kansas, produces a whiskey infused with vanilla beans, and Copper Fox Distillery in Virginia infuses their whiskey by dropping a large tea bag of toasted apple wood into the barrel producing a whiskey with "apple wood notes."

These new styles are challenging whiskey judges, as they have to create new categories to describe the evolving styles. You can see from these examples that the new generation of artisan distillers are not playing by the rules. They are testing the market to see what works. They are out to change the way people perceive and drink whiskey, and like the microbreweries before them, these distillers are creating a whole new market for artisan products.

For the craft distiller, I suggest working with a microbrewery to produce a new generation of washes made from barley, rye and wheat. This way you can easily experiment with different types of mash bills. I would love to taste a whiskey made from a Russian Imperial Stout mash. Big distilleries do not have such flexibility.

And now I want to say a word about vodka. Most people, who contact me about joining the craft distilling industry, want to make vodka. First, I tell them that you cannot make vodka on a pot still, and you will have to spend $250,000 to purchase a small German column still with 15 to 35 plates. I quickly point out that NGS (neutral grain spirits) is readily available in the open market for $5 a proof-gallon. Why would you want to produce vodka when, according the judges, the best vodkas produced in America come from industrial distillers such as Archer Daniels Midland (ADM) or Midwest Grain Processors (MGP)? For that matter, all the vodkas on the world marketplace come from large industrial distilleries. It cannot be profitable for a small firm to distill vodka from scratch. I suggest doing what virtually all the successful vodka marketers do: buy neutral grain spirits (ngs) and redistill it.

Many small distillers, however, insist on making vodka, which requires a huge amount of time and energy, when your time and energy could really be used on distilling something interesting: *whiskey*.

When you go to a bookstore, there are many books on the whiskey industry and nothing on vodka industry. Why? Whiskey has romance, and if you want to be a craft distiller, you have to be a romantic.

Chapter 32

Renaissance of malt distilling in Tasmania (Australia)

Kristy Lark
Lark Distillery, Hobart, Tasmania, Australia

The early days – a brief history

When Hobart was established in 1804 as Tasmania's first colonial settlement, 90% of the population depended on the Commissariat Store for food, clothing and other *refreshments*. As the settlement developed the Commissariat was able to draw on local sources of supply for various manufactured goods to deal with the day to day needs of the colony. Interestingly brewing and distilling got off to a late start primarily due to government regulation, perhaps not so surprising. In the early years scarce resources could not be devoted to such activities and accordingly brewing was prohibited.

Although Hobart remained without any legal alcohol industry for some 16 years there was, however, a reasonable supply of imported spirits and reportedly any number of illegal distilleries. Apparently the drinking habits of Hobart's early inhabitants were notorious by any standards. Thus in January 1820, in an effort to overcome 'grog fever', the government relaxed its attitude towards production of alcoholic drinks. This lead to the establishment of two breweries and, by December 1822, Tasmania's first distillery, The Sorell Distillery, commenced the distillation of spirits. This was subsequently reported in the Hobart Town Gazette (HTG) on 21st December 1822 *"we are glad to find has met with general approbation, as being a spirit of good quality and flavour. This distillery is the first that has been erected in Van Diemen's Land, and is likely in all respects to succeed."*

On 20th December 1823 it was reported in the Hobart Town Gazette *"we have it in our powers to state, that on Monday last the Derwent Distillery began also to distil spirits, which we are glad to find is considered to be of good quality and flavour. – A third distillery, we have the satisfaction to add, is likewise in a rapid state towards commencing its operation."* In September 1824 the distillery placed an advert in the HTG to inform the public that the distillery now sold..., *"clean malt spirit, whisky and spirits of wine as well as imported British gin."*

Again, on 17th September 1824 it was reported in the HTG that *"the public are respectfully informed, that they may be supplied with a good wholesome and pure spirit, at 10s per gallon, exclusive of duty, or 13s. including duty, in quantities of two gallons and upwards. – Applications to be made to Mr Dunn, at the Veranda Stores, or at the above distillery (Constantia Distillery), situated at the New Town Rivulet, near the tannery. –* ***At each of theses places, a constant supply will be always kept for ready money."*** It was also reported that "the product was said to very much resemble the 'fern-tosh' in Scotland".

As we know drunkenness had been rife in the colony for many years, and in 1825 the Hobart Town Gazette drew the attention of the people to the fact 'that more liquor and beer are vended in what are elegantly called 'sly grog shops' than in all the Licensed Houses'. It seemed this was becoming quite an issue with the Governor of the day and accordingly he decided in 1825 "that the duty on imported spirits would be reduced and that the excise on locally produced spirit would be increased. This action almost immediately caused the closure of the Constantia Distillery and most of the other early colonial distilleries.

The only distillery which survived into the 1830's appears to be the original Derwent Distillery, which by then had become known as the Dynnyrne Distillery. However by the late 1830's the action of Governor Brisbane had cast its shadow over the distillery causing its closure and instigating the final death blow to the distilling industry which had started out with such great enthusiasm.

Finally in 1839, Lt Governor Franklin introduced legislation to abolish the local distilling industry in favour of brewing ale only. These ideas were attacked in the local press, but still implemented with the local distilleries being compensated after much legal wrangling.

So ended the whisky industry in Tasmania, after only a few short years until, 153 years later, Lyn & Bill Lark obtained a Spirit Makers General Licence for producing Single Malt Whisky.

The whisky renaissance – modern era

There have been other distilleries in the past on the mainland of Australia which have produced whisky over the years, most notably, Corio, which was established in the 1930's but closed down in the whisky glut of the 1970's. However for various reasons they no longer exist and it is true to say that Tasmania is now making a significant contribution to what is likely to be an emerging Australian industry.

Lark Distillery

Lark Distillery began with a fishing trip to the central highlands of Tasmania, where Bill Lark and his father-in-law Max Stewart pondered, over a dram of single malt, why whisky wasn't made in Tasmania. After all, there is fresh, clean water, locally grown barley, highland peat, and a climate that seemed just right for the production and maturing of fine malt whiskies. Over the next few months and years Bill became very enthusiastic about the possibility of producing a Tasmanian Single Malt Whisky. Having purchased a small 4 litre copper pot still from an antique auction, Bill applied for a General Distillers License. The Distillation Act 1901 was dusted off with much excitement only to reveal that it would be necessary to have a pot still with a minimum wash capacity of 2700 litres. Bitterly disappointed but not totally discouraged Bill decided to approach the local Federal member of Parliament, Mr Duncan Kerr, who also became enthusiastic and immediately phoned his good friend, Barry Jones, the then Federal Minister for Customs, Small Business and Science.

In March 1989 Barry Jones replied to Mr Kerr advising him that:-

> *"Following enquiries made by Mr Lark at the Australian Customs Service Office in Hobart, the matter of the restrictive nature of the legislation has been examined. As a result steps will be taken to amend the Distillation Regulations to provide greater flexibility regarding the capacity of stills.*
>
> *Therefore, the Australian Customs Service will be happy to consider Mr Lark's application for a General Distiller's Licence in anticipation of the Regulation being amended to provide for a still of the capacity required."*

Having changed the legislation in 1989 others were soon encouraged to become involved in whisky production. Currently there are six working whisky distilleries in Tasmania: Lark Distillery, Tasmania Distillery, Hellyers Road, Nant, Old Hobart and Mackeys.

Already the industry is varied in still sizes, brewing with different yeasts, maturing in varying barrel sizes and origins, producing peated and unpeated whisky all of which should produce another level of enjoyment and experience for the malt whisky enthusiast.

Tasmania Distillery

In March 1995 the Tasmania Distillery commenced distilling on the site of the old gas works at Wapping on Hobart's waterfront. Tasmania Distillery has a 2500 litre copper pot still which doubles as wash and spirit still. The distillery does not have its own brewing facility and currently purchases its wash from Cascade Brewery. Up to September 1999, Tasmania Distillery produced some 160 barrels of malt whisky and in September that year the distillery changed hands and immediately increased production to 500 barrels (200 litre) in its first year. The distillery has been silent for the past couple of years but has recently changed hands again and the new owners have relocated their distillery to Cambridge and recommenced distilling. They are currently exporting whisky into Asia and wholesaling a range of other products throughout Australia. In the meantime they have some 700 barrels of whisky lying quietly in their warehouse waiting for maturation to complete.

Whisky Tasmania

It was a very exciting day for Tasmania and the emerging whisky industry when Laurie House announced in 1998 that Betta Milk was in the process of designing a distillery of significant proportions adjacent to their milk factory in Burnie. Indeed they completed their impressive distillery and began producing barrels of malt whisky in late 1998 or early 1999 at a rate of between 300 to 500 barrels per annum.

Whisky Tasmania released their first whisky in 2006 under the name Hellyers Road and have established a visitor centre. Whisky Tasmania currently purchase their malted barley from Cascade Brewery and brew their own wash on site at the distillery. They have also recently purchased some peat smoked barely from the UK and we wait with interest to assess the resultant spirit.

Nant Distillery

Set in Tasmania's Central Highlands, The Nant Estate was first settled in 1821. As part of the National Trust listed farm complex a convict-built sandstone flour mill has been restored and converted into a boutique whisky distillery. The Nant Single Malt will be produced using Tasmanian barley, grown and harvested on the Nant Estate as their primary source of grain. They are aiming to produce 150-200 barrels a year. Maturation will take place on the estate in heritage sandstone buildings.

Old Hobart Distillery

Old Hobart Distillery was established in 2007, and began production straight away. They currently purchase their wash from Lark Distillery, they have an 1800 litre wash still and 600 litre spirit still. They have been laying down barrels to mature since then and are hoping to have their first release is 2012.

Across the Strait

D Baker & Sons

Following a visit to Tasmania and the Lark Distillery in 1998, David Baker returned to Melbourne to established a distillery to produce single malt whisky. After further investigation and consulting he purchased a 1000 litre copper pot still from John Dore & Co in the UK and began to lay down barrels of malt whisky in small casks.

Great Southern Distilling Company

Located in Albany, Western Australia, they commenced distilling in December 2005 and in April 2008 released their first single malt under the name Limeburners. They have an established visitor centre and do all their own brewing and distilling.

All of the above distilleries have their own special stories to tell and they should be contacted for more detailed information regarding their history and current situations.

Environmental

At the time of writing (2008) Australia is in the middle of a drought, so that any amount of waste water is not really beneficial for our environment. Thus when we built our new plant in 2006 we decided to address the issue of water usage. The first decision was that as we did not have room for a holding tank for the third water in brewing (to be then used for the first water in the next brew) we would not have and use a third water.

Next we decided that the condenser water would be run in a large loop (1.6km) through the concrete floor, thus cooling it back down, and then back into the condenser, by doing this we save hundreds of thousands of litres of water every year.

The yeast sludge left at the bottom of the fermenters is given to a pig farmer, and the draff (spent grain) goes to a local sheep farmer. The pot ale and spent ale goes into a pit and is then sprayed onto a nature reserve on the property. Initially some plants were lost but now they are all thriving.

Other distilleries in Australia are also taking up the 'Green' fight including Great Southern Distilling Company. They use a wind farm to generate 75% of their power which means they operate at a base loan of no carbon footprint. Like Lark Distillery they also trap rain water for their condensers and send the draff to a sheep farmer. Other effluent is treated as compost and user for fertiliser for native plants that surround the cellar door.

Peating

We became aware that the Scottish whisky industry had an issue with peat smoking some decades ago. There was a reaction between the green barley and the peat smoke when the starch is being converted to sugar which is overcome by adding sulphur to the kilns. Our own technique for peating suggests that we are eliminating this problem as once the malt has formed it will have no further effect.

We first developed our peat smoker after an evening in the pub, where everyone came home with their hair and clothes smelling of cigarette smoke, and thought that perhaps we could impart a smoke flavour into our malt in the same way! This idea was developed further with our first attempts now being used to hot smoke the salmon that Bill sometimes catches!!! Over the years our process has developed from a tiny peat smoker in the back yard to what it is today.

How our peat smoker works

We receive the malted barley from Cascade brewery in 50 kg bags. The malt is first slightly dampened, and then we peat smoke the malt in 25 kg lots for 60 minutes at a time. The malt is put in a basket to form a downwards cone. The basket is then placed at the top of the smoker. At the base there is a gas fired ring that heats up a metal plate with peat bricks layered on top. As the plate heats up, the peat begins to smolder causing the wonderful peat smoke to waft up through the basket and therefore through the malt. As the malt dries it is imparted with the desirable peat phenols. This gives our single malt a very delicate smoky nose and flavour. In the past we peat-smoked around 16% of our malt, at the moment we peat smoke 50% and in the future we will put some casks down that are 100% peated.

Summary

The travails of the Tasmanian whisky industry since early in the 19th century perhaps reflect the broader history of whisky itself. From its early stuttering start, Tasmania has developed, and is continuing to develop, its distilling capacity and brands. So, next time you're in a specialist whisky shop, whether it's on the Royal Mile in Edinburgh or in the US mid-west, keep your eyes open for some of our lovingly crafted whiskies!

Literature referred to in the composition of this overview

Macfie, Peter, A History and Analysis of The Derwent Distillery & Artillery Brewery (1820 – 1970), May 1995.

Bolger, Peter, Hobart Town, 1973.

Scripps, Lindy, Central Hobart – A Thematic History, Hobart City Council, 1996.

Goodrick, Joan, Life in Old Van Diemens Land, 1978.

"Hobart Town Gazette", various issues.

Chapter 33

Structure of ethanol-water systems and its consequences for flavour

Melina Maçatelli, John R. Piggott* and Alistair Paterson
Strathclyde Institute of Pharmacy and Biomedical Sciences, University of Strathclyde, Royal College Building, 204 George Street, Glasgow G1 1XW, UK

Introduction

Considered the main criterion determining consumer choice of food products (Harrison, 1998), flavour can be used as a powerful instrument to gain and keep reliable market status. Maturation causes a series of changes which are closely related to the quality of whisky aroma. The *pungent, soapy, sour,* and *harsh* notes of new distillates are replaced by *spicy, smooth, vanilla, woody* and *sweet* aroma attributes (Piggott, Conner, Paterson and Clyne, 1993); losses of ethanol and water through the cask wood increase the spirit concentration of many volatile components during maturation (Nishimura, Ohnishi, Masuda, Koga and Matsuyama, 1983; Reazin, 1983); interactions between volatiles and wood-derived components change volatile partition from the liquid into the headspace. The headspace concentration of compounds mainly depends on the temperature, pressure, chemical properties of the liquid medium and the solubility and concentration of the volatile components. Since flavour perception of beverages is directly determined by the release of volatiles to the vapour phase, this may be a critical contribution of maturation, through the addition of compounds which have fluctuating concentrations depending on the maturation variables (i.e. cask type, oak wood species, surface treatments, time and temperature of storage). In aged spirits the reduction of taste stimulation also might be related to changes in the structure of the water-ethanol mixture (Nishimura and Matsuyama, 1989).

Solution properties

Analysis of the DSC thermogram of aged whisky could detect some evidence of the strong interaction between water and ethanol due to ageing (Koga and Yoshizumi, 1977), and Nishimura *et al.* (1983) highlighted that non-volatile extract of oak wood, containing inorganic salts and compounds such as lignin and tannins, largely contributed to the interactions between alcohol and water on maturation. Interactions between water and ethanol in matured whisky disappeared upon distillation, but were recovered when the distillate residue was subsequently added to the solution. Small angle X-ray scattering suggested the existence of a greater degree of non-uniform structure in aged brandies (Aishima, Matsushita and Nishimura, 1992). The mass spectrometric analysis of liquid clusters found that maturation of whisky in a cask increased the amount of large ethanol polymer hydrates, besides the clusters' distribution differed greatly between whisky at 10% alcohol and whiskies of more than 20% v/v ethanol. It was concluded that some volatile and non-volatile compounds could assist in the formation of ethanol-water clusters in whisky, also based on the fact that unaged whiskies induced ethanol-water clusters to a higher extent than that for the simple ethanol water mixture (Furusawa, Saita and Nishi, 1990). Furthermore, the dielectric constants of the matured spirits were lower than those of aqueous ethanol solutions. This indicates that molecules of water and ethanol in matured spirits could not easily be oriented due to cluster formation during maturation (Akahoshi, 1963). Finally, Nishi and Saita (1994), based on their experiments with samples atomized in vacuum, expanded adiabatically and analysed by mass spectrometry (Nishi, Koga, Ohshima, Yamamoto, Nagashima and Nagami, 1988), suggested that the degree of molecular clustering is higher in matured spirits.

Influence of solutes

In spirits, when the solubility limit is exceeded, excess solutes form agglomerates which can incorporate shorter chain esters, alcohols and aldehydes from the bulk, decreasing their free solution, and consequently their headspace, concentrations (Conner, Paterson and Piggott, 1994a). These changes in the activity coefficient of aroma compounds suggest a possible mechanism for the reduced perception of less desirable characteristics of new distillates, described as *oily, soapy,* and *grassy* (Piggott, Conner, Clyne and Paterson, 1992), after the maturation period.

Esters are regarded as key flavour compounds in alcoholic beverages, and especially the acetate, hexanoate, octanoate, decanoate and dodecanoate ethyl esters (Salo, Suomalainen and Nykänen, 1972), which impart important character to whisky aroma. Ethyl esters or compounds of similar polarity showed correlation with immature odour fractions of brandy (Piggott *et al.,* 1992). Esters with longer aliphatic chains, such as ethyl decanoate and dodecanoate, imparted *soapy* notes to the distillate (Ribereau-Gayon, 1978). In addition, ethyl esters are amphiphilic compounds, with a polar head and a hydrophobic hydrocarbon chain, important characteristics to enable micelle formation. These compounds - mainly ethyl dodecanoate and ethyl hexadecanoate - have been found as the primary components of agglomerates formed in diluted distillates (Conner, Paterson and Piggott, 1994b). Furthermore, Paterson, Piggott, Horne and Conner (1994) found that model solutions containing ethyl esters in aqueous ethanol gave similar "micellar" diameters as those found in matured spirits. Conner *et al.* (1994b) demonstrated that addition of wood extract increased the proportion of esters in the agglomerate phase, and decreased both the solution concentration and the activity at which agglomeration occurred. Accumulation of organic acids from ethanol oxidation and breakdown of cask hemicellusoses during the maturation process also influenced volatile release (Conner, Paterson, Birkmyre and Piggott, 1999b). These acids markedly reduced the activity coefficient of ethyl decanoate, a compound that can represent the hydrophobic aroma compounds responsible for immature flavour notes present in spirits (Piggott *et al.*, 1992). In addition, studies of ethyl ester behaviour in redistilled brandies also showed that non-volatiles components, such as tannic acid and oak wood extracts, significantly reduced the activity of ethyl esters in solution, leading to a chain-length-dependent increase in aqueous ethanol solubility of these esters, which reached a maximum for esters with 12 –14 carbons (Piggott *et al.*, 1992).

Dynamic light scattering studies of distillates matured in new and used casks showed that smaller, more stable agglomerates were associated with newer casks, a larger content of wood-derived materials and more mature sensory properties (Paterson *et al.*, 1994). Using the same method, not only with wood extract, but also when catechin was added to the ethanol-water mixture, interactions between water and ethanol seemed to be stronger than in the water-ethanol mixture alone (da Porto and Nicoli, 2002). Paterson *et al.* (1994) also showed that wood extracts affected the size and stability of the ester agglomerates formed on dilution. Then Conner, Paterson, Piggott and Whateley (1998b) found that, in general, distillate components must contribute to the reduction of the interface tension between water and ester as the equilibrium agglomerate size in the new make spirit was significantly lower than in the new distillate model. Alcohol and aldehyde enhanced agglomerate stability, reduced equilibrium diameter, and had noticeable effects on the interfacial tension and the surface tension of water. In addition, the effects of individual compounds appeared to depend on the hydrophobicity of the head and the length of the alkyl chain.

Multidimensional nuclear magnetic resonance (NMR) spectroscopy has proven to be one of the most powerful techniques for determining the structure and conformation of molecules in solution (Aishima *et al.*, 1992; Aishima and Matsushita, 1988; Bovey, 1988; Derome, 1987). In aged spirits, the NMR spectrum of hydroxyl protons was significantly broader than was the case in new beverages. These results indicated that, with the progress of maturation process, there was a decrease in the exchange rate of hydroxyl protons, formation of stable molecular clusters in which the migration of ethanol molecules was restricted, and a decrease in monomeric ethanol (Akahoshi and Ohkuma, 1984). Other researchers based their experiments on the half-bandwidths of ^{1}H or ^{17}O NMR spectra (Aishima and Matsushita, 1988; Okouchi, Ishihara, Inaba and Uedaira, 1994; Okouchi, Ishihara, Inaba and Uedaira, 1995; Tamaki, Matsushita, Hioka and Takamiya, 1986). Ludwig (1995) suggested that the addition of small amounts of alcohols decreased the mobility and increased the structural order of water. Both findings could be associated with hydrophobic hydration. Okouchi, Ishihara, Ikeda and Uedaira (1999) showed that the minimum proton exchange rate increased with longer maturation periods.

In accordance with the quoted results, analysis on the basis of the ^{1}H NMR chemical shift of the OH of water and ethanol showed that the strength of the hydrogen bonding in aged whiskies is directly affected by acidic, (poly)phenols and aldehydes extracted from the oak wood casks (Nose, Hojo, Suzuki and Ueda, 2004b). In this study, the chemical shift toward lower field corresponds to the strengthening of the hydrogen-bonding structure of water. Phenolic acids and aldehydes (gallic, vanillic, and syringic acids; vanillin and syringaldehyde, respectively) exhibited their structure-making effects regardless of the presence or absence of 0.1 or 0.2 mol dm^{-3} acetic acid. Also the OH-proton chemical shift values of the whiskies shifted toward the lower field in proportion to their contents of total phenols. Sugars gave no apparent strengthening effect of the hydrogen-bonding structure in 20% (v/v) aqueous ethanol solution. The effect of undissociated acidic and aldehydes/phenolic components rather than H^+ itself should provide the main contribution to the chemical shift of alcoholic distilled beverages. The same effect was observed in shochu and in fruit cocktail drinks (Nose, Hamasaki, Hojo, Kato, Uehara and Ueda, 2005). In this latter case the effect was attributed to organic acids and (poly)phenols from the fruit juices.

In complementary studies of the OH proton chemical shifts in 20% (v/v) ethanol-water solution, Nose, Hojo and Ueda (2004a) demonstrated that almost all the salts, excluding $MgCl_2$ and KF, caused high-field chemical shifts, which should result in weakening of the water structure. On the other hand, this research highlighted that not only acids and phenols (hydrogen-bonding donors) but also conjugate-base anions (hydrogen-bonding acceptors) from weak acids could cause low-field chemical shifts. The degree of the effect was dependent on the acid strength (p*K*a) and the number of carboxyl (-COOH) and hydroxyl (-OH) functions in the acid molecule. Both undissociated acid molecules (HA) and the proton (H^+) caused the effect of strengthening the structure of water or ethanol-water. The salt effects were related to crystal ionic radii and ionic charges. In this case, no proton transfer with cations or anions should be concerned. As for the effects of weak acids (HA) or of the salts from weak acids (NaA), however, the hydrogen-bonding interaction and proton-transfer with acid molecules or conjugate base anions seem to play an important role. The observed effects of the salts or ions on the structure of water in 20% (v/v) aqueous ethanol solution had the same tendency as observed in pure water, despite the fact that the structure of water in 20% (v/v) ethanol solution is already strengthened as result of the presence of ethanol.

Aroma and taste

For assessment of flavour, distilled spirits are typically diluted to 22 or 23% v/v ethanol to reduce pungency (Hardy and Brown, 1989; Perry, 1989). Dilution, however, has been demonstrated to change the solubility of many volatile compounds that are more soluble in ethanol than water, producing a super-saturated solution (Conner *et al.*, 1994b). Thus, understanding the behaviour of aqueous ethanol solution at different concentrations has been one of the main challenges for determining the rules of solute-solvent interactions.

According to D'Angelo, Onori and Santucci (1994), the molecular structure of ethanol-water solutions is modified by changes in the proportion of the mixture. Compressibility and IR absorption spectra measurements showed that only at ethanol mole fractions below 0.05-0.06 (about 15-17% v/v ethanol) do homogeneous aqueous ethanol mixtures occur, with molecules of ethanol monodispersed in water. At higher concentration, ethanol molecules cluster to reduce hydrophobic hydration and numerous properties of this mixture show notable changes. At this point, water mixtures do not act as true solutions but are in reality microemulsions. In a continued increase of ethanol proportion, the water will lose its hydrogen bonded network completely and the solution will become basically ethanolic. Other studies from the same research group have produced evidence supporting this pattern from a collection of UV (Onori, 1987), dielectric (Fioretto, Marini, Onori, Palmieri, Santucci, Socino and Verdini, 1992), neutron and X-ray (Petrillo, Onori and Sacchetti, 1989) and more compressibility and IR absorption spectra measurements.

There is further evidence of the existence of different behaviour patterns, depending on the ethanol-water ratio, from analysis of some physical properties (Parke and Birch, 1999), dielectric relaxation time and distribution (Sudo, Shinyashiki, Kitsuki and Yagihara, 2002) and low-frequency Raman studies (Amo and Tominaga, 2000). Lamanna and Cannistraro (1996) found that the mobility of water in the solution is lowered when the alcohol concentration is increased, and that ethanol acts as a structure maker at normal temperature. In addition, Wakisaka, Komatsu and Usui (2001), based on mass spectrometric analysis, described three regions (A, B and C) on the basis of the clustering structures. In region A, the ethanol molecules probably participate in the intrinsic water cluster structure, but in region B a layer structure is formed, being more stable and containing almost equal numbers of ethanol and water molecules. In the last region (C), ethanol self-aggregating clusters emerge as an energetic favourable trend. Then, evidence suggested that preferential solvation for substrates should be determined not only by solute-solvent interaction, but also by the clustering structure of the mixed solvent.

Ethyl esters have shown behaviour that seems to be related to the changes in the physico-chemical characteristics of ethanol-water solutions described above. A log linear decrease of their activity coefficients from about 17% (v/v) ethanol was found when these volatiles were dissolved in ethanol-water solutions in increasing ethanol concentration. The intensity of the volatility suppression revealed rates inversely related to the ester acid chain length. At concentrations below 17% v/v ethanol the ester activity coefficients remained constant (Conner, Birkmyre, Paterson and Piggott, 1998a).

Other compounds have followed the same pattern described above. A progressive increase in ethanol strength induced significant reductions in the volatility of alcohols and aldehydes (Escalona, Piggott, Conner and Paterson, 1999). Results of determinations from 5 – 25% v/v ethanol showed a log linear decrease from 17% v/v ethanol for octanal, while for octanol the behaviour appeared to be more a log linear decrease over the whole range of ethanol concentrations. Thus, aldehydes could demonstrate a similar effect to that previously found for ethyl esters. On the other hand, the behaviour of higher alcohols showed no clear relationship with the proposed structural changes in the solution. The important contribution of the hydroxyl group in favour of a solution process could be a plausible explanation, as a negative value of free energy was found for this group in contrast to the positive free energy of the carboxyl group. The mechanism for suppressed volatility of higher alcohols could be their stronger association with the solution bulk, resulting from the hydrophilic character of the alcohol, and increasing incorporation in agglomerates.

Moreover, wood extracts have been shown to decrease the concentration at which aggregation of ethanol molecules occurs. Thus, subsequent lowering of the activity coefficients in solutions with ethanol concentrations between 5 and 30% v/v ethanol were observed. These reductions in the headspace concentrations occurred at both ambient and human mouth temperatures, and also would alter the release of aroma active molecules when mature spirit is consumed (Conner, Paterson and Piggott, 1999a).

Finally, is important to highlight that alteration in the release of aroma compounds has been reported during ingestion by consumers, being related to changes in the agglomerate size and stability (Harrison and Hills, 1997). The binding equilibrium and volatile release kinetics are expected to be changed by the new character of the mouth environment. In studies using model solutions, Boelrijk, Basten, Burgering, Gruppen, Voragen and Smit (2002) showed that under human mouth conditions not all flavours were affected by the addition of ethanol, but ethyl acetate and hexanoate were some of the affected compounds. In these experimental conditions, saliva did not influence flavour release. Nevertheless, direct studies on spirits, exploring details of aroma release for the huge range of compounds concerned under mouth conditions are still lacking in the literature.

Conclusions

Substantial changes occur in the flavour of distilled spirits during maturation in wood, while changes in the composition are relatively small. Some of the changes in flavour appear to be related to changes in volatility of the flavour-active compounds in the spirit. Ethanol-water solutions are not homogeneous mixtures, but show some structure above about 17% ethanol (v/v) which provides a degree of explanation of the observed changes in volatility of aroma compounds. Collectively the studies cited above provide convincing evidence of an increase in the degree of structuring in the solution during maturation, apparently caused by non-volatile materials derived from the wood. It is not clear how the changes in behaviour of ester agglomerates on maturation are related to other structural changes. Understanding the behaviour of aqueous ethanol solutions at different concentrations during maturation is the key challenge for specifying solution properties and predicting their effects on aroma compounds.

Acknowledgements

The first author is grateful to University of Strathclyde for the award of a University Studentship.

References

Aishima, T. and Matsushita, K. (1988). Measurements of food ageing by multinuclear NMR. In: *Frontiers of Flavour*. Edited by Charalambous, G., Elsevier, Amsterdam, pp. 321-337

Aishima, T., Matsushita, K. and Nishimura, K. (1992). Measurements of brandy ageing using O^{17} NMR and small angle X-ray scattering. In: *Elaboration et Connaissance des Spiritueux*. Edited by Cantagrel, R., Lavoisier, Paris, pp. 473-478

Akahoshi, R. (1963). Studies on aged spirits and their dielectricity. Part I. The dielectric coefficient of aged spirit and ethanol aqueous solution which contain some impurities. *Nippon Nogeikagaku Kaishi* **37**: 433-438

Akahoshi, R. and Ohkuma, H. (1984). NMR spectra of hydroxy protons in aged spirits. *Nippon Nogeikagaku Kaishi* **58**: 357-365

Amo, Y. and Tominaga, Y. (2000). Low-frequency Raman study of ethanol-water mixture. *Chemical Physics Letters* **320**: 703-706

Boelrijk, A., Basten, W., Burgering, M., Gruppen, H., Voragen, F. and Smit, G. (2002). The effect of co-solvent on the release of key flavours in alcoholic beverages: comparing *in vivo* with artificial mouth-MS Nose measurements. In: *Flavour Research at the Dawn of the Twenty-first Century*. Edited by Le Quéré, J.-L. and Étiévant, P., Editions Tec & Doc, Paris, pp. 284-287

Bovey, F.A. (1988). *Nuclear Magnetic Resonance Spectroscopy*. Academic Press, San Diego, CA

Conner, J.M., Paterson, A. and Piggott, J.R. (1994a). Interactions between ethyl-esters and aroma compounds in model spirit solutions. *Journal of Agricultural and Food Chemistry* **42**: 2231-2234

Conner, J.M., Paterson, A. and Piggott, J.R. (1994b). Agglomeration of ethyl-esters in model spirit solutions and malt whiskies. *Journal of the Science of Food and Agriculture* **66**: 45-53

Conner, J.M., Birkmyre, L., Paterson, A. and Piggott, J.R. (1998a). Headspace concentrations of ethyl esters at different alcoholic strengths. *Journal of the Science of Food and Agriculture* **77**: 121-126

Conner, J.M., Paterson, A., Piggott, J.R. and Whateley, T.L. (1998b). Contributions of distillate components to disperse phase structures in model spirit solutions. *Journal of Agricultural and Food Chemistry* **46**: 1292-1296

Conner, J.M., Paterson, A. and Piggott, J.R. (1999a). Release of distillate flavour compounds in Scotch malt whisky. *Journal of the Science of Food and Agriculture* **79**: 1015-1020

Conner, J.M., Paterson, A., Birkmyre, L. and Piggott, J.R. (1999b). Role of organic acids in maturation of distilled spirits in oak casks. *Journal of the Institute of Brewing* **105**: 287-291

Da Porto, C. and Nicoli, M.C. (2002). A study of the physico-chemical behavior of diacetyl in hydroalcoholic solution with and without added catechin and wood extract. *Lebensmittel-Wissenschaft und-Technologie-Food Science and Technology* **35:** 466-471

D'Angelo, M., Onori, G. and Santucci, A. (1994). Self-association of monohydric alcohols in water - compressibility and infrared-absorption measurements. *Journal of Chemical Physics* **100**: 3107-3113

Derome, A.E. (1987). *Modern NMR techniques for Chemistry Research*. Pergamon Press, Oxford

Dufour, C. and Bayonove, C.L. (1999) Interactions between wine polyphenols and aroma substances. An insight at the molecular level. *Journal of Agricultural and Food Chemistry* **47**: 678-684

Escalona, H., Piggott, J.R., Conner, J.M. and Paterson, A. (1999). Effect of ethanol strength on the volatility of higher alcohols and aldehydes. *Italian Journal of Food Science* **11**: 241-248

Fioretto, D., Marini, A., Onori, G., Palmieri, L., Santucci, A., Socino, G. and Verdini, L. (1992). Study of aggregation in water n-butoxyethanol solutions by dielectric-relaxation measurements. *Chemical Physics Letters* **196**: 583-587

Furusawa, T., Saita, M. and Nishi, N. (1990). Analysis of ethanol water clusters in whisky. In: *Proceedings of the Third Aviemore Conference on Malting, Brewing and Distilling*. Edited by Campbell, I., Institute of Brewing, London, pp. 431-438

Hardy, P.J. and Brown, J.H. (1989). Process control. In: *The Science and Technology of Whiskies*. Edited by Piggott, J.R., Sharp, R. and Duncan, R.E.B., Longman, London, pp. 182-234

Harrison, M. (1998). Effect of breathing and saliva flow on flavor release from liquid foods. *Journal of Agricultural and Food Chemistry* **46**: 2727-2735

Harrison, M. and Hills, B.P. (1997). Effects of air flow-rate on flavour release from liquid emulsions in the mouth. *International Journal of Food Science and Technology* **32**: 1-9

Koga, K. and Yoshizumi, H. (1977). Differential scanning calorimetry (DSC) studies on the structures of water-ethanol mixtures and aged whiskey. *Journal of Food Science* **42**: 1213-1217

Lamanna, R. and Cannistraro, S. (1996). Effect of ethanol addition upon the structure and the cooperativity of the water H bond network. *Chemical Physics* **213**: 95-110

Ludwig, R. (1995). NMR relaxation studies in water-alcohol mixtures - The water-rich region. *Chemical Physics* **195**: 329-337

Nishi, N. and Saita, S. (1994). Clusters in whisky. *Kagaku to Kogyo* **47**: 168-171

Nishi, N., Koga, K., Ohshima, C., Yamamoto, K., Nagashima, U. and Nagami, K. (1988). Molecular association in ethanol water mixtures studied by mass-spectrometric analysis of clusters generated through adiabatic expansion of liquid jets. *Journal of the American Chemical Society* **110**: 5246-5255

Nishimura, K. and Matsuyama, R. (1989). Maturation and maturation chemistry. In: *The Science and Technology of Whiskies*. Edited by Piggott, J.R., Sharp, R. and Duncan, R.E.B., Longman, London, pp. 235-263

Nishimura, K., Ohnishi, M., Masuda, M., Koga, K. and Matsuyama, R. (1983). Reactions of wood components during maturation. In: *Flavour of Distilled Beverages: Origin and Development*. Edited by Piggott, J.R., Ellis Horwood, Chichester, pp. 225-240

Nose, A., Hojo, M. and Ueda, T. (2004a). Effects of salts, acids, and phenols on the hydrogen-bonding structure of water-ethanol mixtures. *Journal of Physical Chemistry B* **108**: 798-804

Nose, A., Hojo, M., Suzuki, M. and Ueda, T. (2004b). Solute effects on the interaction between water and ethanol in aged whiskey. *Journal of Agricultural and Food Chemistry* **52**: 5359-5365

Nose, A., Hamasaki, T., Hojo, M., Kato, R., Uehara, K. and Ueda, T. (2005). Hydrogen bonding in alcoholic beverages (distilled spirits) and water-ethanol mixtures. *Journal of Agricultural and Food Chemistry* **53**: 7074-7081

Okouchi, S., Ishihara, Y., Inaba, M. and Uedaira, H. (1994) ^{17}O-NMR line-width of distilled spirits. *Nippon Nogeikagaku Kaishi-Journal of the Japan Society for Bioscience Biotechnology and Agrochemistry* **68**: 1215-1218

Okouchi, S., Ishihara, Y., Inaba, M. and Uedaira, H. (1995). Changes in proton-exchange rate in commercial spirits with age. *Nippon Nogeikagaku Kaishi-Journal of the Japan Society for Bioscience Biotechnology and Agrochemistry* **69**: 679-683

Okouchi, S., Ishihara, Y., Ikeda, S. and Uedaira, H. (1999). Progressive increase in minimum proton exchange rate with maturation of liquor. *Food Chemistry* **65**: 239-243

Onori, G. (1987). Adiabatic compressibility and structure of aqueous-solutions of methyl-alcohol. *Journal of Chemical Physics* **87**: 1251-1255

Parke, S.A. and Birch, G.G. (1999). Solution properties of ethanol in water. *Food Chemistry* **67**: 241-246

Paterson, A., Piggott, J.R., Horne, D.S. and Conner, J.M. (1994) Solute structures in aged malt distillates. In: *Proceedings of the Fourth Aviemore Conference on Malting, Brewing and Distilling*. Edited by Campbell, I. and Priest, F.G., Institute of Brewing, London, pp. 222-225

Perry, D.R. (1989). Odour intensities of whisky compounds. In: *Distilled Beverage Flavour: Recent Developments*. Edited by Piggott, J.R. and Paterson, A., Ellis Horwood, Chichester, pp. 200-207

Petrillo, C., Onori, G. and Sacchetti, F. (1989). Hydration structure of ethanol water solution at low alcohol concentration. *Molecular Physics* **67**: 697-705

Piggott, J.R., Conner, J.M., Clyne, J. and Paterson, A. (1992). The influence of nonvolatile constituents on the extraction of ethyl-esters from brandies. *Journal of the Science of Food and Agriculture* **59**: 477-482

Piggott, J.R., Conner, J.M., Paterson, A. and Clyne, J. (1993). Effects on Scotch whisky composition and flavour of maturation in oak casks with varying histories. *International Journal of Food Science and Technology* **28**: 303-318

Reazin, G.H. (1983). Chemical analysis of whisky maturation. In: *Flavour of Distilled Beverages: Origin and Development*. Edited by Piggott, J.R., Ellis Horwood, Chichester, pp. 225-240

Ribereau-Gayon, P. (1978). Wine flavour. In: *Flavour of Foods and Beverages*. Edited by Charalambous, G. and Inglett, G.E., Academic Press, New York, pp. 355-380

Salo, P., Suomalainen, H. and Nykänen, L. (1972). Odor thresholds and relative intensities of volatile aroma components in an artificial beverage imitating whisky. *Journal of Food Science* **37**: 394-398

Sudo, S., Shinyashiki, N., Kitsuki, Y. and Yagihara, S. (2002). Dielectric relaxation time and relaxation time distribution of alcohol-water mixtures. *Journal of Physical Chemistry A* **106**: 458-464

Tamaki, T., Matsushita, K., Hioka, K. and Takamiya, Y. (1986). ^{1}H-NMR and ^{17}O-NMR studies of distilled spirit - New methods for assessing the aging process of awamori. *Journal of the Agricultural Chemical Society of Japan* **60**: 191-197

Wakisaka, A., Komatsu, S. and Usui, Y. (2001). Solute-solvent and solvent-solvent interactions evaluated through clusters isolated from solutions: Preferential solvation in water-alcohol mixtures. *Journal of Molecular Liquids* **90**: 175-184

Chapter 34

The influence of wood species of cask on matured whisky aroma - the identification of a unique character imparted by casks of Japanese oak

Yushi Noguchi[1,3], Paul S Hughes[1], Fergus G Priest[1], John M Conner[2], and Frances Jack[2]

[1]International Centre of Brewing and Distilling, Heriot-Watt University, Riccarton, Edinburgh, EH14 4AS, UK; [2]The Scotch Whisky Research Institute, The Robertson Trust Building, Research Park North, Riccarton, Edinburgh, EH14 4AP, UK; [3]Suntory Limited, Yamazaki Distillery, 5-2-1 Yamazaki, Shimamoto-cho, Mishima-gun, Osaka, 618-0001, Japan

Introduction

Traditionally, whisky is matured in casks made of oak and the flavour of the maturing spirit is influenced by both wood species and previous cask history. Currently, bourbon casks made of American oak (*Quercus alba*) are mainly used. These casks impart a light and floral flavour to a whisky (Conner, Reid and Jack, 2003). Alternatively, sherry, brandy, or French wine casks, made of European oak (*Quercus robur* or *Quercus sesslilis*) are used. These are quite different from American oak, with spirit matured in these casks containing higher levels of colour and cask extractives (Conner et al 2003). Sherry casks, made from European oak, produce whiskies with typical 'sherry wood whisky' characteristics, combining vanilla, fruity and sweet aromas (Conner et al 2003). Both types of cask are used in Japan to mature malt and grain spirits. However, for more than 50 years, a small number of casks made from Japanese oak (*Quercus mongolica*) have also been used. Maturation in Japanese oak cask is known to give unique flavours.

The habitat of Japanese oak is East Asia, including Japan, Korean Peninsula, north east of China, and south Sakhalin, and its formal scientific name is *Quercus mongolica Fisch. ex Turcz.var. grosseerrata (Bl.) Rehd et Wils*. The characteristics of this oak are that it is softer and has less tyloses than American oak (Kato 1985). Japanese oak casks, of 500 litre capacity, are generally seasoned with oloroso sherry wine for 1 year. After seasoning, the cask is used for whisky maturation. At a younger age the Japanese oak matured whisky has fresh and light characteristics, similar to those obtained using a bourbon cask. However, over twenty years, the flavour changes into a unique one, which is different from that produced by other oak casks. In Japan these flavours are described as "well ripened pineapple", "melted butter and cinnamon", "Japanese shrine and temple", and "heavy oriental smell".

Here, we report the sensory properties of these Japanese oak whiskies, relative to the other whisky types. We also report our observations regarding the impact of oak species on the isomeric ratio of whisky lactones, which are known to make an important contribution to mature character (Masuda and Nishimura 1971). Whiskies matured in Japanese oak casks for up to forty years develop substantially higher levels of *trans*-whisky lactone, relative to whiskies matured in either American or Spanish oak. This raises the possibility that the whiskies matured in Japanese oak can be distinguished analytically, by the determination of the whisky lactone ratio and content.

Materials and methods

Whisky samples

Whiskies (Table 1) were used for the sensory analysis and the chemical analysis. These were selected as typical long matured whiskies of three ages. In this report, the whiskies are referred to as Japanese oak whisky (whisky matured in Japanese oak casks), American oak whisky (whisky matured in American oak casks) and Spanish oak whisky (whisky matured in Spanish oak casks). The American and Spanish oak whiskies approximately correspond in age to the Japanese oak whiskies.

Chemical analysis

The volatiles and phenolics analysis of whiskies was carried out with GC (Shimadzu, Kyoto, Japan) and HPLC (Shimadzu, Kyoto, Japan). These component concentrations are shown at sample strength. The analysis of whisky lactone was carried out with HP5971-GC-MS (Agilent, U.K.). The concentrations of lactones are shown at sample strength.

Whisky lactone

The whisky lactone used in this study was obtained from Aldrich. It is reported to contain the same ratio of 4 isomers (Guichard, Fournier, Masson and Puech, 1995). The isomers of this reagent were separated to both *cis*-lactones, 3S,4S (*cis*) and 3R,4R (*cis*), and both *trans*-lactones, 3S,4R (*trans*) and 3R,4S (*trans*), by silica-gel chromatography through the solvent of diethyl ether- pentane (1:6). The purities of these separated lactones were quantified by GC-MS. No *cis*-lactones were detected in the separated *trans*-lactones but the *cis*-lactones contained 1.1% of *trans*-lactones. This contamination level is thought to be low enough to disregard. When the separated *cis*-lactones and *trans*-lactones, which include the natural and unnatural lactones, were compared with the natural lactones in whisky using GC-Olfactometry, the separated lactones showed almost the same flavour as the natural lactones. Thereby, these separated lactones were used respectively as *cis* or *trans*-lactone for our study.

Sensory analysis

All sensory analysis was carried out using Quantitative Descriptive Analysis by the Scotch Whisky Research Institute's trained sensory panel. Attributes were scored using a scale of 0.0 to 3.0 and average scores calculated across the panel. Whiskies were reduced to about 20% (v/v) alcohol strength and blind coded prior to assessment.

Threshold measurement

The samples were prepared in 20% (v/v) ethanol solution, which included each concentration of lactone or lactones, *cis*-lactone; 0.00, 0.05, 0.10, 0.15, 0.20, 0.25 mg/L, *trans*-lactone; 0.00, 0.40, 0.80, 1.20, 1.60, 2.00 mg/L, mixture (*trans* : *cis*

Table 1. Whisky samples.

Name	Japanese (JPN) oak whisky			American (USA) oak whisky			Spanish (SPN) oak whisky		
	Type	*Spirit*	*Distilled*	*Type*	*Spirit*	*Distilled*	*Type*	*Spirit*	Distilled
20 yo	Grain	Chita	1987	Grain	Chita	1988	Grain	Chita	1988
27 yo	Malt	Yamazaki	1980	Malt	Yamazaki	1980			
40 yo	Malt	Yamazaki	1960	Malt	Yamazaki	1968			

= 1:1); 0.00, 0.05, 0.10, 0.15, 0.20, 0.25 mg/L. The threshold was calculated by determining the point at which 50% of the panel can first detect the aroma.

Results and discussion

Sensory analysis using general flavour descriptions

The spider chart (Figure 1) shows the comparison of twenty-seven-year-old Japanese oak and American oak whiskies using flavour descriptions generally used to profile mature Scotch whiskies. The two whiskies were found to be very similar in terms of these flavour descriptions. Although slight differences were found in Feinty and Sulphury, they do not completely describe the typical flavour of Japanese oak whisky.

Special flavour descriptions

Panellists were also asked to comment on other flavours present in the whiskies. Descriptions obtained included Musty, Earthy, Varnish, Incense, Aniseed, Matured pineapple, Coconut, Beeswax, Melted butter. From these comments, the descriptions of "Incense" and "Coconut" were identified as possible flavours that typify Japanese oak whiskies. The sensory analysis was carried out again using these descriptions, in order to determine whether or not these attributes characterised the unique flavour of Japanese oak whisky. All ages of whiskies were compared in the flavour description of Incense and Coconut (Figure 2). From this, it is clear that Japanese oak whiskies had higher scores for "Incense" than the American oak whiskies, with these differences becoming statistically significant for the older products. This indicates that Incense is one of

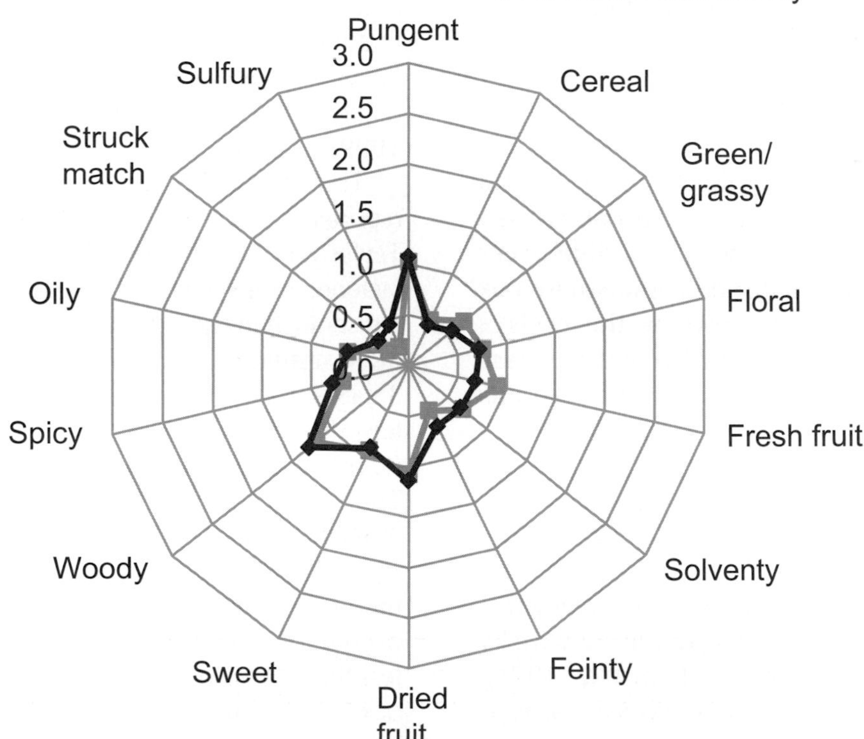

Figure 1. Result of general sensory analysis.

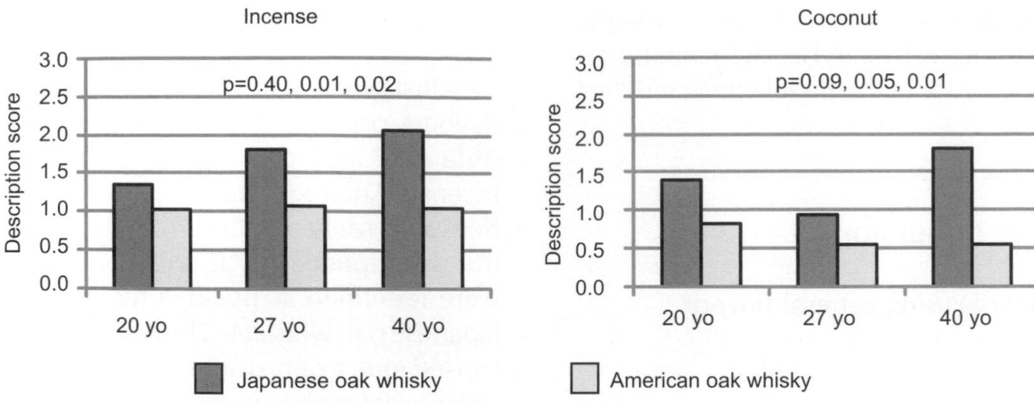

Figure 2. Sensory result in special flavour description, incense and coconut.

the unique flavour descriptions of Japanese oak whisky. Similarly, for "Coconut", Japanese oak whiskies showed significantly higher score in all three ages of whisky. This indicates that Coconut is another unique flavour description of Japanese oak whisky. Although Coconut is a flavour typically associated with American oak whisky, this sensory result indicates that Japanese oak gives even more of this characteristic.

General chemical analysis

A comparison of the volatiles analyses of American, Spanish, and Japanese oak whisky (Table 2) showed no compositional differences were found that distinguished the Japanese oak whiskies from the others. However, the levels of phenolic compounds in Spanish and Japanese oak whiskies are higher than in American oak whiskies.

Whisky lactone analysis

Whisky lactone is a well known wood extractive responsible for coconut flavour in whisky (Otuska, Zenibayashi, Itoh and Totsuka, 1974). This molecule contains two chiral carbons and as such can exist as 4 isomers, 3S,4S (*cis*), 3S,4R (*trans*), 3R,4R (*cis*), and 3R,4S (*trans*). Although each isomer has a slightly different flavour, they all have coconut notes and could potentially contribute to coconut flavour in whisky (Koppenhoefer, Behnisch, Epperlein and Holzschuh, 1994). However, only two of these isomers are reported to exist naturally, 3S,4S (*cis*), 3S,4R (*trans*) (Masson, Guichard, Fournier and Puech, 1995). It is also reported that the isomerisation of these lactones will not occur in wine or whisky because of the acidic nature of these media (Pollnitz , Jones and Sefton, 1999).

The thresholds of 4 lactone isomers were reported in white and red wine (Brown, Sefton, Taylor and Elsey, 2006). In this report, each *cis*-lactone, 3S,4S (*cis*) and 3R,4R (*cis*), has a lower threshold than each *trans*-lactone, 3S,4R (*trans*) and 3R,4S (*trans*). Furthermore, the threshold of natural 3S,4S (*cis*) lactone is lower than unnatural 3R,4R (*cis*). Natural 3S,4R (*trans*) and unnatural 3R,4S (*trans*) have almost the same threshold.

The amount of lactones found in the whiskies at each age (Table 3) showed that for all ages, Japanese oak whiskies contained higher levels of *trans*-lactone than American oak whiskies. The ratio of *cis/trans* in all of the Japanese oak whiskies were less than 1.0, while in the Spanish and American oak whiskies the ratios were all well in excess of 1.0. Hence, only in the Japanese oak whiskies is the level of *trans*-lactone higher than *cis*-lactone.

Table 2. Result of general chemical analysis.

mg/L, as is

Group	Compound name		Whisky						
			USA	SPN	JPN	USA	JPN	USA	JPN
			20 yo	20 yo	20 yo	27 yo	27 yo	40 yo	40 yo
Fusel alcohols	n-PrOH	n-Propyl Alcohol	405.3	410.0	408.0	408.6	526.0	455.8	495.7
	i-BuOH	i-Butanol	640.9	745.7	567.3	551.7	656.7	531.0	1486.8
	i-AmOH	i-Amyl Alcohol	104.1	52.2	55.0	1231.7	1823.8	1728.7	3472.8
	a-AmOH	a-Amyl Alcohol	29.5	12.7	15.5	346.3	556.6	374.8	929.9
	β-PheOH	β-Phenethyl Alcohol	10.3	5.30	6.71	73.2	91.6	82.9	131.2
Fatty acid esters	Et-C2	Ethyl Acetate	662.7	745.7	587.5	1334.1	2230.1	1771.5	2660.9
	Et-C6	Ethyl Caproate	N.D.	N.D.	N.D.	13.5	29.9	12.9	15.2
	Et-C8	Ethyl Caprylate	N.D.	3.57	4.76	71.9	153.1	70.7	62.0
	Et-C10	Ethyl Caprate	1.75	5.77	8.78	111.7	220.4	135.8	116.5
	Et-C12	Ethyl Laurate	1.48	4.50	6.39	76.2	138.0	86.9	64.6
	Et-C14	Ethyl Myristate	N.D.	N.D.	N.D.	7.07	12.7	13.8	8.59
	Et-C16:1	Ethyl Palmitleat	N.D.	N.D.	N.D.	14.2	22.4	2.35	1.77
	Et-C16	Ethyl Palmiate	2.04	2.74	2.04	26.1	45.8	19.1	17.1
	Et-Lac	Ethyl Lactate	3.39	9.14	4.77	42.5	82.5	16.7	61.0
	i-AmC2	i-Amyl Acetate	N.D.	N.D.	N.D.	3.09	4.63	4.46	18.6
Fatty acids	C2-acid	Acetic Acid	509.6	618.9	524.3	891.1	798.9	773.2	1404.9
	C3-acid	Propionic Acid	N.D.	2.23	N.D.	1.89	2.45	1.75	7.04
	i-C4-acid	i-Butylic Acid	N.D.	N.D.	N.D.	1.66	1.61	0.58	1.89
	i-C5-acid	i-Valeric Acid	N.D.	N.D.	N.D.	3.63	4.71	1.43	4.00
	C6-acid	Caproic Acid	N.D.	0.67	0.75	7.73	10.2	5.65	7.42
	C8-acid	Caprylic Acid	N.D.	2.28	3.39	40.6	54.6	30.8	30.7
	C10-acid	Capric Acid	0.95	4.06	6.28	67.6	82.8	64.7	63.3
	C12-acid	Lauric Acid	N.D.	2.27	3.66	45.1	53.9	39.8	34.8
Aldehydes	Acetaldehyde		202.1	258.2	212.6	223.3	260.0	308.4	325.2
	Acetal		66.4	77.4	57.9	80.5	219.1	190.2	164.0
	Furfral		6.84	5.16	22.4	23.6	34.1	19.0	31.9
Phenolic compounds	Gallic Acid		20.3	70.9	94.9	25.8	79.6	37.9	141.5
	p-Hydroxybenzoic Acid		0.38	0.30	0.31	0.46	0.87	0.67	1.87
	Vanillic Acid		2.67	3.39	3.37	4.26	9.17	6.61	18.4
	Syringic Acid		4.04	6.71	5.52	7.98	13.9	11.0	25.7
	Vanillin		2.65	5.45	5.97	4.05	7.87	7.23	18.4
	Syringaldehyde		6.52	11.6	12.1	12.4	18.3	16.7	34.8
	Coniferaldehyde		0.59	0.87	1.02	0.92	1.52	1.27	2.50
	Sinapaldehyde		0.48	1.03	1.33	0.70	0.86	0.59	1.21

Nabeta (Nabeta, Yonekubo and Miyake, 1986) reported the amounts of lactones in three types of oak including *Q. mongolica* (Table 4). Japanese oak showed higher levels of *trans*-lactone. Therefore, the greater amounts of *trans*-lactone in Japanese oak whisky are very likely to be derived from the wood itself.

Many studies about the ratio of lactone isomers are reported in wine (Waterhouse and Towey 1994; Diaz-Plaza, Reyero, Pardo, Alonso and Salinas 2002; Simón, Cadahia and Jalocha, 2003). From these reports, in the case of American oak, the ratio of *cis/trans* is from about 7 to 10, and European oak case, from

Table 3. Result of whisky lactone concentration in whisky (mg/L, as is).

Whisky		*cis*	*trans*	*ratio*
20 yo	USA	3.02	0.30	10.24
	SPN	2.08	0.28	7.56
	JPN	1.22	2.47	0.49
27 yo	USA	2.72	0.47	5.79
	JPN	2.27	2.52	0.90
40 yo	USA	6.37	1.54	4.14
	JPN	14.78	29.60	0.50

Table 4. Data of whisky lactone amounts in wood (mg/L, as is).

Wood species	*cis*	*trans*	*ratio*
Q. mongolica	1200.0	974.0	0.81
Q. serrata	60.2	170.0	2.82
Q. dentata	34.8	441.0	12.67

1 to 5. Therefore in these oaks the *cis*-lactone is the more abundant isomer. Only Japanese oak has higher ratio of *trans*-lactone. Therefore lactone ratio may provide an analytical means of identifying whether or not a whisky has been matured in Japanese oak.

The threshold of lactones

The threshold of *cis*-lactone in 20% (v/v) ethanol was 0.15 mg/L, which is 5.5 times lower than that of *trans*-lactone, 0.83 mg/L. The result is very close to former studies carried out in 30% ethanol solutions, where the threshold of *cis*-lactone was 0.067 mg/L and of *trans*-lactone was 0.79 mg/L (Otuska et al 1974). In wine research, the threshold of each lactone has also been reported and again the results show that *cis*-lactone has a lower threshold (Brown et al 2006). In the past, due to the higher ratio of *cis*-lactone in American oak and European oak, most studies have focussed on only this isomer.

In addition to the thresholds of only *cis* and *trans*-lactone, the threshold of 1:1 mixture of both lactones was measured. This threshold, 0.11 mg/L was lower than that of either *cis*-lactone (0.15 mg/L) or *trans*-lactone (0.83 mg/L) when measured individually. This indicates that mixed lactones are more active flavour than only *cis*-lactone or *trans*-lactone individually.

Coconut flavour intensity

It is surprising that "Coconut" is a typical flavour of Japanese oak when these whiskies show higher amounts of *trans*-lactone, which is less flavour active, than *cis*-lactone. The equation below can be used to predict coconut flavour based on a combination of the levels and thresholds of the two lactones.

$$\textbf{Coconut Flavour Intensity} = [cis] / 0.15 + [trans] / 0.83$$

Sensory analysis was carried out in a 20% (v/v) ethanol solution including 1 mg/L of each lactone in order to test this prediction. By the calculation of the intensity using this formula, the intensity of *cis*-lactone (1 mg/L) is 6.7, and of the *trans*-lactone (1 mg/L) is 1.2. Of course, the intensity of *trans*-lactone 1 mg/L solution is lower than *cis*-lactone 1 mg/L solution. Results of the sensory evaluation, shown in Table 5, agree with the predicted values.

Table 5. Confirmation of Coconut intensity.

Sample	*Amount (mg/L)*		*Intensity*	*Coconut score*[a]
	cis	*trans*		
cis	1.00	0.00	6.7	1.33
trans	0.00	1.00	1.2	0.47

[a]N = 15 (p = 0.0001)

Next, this intensity calculation was applied for a whisky, based on the levels of each of the lactones that they contained. The predicted coconut intensity of Japanese oak whisky was 3.7, which was about half that of American oak whisky (6.8). However, the sensory results showed the inverse of this, with the Japanese oak whisky being given higher scores for this aroma (Table 6).

In order to examine this difference between predicted and actual coconut intensity, we focused on the influence of each lactone in the

Table 6. Coconut intensity and sensory result in whisky.

Sample	*Amount (mg/L)*		*Intensity*	*Coconut score*[a]
	cis	*trans*		
USA	1.01	0.10	6.8	0.82
JPN	0.41	0.82	3.7	1.39

[a]N=9 (p=0.09)

whisky media and carried out further studies with each lactone added to whisky. The tests were carried out using both American oak whisky and Japanese oak whisky, which contain different original ratios of lactones. In the first test 1 mg/L of each lactone was added to American oak whisky. The predicted intensity of coconut aroma was lowest in the sample containing no added lactone, highest in the one with added *cis*-lactone and at an intermediate level in the one with added *trans*-lactone (Table 7). However, in the sensory results the score for the *trans*-lactone addition was almost the same, or even slightly higher, than the *cis*-lactone addition. Addition of lactones to the Japanese oak whisky gave similar results. In conclusion, *trans*-lactone shows a highly active coconut flavour when added to whiskies containing different ratios of lactones.

Synergy effect between whisky lactones

We considered why the *trans*-lactone shows this highly active flavour, and prepared 20% (v/v) ethanol model samples which contained the same amounts of each lactone as the Japanese oak whiskies used in the previous test. The sensory result for these model samples are shown in Figure 3, alongside the original whisky sensory results. The model samples showed higher overall scores than original whiskies, because the coconut flavour is easier to detect in this simple ethanol solution than in a complex whisky matrix. When the results for the model samples are compared, the sample containing *trans*-lactone showed higher scores than the sample containing no lactone and almost same score as the *cis*-lactone sample. This tendency indicates two points. The first is that the coconut flavour in whisky is mostly influenced by the ratio of lactones. The second point is that *trans*-lactone has a more active flavour when the lactones are mixed.

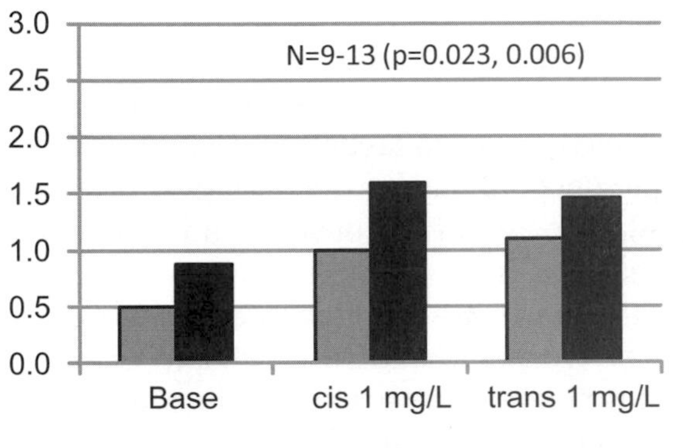

Figure 3. Result of 20% ethanol model samples.

The previous threshold results showed that the thresholds of 1:1 (w/w) mixture of both lactones was clearly lower than only *cis*-lactone or *trans*-lactone, and the mixed lactones were more flavour-active than individual isomers. Considering the two results, this model sample behaviour and the threshold of mixed lactones demonstrates a multiplier effect between *cis*-

Table 7. Result of additional test.

Addition	*American oak whisky*[a]				*Japanese oak whisky*[a]			
	Amount (mg/L)		*Intensity*	*Coconut score*[b]	*Amount (mg/L)*		*Intensity*	*Coconut score*[b]
	cis	*trans*			*cis*	*trans*		
Base	1.01	0.10	6.8	0.44	0.41	0.82	3.7	0.49
cis 1 mg/L	2.01	0.10	13.5	0.72	1.41	0.82	10.4	1.00
trans 1 mg/L	1.01	1.10	8.1	0.94	0.41	1.82	4.9	1.09

[a]Whisky: 20 yo, [b]N=13, 14 (p=0.034, 0.023)

lactone and *trans*-lactone, explaining the high flavour activity of *trans*-lactone in whisky.

Conclusions

"Incense" and "Coconut" were found to be typical characters of Japanese oak whiskies. The coconut flavour appears to be mainly derived from the higher *trans*-lactone concentration which is extracted from Japanese oak wood during maturation. Furthermore, it was shown that in a mixture of *cis* and *trans*-lactones, *trans*-lactone has a more active flavour possibly due to an interaction between the isomers. From these results, we suggest two points. The first is that future studies should not only focus on *cis*-lactone but also *trans*-lactone. The second is that whiskies matured in Japanese oak casks have a unique coconut flavour due to higher levels of *trans*-lactone which are never found in bourbon or sherry casks.

In the future, we will compare some different ages of whiskies, and research the effect of charring conditions, oak tree locations, and other factors on lactone levels of Japanese oak. Further work is also planned to identify the alternative Japanese oak character, "Incense".

Acknowledgements

The authors would like to thank the SWRI panellists for the sensory analysis , and the ICBD for help with the experimental work. Thanks are also due to colleagues at Suntory and Dr. Inatomi for their helpful and informative discussions.

References

Brown, R. C., Sefton, M. A., Taylor, D. K., and Elsey, G. M. (2006) An Odour detection threshold determination of all four possible stereoisomers of oak lactone in a white and a red wine. *Australian Journal of Grape and Wine Research* **12**: 115-118

Conner, J., Reid, K., and Jack, F. (2003). Chapter 7 Maturation and blending. In: *Whisky Technology, Production and Marketing*. Edited by Russell, I., Bamforth, C., and Stewart, G. G., Academic Press, UK, pp. 211-242

Díaz-Plaza, E. M., Reyero, J. R., Pardo, F., Alonso, G. L., and Salinas, R. (2002) Influence of Oak Wood on the Aromatic Composition and Quality of Wines with Different Tannin Contents. *Journal of Agricultural and Food Chemistry* **50**: 2622-2626

Guichard, E., Fournier, N., Masson, G., and Puech, J. L. (1995) Stereoisomers of β-Methyl-γ-Octalactone. I. Quantification in Brandies as a Function of Wood Origin and Treatment of the Barrels. *American Journal of Enology and Viticulture* **46**(4): 419-423

Kato, S., (1985) Chapter 1. In: *Textbook of Cooperage Technology*. Edited by Katoh, S., pp. 140-146

Koppenhoefer, B., Behnisch, R., Epperlein, U., Holzschuh, H. (1994). Enantiomeric Odor Differences and Gas Chromatographic Properties of Flavours and Fragrances. *Perfumer & Flavorist* **19**(5): 1-14

Masson, G., Guichard, E., Fournier, N., and Puech, J. -L. (1995). Stereoisomers of β-Methyl-γ-Octalactone. II. Contents in the Wood of French (Quercus robur and Quercus petraea) and American (Quercus alba) Oaks. *American Journal of Enology and Viticulture* **46**(4): 424-428

Masuda, M. and Nishimura, K., (1971). Branched Nonalactones from Some Quercus Species. *Phytochemical Reports* **10**: 1401-1402

Nabeta, K., Yonekubo, J., Miyake, M. (1986). Analysis of Volatile Constituents of European and Japanese Oaks. *Mokuzai Gakkaishi* **32**(11): 921-927

Otuska, K., Zenibayashi, Y., Itoh, M., and Totsuka, A. (1974). Presence and Significance of Two Diastereomers of β-Methyl-γ-octalactone in Aged Distilled Liquors. *Agricultural and Biological Chemistry* **38**(3): 485-490

Pollnitz, A. P., Jones, G. P., and Sefton, M. A.

(1999). Determination of oak lactones in barrel-aged wines and in oak extracts by stable isotope dilution analysis. *Journal of Chromatography A* **857**: 239-246

Simón, B. F., Cadahía, E., and Jalocha, J. (2003) Volatile Compounds in a Spanish Red Wine Aged in Barrels Made of Spanish, French, and American Oak Wood. *Journal of Agricultural and Food Chemistry* **51**: 7671-7678

Waterhouse, A. L. and Towey, J. P., (1994) Oak Lactone Isomer Ratio Distinguishes between Wines Fermented in American and French Oak Barrels. *Journal of Agricultural and Food Chemistry* **42**: 1971-1974

Chapter 35

New highly aromatic products and distillates from smoked malt

J. Voigt[1], A. Richter[2], B. Weckerle, R. von der Recke[3]

[1]Technische Universität München, Center of Life Sciences Weihenstephan, Am Forum 2, 85354 Freising Weihenstephan, Germany; [2]Weyermann Specialty Malting, Brennerstrasse 17-19, 96052 Bamberg, Germany; [3] SymriseSymrise GmbH & Co KG, Anton-Jaumann-Industriepark 986720 Nördlingen, Germany

Abstract

The production of beers from smoked malt can vary in a wide range of smoked malt additions. On the basis of Pilsner malt different percentages of Bamberg Rauch malt were added to achieve different characteristics of smoked beer flavours. Two different fermentation procedures with top and bottom-fermenting yeasts were investigated with respect to the profile of aromatic compounds. The main target was to optimize fermentation conditions such as temperatures. All beers were analysed and tested sensorially. In a second trial series, the products were distilled in order to produce distillate products which can be used as flavourings. The process of distilling was performed in a column under various conditions (eg number of trays and flow rates). The resulting distillates were characterised by sensory and chromatographic methods. These can be used for the flavouring of innovative alcoholic beverages.

Introduction

This work was initiated in order to follow the behaviour of aroma compounds from smoke-flavoured malts from the typical "Bamberg Rauchmalz". This aroma is used typically in beers with an addition of this special malt as an ingredient. The flavour can give a smoky aroma and taste to beers and intermediate wort products. The investigation of the behaviour of such flavour compounds are also of interest for other foods and beverages. Distillates of fermented beers may be interesting for spirits since the smoky aromas have not yet been described. The aroma compounds are believed to be different from those caused by smoky compounds from wood or toasted casks as they are used in whiskey.

Goals

The project was set up in order to investigate the behaviour of smoked malt aroma compounds during beer production and the distilling of unhopped beers for the production of distillates. These distillates were described regarding the optional use in whiskey production and as flavouring agent in other food applications.

Materials and methods

- Percentage of smoked malt in the grist charge 0 - 90%
- Comparison of two different yeast strains

- pH in Wort and Fermentation
- Original gravity
- Colour
- Final degree of attenuation

The raw materials used for brewing are shown in table 1 below:

Table 1. Different malt charges for the trials.

	Smoked malt	*Pilsner malt*	*Acid malt*	*Caraaroma*
Brew 1	0%	90%	2%	8%
Brew 2	25%	65%	2%	8%
Brew 3	50%	40%	2%	8%
Brew 4	90%	0%	2%	8%

Brewing

Beers were produced in pilot scale 2,5 hl in the Weyermann Research Brewery. Same wort were fermented with W34/70 and M1 (Whiskey) dry yeast. The raw materials as in table 1 were milled and mashed in an infusion mashing programm with 52°C Mash-in temperature, 35 mins at 64°C, 5 mins at 68°C, 20 mins. At 72°C the gravity of the cast-out wort was 15 % OG. Boiling was 5 minutes for sterilisation without hopping. After sedimentation in the whirlpool, the fermentation temperature was 20 °C for bottom fermentation, up to 25°C with the whiskey yeast and 12 °C for the bottom fermentation up to 15°C.

Distilling

The beer from the brewing trials were distilled in a in pilot scale 125 liter still (Fig. 1) with 3 bottoms, a dephlegmator and a cynid separator. First runs were stopped at 0,9 l, second runs were collected at 54% vol. alcohol and last runs from 54 to 14%. Samples were taken from wort, beer, first, second and last runs as well as spent grains residual wash.

Gas chromatography

The GC/MS analyses were made for structure, whilst GC/FID analyses were used for quantitation. The mass spectrometer was operated at 70 eV ionization energy in EI mode in full scan mode with a mass range from 25-370. Mass spectra as well as linear retention indices (based on hydrocarbon indices) were compared to those of authentic components and to the in-house database. The analyses were carried out by Symrise®. At this stage,

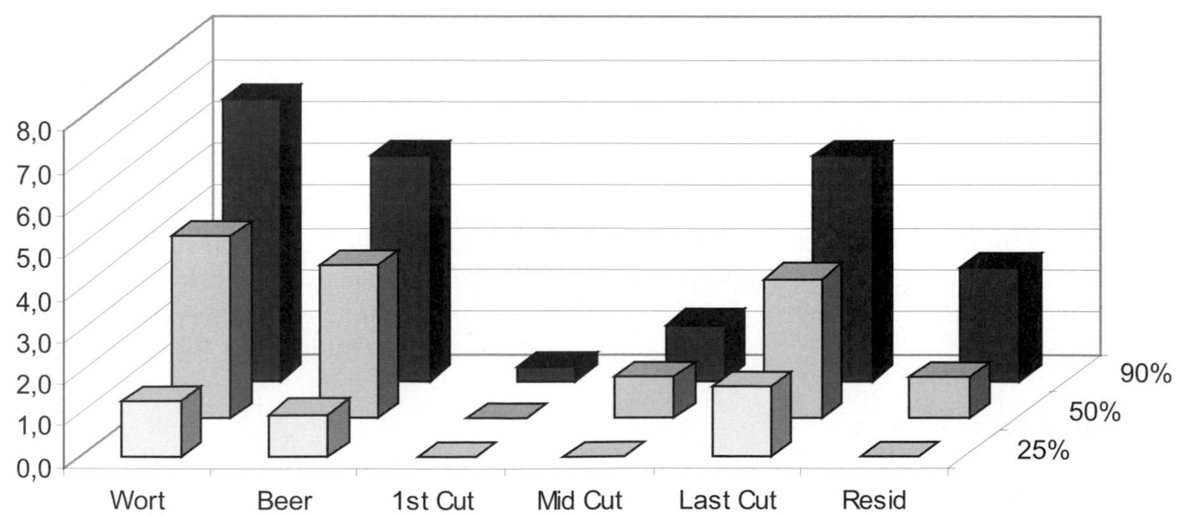

Figure 1. Intensity of aroma in top fermentation with varying smoked malt additions.

the characterization of the compounds measured by GC do not allow a quantitative identification of the smoke aroma found by the sensory analyses. Even though some compounds are defined as having a smoky aroma, they are also compounds found in normal beer fermentation without correlation to this specific aromatic impression.

Sensory analysis

The sensory analysis focused on tracing the intensity of smoky smell or taste of: wort, beer, first, middle and last run of distilling and the remaining wash.

The tasting was done by a panel familiar with tasting aroma compounds in wort, beer and distillates. The intensity of smoky flavour was described on a scale of 0 to 10, where 0 represents no detectable smoke flavour and 10 indicates a very strong smoke impression. The sensory analyses was made for both the aroma and the taste of the samples.

Results and discussion

Sensory results

The sensory analyses indicated that the smoky aromatic fractions are found in wort and beer. The concentration of smoky aromas significantly correlates with the addition of smoked malt to the original product. 90% use of smoked malt always gave the highest impression of smoky aroma or taste while 25% always gave the least. The intensities of smoke aromas in first and middle run of the distillation are small, but detectable. The first run of distillation, which is normally not used, may also contain smoky compounds but this is suppressed by the presence of other more intense compounds.

Most of the smoky flavours can be detected on both aroma and taste in the last runs. Also in the residual wash some smoke aromas were detected by sensory analysis. By monitoring the amount of smoke aromas during the distilling process the most intense fractions can be found. Top fermentated worts has slightly higher flavours on the basis of taste than their bottom fermented counterparts.The intensity decreased from wort to beer. The smoke components are more easily detected by taste than by smell. Figures 1-4 show the aroma and taste results of top and bottom fermented products with 25, 50 an 90% smoked malt additions. The GC aroma-analysis and evaluation for tracing the smoked aroma components indicates some key components are: 4-vinylguaiacol, furfural, 2-acetylfuran and guaiacol. These Methoxyphenols are also often part of whiskey aroma. These products are also

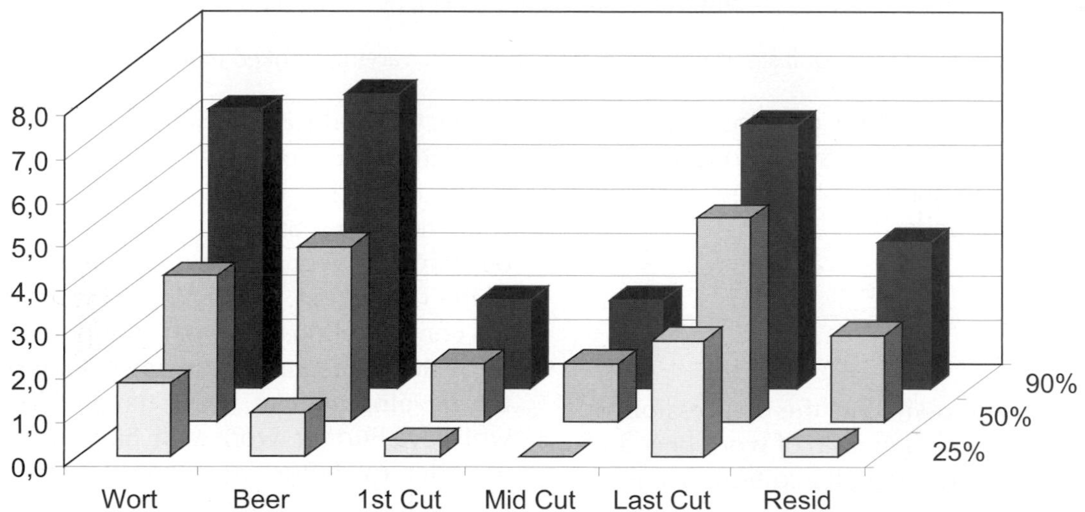

Figure 2. Intensity of taste in top fermentation with varying smoked malt additions.

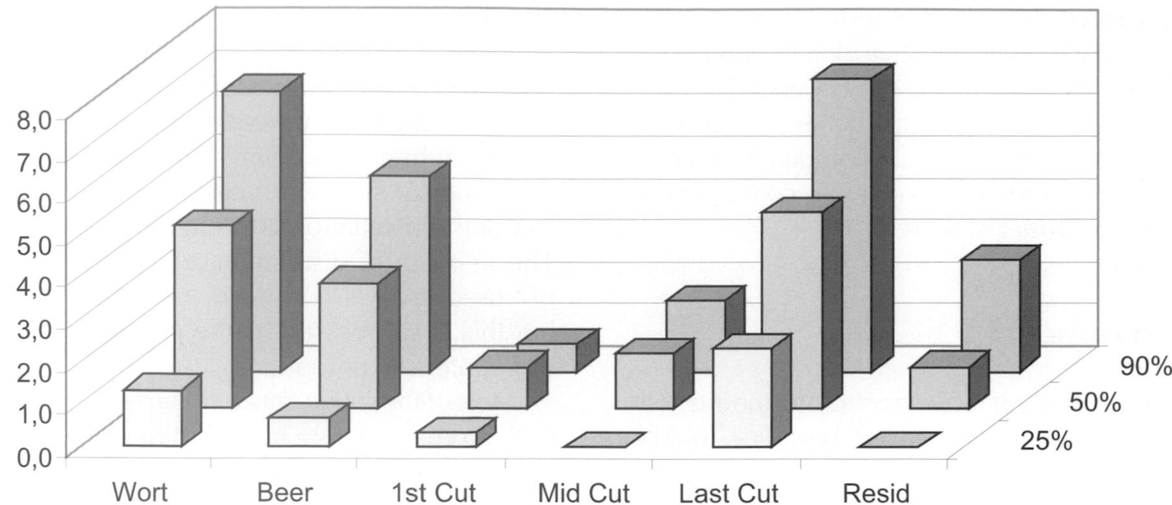

Figure 3. Intensity of aroma in bottom fermentation with varying smoked malt additions.

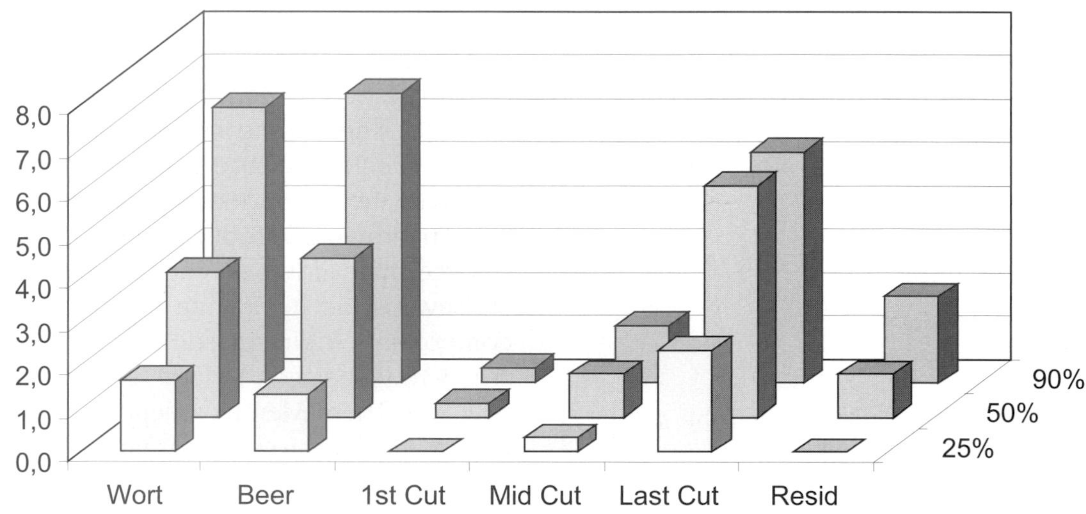

Figure 4. Intensity of taste in bottom fermentation with varying smoked malt additions.

found in the fermentation of standard malts. Most likely the intensity caused by concentration plays the most important role in their attribute as smoke compounds.

Summary

It was clearly shown that the impression of smoke in the aroma and taste of wort, beer and distillates from smoked malt additions becomes more intense with the amount of smoked malt added. The fermentation process in beer production reduces the smoke flavour. During distillation most of the smoky compounds are traced in the last runnings. For further work it is intended to search for the most suitable cut-off point between the middle run and last run of the distillation. This is expected to enhance the concentrations of smoky compounds in the distillates. This can be an interesting route to the development of novel flavour profiles in whiskey. Further work will have to be done in order to define correlations between the chromatographically found fractions and the smoke flavour.

References

Câmara, J., Marques, J.C., Perestrelo Rodrigues, R. F., Oliveira, L., Andrade, P., Caldeira M.(2006), Evaluation of volatile constituents profile in Scotch whisky by SPME/GC-ITMS, Proceedings IUFoST World Congress, 13th World Congress of Food Science & Technology

Demyttenaere, J. C. R.; Sanchez Martinez, J. K.; Verhe, R.; Sandra, P.; De Kimpe, N. (2003), Analysis of volatiles of malt whisky by solid-phase microextraction and stir bar sorptive extraction J. Chromatogr., A 2003 985 221 232

De Rijeke, D.; TerHeide, R.(1983), Flavour compounds in Rum, Cognac and Whisky In *Flavour of Distilled Beverages: Origin and Development.* Piggott, J. R. Eds.; Ellis Horwood: Chichester, 1983; pp 192 – 202

Glabasnia A., Hofmann T. (2006), Sensory-directed identification of taste-active ellagitannins in American (Quercus Alba L.) and European oak wood (Quercus robur L.) and quantitative analysis in Bourbon whiskey and oak-matured red wines. *J. Agric. Food Chem.*, 54, 3380-3390.

Lee K.-Y. M., Paterson A., Pigott J. R., Richardson G. D.,(2001) Sensory discrimination of blended Scotch whiskies of different product categoriesFood quality and preference, 2001, vol. 12, no2, pp. 109-117 (40 ref.)

Lee K.-Y. M., Paterson A., Piggott J. R., Richardson G. D., (2000) Perception of whisky flavour reference compounds by Scottish distillers Journal of the Institute of Brewing 2000, vol. 106, no4, pp. 203-208 (26 ref.)

Lehtonen, M. (1982) Phenols in Whisky, Presented at the 14th International Symposium on Chromatography London, September, 1982

MacNamara, K.; Brunerie, P.; Squarcia, F.; Rozenblum, A. (1985), Investigation of Flavour Compounds in Whiskey Spent Lees. In *Food Flavors: Generation, Analysis and Process Influence*; Charalambous, G. Eds.; Elsevier Science: New York, 1995; pp 1753 – 1766

Perry, D. R. (1989), Odour Intensities of Whisky Componds In Distilled Beverage Flavour, Piggott, J. R.; Paterson, A. Eds.; Ellis Horwood, Series in Food Science and Technology; VCH: Weinheim, Germany, 1989; pp 151 – 169

Poisson L., Schieberle, P.(2008), Characterization of the Most Odor-Active Compounds in an American Bourbon Whisky by Application of the Aroma Extract Dilution Analysis *J. Agric. Food Chem.*, 2008, 56 (14), pp 5813–5819

Postel, W.; Adam, L.(1979), Characterization of American and Canadian whiskies by their volatile profile (in German) *Branntweinwirtschaft* 1979 119 172 176

Chapter 36

Reactive oxygen scavenging ability of whisky

Yuri Yamada[1], Sei-ichi Koshimizu[1], Norifumi Shirasaka[2],Hajime Yoshizumi[2], Kunimasa Koga[3]

[1]Suntory Ltd. Yamazaki Distillery 5-2-1 Yamazaki, Shimamoto-cho, Mishima-gun, Osaka 618-0001 Japan; [2]Department of Applied Biological Chemistry, Faculty of Agriculture, Kinki University, Nara, Japan; [3]School of High Technology for Human Welfare, Tokai University, Shizuoka, Japan

Introduction

Reactive oxygen species is a general term for superoxide radical, hydroxyl radical, hydrogen peroxide, singlet oxygen, and so on. It is known that an excess of reactive oxygen injures cells, causes symptoms of aging, and accelerates the growth of cancer (T. Finkel and N. J. Holbrook, 2000; N. Hogg, 1998). Therefore, the ability of the body to scavenge reactive oxygen is important (Fig. 1). It has also been reported that whisky induces antioxidant capacity in humans (Duthie *et al.*, 1998).

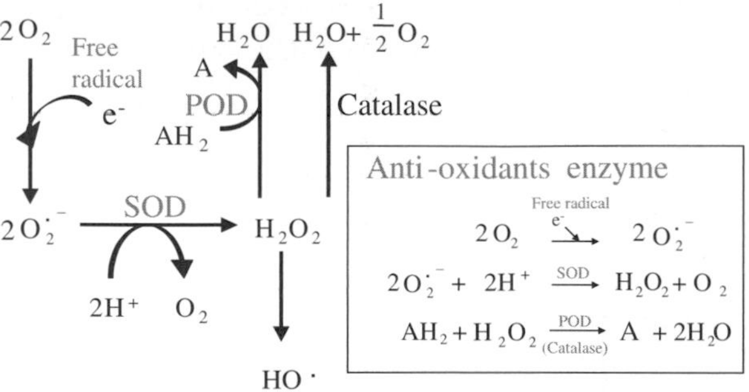

Figure 1. Reactive oxygen scavenging system.

In this study, we evaluated the reactive oxygen scavenging ability of single malt whiskies with a maturation age of 10-30 years, and clarified the relationship between this ability and the maturation age. In order to evaluate this ability, we measured three activities: free radical scavenging activity, peroxidase (POD)-like activity, and superoxide dismutase (SOD)-like activity of the whiskies.

Materials and methods

Whisky samples

Twenty-three commercially bottled single malt whiskies were used. These, together with the locations in which they were produced, are described in Table 1. These samples were used to determine free radical scavenging activity, POD-like activity, and SOD-like activity.

Table 1. Whisky samples for evaluation with the locations.

Japanese A 10	Islay A 10	Speyside A 10
Japanese B 10	Islay B 12	Speyside B 10
Japanese C 12	Islay C 15	Speyside C 12
Japanese D 12	Islay D 15	Speyside D 12
Japanese E 12	Islay E 17	Speyside E 12
Japanese F 18	Islay F 30	Speyside F 12
Japanese G 25	Highland G 10	Speyside G 15
		Speyside H 18
		Speyside I 18

Analysis of reactive oxygen scavenging ability

Free radical scavenging activity of whisky

Free radical scavenging activity was determined by the diphenylpicrylhydrazyl (DPPH; Wako Pure Chemical Industries, Osaka, Japan) method (Yamaguchi *et al.*, 1998). 500 μl of 0.5 mM DPPH solution and 2 ml of 75% (v/v) ethanol aqueous solution were mixed with 25 μl of a whisky sample. The decrease in absorbance was determined at 517 nm after incubation at 37°C for 30 min. A 43% (v/v) ethanol aqueous solution was used as a control. The free radical scavenging activity of whisky was expressed as Trolox (a water soluble Vitamin E: EMD Biosciences, USA) equivalents.

Peroxidase (POD)-like activity of whisky

50 μl of a 3 mM H_2O_2 aqueous solution, 20 μl of whisky and 930 μl of a 0.5 mM phosphate buffer (pH 7.0) were mixed and the absorbance measured at 500 nm after incubation at 37 °C for 10 min.

The H_2O_2 scavenging rate was calculated from the absorbance with the following equation:

$$\text{POD-like activity} = [1-(A_3 - A_1)/(A_2 - A_0)] \times 100\ (\%)$$

A_3 : the absorbance of whisky samples, A_1 : the absorbance of the control without H_2O_2, A_2 : the absorbance of the sample without whisky, A_0 : the absorbance of the control without H_2O_2 and whisky.

Superoxide Dismutase (SOD)-like activity of whisky

SOD-like activity was measured with the SOD Assay Kit-WST (Dojindo laboratories, Kumamoto, Japan). 20 μl of whisky (whisky and blank2) or double distilled water(blank1 and blank3), 10 μl of WST solution, 190 μl of buffer solution and 20 μl of enzyme working solution (whisky and blank1) or dilution solution (blank2 and blank3) were mixed. The absorbance was determined at 450 nm after incubation at 37°C for 20 min. The SOD-like activity was calculated from the absorbance with the following equation:

$$\text{SOD-like activity} = [(A_7 - A_5)-(A_6 - A_4)]/(A_7 - A_5) \times 100\ (\%)$$

A_7 : the absorbance of blank1, A_5 : the absorbance of blank3, A_6 : the absorbance of whisky, A_4 : the absorbance of blank2

Reactive oxygen scavenging ability of distillate and residue after evaporation

After evaporation of whisky samples (20 ml) with various maturation ages (Yamazaki 10, 12, 18, 25), each residue after evaporation of whisky samples was kept in a desiccator containing silica gel for 24-48 h and the quantity of the each residue after evaporation was determined.

Results and discussion

Free radical scavenging activity of whisky

The relationship between free radical scavenging activity and maturation age of all 23 single malt whiskies is shown in Fig. 2. There is some evidence here that the free radical scavenging activity of whisky increased with years of aging.

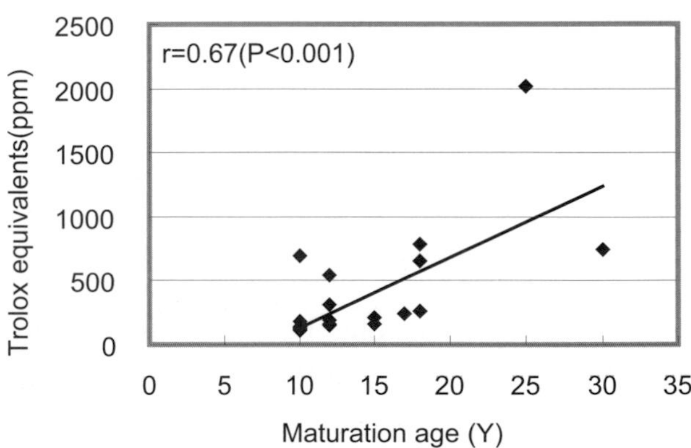

Figure 2. Free radical scavenging activity of whisky.

POD-like activity of whisky (H_2O_2 scavenging activity of whisky)

The relationship between POD-like activity and maturation age of all 23 single malt whiskies is shown in Fig. 3. The results clearly show that there is a significant positive correlation between POD-like activity of whisky and its age after maturation.

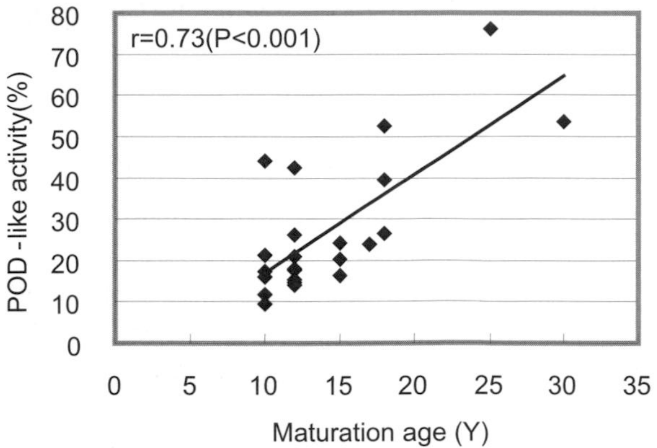

Figure 3. POD-like activity of whisky.

SOD-like activity of whisky

The relationship between SOD-like activity and maturation age of all 23 single malt whiskies is shown in Fig. 4. The results clearly show that there is a significant positive correlation between SOD-like activity of whisky and its age after maturation.

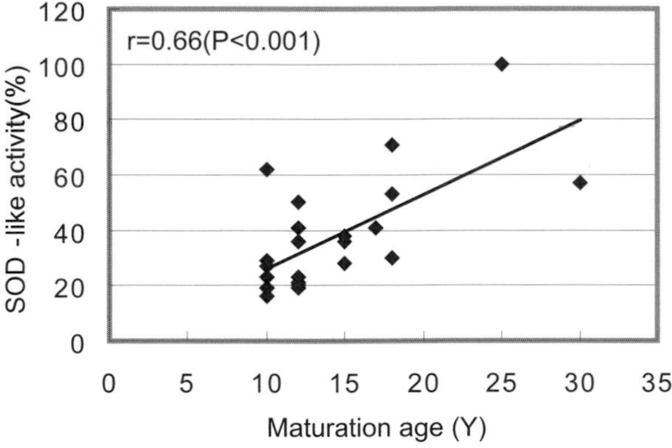

Figure 4. SOD-like activity of whisky.

The coefficient of correlation (r) between the maturation age and each activity was high, with that for free radical scavenging activity being 0.67, that for POD-like activity 0.73, that for SOD-like activity 0.66. These results show that the contents of substances responsible for each activity gradually increase in whisky during the aging process.

Reactive oxygen scavenging ability of distillate and residue after evaporation of single malt whisky

Reactive oxygen scavenging ability (free radical scavenging activity, POD-like activity and SOD-like activity) was assessed in both distillate and residue after evaporation of Yamazaki 18 whisky. The reactive oxygen scavenging ability of the residue after evaporation sample was higher than that of the distillate sample. Accordingly, the reactive oxygen scavenging ability of the whisky (Yamazaki 18) is considered to be due to the materials present in the residue after evaporation in the whisky, and presumably originate from the cask rather than from the distillate itself.

Table 2. RO scavenging ability of distillate and evaporation residue of single malt whisky.

	Free radical scavenging activity as Trolox equivalents (ppm)	*SOD-like activity (%)*	*POD-like activity (%)*
Distillate	0	0	5.8
Evaporation residue	763	>98	59.9

Conclusions

It was shown by analysis of free radical scavenging activity, SOD-like or POD-like activity that the reactive oxygen scavenging ability of whisky increased with years of aging. Because the residue left after evaporation contributed to the reactive oxygen scavenging ability, these results suggested that reactive oxygen scavenging ability originated from the wooden cask rather than the distillate.

References

Duthie, G.G., Pedersen, M.W., Garder, P. T., Morrice, P. C., Jenkinson, A. McE., McPhail, D. B., Steele, G. M. (1998). The effect of whisky and wine consumption on total phenol content and antioxidant capacity of plasma from healthy volunteers. *European Journal of Clinical Nutrition* **52:** 733-736

Finkel, T. N., Holbrook, N. J. (2000). Oxidants, oxidative stress and the biology of ageing. *Nature* **408**: 239-247

Hogg, N. (1998). Free radicals in disease. *Seminars in Reproductive Endocrinology* **16**(4): 241-248

Chapter 37

2-Acetyl-1-pyrroline, a contributor to cereal and feinty aromas in Scotch whisky

John Conner[1], Frances Jack[1] and David Walker[2]

[1]The Scotch Whisky Research Institute, The Robertson Trust Building, Research Avenue North, Riccarton, EH14 4AP; [2]International Centre for Brewing and Distilling, Heriot-Watt University, Riccarton, Edinburgh, EH14 4AS

Introduction

In malt whisky distillation, "feints" are the third and final fraction of distillate received from the malt spirit still. Feints are considered to be the undesirable last runnings of spirit and are returned, with the foreshots, to the spirit still when it is recharged with low wines. When aromas from these last runnings are detected in spirit it is often described as "feinty". In the Scotch Whisky Flavour Wheel feinty aroma is sub-divided as shown below.

During spirit distillation aromas emerge as a continuum rather than as sudden changes. Aromas that develop during the latter half of spirit distillation are initially described as "pleasant and biscuity with toasted scents". These evolve into "tobacco-like and honeyed" and then to "sweaty". The spirit collection usually stops at the honeyed stage, as quality deterioration can be dramatic thereafter. The initial biscuity and toasted aromas contribute to the cereal character of whisky and indicate a degree of overlap between cereal and feinty characters.

Most research on whisky aroma has, not surprisingly, concentrated on the spirit fraction. However some characteristic aromas are more prevalent in the feints fraction, where the higher concentrations present may facilitate the identification of the compounds responsible.

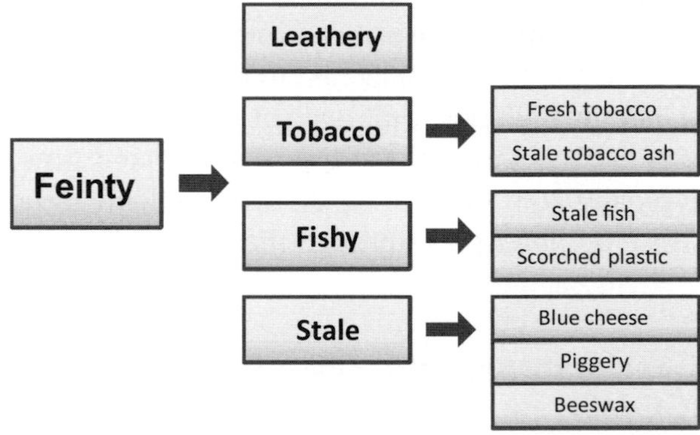

Figure 1. Sub-divisions of feinty aroma in the Scotch Whisky Flavour Wheel.

Gas chromatographic analysis of feints showed elevated levels of furfural, 2-phenethyl acetate, 2-phenethyl alcohol, hexanoic, octanoic, decanoic and dodecanoic acids (Kahn, 1969; Muller 1992). However the compounds responsible for the different aspects of feinty aroma are largely unknown and their identification would open the door to a better understanding of their impact in new make and mature whisky aroma.

Materials and methods

Samples of feints were collected from 3 malt distilleries using lightly or non-peated malted barley for spirit production. Samples, typically

9% ethanol v/v were refrigerated until required for analysis.

Headspace analysis

Apparatus to trap volatiles from the headspace above liquid feints samples was constructed by combining a Quickfit® 3-necked flask and inert stainless steel tubing. Varying the vessel or liquid sample volume and equilibrium time controlled the amount of volatile material for collection. Tenax absorption tubes fitted to the sampling apparatus were used to trap the volatiles generated. Both static and dynamic headspaces were collected from this apparatus. For static, the headspace was allowed to equilibrate for a set time, typically 30minutes and then drawn through the absorption tube using a large volume gas syringe attached to the tube exit. For dynamic, high purity nitrogen at a controlled flow was passed through the liquid for a fixed time, typically 20 minutes, displacing volatile material from the headspace through the Tenax tube.

Gas chromatography – mass spectrometry (GC-MS)

Volatiles adsorbed by the Tenax tube were analysed using a Perkin Elmer ATD400 automated thermal desorber combined with a Hewlett Packard HP5973 gas chromatograph - mass spectrometer. The effluent from GC was split between the mass spectrometer and a nosing port to allow selected trained sensory assessors to comment on the odour of the separated components. The effluent from the GC could also be transferred to a Gerstel Preparative Fraction Collector (PFC) that could be used to trap and concentrate selected peaks from repeated chromatographic analyses.

Gas chromatography – olfactometry (GC-O)

Initially, tests were conducted to ensure that there was no alteration to the odour components by heat during the analytical process. A length of deactivated silica capillary tubing was used to connect the ATD 400 directly to the nosing port through the GC oven, which was set at the highest temperature used in the analysis. Samples of feints were desorbed and assessors asked to compare the odour at the nose port with a reference sample. All assessors described the odours at the nosing port as being similar to the corresponding sample of feints, indicating that the aromas trapped by the Tenax were representative of feints and not altered by the gas chromatographic analysis.

The gas chromatography-olfactometry used a modified version of aroma extract concentration analysis (Grosch, W., Kerscher, R., Kubickova, J. and Jagella, T., 2001) in which five levels of feints (0, 0.1, 0.5, 1.0, 5.0 and 10.0% v/v) from each distillery were added to 20% v/v reagent grade ethanol in Ultrapure® water for analysis. Four assessors performed GC-O on all feints dilutions from all distilleries, including blanks. Some replication was undertaken when time permitted. Assessors commented on one or two GC-O runs per day, time permitting.

Selective solvent extraction of 2-acetyl-1-pyrroline

The pH of 250mL of feints was increased to 12 using 5mL of 1.0 molar NaOH and 20mL of a saturated salt solution (sodium chloride) added to aid phase separation. This was then extracted with 2 portions of 150mL Freon 11 and the combined extracts reduced to approximately 50μL under a gentle stream of nitrogen for analysis. The feints were further extracted with 2 portions of 200mL dichloromethane and the combined extracts similarly reduced to approximately 50μL for analysis.

Results and discussion

First attempts at GC-O analysis of both feints headspace and liquid extracts were performed on samples from one distillery at "natural pH" (3.4). Areas of odour interest in the resulting chromatograms were frequently masked by large responses from relatively non-odorous compounds, such as the longer chain ethyl esters. Volatile free fatty acids, shown to be present in the feints headspace by GC-MS, had the potential to mask both odour and signal from minor chromatographic peaks, due to their relatively intense odours and low odour thresholds. The aroma of the short chain acids is described as cheesy, sweaty and rancid and these compounds undoubtedly contribute to certain aspects of feinty aroma. Sensory assessment showed that raising the pH of the feints dramatically reduced the odour impact of these acids and revealed other feinty and cereal aromas that were more typical of those that developed towards the end of spirit distillation.

Using base modified feints, many of the detected aromas did not coincide with recognisable GC peaks. An example of this phenomenon is illustrated in Figure 2, with intense odours being reported when the GCMS signal was low, i.e. at baseline level. This implies that components at extremely low concentrations are responsible for some of the most intense odours in feints. The peak profile obtained by the 'chemical' detector did not reflect the aroma profile of feints.

When odour comments from all the GC-O data were scrutinised, it was clear that all the assessors had used consistent personal descriptors and the odour times of these descriptors had remained extremely consistent throughout the five month exercise. From these odour comments, the nines aromas were selected (Table 1), based on their frequency of use by assessors and commonality between distilleries.

Only two of these aromas were detected at the same time as peaks on the total ion chromatogram of the GC-MS. Aroma 3 eluted at the same retention time as the peak for 2- and 3-methylbutanoic acids. Aroma 9 eluted at the same retention time as the peak for 2-phenylethanol. In both cases the recorded description is consistent with that of the pure compound.

At this stage a simple linear scoring system was evolved so that the key odours could be

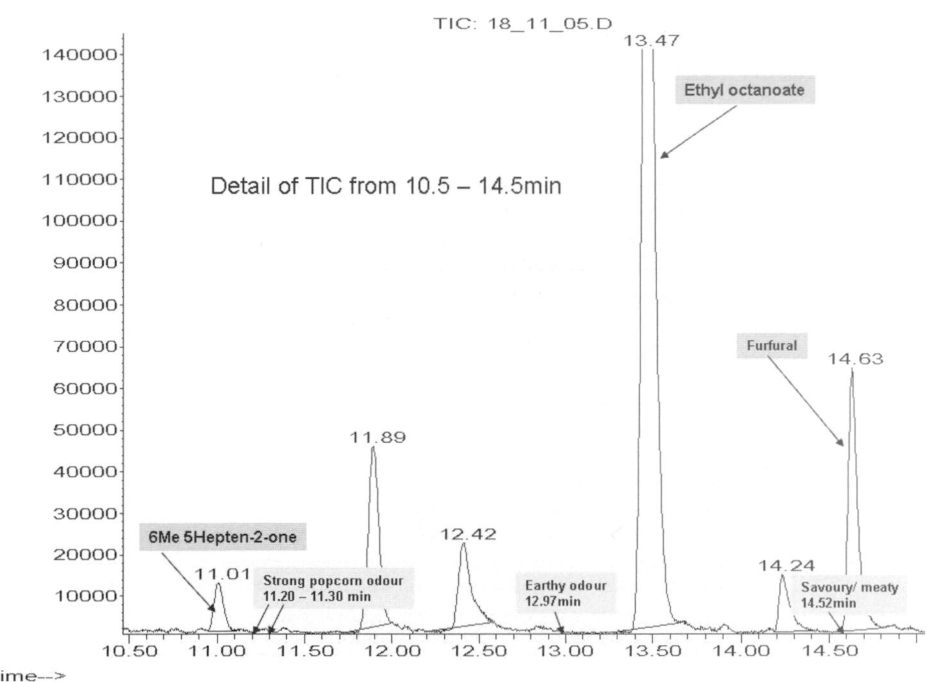

Figure 2. Detail from a total ion chromatogram showing areas of intense odours but little or no signal.

Table 1. GC-O descriptions used by four assessors of the nine major aromas in feints.

1	A	mushrooms	4	A	popcorn	7	A	mushrooms
	B	mushroom		B	cooked rice/ cereal		B	mushrooms
	C	mushrooms		C	biscuity		C	mushroom/ mouldy
	D			D	popcorn		D	
2	A	cooked mince & tatties	5	A	PVC/plastic sheeting	8	A	nutty/oily/
	B	potatoes		B			B	greasy/fatty
	C	potatoes/ veg/ sulfurs		C	earthy/stale		C	roasted almonds
	D	cooked mince/ potatoes		D	mouldy leaves/ oily		D	stale/(bees)wax
3	A	smelly feet	6	A	smoked sausage	9	A	floral/ roses
	B	cheesy/sweaty feet		B	phenolic or caramel		B	nose spray
	C	stale/ sweaty		C	sweet phenolic/medicinal		C	floral/waxy
	D	Edam cheese/ cheesy		D	spicy/guaiacol		D	biro ink/ floral

ascribed numerically and given an odour priority for further investigation. Odours detected at the highest dilution were given the highest score and the scores for each assessor and each distillery were summed to yield compiled odour scores (Figure 3). The aroma "popcorn/ cereal" scored highest out of the nine, followed by "biro ink/ floral" (2-phenylethanol). All assessors recorded "popcorn/ cereal" in all distilleries examined, but there was no peak attributable to this aroma on the chromatograms. As this odour scored highest, it can be considered the most important component in base modified feints and, as such, merited isolation and identification.

initially, the Gerstel PFC was selected as a potential isolation route, since the fraction collector plumbing was equivalent in dimension to the odour port plumbing on the modified GC-O system. However, the PFC provided incomplete evidence for the identity of the "popcorn" aroma. There was insufficient component trapped to produce a chromatographic peak to match the retention time measurement, nor was enough material isolated to produce a full scan

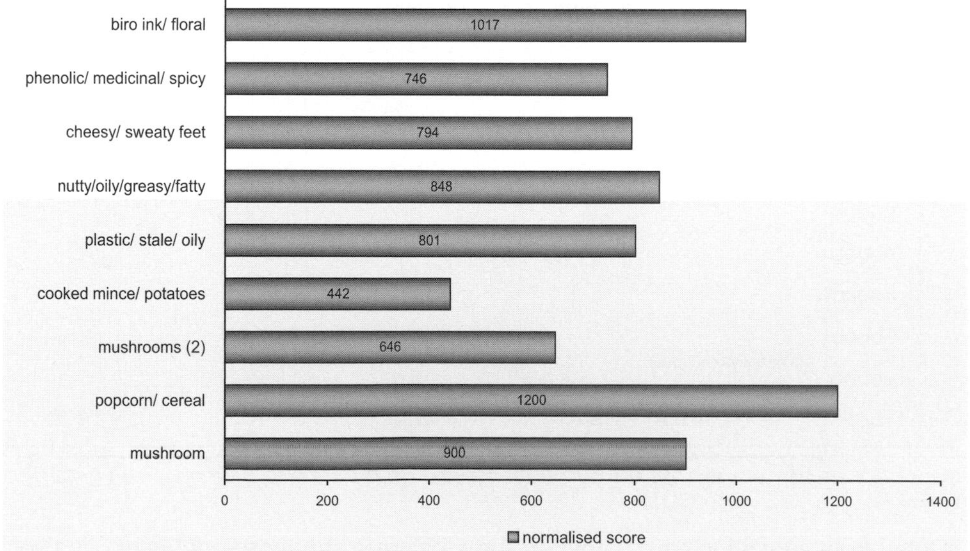

Figure 3. GC-O odour scores for the nine major aromas in feints.

mass spectrum from the strong popcorn odour observed from the trapped concentrate. An alternative strategy based on selective solvent extraction of pH modified distillery feints was evolved, where initial extraction with Freon 11 was followed by a final extraction with dichloromethane.

The relevant section of the full scan total ion current chromatogram of the concentrated final extraction with dichloromethane is shown in Figure 4. The peak corresponding to the "popcorn" aroma recorded between 15.50 and 15.65 minutes is highlighted. The mass spectrum from this peak is also shown and matched with the NIST 2002 library spectrum of 2-acetyl-1-pyrroline. An authentic standard of 2-acetyl-1-pyrroline was kindly provided by Professor Schieberle of the Technical University of Munich and this gave the same retention time and mass spectrum as the peak in the dichloromethane extract. This standard also possessed the same characteristic popcorn odour, as analysed by GC-O.

The aroma of wheat, rice and popcorn. In wheat bread the amino acids proline and ornithine are precursors and it is one of the character impact compounds in wheat bread crust (Schieberle and Grosch, 1985; Buttery, Turnbaugh and Ling 1988; Schieberle, 1990; Schieberle 1991). 2-Acetyl-1-pyrroline is a highly potent aroma compound. Its detection threshold was 67ng/L in 20% ethanol v/v, the strength used for the sensory analysis of whiskies at SWRI. However, due to the absence of characteristic ions in its mass spectrum, it has not been possible to develop a convenient analytical method capable of detecting these concentrations in whisky. GC-O analyses have since identified the presence of 2-acetyl-1-pyrroline by retention time and characteristic aroma in both new make and mature whiskies.

Conclusions

The principal aromas identified in feints were short chain organic acids (e.g2-methylbutanoic acid), 2-phenylethanol and 2-acetyl-1-pyrroline. 2-Acetyl-1-pyrroline has been identified by retention time and aroma in GC-O analyses of

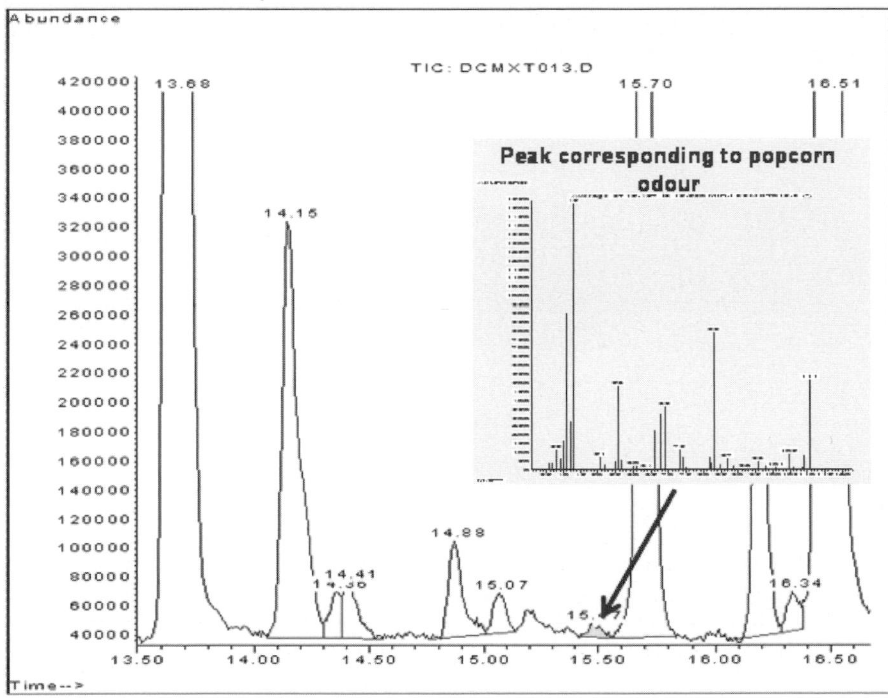

Figure 4. Section of the full scan total ion current chromatogram from the selective extraction showing the peak and mass spectrum corresponding to the "popcorn" aroma recorded between 15.50 and 15.65 minutes

new make spirits and mature whiskies, but as yet, a chromatographic method with adequate sensitivity has not been developed. The low odour threshold and characteristic popcorn aroma suggest that it is an important contributor to both cereal and feinty aromas in Scotch whisky.

Acknowledgement

The authors would like to thank Professor Peter Schieberle of the Technical University of Munich for supplying an authentic sample of 2-acetyl-1-pyrroline.

References

Buttery, R., Turnbaugh, J. and Ling, L. (1988). Contribution of Volatiles to Rice Aroma. *Journal of Agricultural and Food Chemistry*: **36**, 1006 – 1009.

Kahn, J.H., LaRoe, E.G., Conner, H.A. and Shipley,P.A. (1969). Whisky Composition: Identification of Additional Components by Gas Chromatography-Mass Spectrometry. *Journal of Food Science*: **34**, 587 – 590.

Muller, S. (1992). *The Analytical Composition of the Feints Fraction of Scotch Malt Whisky.* MSc Thesis.

Grosch, W., Kerscher, R., Kubickova, J. and Jagella, T. (2001). Aroma Extract Dilution Analysis versus Aroma Extract Concentration Analysis. In: *Gas Chromatography – Olfactometry: The state of the art,* edited by Leland, J., Schieberle, P., Buettner, A. and Acree, T. American Chemical Society, Washington, DC, pp. 138 – 147.

Schieberle, P. and Grosch, W. (1985). Identification of the Volatile Flavour Compounds of Wheat Bread Crust - Comparison with Rye Bread Crust. *Zeitschrift fur Lebensmittel - Untersuchung und Forschung*: **180**, 474 – 478.

Schieberle, P. (1990). The Role of Free Amino Acids Present in Yeast as Precursors of the Odorants 2-acetyl-1-pyrroline and 2-acetyltetrahydropyridine in Wheat Bread Crust. *Zeitschrift fur Lebensmittel-Untersuchung und-Forschung:* **191**, 206 – 209.

Schieberle,P. (1991). Primary Odorants in Popcorn. *Journal of Agricultural and Food Chemistry*: **39**, 1141 – 1144.

Chapter 38

The role of water composition on malt spirit quality

C.A. Wilson[1], F.R. Jack[1], F.G. Priest[2]
[1]*Scotch Whisky Research Institute, The Robertson Trust Building, Riccarton, Edinburgh, UK;* [2]*International Centre for Brewing and Distilling, Heriot-Watt University, Edinburgh, UK*

Introduction

Water is seen as an important raw material in whisky production, both from distilling and marketing viewpoints, although little is currently known about the influence of water composition on spirit quality. The concept of *terroir*, a term coined by the French wine industry is regarded as the influence of factors such as soil, climate and elevation. This concept is becoming integrated into the malt distiller's vocabulary, taking in the influence of water chemistry and the environment in which the barley is grown. Theoretically, the influence of *terroir* on spirits should be more pronounced than that of wine, as wine is merely the product of grape juice, whereas spirits consist predominantly of water, often drawn directly from the ground.

Distillers use a variety of water sources. Surface water, such as streams, rivers, lochs and canals may receive a large organic influence from contact with peat and vegetation. Springs sourced from the static, underground void in-fill of rocks are more heavily influenced by underlying geology. Certain distilleries use mains water, which offers a consistent, if expensive, supply. Water is used for a variety of purposes; for steeping of grains, mashing and wort production, reducing spirit strength prior to racking in casks and reducing spirit strength prior to bottling. Indirect uses also include cooling water for spirit condensing and for use in distillery boilers. The majority of malt distilleries in Scotland use spring water or burn / river water, with only a small proportion using loch and mains water.

Good quality water is required, although distillery mashing waters (process waters) vary greatly in terms of organic and mineral content. These variables are thought to be important in determining the quality of the spirit produced (Bathgate 2000), due to the large volumes involved and the concentration effect of distillation (Gray and Swan 1977). The activity of bacteria present in process water, particularly lactic acid bacteria, also contributes to the organoleptic qualities of the final spirit (Priest 2004).

The use of steeping water is merely to swell the grains, which are dried during kilning, therefore minimal flavour impacts are likely. In the case of mashing water, the chemical composition is more likely to affect the fermentation process. Although distillation is in itself a purification technique, it is thought that certain compounds may pass through into the resulting new make spirit. Howie and Swan (1984) state that only a small proportion (in the order of 4%) of phenolic compounds find their way into the final spirit, therefore the direct flavour impacts of organic compounds are likely to be minimal. Cooling water, for condensing spirit during distillation, does not come into contact with the spirit. However, the temperature can affect spirit style, as winter-cold water leads to a heavier spirit by reducing the effect of copper.

Reducing water used prior to racking into casks is usually from the same source as the mashing liquor, although since only a small amount is required to bring strength down from 70% to 65%, little flavour impact is likely to be contributed. Demineralised water is invariably used for reduction prior to bottling to ensure no flavour impacts. Depending on its source, water used for distilling can contain a variety of plant-derived compounds from lignin, carbohydrates, amino acids, proteins, lipids and fatty acids, as well as inorganic ions, a variety of micro-organisms and particulate matter.

Presently, Scotland has over 1,100,000 ha of peatland - areas of high rainfall where few plants can survive, with the ecosystem being dominated by *Sphagnum* mosses, grasses and heather. Successive layers of dead plant material accumulate over thousands of years, forming a layer of peat, a proportion of which fluxes to aquatic sources as dissolved carbon, particulate matter and dissolved CO_2. As the peat becomes subjected to anaerobic conditions in the deepest layers of the deposit, it is preserved and changes comparatively little over time. This is an extremely slow process, with formation of 1 m of peat taking around 1000 years.

Typically, over 50% of aquatic dissolved organic matter exists as humic substances - phenolic compounds linked by polysaccharides, amino acids, aliphatic compounds and peptides formed by microbial breakdown and synthesis of plant matter, such as lignins, polyphenols, polysaccharides, lipids and pigments. Non-humic substances include those with still recognisable chemical characteristics, such as carbohydrates, proteins, fats and waxes (Schulten 1999). Humic substances play a fundamental and versatile role in the aquatic environments by influencing physico-chemical properties of water, such as colour, acidity and buffer capacity, participating in carbon and nutrient cycling, interacting with metals, acting as catalysts, and affecting the mobility, bioavailability and toxicity of anthropogenic environmental pollutants. From a distilling viewpoint, the capacity for complexation with metals is significant, as bioavailability is reduced, with potential effects for the fermentation process (Jacobsen and Lie 1977).

Lignin-derived compounds comprise a large proportion of humic macromolecules depending on plant source, consisting of three sub-units; the substituted phenols guaiacyl, syringyl and *p*-coumaryl. Softwood lignin is composed mainly of guaiacyl units, whereas hardwood lignin consists of predominantly guaiacyl and syringyl units. Grass lignins contain a mixture of guaiacyl, syringyl and *p*-coumaryl units. While bryophytes such as *Sphagnum* spp. do not contain true lignin, they contain a variety of similar methoxylated phenolic compounds existing mainly as polyphenols (Kracht and Gleixner 2000). Such compounds exist within humic molecules in various stages of humification, converted by microbial degradation and metabolism, into large macromolecules and aggregates.

The mineral content may also vary, depending on the underlying geology of the water source and interactions with organic compounds. Information from the brewing industry suggests that ion concentrations in water affect mashing and fermentation, through altering yeast activity, pH, flocculation or similar effects. However, the solubility of such ions is dependent on mashing conditions, primarily pH, with the ions often existing chelated with proteins, polyphenols and other macromolecules (Holzmann and Piendl 1976). Distillery process water is generally softer and contains fewer minerals than most brewing process waters, with several notable exceptions. The influence of inorganic constituents in distillery fermentations has received relatively little attention in the past, and their impact on spirit character is unknown.

Although the image of pristine water flowing over granite and peat forms a large part of Scotch whisky marketing, this is an environment which is constantly under threat. Whilst distilling is among the most energy conscious and sustainable industries, many aspects of water use are becoming subject to environmental legislation. Also, the chemical nature of water supplies is expected to change as a consequence of climate change, with increased levels of peat-derived compounds in water courses (Evans *et al.* 1999).

The aim of this study was to gain insights into the influence of water composition on spirit quality by characterising a variety of distillery process waters both chemically and physically. These waters were used for mashing and lab-scale fermentation and distillation to produce new-make spirits for chemical and sensory analysis to assess the impact of water composition on spirit quality and character. Based on these initial findings, artificially-spiked waters were prepared to produce spirit under carefully controlled laboratory conditions to ascertain the influence of individual chemical parameters upon spirit character and quality.

Characterisation of industrial process waters

Process waters exhibiting a range of organic and inorganic influences from a variety of locations and geologies were collected from 10 malt distilleries. Analysis of these process waters involved ion exchange chromatography and pyrolysis-GC/MS for aquatic humic substances (AHS), HPLC for marker phenolic compounds, ion chromatography and colorimetric tests for major anions, cations and metals and organic carbon by CHN analysis.

Pyrolysis results from the process water samples demonstrated a complex range of pyrolysis products, with over 70 compounds identified. The results showed pyrolysis products dominated by long-chained fatty acids, alkanes, alcohols and aromatic compounds. Pyrolysis products from the water samples were generally dominated by aliphatic compounds sourced from the breakdown of plant lipids and triglycerols. Substituted phenolic compounds were found in varying proportions in all samples, predominantly phenolic acid derivatives, guaiacyl- and syringyl-sourced benzaldehydes and benzene di- and tricarboxylic acids.

The pyrolysis data was summarised using Principal Components Analysis (PCA), shown in figure 1, which showed a clear relationship existed between distillery location and process water composition. Water from the Highland distilleries contained relatively high levels of guaiacyl-derived compounds. Process water from the three Islay distilleries contained a mixture

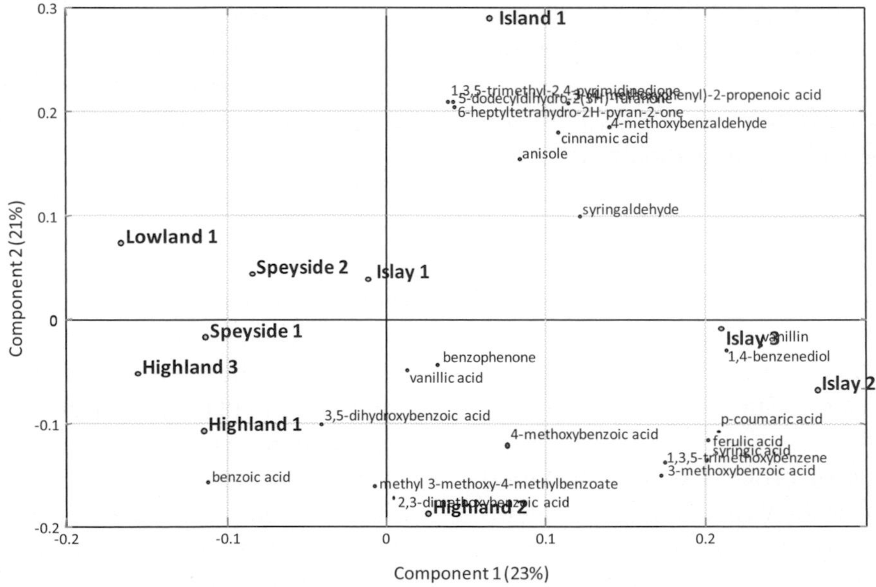

Figure 1. PCA biplot of loadings and sample scores excluding aliphatic compounds.

of all three lignin types, defined by higher proportions of syringyl-derived compounds indicating greater input from humification of angiosperms such as heather and mosses. Process water from the Island distillery was distinct from the other distilleries, due to higher levels of *p*-coumaryl and carbohydrate-derived compounds.

PC 1 relates to overall lignin source diversity, with more complex samples at the positive end of the component. Speyside process water samples were proportionally low in lignin-sourced compounds, with guaiacyl-derived compounds being the most abundant.

Generally, waters sourced from lentic (standing) waters such as lochs contained the highest total amounts of organic input. However, waters sourced from lotic (running) water systems contained the highest amounts of lignin-derived compounds. Groundwater sources generally exhibited the lowest levels of AHS. Levels of organic input were often proportional to the size of the river basin and hence the area of vegetation, both living and humified, traversed. Geographic location was a major determinant of aquatic humic substance composition, with sites from northern and western areas of Scotland possessing an organic composition more heavily influenced by peatlands, whereas the organic content of waters from eastern and southern areas was more influenced by arable vegetation.

Total organic carbon levels varied between samples, although not proportionally to levels of AHS. All sites exhibited a considerably higher level of DOC than particulate organic carbon (POC), implying that the majority of organic input is sourced from leaching from pedogenic sources such as peat or soils, rather than allochthonous sources such as run-off or autochthonous sources such as algae (Leenheer and Croué 2003).

HPLC analysis of process waters provided little information, as the vast majority of analytes were shown to be near or below limits of detection. This shows that the vast majority of peat-derived compounds in water do not exist dissolved in solution, but instead as part of larger humic aggregates or macromolecules. Hence, it can be concluded that the compounds traditionally associated with 'peaty', 'smoky' and 'phenolic' character in whisky are not sourced from water, but exclusively due to adsorption of such compounds to malt during the kilning process.

The results from ion chromatography analysis of the water samples showed clear groupings for waters from Hebridean sites (Islay and Island), Northern Scottish sites (Speyside and Highland) and Lowland sites, influenced primarily by underlying geology. Little correlation between ionic concentration and water source type (burn, loch, spring) was evident.

Analysis of new make spirits produced using industrial process waters

In order to understand fully the consequences of variation in process water on spirit character, it was necessary to produce spirits from these waters in the laboratory using methods which replicated industrial practices. The spirits were analysed by the Scotch Whisky Research Institute's in-house sensory panel to elucidate the relationship between water chemistry and spirit character.

The overall sensory character of these spirits was largely similar, although statistically significant variation was found in sulphury, meaty, green / grassy, cereal, feinty, clean, and sweet attributes. Differences in sensory character were found to relate to the geographical source of the process water, with Speyside and Island waters producing heavier spirits, whereas Islay, Highland and to a lesser degree, Lowland waters produced lighter, sweeter spirits (figure 2). The ionic content of process waters appeared to have little influence on spirit character.

The peaty attribute scored low in all samples, proving peaty character is not sourced from water, but exclusively from the burning of peat during malt kilning, which agreed with compositional analysis outlined previously

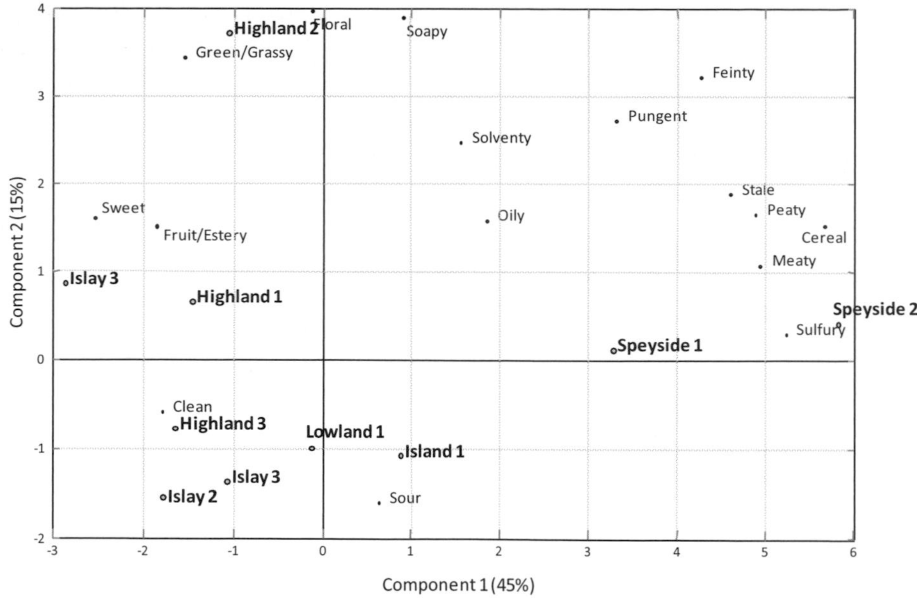

Figure 2. PCA biplot of sensory results.

which showed minimal phenolic compounds existing in solution in process water. Any effects on spirit flavour are likely to be due to a number of competing factors in water composition, therefore it was imperative to investigate the influence of inorganic and organic content in isolation.

Production of new-make spirit using artificially spiked waters

Waters containing a variety of organic and inorganic compositions reflecting those found in industrial process waters were produced to assess each factor in isolation, and new-make spirits created for sensory analysis. Levels of key higher alcohols and residual sugars were measured, along with wash pH and alcohol strength to fully understand any effects of process water composition on the fermentation process.

Analysis of worts for fermentable sugars showed little variation between samples of differing ionic profile, which showed that the mashing process was largely unaffected by changes in ionic composition at the levels used in this study. Overall effects of increased ionic concentration in mashing waters on the fermentation process were minimal, with high ionic concentration waters having a slight positive effect on production of some volatile wash components, and a slight negative effect on the production of others. An inhibitory effect on certain congener production was found in early stages of fermentation in samples made from iron- and zinc-supplemented waters.

Spirits made from deionised and mid level ionic waters exhibited cleaner, sweeter aromas while those made from high level ionic waters possessed heavier notes, but no general trends were observed. The minimal influence of ionic composition is thought to be primarily due to binding of inorganic constituents to wort solids, thus leading to their removal during the mashing process.

Analysis of yeast growth in the organically-supplemented samples during fermentation showed overall ester production by yeasts during fermentation was stimulated in samples made from peat-supplemented waters, possibly as a consequence of greater concentrations of precursors, and was especially pronounced in samples made from waters with high dissolved organic carbon. Higher alcohol production occurred at a slower rate in peated waters.

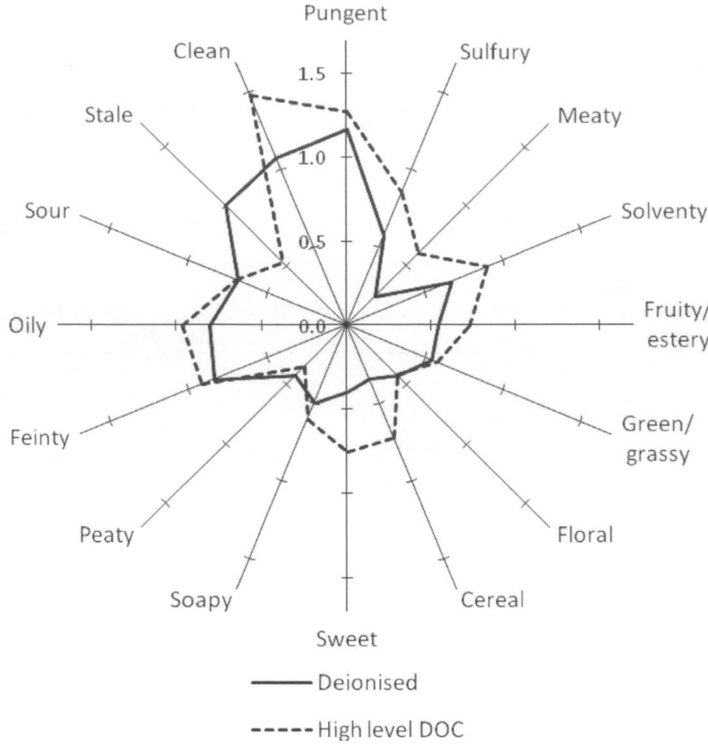

Figure 3. Spider plot of sensory results.

Spirits made from waters containing Highland peat showed a more complex character, whereas those made from waters containing Islay peat scored lower for 'heavy' attributes, such as cereal and meaty. The presence of dissolved organic carbon in artificially high levels produced spirits with 'heavier' characteristics such as meaty, solventy and sulphury (figure 3), which confirmed earlier findings. No significant correlation was found between levels of humic substances and sensory character.

Overall, iron- and zinc-spiked samples possessed a reduced fruity / estery, sweet and pungent character, ionic-supplemented waters had a greater sulphury, meaty and cereal character and peated waters produced a spirit with generally heavier, more complex character. The extent of separation found showed that the presence or absence of ions, peat-derived compounds and metals was affecting the character and quality of new-make spirit. The differences found, however minimal, are an integral part of the process which creates the unique character of Scotland's whiskies, where modifications to over 100 processing parameters can produce the vast array of malt whisky styles found in the modern marketplace.

With predicted changes in climate leading to a greater flux of carbon from peatlands, this study shows the type and extent of potential changes to spirit character that would be expected. Also, proposed changes to water abstraction regimes and potential threats to water supplies could force distillers to consider alternative process water sources in order to remain economically viable. The results elucidated will allow informed decisions to be made to facilitate such changes.

References

Bathgate, G.N. (2000). The Recipe for Scotch Whisky. In: Paul's Malt - Brewing Room Book 1998-2000 pp. 81-84. Cargill Malts, Sheboygan, WI, USA.

Evans, M.G., Burt, T.P., Holden, J., Adamson, J.K. (1999). Runoff Generation and Water Table Fluctuations in Blanket Peat: Evidence from UK Data Spanning the Dry Summer of 1995. *J. Hydr.* **221:** pp. 141-160.

Gray, J.D. Swan, J.S. (1977). Observations on the Flavour and Aroma of Scotch Whisky. *Inst. Brew. Conf. Proc. Edinburgh 1977.* Institute of Brewing, Edinburgh.

Holzmann, A., Piendl, A. (1976). Malt Modifications and Mashing Conditions as Factors Influencing the Minerals of Wort. *J. Am. Soc. Brew. Chem.* **35:** pp. 1-8.

Howie, D., Swan, J.S. (1984). Compounds Influencing Peatiness in Scotch Malt Whisky Flavour. *Alko Symp. Flav. Res. Alc. Bev., Helsinki 1984* pp. 280-289.

Jacobsen, T. and Lie, S. (1977). Chelators and metal buffering in brewing II. *J. Inst. Brew.* **83:** pp. 208-212.

Kracht, O., Gleixner, G. (2000). Isotope Analysis of Pyrolysis Products from Sphagnum Peat and Dissolved Organic Matter from Bog Water. *Org. Geo.* **31:** pp. 645-654.

Leenheer, J.A., Croué, J-P. (2003). Aquatic Organic Matter. *Env. Sci. Tech.* **19:** pp. 1-14.

Priest, F.G. (2004). Lactic acid bacteria - the uninvited but generally welcome participants in malt whisky fermentation. *Micro. Today* **31** (1): pp. 16-19.

Schulten, H.R. (1999). Analytical Pyrolysis and Computational Chemistry of Aquatic Humic Substances and Dissolved Organic Matter. *J. Anal. Appl. Pyr.* **49:** pp. 385-415.

Chapter 39

Characteristics of the production and flavour of sweet potato shochu

Toshiharu Nakajima, Kazuyuki Torii
Suntory Ltd., Product Development Center, 57 Imaikami-cho, Nakahara-ku, Kawasaki 211-0067, Japan

Introduction

Shochu, a traditional distilled spirit unique to Japan, has a number of features that set it apart from other distilled spirits. Shochu is made using Koji as one of its raw materials. Shochu mash is very characteristic. The pH is very low and the final alcohol strength is high at about 14% (v/v). In addition, the mash is single distilled to a final strength of about 35 to 45% (v/v). It is usually drunk without any maturation period, ensuring that the shochu retains the characteristic flavour derived from the raw materials, namely barley, rice or sweet potato. (Figure 1) Shochu is consumed as an accompaniment to food.

Here we introduce the characteristic method of production and report on the flavour differences between sweet potato shochu and those made from other raw materials.

The market for spirits in Japan

In Japan, total spirits consumption is growing. The ratio of shochu in the spirits market is about 90%. The whisky and brandy market has been decreasing, but only the shochu market has continued to grow for a number of years. (Figure 2)

Shochu has a characteristic flavour derived from its raw materials of barley, rice or sweet potato. In particular, only the market for sweet potato shochu is continuing to grow, unlike the other kinds of shochu. (Figure 3)

How to make shochu

Figure 4 shows the process of making shochu. There are some characteristic points in this

Figure 1. Shochu is made from many types of raw materials.

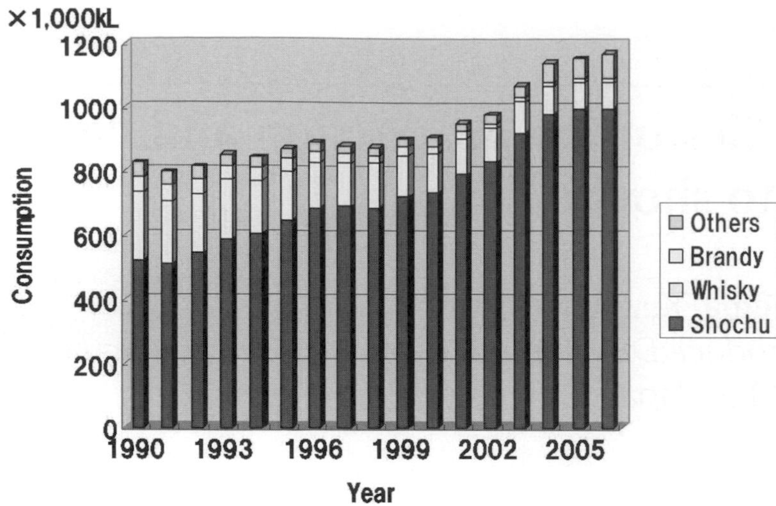

Figure 2. Spirits consumption in the Japanese market.

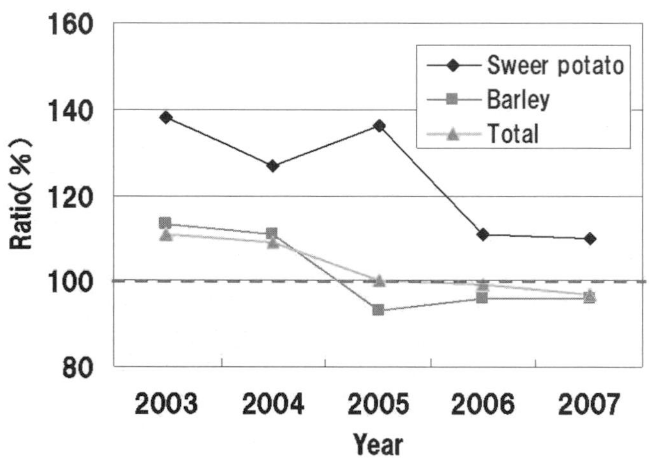

Figure 3. Growth rate of various types of shochu.

process. The first is the use of Koji as one of the raw materials, which is the most important point in shochu manufacturing. Koji is made from barley or rice cultured with Aspergillus and has been used for the production of fermented foods in Japan and countries in East Asia from ancient times. In the fermentation of liquor, it is used as a source of saccharification enzyme (Figure 5), because it has some enzymes like malt, including alpha-amylase, glucoamylase and proteases.

Another characteristic is simultaneous saccharification and fermentation. Figure 6 shows the comparison of the three types of fermentation. The fermentation of wine uses only yeast. That of beer and whisky uses yeast after the saccharification of starch with the enzymes from malt. In the shochu mash, both saccharification with Koji and fermentation with yeast take place at the same time. As a result of this process, the final alcohol strength is up to 14-18% (v/v).

The points in sweet potato processing

Sweet potato shochu uses sweet potatoes as a main raw material (Figure 4). Before brewing, the treatment of the sweet potato is very important for the quality of sweet potato shochu. The sweet potato has to be fresh, as old or rotten sweet potato has a strong flavour of terpene, like citrus

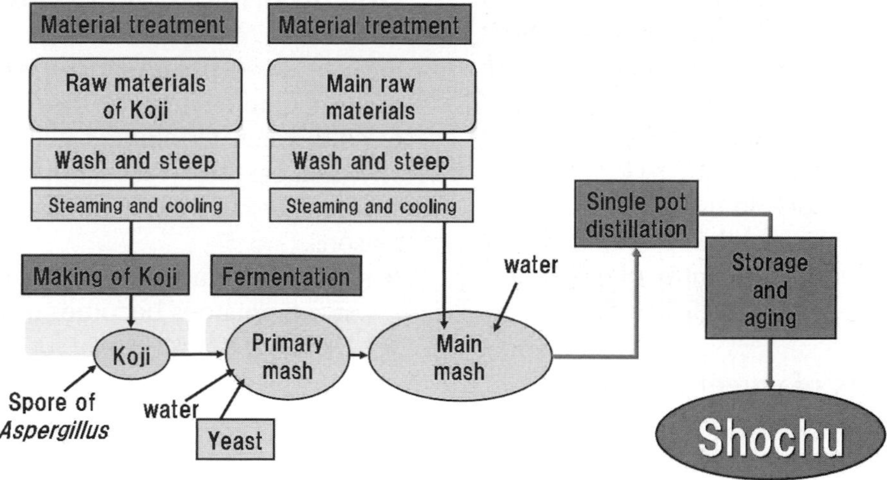

Figure 4. The process of making shochu.

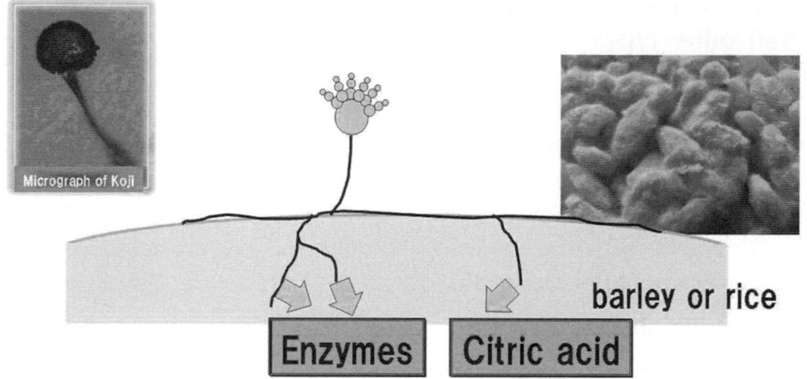

Figure 5. A sectional schematic view of Koji.

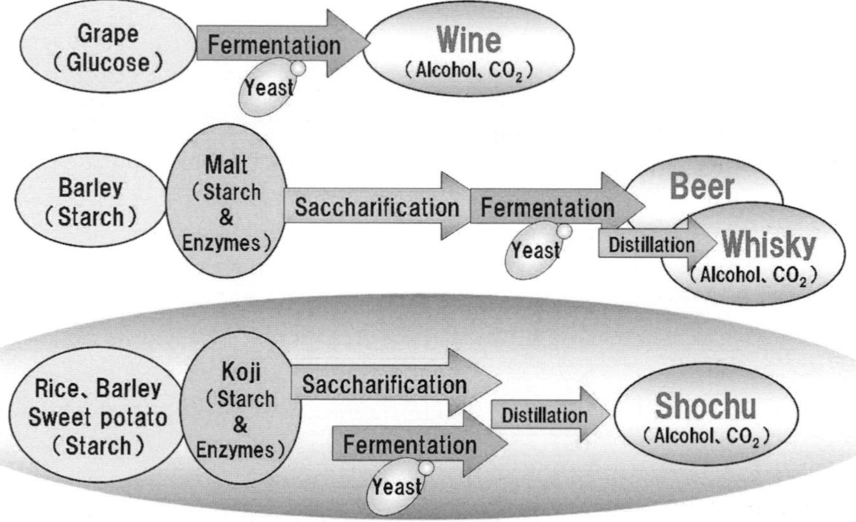

Figure 6. Comparison of three types of fermentation.

or rose. Therefore, we have to use the sweet potato immediately after it is harvested. Both ends of the sweet potato have to be removed, as the ends also include a significant amount of terpenes. Although terpenes are an important flavour in sweet potato shochu, excessive levels have a negative impact on quality. We believe that the remaining parts of the sweet potato that we use have a moderate quantity of terpenes.

The ingredients of sweet potato shochu

Table 1 shows the ingredients of various types of shochu, namely sweet potato, barley and rice. Sweet potato shochu contains higher levels of fusel alcohols than other types of shochu. This is a characteristic of sweet potato shochu in components, although the flavour of fusel alcohols is not a typical flavour of sweet potato shochu. Further study to clarify the characteristic flavour of sweet potato shochu is underway.

Table 1. The characteristics of sweet potato shochu.

	Sweet potato	*Barley*	*Rice*	
pH	4.81	5.73	4.66	
Acidity	0.77	0.25	0.41	
n-Propyl alcohol	97	91	152	
i-Butyl alcohol	236	137	198	
j-Amyl alcohol	454	421	435	
Acetaldehyde	40.9	0.2	31.2	
Furfural	0.23	0.53	0.23	(mg/100ml)
Ethyl acetate	79.2	49.8	34.4	
j-Amyl acetate	9.1	8.4	6.2	
Ethyl caproate	0.4	0.8	0.6	(ppm)

How to drink sweet potato shochu

In Japan, sweet potato shochu is drunk in various styles, including neat, on the rocks and with hot or cold water. Drinking it with hot water is the style that best suits sweet potato shochu. This is generally thought to be the case for the following reasons:

- The sweet fragrance of shochu derived from sweet potatoes becomes more attractive
- Drinking it hot is good for relieving fatigue

Chapter 40

Alcohol and cardiovascular health

Arthur L. Klatsky
Senior Consultant in Cardiology, Oakland Medical Center, Adjunct Investigator, Division of Research, Kaiser Permanente Medical Care Program, 280 West MacArthur Blvd, Oakland CA 94611 USA

Synopsis

The substantial medical risks of heavy alcohol drinking as well as existence of a probable safe drinking limit have been evident for centuries. Modern epidemiologic studies show lower risk of both morbidity and mortality among lighter drinkers. Defining "heavy" as ≥ 3 standard drinks per day, the alcohol – mortality relationship is a J-curve with risk highest for heavy drinkers, lowest for light-moderate drinkers and intermediate for abstainers. A number of non-cardiovascular and cardiovascular problems contribute to the increased mortality risk of heavier drinkers. The lower risk of light drinkers is due mostly to lower risk of the most common cardiovascular condition, coronary heart disease (CHD). Thus, disparate relationships of alcoholic drinking to various cardiovascular and non-cardiovascular conditions constitute a modern concept of alcohol and health.

Increased cardiovascular risks of heavy drinking include: 1) heart muscle damage in susceptible persons, called alcoholic cardiomyopathy, 2) systemic hypertension (high blood pressure), 3) heart rhythm disturbances in binge drinkers, and 4) hemorrhagic stroke. Lighter drinking is unrelated to increased risk of any cardiovascular condition and, in observational studies, is consistently related to lower risk of CHD and ischemic stroke. A protective hypothesis for CHD is robustly supported by evidence for plausible biological mechanisms attributable to ethyl alcohol. International comparisons and some prospective study data suggest that wine may be more protective against CHD than liquor or beer, and possible non-alcohol beneficial components in wine (especially red) support hypothetical extra protection by wine. However, most population study data suggest that choice of beverage is not an important factor and that a healthier pattern of drinking or more favorable risk traits in wine drinkers may account for observed differences in benefit. Advice about drinking by health professionals to concerned persons is best individualized.

Introduction

Few areas of study of life-style habits and cardiovascular diseases have been as exciting in recent decades as the relationships to alcohol drinking. Because historical perspective is interesting and instructive, this brief review includes discussion of concepts that developed over the past two centuries. Disparities with respect to various cardiovascular conditions are increasingly evident (Klatsky 2003, 2007). Some conditions needing separate consideration are cardiomyopathy, arsenic and cobalt beer drinkers' disease, cardiovascular beri-beri, systemic hypertension, cardiac arrhythmias, stroke, and atherosclerotic coronary heart disease (CHD). Basic disparity between effects of lighter and heavier drinking underlies all alcohol-health relationships.

Definition of moderate and heavy drinking

These definitions are arbitrary. The operational boundary used here is the drinking level above which net harm is evident in epidemiologic studies. Thus, 3 or more drinks per day is called "heavy", and lesser amounts "light", "lighter", or "moderate" drinking. Individual factors, including sex and age, lower the safe boundary for some persons and raise it for others. Survey-based data always are confounded by systematic underestimation, with some heavy drinkers alleging lighter intake. One common result of this underestimation is a lower apparent threshold for harm.

Since most persons think in terms of "drinks", not milliliters or grams, it is fortunate that a standard-sized drink of wine, liquor, or beer contains approximately the same amount of alcohol (12-14 g). It seems best to describe relationships to health in terms of drinks per day or week. When talking with clients, health professionals need to define the size of drinks.

Alcoholic cardiomyopathy

A relationship of chronic heavy drinking to heart disease was repeatedly observed in the 19th century. Noting a mean yearly beer consumption of 432 liters in Munich vs. 82 liters per year elsewhere in Germany, Bollinger (1884) described the "M nchener bierherz", characterized by cardiac dilatation and hypertrophy. Graham Steell (1893) stated "not only do I recognize alcoholism as one of the causes of muscle failure of the heart but I find it a comparatively common one". However, after a heart disease epidemic due to arsenic contaminated beer occurred in Manchester, England in 1900, he wrote "in the production of the combined affection of the peripheral nerves and the heart met with in beer drinkers, arsenic has been shown to play a conspicuous part" (Steell 1906). William MacKenzie (1902) described heart failure from alcohol and used the term "alcoholic heart disease." After early descriptions of beri-beri (Aalsmeer and Wenckebach 1929, Keefer 1930), which later was understood to vitamin B1 (cocarboxylase) deficiency, the concept of "beri-beri heart disease" dominated thinking about alcohol and the heart.

There is renewed interest in direct myocyte toxicity from alcohol, and the concept of alcoholic cardiomyopathy is now solidly established by clinical observations, evidence of decreased myocardial function in many heavy chronic drinkers, and a few controlled studies. Since the entity is indistinguishable from dilated cardiomyopathy of other causes, epidemiologic study is impaired. Most cases of dilated cardiomyopathy in 2008 remain of unknown cause, with post-viral auto-immune processes and genetic predisposition the leading etiologic hypotheses. Lifetime alcohol consumption is quantitatively related to myocardial abnormalities in alcoholics above a threshold dose of 120 grams alcohol/day for 20 years (Urbano-Marquez et al. 1989).

Only a small proportion of alcoholics develop cardiomyopathy, thus creating interest in other traits affecting risk. It is believed probable that a genetic substrate underlies a large proportion of cases of idiopathic dilated cardiomyopathy and of alcoholic cardiomyopathy (Pasotti et al. 2004). In the context of other factors in alcoholic cardiomyopathy, it is appropriate to examine the arsenic and cobalt beer drinker episodes and thiamine (cocarboxylase) deficiency.

Arsenic-beer drinkers' disease

In 1900 an epidemic (>6000 cases with >70 deaths) in and near Manchester, England, was proved due to accidental contamination of beer by arsenic. Manifestations involved the skin, nervous system, gastrointestinal system and, prominently, the cardiovascular system. An investigative committee (Royal Commission 1903) suggested that "alcohol predisposed people to arsenic poisoning".

Cobalt-beer drinkers' disease

Recognized sixty-five years after the arsenic-beer episode, this condition had similarities. Heart failure epidemics occurred among beer drinkers in Omaha, Minneapolis, Quebec, and Belgium, with symptoms developing fairly abruptly in chronic heavy beer drinkers. The North American patients suffered a high mortality rate, but survivors did well despite frequent return to previous beer habits. The explanation proved to be addition of small amounts of cobalt chloride to improve the foaming qualities of beer. Quebec investigators (Morin and Daniel 1967) tracked down the etiology; the condition became justly known as Quebec beer-drinkers cardiomyopathy. Removal of the cobalt additive ended the epidemic in all locations. Both cobalt and substantial amounts of alcohol were needed to produce this condition in susceptible persons. Biochemical mechanisms were not established. Viewing the arsenic and cobalt episodes Alexander (1969) commented: "This is the second known metal induced cardiotoxic syndrome produced by contaminated beer". Speculative possibilities mentioned as possible cofactors for alcoholic cardiomyopathy include cardiotropic viruses, drugs, selenium, copper, and iron. Deficiencies (zinc, magnesium, protein, and vitamins) have also been suggested as cofactors, but only thiamine deficiency is proven.

Cardiovascular beriberi

Aalsmeer and Wenckebach (1929) defined, in Javanese polished-rice eaters, high-output heart failure resulting from decreased peripheral vascular resistance. Many assumed that heart failure among Western heavy alcohol drinkers was due to associated nutritional deficiency states (Keefer 1930). A few heart failure cases in North American and European alcoholics suited this hypothesis. Most did not, however, as they had low output heart failure, were well-nourished, and responded poorly to thiamine. Chronicity and ultimate irreversibility of beri-beri, was used by some to explain the situation. Blacket and Palmer (1960) sorted the conditions out: "It (beri-beri) responds completely to thiamine, but merges imperceptibly into another disease, called alcoholic cardiomyopathy, which doesn't respond to thiamine". In beriberi there is generalized peripheral arteriolar dilatation creating a large arteriovenous shunt and high resting cardiac outputs. A few cases of complete recovery with thiamine within 1-2 weeks have been documented.

Thus, many cases earlier called "cardiovascular beriberi" would now be called "alcoholic heart disease". Does chronic thiamine deficiency play a role in alcoholic cardiomyopathy? This hypothesis has not been proved or disproved.

Hypertension

Almost 90 years ago Lian (1915) reported a relation of heavy drinking (mostly as wine) to hypertension (HTN) in WW1 French servicemen. Unless these soldiers exaggerated, they were prodigious drinkers, as the HTN threshold appeared at $\geq$ 2 liters/wine per day. No further attention was given to this subject for almost 60 years. Since the mid 1970s, dozens of cross-sectional and prospective epidemiologic studies (Beilin and Puddey 1992, Klatsky and Gunderson 2008) have solidly established an empiric alcohol-HTN link. The apparent threshold for this relationship is approximately 3 drinks per day. The studies involve both sexes, various ages and populations in North American, Europe, Australia, and Japan. Importantly, most studies show no increased HTN with lighter drinking; in fact, several show an unexplained J-shaped curve in women with lowest pressures in lighter drinkers. The relationship is independent from several potential confounders such as adiposity, salt intake, education, smoking, and beverage type (wine, liquor, or beer).

An experiment in hospitalized hypertensive men showed pressure increases with 3-4 days of drinking 4 pints of beer and decreases with 3-4 days of abstinence (Potter and Beevers 1984). Similar results were later seen in ambulatory persons with both normal and high pressures. Heavier drinking impairs drug treatment of HTN, and moderation supplements other nonpharmacologic interventions such as weight reduction, exercise, or sodium restriction (Keil 1993, Klatsky and Gunderson 2008). Experiments do not support the hypothesis that acute withdrawal is the major cause of alcohol-associated HTN. Even without an established mechanism, intervention studies support a causal hypothesis.

Arrhythmias

The observation that heart rhythm disturbances were more frequent on Mondays and in the Christmas-New Year's period led to the term "holiday heart syndrome" (Ettinger 1978). Association of heavier drinking, especially with a large meal, and atrial arrhythmias had been suspected for decades. Atrial fibrillation is commonest, typically resolving with abstinence, with or without other treatment. In 1,322 persons reporting intake of $\geq$ 6 drinks per day a Kaiser Permanente study found a doubled relative risk of atrial fibrillation, atrial flutter, supraventricular tachycardia, and atrial premature complexes (Cohen et al. 1988). A prospective analysis of risk of atrial fibrillation in men and women (Mukamal et al. 2005) showed that risk was increased at $\geq$ 35 drinks per week, but was not increased at light-moderate drinking levels.

Stroke

Prior to modern imaging techniques imprecise diagnosis of stroke type was a limitation in analysis of alcohol-stroke relations. Studies of alcohol and stroke have to deal with the complex disparate inter-relationships of stroke, alcohol, and other cardiovascular conditions. Some reports deal only with drinking sprees; others fail to differentiate hemorrhagic and ischemic strokes. Several of these reports suggested that alcohol drinking (heavier especially) carried increased risk of stroke (Van Gign et al. 1993). HTN is an important risk factor for all types of stroke and could be an intermediary between heavy alcohol drinking and increased risk of all stroke types. Anti-thrombotic effects of alcohol might increase hemorrhagic, but lower ischemic stroke risk. Blood lipid effects of alcohol (see CHD discussion below) might favorably affect ischemic stroke risk

The importance of these deficiencies is highlighted by several recent studies suggesting that regular lighter drinkers may be at higher risk of hemorrhagic stroke types, but at lower risk of several types of ischemic stroke. For example, The Nurse's Health Study (Stampfer 1988) showed drinkers to be at higher risk of subarachnoid hemorrhage, but lower risk of occlusive stroke. Kaiser Permanente studies (Klatsky 2007) showed that only daily consumption of $\geq$ 3 drinks was related to higher hospitalization rates for hemorrhagic stroke, and higher blood pressure was a partial mediator of this relationship. However, alcohol use was associated with lower hospitalization rates for ischemic stroke, a relationship present in both sexes, whites and blacks, and for extracranial and intracerebral occlusive lesions. In summary, except for increased risk of hemorrhagic stroke, there is no current consensus about relationships of alcohol drinking to various types of stroke.

Coronary heart disease (CHD)

Although incidence is decreasing in developed countries, CHD remains the leading cause of death in men and women. Comprising a majority of cardiovascular deaths, CHD dominates statistics for cardiovascular mortality and has substantial impact upon total mortality. Population studies have uncovered several, probably causal, risk factors, including smoking, HTN, diabetes mellitus, high low-density lipoprotein (LDL) cholesterol, and low high-density lipoprotein (HDL) cholesterol. Sometimes, the LDL is called the "bad" cholesterol and HDL the "good" cholesterol. Atherosclerotic narrowing of major epicardial vessels is the usual basis, with clot formation in narrowed vessels playing a critical role in major events, such as acute myocardial infarction ("heart attack") or sudden death. Angina pectoris is a common symptom of CHD. Early studies of alcoholics and problem drinkers suggested a high CHD rate, but these studies did not allow for the role of traits associated with alcoholism, such as cigarette smoking. Studies of heavy drinkers can tell nothing about the role of light-moderate drinking.

The classic description of angina pectoris (Heberden 1786) included: *"Wine and spirituous liquors and opium—afford considerable relief"*. Thus, it was widely presumed that alcohol is a coronary vasodilator (Osler 1899, White 1931, Levine 1951). However, exercise ECG test data (Russek *et al.*,1950, Orlando 1976) suggest that alcohol does not improve myocardial oxygen deficiency, and may mask symptoms by a sedative/analgesic effect. Thus, symptomatic benefit is likely to be dangerously misleading in patients with angina who drink before exercise, since available data suggest no major immediate effect of alcohol upon coronary blood flow (Renaud et al. 1993, Klatsky 2007). In the early 1900's an inverse relationship between alcohol consumption and atherosclerotic disease (including CHD) was reported (Cabot 1904, Hultgen 1910, Leary 1931). A "solvent" action of alcohol was suggested, another explanation offered was that premature deaths in heavier drinkers precluded development of CHD (Wilens 1947, Ruebner *et al.*, 1961). Population and case-control studies in the past few decades have solidly established an inverse relation between alcohol drinking and fatal or nonfatal CHD (Renaud *et al.*,1993, Klatsky 2007). Data about plausible protective mechanisms against CHD by alcohol (Renaud *et al.*,1993, Klatsky 2007) make it now seem likely that alcohol drinking protects against CHD.

In 1819 Dr. Samuel Black, an Irish physician interested in angina pectoris perceptive about epidemiologic aspects, wrote (Black 1819) what is probably the first commentary about the "French Paradox". Noting much angina in Ireland but observing little discussion in the writings of French physicians, his explanation of the presumed disparity was "the French habits and modes of living, coinciding with the benignity of their climate and the peculiar character of their moral affections". It was 160 years until the presentation of international comparison data showing less CHD mortality in wine drinking countries (St. Leger et al. 1979). Confirmatory international comparisons plus reports of nonalcoholic antioxidant phenolic compounds and antithrombotic substances in wine, especially red wine (Renaud et al. 1993, Klatsky 2007), have created great interest in this area. However, prospective population studies show no consensus about the wine/liquor/beer issue (Rimm et al. 1996, Klatsky 2007). The beverage choice issue remains unresolved at this time.

Advice about drinking

Attempts to define a safe limit are hardly new, since the medical risks of heavier drinking and the relative safety of lighter drinking have long been evident. Probably the most famous such limit has been known for more than 100 years as "Anstie's Rule (Anstie 1870). The rule suggested an upper limit of approximately three standard drinks daily. In the mid-19th century, the limit was intended to apply primarily to mature men, but Sir Anstie was a distinguished neurologist and public health activist who emphasized individual variability in the ability to handle alcohol. Modern scientific advances have added little; the threshold for net harm in most population studies is exactly where Anstie, using common-sense observation, placed his limit. Now, as then, considerations of age, sex, and individual risks and benefits become the foci of any discussion (Friedman and Klatsky 1993, Klatsky 2001) in which a health practitioner advises his or her client about alcohol drinking.

References

Aalsmeer, W.C. and Wenckebach, K.F. (1929). Herz und Kreislauf bei der Beri-Beri Krankheit. *Wien Arch Inn Med* **16**:193- 272.

Anstie, F. E. (1870). *On the uses of wines in health and disease*. J.S. Redfield, New York. New York, pp. 11-13.

Alexander, C.S. (1969). Cobalt and the heart. *Annals of Internal Medicine* **70**: 411-413.

Beilin, L.J. and Puddey, I.B. (1992). Alcohol and hypertension. *Clinical Experiments in Hypertension Theory and Practice* **A14**: 119-138.

Black, S. (1819). *Clinical and Pathological Reports*. Alex Wilkinson, Newry, England. pp. 1-47.

Blacket, R. B. and Palmer, A.J. (1960). Haemodynamic studies in high output beri-beri. *British Heart Journal* **22:** 483-501.

Bollinger, O. (1884). Ueber die Haussigkeit und Ursachen der idiopathischen Herzhypertrophie in Munchen. *Disch Med Wochensch (Stuttgart)* **10**: 180.

Cabot, R.C. (1904). The relation of alcohol to arteriosclerosis. *Journal of the American Medical Association* **43**: 774-775.

Cohen, E. J., Klatsky, A.L. and Armstrong, M.A. (1988). Alcohol use and supraventricular arrhythmia. *American Journal of Cardiology* **62**: 971-973.

Ettinger, P.O., Wu, C.F., De La Cruz, C. Jr., Weisse, A.B., Ahmed S.S. and Regan T.J. (1978). Arrhythmias and the "holiday heart": alcohol-associated cardiac rhythm disorders. *American Heart Journal* **95**: 555-562.

Friedman, G.D. and Klatsky, A.L. (1993). Is alcohol good for your health? (Editorial). *New England Journal of Medicine* **329**: 1882-1883.

Heberden, W. (1786). Some account of a disorder of the breast. *Medical Transactions of the Royal College of Physicians (London)* **2**: 59-67.

Hultgen, J.F. (1910). Alcohol and nephritis: Clinical study of 460 cases of chronic alcoholism. *Journal of the American Medical Association* **55**: 279-281.

Keefer C.S. (1930). The beri-beri heart. *Archives of Internal Medicine* **45**: 1-22.

Keil U., Swales J.D. and Grobbee, D.E. (1993). Alcohol intake and its relation to hypertension. In: *Health Issues Related to Alcohol Consumption (Ed. Verschuren P M)*. ILSI Press, Washington DC pp. 17-42.

Klatsky, A.L. (2001). Should patients with heart disease drink alcohol? (Editorial). *Journal of the American Medical Association* **285**: 2004-2005.

Klatsky, A.L. (2003). Drink to your health? *Scientific American* **288**: 74-81.

Klatsky, A.L. (2007). Alcohol, cardiovascular diseases and diabetes mellitus. *Pharmacological Research* **55**: 237-247.

Klatsky A.L. and Gunderson, E. (2008). Alcohol and Hypertension: A Review. *Journal of the American Society of Hypertension*. In Press.

Leary, T. (1931). Therapeutic value of alcohol, with special consideration of relations of alcohol to cholesterol, and thus to diabetes, to arteriosclerosis, and to gallstones. *New England Journal of Medicine* **205**: 231-242.

Levine, S.A. (1951). *Clinical Heart Disease, 4th ed.*, Saunders, Philadelphia, PA. p. 98.

Lian, C. (1915). L'alcoholisme cause d'hypertension arterielle. *Bull Acad Med (Paris)* **74**: 525-528.

MacKenzie, J. (1902). The Study of the Pulse. *YJ Pentland, Edinburgh and London, UK.*

p. 237.

Morin, Y. and Daniel, P. (1967). Quebec beer-drinkers' cardiomyopathy: Etiologic considerations. *Canadian Medical Association Journal* **97**: 926-928.

Mukamal, K.J., Tolstrup, J.S., Friberg, J., Jensen, G. and Grønbæk, M. (2005). Alcohol consumption and risk of atrial fibrillation in men and women. The Copenhagen City Heart Study. *Circulation* **112**: 1736-1742.

Orlando, J., Aronow, W.S., Cassidy, J. and Prakash P. (1976). Effect of ethanol on angina pectoris. *Annals of Internal Medicine 84*: 652-655.

Osler, W. (1899). *The Principles and Practice of Medicine, Third Edition*. Appleton, New York, New York.

Pasotti, M., Repetto, A., Tavazzi, L. and Arbustini E. (2004). Genetic predisposition to heart failure. *Medical Clinics of North America* **88**: 173-192.

Potter, J.F. and Beevers, D.J. (1984). Pressor effect of alcohol in hypertension. *Lancet **i***: 119-122.

Renaud, S., Criqui, M.H., Farchi, G. and Veenstra, J. (1993). Alcohol drinking and coronary heart disease. In: *Health Issues Related to Alcohol Consumption*. Verschuren, PM, Ed. ILSI Press, Washington, D.C. pp. 81-124.

Rimm, E., Klatsky, A.L., Grobbee, D. and Stampfer, M.J. (1996). Review of moderate alcohol consumption and reduced risk of coronary heart disease: Is the effect due to beer, wine, or spirits? *British Medical Journal 312*: 731-736.

Royal Commission Appointed to Inquire into Arsenical Poisoning from the Consumption of Beer and other Articles of Food or Drink. "Final Report," Part I. (1903) Wyman and Sons, London, England.

Ruebner, B.H., Miyai, K.J. and Abbey, H. (1961). The low incidence of myocardial infarction in hepatic cirrhosis - a statistical artefact? Lancet **ii:** 1435-1436.

Russek, H.I., Naegele, C.F. and Regan, F.D. (1950). Alcohol in the treatment of angina pectoris. *Journal of the American Medical Association* **143**: 355-357.

St. Leger, A.S., Cochrane, A.L. and Moore, F. (1979). Factors associated with cardiac mortality in developed countries with particular reference to the consumption of wine. *Lance **i***: 1017-1020.

Stampfer, M. J., Colditz, G.A., Willett, W.C., Speizer, F.E. and Hennekens, C.H. (1988). Prospective study of moderate alcohol consumption and the risk of coronary disease and stroke in women. *New England Journal of Medicine* **319**: 267-273.

Steell, G. (1893). Heart failure as a result of chronic alcoholism. *Medical Chronicles of Manchester* **18**: 1-22.

Steell, G. (1906). In: *Textbook on Diseases of the Heart*. Blakiston, Philadelphia. p. 79.

Urbano-Marquez, A., Estruch, R., Navarro-Lopez, F., Grau, J.M., Mont, L. and Rubin E. (1989). The effects of alcoholism on skeletal and cardiac muscle. *New England Journal of Medicine* **320**: 409-415.

Van Gign, J., Stampfer, M.J., Wolfe, C. and Algra, A. (1993). The association between alcohol consumption and stroke. In: *Verschuren PM, Ed. Health Issues Related to Alcohol Consumption*. Washington, DC, ILSI Press. pp. 43-80.

White, P.D. (1931). *Heart Disease*. Macmillan, New York, New York. p. 436.

Wilens, S.L. (1947). The relationship of chronic alcoholism to atherosclerosis. *Journal of the American Medical Association* **135**: 1136-1138.

Chapter 41

Scotch whisky: Threats and opportunities

Professor Alan Rutherford
West Wing, Stelling Hall, Newton, Stocksfield, Northumberland, NE43 7UR

Introduction

Many of you will be regular readers of The Annual Scotch Whisky Industry Review published by my friend of many years, Alan Gray. Every year, Alan includes a section entitled "Issues and Problems Affecting the Industry" and in his latest Review, he lists 27 issues that are shown in my first slide (Table 1). If we take only the last of these: "Trade Barriers" and move to page 75 of the Review, we find 16 examples under this heading alone (Table 2).

These are the threats but incidentally, when I sat down and wrote out a list of opportunities, the topics were very similar. In the main, opportunities arise from analysing threats and addressing them.

Most of us here have a backgound in the technical or production areas of the industry and probably feel that there is very little we can do to influence most of these threats or opportunities. Indeed most lie in the hands of our commercial colleagues, politicians, lawyers, overseas ambassadors and the officers of the Scotch Whisky Association who do tremendous work on behalf of the industry.

My intention is to select only three or four of these issues all of which are topical and over which we in this audience can exert some influence. Those I have chosen are: deep

Table 1. Threats to the Scotch Whisky Industry (After Gray, 2007)

• Deep Economic Recessions	• Fall in Popularity in USA
• Parallel Trading	• Minimum Spirits Strength
• Changing Fashions in Drinks	• Bottle sizes
• Opposition to Bulk Exports	• Abolition of Duty Free
• Drink Driving	• Import Duties
• High UK Duty Levels	• Fuel Costs
• Cross Border Trading (EU)	• Strip Stamps
• Inadequate Selling Prices	• Definitions
• Anti-drink Lobby / Alcohol abuse	• Discrimination in India
• Need to Appeal to Younger Markets	• Counterfeiting
• Locally Produced Whisky	• Need for fair play
• Failure to Innovate	• EU Excise Duties
• Need for More Effective Marketing	• Trade Barriers in Overseas
• Poor image among females	

Table 2. Trade barriers against Scotch Whisky (After Gray, 2007)

• Bans and Partial Restrictions	• State Monopolies
• Minimum Values for Duty/Tax	• Advertising Restrictions
• Discriminatory mark-ups	• Ingredient Listing
• Profit Margin Controls	• Nutrition Requirements
• Import Deposits	• Tariff Barriers
• Discriminatory Duties/Taxes	• Pre-shipment Inspection
• Quotas	• Strip Stamps
• Foreign Exchange and/or Credit Control	• Mark-ups

economic recessions, failure to innovate, fuel costs and product definitions.

Economic recessions

There may be some eternal optimists among you who feel that we are not entering a global recession or if we are, then it will be very short lived. If you were working in the finance or housing sectors you might feel differently and if you compound the downturn in economic activity with soaring prices for mankind's most essential commodities - namely food and energy - then even the most optimistic among you must have some concern. So why is it that Scotch Whisky is completely bucking the trend? Exports are booming, distilleries are working 24/7, closed distilleries are re-opening, new ones being built and there are shortages of almost everything including mature stocks, warehouse space and casks. We have all heard of the growth of Scotch Whisky sales, in double digit percentages, in the so called BRIC economies (ie Brazil, Russia, India and China) as well as healthy price rises in the developed markets. I hear confident predictions that this growth is unstoppable and will see everyone out to retirement and I hear very few voices expressing fears of overproduction.

However, I have a growing sense of "deja vu". Being somewhat older than most of you, I have experienced this scenario three times before. The first time was in the mid-seventies and I must confess that I believed it! After all, we had experienced continuous annual growth, averaging about 6%, since the end of the Second World War. I must stress that I am personally delighted by the current whisky boom and I believe that it will continue for a while yet but I also believe that it is a cycle and cycle it will. Everything in this world does: economics, empires, ecosystems, the weather, morals, fashion - and of course life itself!

A colleague of mine at United Distillers was fond of saying that forecasting is very difficult - especially when it concerns the future. We will always get it wrong, the question is simply how wrong? In whisky, we have to make long term demand forecasts, and even if we get close on an industry average, every brand manager chasing a bonus will be forecasting that his/her brand will do better than the average. An interesting dynamic of Scotch Whisky cycles is that they are in some measure self-induced. History tells us that unlike motor cars or houses, cycle downturns for whisky production have not been caused by a collapse in sales but by over-forecasting and the consequent over-production. So let's have a look at some recent history:

Figure 1 shows how production, export sales and industry stocks have progressed with time.

Figure 2 shows, over a much longer timescale, the number of operational distilleries in Scotland.

If the optimists are still unmoved, I would point to some recent developments which may persuade you to pause for thought:

Firstly, in Pernod Ricard's most recent annual report - published in July, I noted that the market for Scotch in China fell by 2% in 2007. This was attributed not to economics but to fashion. We saw similar effects historically in other more mature markets such as the USA, Japan and more recently in Spain - where rum has been in the ascendency.

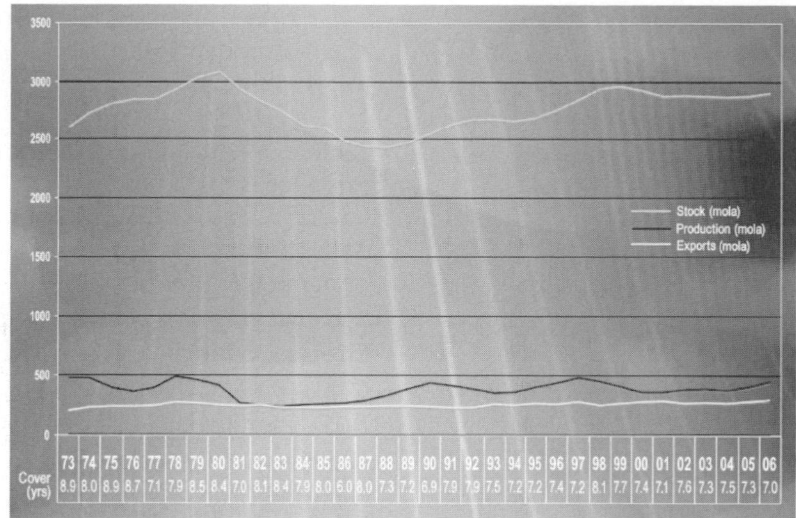

Figure 1. Scotch whisky production, exports and stock (1973 – 2006)

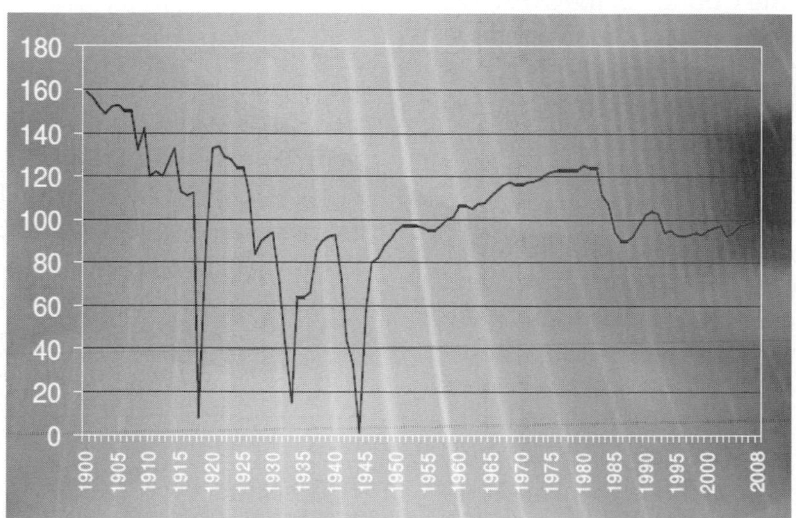

Figure 2. Whisky distilleries in operation in Scotland (1900 – 2008)

Secondly, if we look at the SWA's most recent statistics, for the first four months of 2008 (Table 3) the picture is not universally bullish.

Thirdly, we should look at the costs of laying down replacement stocks in an era where cereal prices have doubled and oil prices have trebled

Table 3. Changes in the whisky market from January – April 2008

Country/region	*Volume (%)*	*Value (%)*
Asia	-6.65	-1.0
Central and South America	-24.0	-8.0
North America	-3.5	-1.0
EU	+8.0	+40.0
China	-19.0	-26.0
India	+3.0	-24.0
Brazil	-38.0	-15.0
Total exports	-1.66	+13.0

in the space of less than two years. These are our two main input costs and even in the most efficient grain whisky distillery, a distillation cost of about 40p per litre two years ago has risen to over 80p per litre today. It has become quite normal in the whisky industry to build stocks using bank debt for the additional working capital - and by securitising this debt on the increasing value of the stock. Does this have parallels with the housing sector? I sincerely hope not.

So is there a solution? Are there opportunities?

During my time on the Council of the SWA, we thought that two factors would greatly improve the accuracy of our forecasting : the first was the sharing of information regarding stocks and production levels amongst members and the second was industry consolidation i.e. the steady stream of mergers and acquistions which was reducing the number of decision makers.

Information has certainly been shared and published and I had thought that there were fewer players owning distilleries but when I researched the facts, the true position surprised me:

When I lived on Speyside in the 1970s, these are the companies whom I remember as owning distilleries but who no longer exist as independent companies today (Table 4).

I have grouped together the bigger companies who have grown by acquisition and mergers, plus the foreign entrants since 1975, the smaller companies who have acquired or built distilleries and, of course, there are some who have sailed through the past thirty years without being substantially changed (Table 5). So all in all, contrary to the folklore, the number of distilling companies has actually increased! For many reasons this must be welcomed.

So is there any solution to boom and bust - under and over production? I would like to suggest one and that is to work much harder at decoupling the perception in many markets that age of itself means quality. Having a 10, 12, 15 year age statement on a volume brand makes production and stock management almost impossible.

Table 4. A selection of distilling companies in existence in 1978

Amalgamated Distilled Products plc
Arthur Bell & Sons plc
S. Campbell & Son Ltd (Pernod Ricard)
Charles Mackinlay & Co Ltd
Chivas Bros Ltd
Eadie Cairns Ltd
Glenlivet Distillers Ltd
Highland Distilleries Ltd
Hiram Walker & Sons (Scotland) plc
International Distillers & Vintners Ltd
Invergordon Distillers Ltd
Long John International Ltd
Macallan-Glenlivet plc
Macdonald Martin Distillers plc
North British Distillery Co Ltd
North of Scotland Distilling Co Ltd
Robertson & Baxter Ltd
Scottish Malt Distillers (DCL)
Stanley P Morrison Ltd
William Lawson Distillers Ltd
Wm Teacher & Sons Ltd

When dealing with unaged whiskies, we can manage stock levels quite successfully by over- or under-ageing. During the years of surplus in the eighties, almost all of UD's standard blends were over 8yo - so what did we do? We re-launched Bells as an 8yo - it is a sign of the times that Bells is now being relaunched again as Bells Original - without an age statement - a sensible decision. It is even more important that we launch unaged flagship brands in the premium and super-premium categories. JW Blue Label and JW Premier show that it can be done (Figure 3) by the big companies and at the other end of the scale, by craft whisky makers such as Compass Box (Figure 4) There are also some signs that it can be done with premium expressions of single malts such as Jura Superstition (Figure 5), Bowmore Legend

Table 5. Landscape of the Scottish whisky distilling industry in 2008

Diageo	LVMH (Glenmorangie, Ardberg)
Pernod	Bacardi (John Dewar, Wm Lawson)
Edrington Group	Campari (Glen Grant)
Wm Grant & Sons	Nikka (Ben Nevis)
	Suntory (Morrison Bowmore)
	Takara, Kokubu & Morubeni (Tomatin)
	Fortune Brands (Beam Global)
	Pacific Spirits (Inverhouse)
	UB Group (Whyte & Mackay)
	CL Worldbrands (Burn Stewart)
Gordon & MacPhail (Benromach)	
Isle of Arran	
Angus Dundee (Tomintul, Glencadam)	
Ben Riach	(Glenglassaugh)
Tullibardine	(Glendronach)
Kilchoman	(Glen Moray)
Bladnoch	(Falkirk)
Bruichladdich	
Signatory (Edradour)	
Speyside	Glenfarclas
Ian Macleod (Glengoyne)	Springbank/Glengyle
Daftmill	Loch Lomond

and Aberlour a'bunadh where an innovative name, instead of an age statement is used to create brand equity.

After all, our industry was built on non-aged blends and these products continue to represent the largest volume category.

Staying with the issue of quality - there is one very serious threat in boom times which is not always acknowledged but which those on the technical and production sides of the industry know well and are able to influence - that is the threat of working our distilleries, particularly our malt distilleries too hard. Obviously there is pressure to maximise capacity - more malt in the mash, shorter fermentations, filling the stills, driving them harder, failure to rest the stills and let air get at the copper, higher condensing temperatures, less maintenance, and refilling casks too many times - all of which should be resisted if quality and consistency are to be maintained.

Figure 3. Diageo brands lacking an age statement

Figure 4. Compass Box brands lacking an age statement

Figure 5. Jura Superstition, a premium single malt expression lacking an age statement

Cereal costs and fuel costs

My second area of threats and opportunities lies in the rapidly rising prices of cereals and energy.

Figure 6 shows wheat and oil prices. Dealing firstly with wheat, although the price rises are severe, we have enjoyed artificially low wheat and barley prices for many years and I am more sanguine about cereal prices than I am about oil, at least in the short term, because cereals are renewable and the market can respond. There are many thousands of acres in Europe alone which can be brought into production and I do not believe that biofuels from cereal starch will gain universal support. Most research money in this field is aimed at lignocellulose conversion which will eventually produce biofuels from wastes and from non-food crops.

However, we can't do without cereals and we can't entirely buck the markets but what we can do, is to secure quality supplies - by giving rolling contracts of at least three years to UK farmers which will ensure that our chosen varieties are grown with full traceability and a price hedge against poor harvests, currency fluctuations and world markets. We have a futures market in wheat, which works well - there is no reason why this should not also operate for barley. This is especially important in the North of Scotland where the supply chain is attractively short and superb wheat and barley varieties can be grown - but not much else. Use it or lose it!

I also believe that organic whisky represents a small but growing opportunity at a premium price. I know of at least three malt distilleries who are already accredited for organic production with another two having plans to do so. More controversially, I do believe that if we are to feed

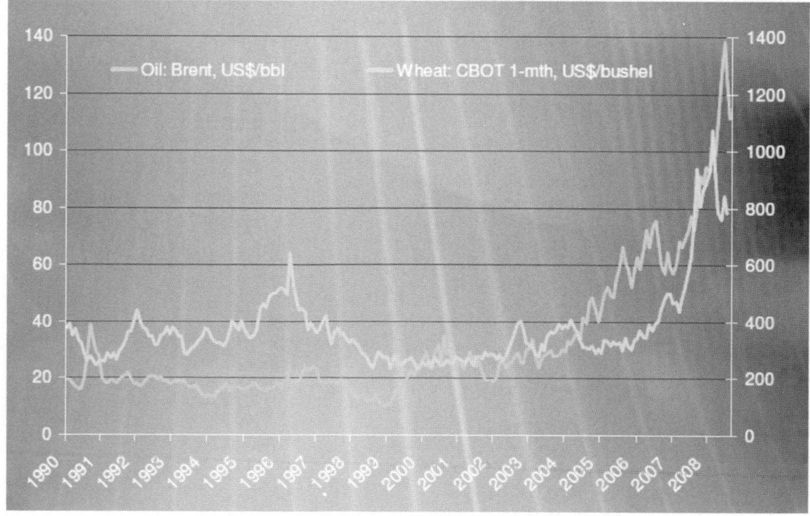

Figure 6. Wheat and oil prices since 1990

the world, then in the longer term the scientific community, including those in the drinks industry will have to embrace GM crops.

Moving now to oil. Whilst the price has eased in recent weeks, I attended this summer's Executive briefing of the Energy Institute where a speaker from one of the major oil companies was predicting an oil price of $200 by Christmas and $400 by 2010. This may or may not happen, but oil supplies are finite and global consumption continues to accelerate. A year ago it was difficult to envisage oil going above $100 per barrel, now it is difficult to envisage it below $100!

Distilling is a very energy intensive industry, which makes us vulnerable to energy prices as well as to criticism from environmentalists and punitive carbon taxes from governments. From fertilisers to grain driers, distilleries to bottling halls, glass manufacture and transport, our carbon footprint is considerable.

Despite these dire warnings on carbon emissions and fossil fuels, I know of at least two distilleries who have just ordered new oil boilers! I can only assume that their margins are so good that they have no need to consider alternative energy technologies. I must applaud Diageo for their plans to become virtually independent of fossil fuels at Cameronbridge Distillery by investing in a combination of anaerobic digestion and biomass combustion (including draff) to raise steam. I know that at least one other grain distiller has similar plans. Also Pulteney Distillery at Wick for pioneering gasifier technology (Figure 7) in their CHP system and Deanston Distillery for continued investment in its flow of river turbines which have operated since the 1930's. There are also huge wind and marine opportunities, especially on Islay, and I do hope that these will soon be embraced by the distilling companies.

There are a number of renewable energy options depending primarily on location (Table 6). If anyone tells you that wind energy is uneconomic, then ask them why so many wind farms are being built or in the pipeline or why Tesco are planning to put turbines onto so many of their sites or why there is a waiting list of several years for the larger sizes of wind turbines. However, if wind does not appeal, then please look at small scale hydro - although this, like wind, will only provide you with electricity. The real answer for any distillery at present is biomass - burning or gasifying woodchips, chaff, straw and small corns, draff and anything else permissable via a steam turbine set or a gas engine. If this is combined with an anaerobic digester for liquid wastes then any distillery can become totally independent of fossil fuels as well as feeding some green energy into the grid and getting some really green PR for Scotch Whisky.

Figure 7. Gasifier technology at Pulteney Distillery, Wick

Table 6. Renewable energy technologies

Biomass CHP
Anaerobic Digestion (AD)
Wind
Small Hydroelectric
Solar Thermal
Solar Photovoltaic (PV)
Geothermal
Biofuels
Wave
Tidal
Hydrogen
Fuel Cells

I firmly believe that pressures of fuel prices, carbon abatement legislation and the need for green credentials will force all of us down the renewables route. Wave, tidal, hydrogen and other forms are for the future but distilleries with their balance of Combined Heat and Power are ideally suited to the already proven CHP technologies that I have just described. Scotland's First Minister wants his country to lead the world in renewables so it is entirely appropriate that Scotland's flagship industry should lead the way

Definitions and innovation

For my final topic of threats and opportunities, I have chosen definitions coupled to - or perhaps pitted against - innovation. This conflict is inevitable, because definitions are by their very nature restrictive, requiring convergent thinking whilst innovation is by nature creative and expansive, requiring divergent thinking.

I have not been involved in the recent consultation on the new legal definitions for Scotch but I did serve for seven years on the SWA Council and on its Product Integrity sub-committee. I was involved in the previous tightening of definitions back in the Scotch Whisky Act of 1988 and the Scotch Whisky Order of 1990 when the outgoing and much respected Chairman of the SWA, John MacPhail, said to us all: "I hope you chaps don't regret these tighter definitions because they will surely inhibit your ability to innovate". Sadly, John is no longer with us, but I am sure that 20 years on he will watching with a wry smile as we tighten the regulations much further than he could have imagined. The sub-committee I referred to earlier was set up in the 1990's primarily to address the vexed question of long closed and fictitious distilleries but these concerns seemed to grow legs after the Cardhu controversy.

The new proposals are very logical and legalistic but we are setting in stone the practices which make sense in 2008 and for which our successors might not thank us. My main concern is the use of the word "blended" when applied to vatted malts. For more than a century, the word "blended" has meant malt and grain whiskies combined and whilst I cannot question the logic of "blended malts", I do question its wisdom. I would have voted for two categories called simply "malt whisky" and "single malt whisky". Another possible concern is the regulation that single malts must be bottled in Scotland - thus ensuring that they have the highest possible carbon footprint by the time they reach say California where moves are already afoot to tax imports on this basis. I also worry about the unnecessary restriction on types of still. And should we really be forbidding the use of Gaelic in a Scotland which may soon aspire to independence? When we have exhausted the finite range of cask finishes, including perhaps herring casks and butter barrels, then innovation at the production end will become very difficult indeed.

However, I suspect that my general discomfort with ever tightening regulation is my inbred aversion to red tape and my concern is that in the main we are legislating against ourselves. We are telling future generations of Scotch Whisky distillers what they must not do and what is more, we are embedding these rules in law so that an Act of Parliament will be needed to change them. How much better if the rules of the club could be amended by the club members as and when they need to be changed.

Looking finally at innovation, there have been many efforts before and since the 1988 Act but the legal definition has been tight enough to ensure that creativity was strictly limited. I have listed some of these products on my next slide (Table 7) where the obvious successes have been in line-extensions and in the packaging of super-premiums. The effort to improve mixability is a common theme but of course ready to drink whisky and water is illegal due to the minimum strength regulation!

At Compass Box John Glaser has been breaking new ground using craft whisky making. That is, whisky based on style and quality - without any age statements or named distilleries.

Table 7. Examples of innovations in the Scotch whisky industry

1960's	
Glenfiddich	- Single Malt
1980's RTD's	
James Burrough	- Whisky & Lemonade
	- Whisky & Ginger
Arthur Bell	- Bells & Irn Bru
	- Bells & Cola
Highland Distilleries	- Madison
Slater & Scott (DCL)	- Grassy Green
Teachers 60	
Bell's Islander	
1990's	
Line Extensions	- e.g. Johnnie Walker Green, Gold, Blue, Famous Grouse Malt
Wood Finishes	- e.g. Glenmorangie, Port, Sherry, Madeira, etc.
Classic Malts + Selection + Wood Finishes	
2000's	
Rare Malts, Hidden Malts	
J & B -6°C	
Bowmore Dusk & Darkest	
Jura Superstition	
Compass Box	- Asyla, Eleuthra, Hedonism, Oak Cross, Flaming Heart, Peat Monster

Whisky Magazine has awarded Compass Box its Innovator of the Year Award in four of the past seven years so John must be doing something right!

To round off on this topic, innovation in Scotch Whisky is absolutely essential and I am sure it will continue, but tightening definitions will ensure that these innovations will be less and less likely to originate in the distillery.

Conclusion

So in conclusion, I see four major opportunities which we and our successors can grasp to advantage:

- Smooth production levels by moving away from age statements.
- Secure long term varietal wheat and barley contracts.
- Abandon fossil fuels.
- Defend quality at all costs!

All four are do-able as of now and if we can do these four simple things then I have no doubt that the future is bright.

Reference

Gray, A.S., Scotch Whisky Industry Review, Sutherlands Edinburgh, 2007.

Chapter 42

Tradition and authenticity – where marketing and production meet

Ian Buxton
Brollachan Ltd, Distillery House, Tomdachoille, by Pitlochry PH16 5NA, Perthshire, UK

Recent trends in the marketing of distilled spirits have seen increased emphasis placed on the distillery as the 'brand home-place' and the phenomenon of 'brand centres' and 'brand experiences' being developed in place of the more traditional distillery visitor centre and tour. At the same time, the role of Distillery Manager has evolved to require the personnel concerned to behave as 'Brand Ambassador' (or 'Master Distiller' or 'Master Blender' – titles often created as much by a marketing imperative as any strictly functional need), often travelling to consumer events and being required to give presentations and tastings to an informed and enthusiastic audience. In turn, this requires new performance and presentational skills not previously strongly associated with this function.

The marketing of many distilled spirit brands is now laying great emphasis on claims of heritage, tradition and provenance and the distillery itself is increasingly used as a resource to support and demonstrate these claims. 'Experience' and 'authenticity' have become critical values in brand marketing – though it is debatable how far these are absolute measures, as opposed to relative and subjective ones. Pressures to achieve greater yields and increase efficiency in the distillery itself may also be at odds with marketing messages about heritage. In addition, production facilities are now being opened up to the consumer who expects to see into hitherto secret corners. This trend challenges the traditional relationship between the marketing and production functions and sets new challenges for the production department as their role, beliefs and practices come under greater scrutiny, not necessarily all of it fully informed.

Here we will explore the background to these trends (the development of the so-called 'Experience Economy'), their practical effects and implications and the tensions that may result between technical innovation and the marketing of heritage.

The practical effect is that you are going to see a lot more of your marketing and sales colleagues in territory which was traditionally production's fiefdom. It is happening all across alcohol beverage marketing.

Here are five examples from Scotland, from Ireland, from Puerto Rico and from the USA. The distillery visitor centre is well established in Scotland. Two examples, at The Glenlivet and Highland Park, where I recently re-modelled their small brand home, are typical. The Guinness Storehouse is Dublin's largest tourist attraction: the Jack Daniels Centre in Lynchburg, Tenessee has put that otherwise unremarkable part of rural America on the international tourist map and overnight the Casa Bacardi in San Juan, Puerto Rico became the island's number one tourist attraction. Again, I led the design team for the development of the Bacardi centre.

Dewar's World of Whisky in Aberfeldy is another example from Scotch Whisky. Dewar's use the centre both for consumer visits and for trade entertaining and brand education. Importantly the public operation covers the operating cost providing a trade entertainment and hospitality effectively free of charge. I was extensively involved in the design and project management of this example too.

And beyond distilled spirits, two examples from the world of brewing. Dublin's Guinness Storehouse attracts around three-quarters of a million visitors annually and also houses the Guinness archive together with significant training and conference facilities. The capital cost of this development was something in excess of £40million.

Finally in Amsterdam, the Heineken Experience, located in a redundant brewery in the heart of the city, draws substantial visitor numbers and is currently in its third major remodelling and expansion since its opening. So the brand home-place is an increasingly familiar marketing tool that is being embraced by every part of the alcohol marketing fraternity with increasing enthusiasm. To understand why this is we need a short diversion into the recent history of post-War and contemporary marketing.

Today's marketers face a challenge unknown to even their recent predecessors. The problem is 'stuff'.

A whistle stop tour of the contemporary marketing scene reveals six key trends. First, the breakdown of monolithic communication channels: a proliferation of media and the development of the world wide web. The classical post war Proctor and Gamble model of brand development relied upon easy if expensive access to the mass audiences delivered by commercial television since its advent in the 1950's and 60's. It's hard to recall today that as recently as 20 years ago a substantial part of the UK population could be captured with a series of commercials in popular TV shows that as often as not would be discussed at work the next day. This was the heyday of television advertising with very high production values and budgets to match. As a young brand manager working on Carling Black Label I thought little of buying a national TV audience of 5 million and more viewers for a single exposure to one commercial. Today that's impossible. Media have fragmented and along with that audiences have grown more niche, elusive and challenging to find.

If that were not complex enough, this has gone hand in hand with greatly increased concentration of retail power and the dominance of a few multiple grocers has had an extraordinary influence especially in the marketing of popular alcohol brands. Conversely, in recent years, we have seen the emergence of a new breed of specialist retailers and dedicated on-line offers of niche and premium brands.

For the increasingly harassed marketing department, quality was the answer a decade or so ago, but quality is now taken for granted. The consumer assumes as of right the functional performance of the products they buy. There simply isn't any bad 'stuff' and if you doubt that basic truth consider the car you would have driven less than 20 years ago and compare it to the vehicle you drive today. Whereas manufacturers such as BMW and Audi were able to compete against Ford, Leyland and others on the promise of product delivery and quality, today even the quality of a humble Skoda is taken for granted. Simplistically, there's no bad stuff out there anymore, so you can't sell on product quality when every product delivers functionally.

And whilst that has been going on the Western consumer has enjoyed nearly two decades of more or less continuous economic growth and is now saturated with 'stuff'. If you recall from your management training programme the theory behind Maslow's Hierarchy of Needs, you'll understand that the basic human drives have been satisfied. Now we're moving to a world where we seek to fulfil social needs, esteem needs and even, for a fortunate few, pursue self actualisation.

As a result, especially in developed Western markets, the consumer now searches for personalisation, authenticity and 'real' brands as they seek to make emotional connections with the brands and products they continue to voraciously consume.

This is classically described as 'creating the Experience Economy'.

The term 'The Experience Economy' was first coined in April 1999 by two American management authors, Joseph Pine and James Gilmore, in a book of the same title. Remarkably for a management text, it is still in print and, due to its continuing sales, still only available in hard back. This text has been massively influential in the marketing and design community to the extent that even practitioners who have not read it and may even be unaware of it are in fact influenced by its fundamental proposition. If I can recommend one seminal text for you to visit I would suggest picking up a copy of The Experience Economy and surprising your marketing colleagues. At the heart of the book is a proposition at once startling, but elegant.

Pine and Gilmore's central proposition holds that in the developed West we have moved to a new level of economic activity. The graph demonstrating this contains three axes. On the left hand side we move from undifferentiated to differentiated product offerings as we move up the axis. Along the bottom of the graph the axis indicates a move from pricing determined by the dictates of the wider market to premium pricing determined by the brand owner. The right hand axis indicates the relevance of the brand offer to individual consumers. A move up and into the right hand quadrant implies increasing customisation of the product or brand and the corollary is that as products slip down and to the left hand quadrant they are subject to an increasing degree of commoditisation – anathema to the brand owner.

To put a tangible example on this process, consider the humble coffee bean. At the bottom in the left hand corner in the agrarian economies of the so-called developing world, economic activity is, broadly speaking, limited to the extraction of commodities. These are undifferentiated, irrelevant to the individual consumer and all too often, pricing is at the whim of a global market. This characterised the state of the economy in pre-industrial Britain up to the advent of the first Industrial Revolution around the middle of the 18th century.

At that point the western world moved to Pine and Gilmore's second level of economic activity and began the production of manufactured goods. In our example, the raw coffee beans of the developing world have been processed and graded, in the course of which the products have gained value through becoming increasingly differentiated, somewhat more relevant to individual consumers and capable of commanding a higher price. Western society continued to develop along these lines until the advent of the first brands, formally recognised with the creation of the legally recognised trade mark in 1876 (interestingly, the red triangle of Bass' beer) and the rapid expansion of trade and commerce in the Victorian era. Brand marketing as we know it today got into its stride in the post-WW2 era of peace and prosperity characterised by sustained economic growth and the development of the so-called service economy from circa 1950. As Harold Macmillan memorably remarked in a speech in 1957 "..most of our people have never had it so good." For a newly emergent purchasing class, that was strikingly true. In the service economy our coffee beans have been processed to provide strongly branded varieties of instant coffee – increasingly differentiated, increasingly premium priced and increasingly relevant and capable of appealing to discrete groups of individual consumers.

At this point, Pine and Gilmore's theory of the 'Experience Economy' kicks in and some ten years ago they posited that the developed Western world was in the process of moving to a new economic model which they termed 'staging experiences'. To continue the coffee example, Gold Blend has given way as aspirational to a

Starbucks', or its host of imitators', cappuccino. If you call to mind for just a moment a typical Starbucks, Costa Coffee, Cafe Nero or Coffee Angel menu, the bewildering range of choices and the deliberately complex new language that is required to order a cup of coffee from the 'barista', this demonstrates Pine and Gilmore's theory. These products are highly differentiated, relevant to individual consumers through the plethora of choice and opportunity for customisation and, as we can all no doubt painfully attest, certainly they command premium prices. In fact, in the 'Experience Economy' a single take away coffee commands a price higher than the value of an entire coffee bush for the unfortunate subsistence farmer of the third world. It's a compelling rationale.

So what does this mean as an increasingly saturated and over indulged consumer engages with the world of distilled spirits. The brand centre has emerged as a child of the Experience Economy so let's consider how brand centres are considered critical to the promotion of brand values.

The brand centre, or at least those founded in an intellectual perception of their role within brand positioning and promotion, is a carefully designed world of artifice which seeks to express three key brand values and to take the unwitting consumer visitor through a carefully moderated process. In the search for authenticity, the brand owner seeks to demonstrate his or her product integrity, a sense that the product is the result of passion and pride, hence the increasing overuse of "passion" in marketing which is rapidly becoming something of an embarrassing cliché. Beyond demonstrating authenticity, the brand centre seeks to create a sense of belonging, of recruiting the consumer into a like minded tribe where the resonance and cultural relevance of the brand's icons, symbols, values, badges and rituals are summarised in the brand myth.

And finally the marketer seeks the engagement of his consumer. At the apex of belonging is engagement where the brand achieves a status of being culturally 'cool' where its stories are talked about by the 'right people' in the 'right places'. In the brand centre, according to the design theory, the consumer will see and believe, touch and own, and ultimately share the brand's values with their peer group. And that's why marketing has now laid claim to the distillery and why you aren't getting the distillery back any time soon.

There is a very simple relationship ladder that marketing are seeking to encourage their audience to climb. From prospect to customer, customer to client, client to supporter, and ultimately supporter to advocate, the theory of the experience economy is brought to life in the brand centre. It's a simple ladder but, I should mention, a slippery one.

To consider this model in more detail, the brand experience space works as follows: awareness is created amongst the desired target market; traffic driven to the brand experience space where the visitors receive distinct brand messages tailored to their position on the relationship ladder. Here they are introduced, educated, or reinforced in the key aspects of the brand essence. And again, depending on the depth of their pre-existing relationship with the brand, they move through the stages of trial, adoption, consumption or loyalty to the point where eventually they become informal, unofficial, unpaid, but all the more compelling brand ambassadors. They, in turn, through personal recommendation and word of mouth endorsement contribute to the process of creating awareness amongst the target market - and so the wheel goes round. Through an increasingly sophisticated relationship e-marketing programme, today delivered almost invisibly to those outside the desired target group, consumers are encouraged to progress from client to supporter to advocate and, if your marketing department are not collecting visitor data to continue their relationship marketing after the visit, they most certainly should be. Your competitors are.

So, within the experience economy, we see a search for personalisation, authenticity and "real brands" as sated consumers seek those elusive emotional connections. This is expressed in other ways as well as we shall see in a moment, but, contrary to the common sense view, authenticity is a relative construct. An increasing trend to demonstrate authenticity and make real connections is seen in the proliferation of whisky festivals, again a phenomenon of the past decade.

Remarkably, the first whisky festival of any significance can be dated to the "Meet the Maker" feature in New York's WhiskyFest of November 1998 when a small group of distillers were tentatively exposed to an intrigued audience equally unsure of what they would find. Today WhiskyFest goes from strength to strength. We have the world wide explosion of the Whisky Live event, Edinburgh's Whisky Fringe forming part of the Festival, the Speyside and Islay festivals and further similar events in Stockholm, Kentucky, Limburg, Louvain, Moscow and so on. The result of this continued exposure has been a new role for the Distillery Manager, that of Brand Ambassador, Master Distiller, Master Blender or a range of similarly exotic new job titles.

But, if marketing expects, Finance dictates. As production practitioners, you will recognise the constant pressure to reduce costs, increase yields and a trend to increased automation in the distilling process. These imperatives, driven by financial considerations, conflict with a consumer demand for authenticity and heritage. In a world where almost every aspect of distilling production has evolved to meet these demands, marketing continue to spin the distillery as if Alfred Barnard had only just departed. So, in conclusion, of this presentation some questions to stimulate discussion. I say quickly that I don't have all of the answers but, in closing, we might care to consider:

- How far should marketing reflect the reality of distilling practice?
- As brand education creates an increasingly well-informed consumer, can we continue to fool all of the people all of the time?
- As we open the distillery, should we show everything?
- More fundamentally, who is the distillery for? In corporate terms, who *owns* it?
- Who decides on the above issues and, critically, *how*?

References

Pine, B Joseph and Gilmore, James (1999). *The Experience Economy: Work Is Theater & Every Business a Stage*. Harvard Business School Press, Boston, USA.

The CEOs Panel

It was great to meet the CEOs and a bit of a coup for the distillers for they turned up in person when the previous year's IBC in Manchester could only manage videos! Diageo's **Paul Walsh** said distillers were used to taking the long term view and now were ensuring long term sustainability particularly with his investments at Roseisle (£45m) and Cameronbridge (£65m), this latter being the largest single energy investment outside of a utility company. It was important to protect the local environment and while production was 4% up, energy usage was down by 10%. It is possible to engage with the regulators, Walsh said, and also consumers who appreciate products with green credentials.

Protectionism was a problem in some parts of the world but there were hopeful signs of improved product recognition in the larger emerging markets where there was a growing incidence of imitation. The 28 states of India continue to beguile and yet frustrate at the same time!

Higher taxes and less accessibility were not the solutions to product abuse with the Scottish parliament particularly lacking in joined up thinking. There is no quick or easy solution to Scotland's drinking habits. The danger was 'here today and gone tomorrow' politicians may well try to grab the headlines which could well lead to unwelcome consequences. Better to enforce the current laws by not serving inebriated individuals or indeed children, and reinforce both parental and personal responsibility. Higher taxes and less accessibility are not the answer; 'target not blanket', he suggested.

There were problems with some credit-crunched consumer spending power but Walsh asserted that the presence of Diageo products in 200 markets were an affordable indulgence in challenging financial times. Brands have seen more wars, economic downturns than each of us is ever likely to see so he looked into the future with quiet confidence.

Edrington's **Ian Curle** (Macallan, Famous Grouse and Highland Park) agreed over market access and the right to promote brands responsibly and that 'ethical consumerism' was on the rise. It was often a challenge to know where and how to spend advertising budgets to reach consumers in a fast fragmenting media market. He reckoned it was still possible to grow a brand in mature categories and highlighted the importance of forecasting. He quoted Charles Dickens "it is not the strongest or most intelligent of species which survive, it is the one most responsive to change".

The last of the three accountants now leading major companies was **Mike Keillor** from single malt specialist and Suntory subsidiary Morrison Bowmore (Auchentoshan, Bowmore and Glen Garioch). He agreed that the three companies of different sizes and complexity had a lot in common. Whisky was a hot category at the moment and the industry needed cash (lots of it) to invest in stock and to make a return on that capital that justifies it. We must retain customer confidence in quality and use creative marketing to bring the category to that consumer.

As a panel the CEOs felt that consolidation in the industry was inevitable particularly where companies were caught without category depth or geographic presence. The very focused or very broad will survive and grow. Walsh even divulged that his company had walked away from 'crazy' supermarket price proposals and the volume that went with them. His view was that if you start on this slippery slope, they would come back again next year and go a little deeper.

Index